WHAT MAKES THE MONKEY DANCE

THE LIFE AND MUSIC OF
CHUCK PROPHET AND GREEN ON RED

STEVIE SIMKIN

WHAT MAKES THE MONKEY DANCE
The Life And Music Of
Chuck Prophet And Green On Red
Stevie Simkin

A JAWBONE BOOK
First edition 2020
Published in the UK and the USA by
Jawbone Press
Office G1
141–157 Acre Lane
London SW2 5UA
England
www.jawbonepress.com

ISBN 978-1-911036-61-6

Jacket design by Paul Palmer-Edwards,
www.paulpalmer-edwards.com

Printed by Everbest Printing Investment Ltd.

1 2 3 4 5 24 23 22 21 20

CONTENTS

▌Recording *Homemade Blood*, Toast Studios, San Francisco, 1996. (*Tom Erikson*)

FOREWORD BY CHUCK PROPHET

I'm not that crazy about the idea of writing a biography. Or sitting down for one. What the heck? I mean, really. When do these books get anything right? I don't like to confront myself in the mirror from one day to the next, let alone all this.

But, then again, I suppose I've been happy to do it. Still, talking about or explaining songwriting has always kind of weirded me out. I don't like to hear myself do it. But I keep doing it anyway! With some of that explaining stuff, I wish I wasn't so forthcoming. They say a real magician doesn't give up his secrets. The 'secret' is actually worthless to the audience. They're just left with an incomplete idea of how you fooled them. So why do it? And where's the mystique in that? And who's going to find this interesting? All good questions.

Plus there's all this recurring talk of success, or the lack of it, however people define it. People must be interested in it. It sure comes up a lot. Yet, if it's been such a struggle, then why do I feel so lucky? So there you go. Are you getting the picture? I'm a walking contradiction—one part fact, one part fiction. And, yes, there's been a lot of both in my life.

At first I might have thrown out some stock zingers. I think, *Oh, I know how to do this.* (What comes first? The music or the lyrics? The advance! Next question.) But eventually the sound bites kind of melt away. I mean, why try to fool anyone? What good would it do?

Speaking to Stevie has felt comfortable for the most part. We have a lot in common. We share a love for much of the same music. And he seems like a nice guy. I like to think I know these things, that I'm a good judge of character. (Though I have made some colossal mistakes in that department too. So read on, if that piques your interest.) I try to be candid. We touch on it. The tumultuous relationships, collaborators, adversaries, fights, losses, scores to settle, and a whole lot of foolishness. Plus a mess of gigs along the way. Stevie was able to talk to people who've learned to forgive me my transgressions and maybe share some kind words too.

During all the times Stevie and I sat around talking about things, we happily went on tangents. And maybe it is interesting. That's the stuff I like.

Sure, there's been plenty of struggle and hard knocks along the way. Yet it hasn't been easy for me to express how much fun and, well, joy I've had playing music either. It's difficult to convey. Traveling around the world. Meeting people. Playing music has afforded me all kinds of opportunities. And it has always been an adventure. At times this project has felt like the dreaded box set where it's generally understood that, once they box you up, its over. It's pretty unlikely that you will ever transcend anything in that box. You've peaked, pal! Hit the bricks. One writer described me nearly thirty years ago as a man with a 'great future behind him'.

I guess there's a kind of boilerplate for these things. Chuck went here. Chuck went there. And usually there's some forensic study of the songs. But, ultimately, this is a book about the music. And, without being overly dramatic, music has sustained me in many ways. It's given me a purpose, I suppose. And, as a bonus, I have managed to eke out a living. I don't know what kind of a living it is. Somewhere between a grad student and a guy who has a talent for rebuilding imported car transmissions or something. But it has sustained me. And brought me much of the good stuff in my life. Including Stephanie. Mostly Stephanie.

Speaking of the good stuff, I'm grateful for some kind of fan base. At all. I don't think money was ever the driving force for me. But people who are engaged? They are gold. There are two or three of them. People like Stevie. They bring something to the party. What exactly? I don't know. But it feels like love. If not love, certainly something like it.

ONWARDS,

–CP

AUTHOR'S NOTE

Chuck can say a lot by not saying very much. Maybe that's a songwriter's specific gift. My own talents and training have led me down a different path.

I should confess that part of the motivation to write this study of Chuck Prophet's work and career has been a desire to bring him to the attention of more people. I started out as a fan, and it is a natural urge to want to share with the wider world what moves us; for many of us, music is a more powerful force than anything else. At the same time, this study is also an attempt to make sense of Chuck Prophet's thirty-five years as a recording artist in an objective frame. From Green On Red's *Gas Food Lodging* in 1985 to his most recent solo LP, *The Land That Time Forgot*, in 2020, there have been a lot of songs, a lot of gigs, and a lot of road.

Inevitably, there is a degree of subjectivity in these pages, especially when it comes to writing about the music itself; how could there not be? In my defence, researchers working in the humanities have more recently been expected to situate themselves in relation to their subject matter. So, here goes. Back in the 80s and early 90s, I spent nine years being trained (or training myself) to write about literature; my PhD, for what it's worth, was a study of the work of the Victorian poet Gerard Manley Hopkins, revered by many and dismissed by others as (ironically) unmusical and wilfully obscure. It's a winding path to end up writing about popular music. But something about Hopkins's work fascinated me. As so often for those in my trade, four years' work began with a personal connection, a preoccupation, an obsession.

I teach a Shakespeare class every year, so I am very familiar with the debates about the 'canon'—that is to say, what constitutes 'great' art, and who decides. The way that a canon is constructed has much to do with the whims of fashion, commerce, and how people at any point in history make sense of themselves and the world around them. I have spent more than half my life teaching and writing about literature, drama, and film, as well as popular music. Some of the texts that I've studied and taught (poems, novels, plays, films, songs) I can take or leave on a personal level, even while acknowledging their significance; others—songs in particular—have informed my identity, my sensibilities, and have shaped my understanding of the world in fundamental ways. The writer George Steiner suggests that the way a work of art grips our consciousness can be 'value-free' and 'indiscriminate'. He argues that there may be a 'syllabus of great art' established by consensus over time (in the UK, for instance, every schoolchild must study a Shakespeare play). But we also have our own 'canons' of works of art that move *us* specifically, he writes, and such a collection for any individual can be 'a profoundly personal construct'.[1] One key motivation when analysing art is simply to invite others to recognise what we value in it ourselves. And there's nothing wrong with that.

Green On Red popped up on my music radar relatively late, around the time Prophet and bandleader Dan Stuart were appearing on the front pages of UK music weeklies *Sounds* and *Melody Maker* promoting their album *Here Come The Snakes* (1988)—eight years after the band first formed, and four years after Prophet joined them. We were still in the pre-internet era, so keeping up with our favourite artists' movements remained a hit-and-miss affair, even for bands and artists with a higher profile than Chuck Prophet. In 1991, for instance, I flew to California to see Tom Petty & The Heartbreakers in LA and San Diego, convinced they were never coming back to the UK. A few weeks later, they announced an imminent European tour.

I came across Prophet's first solo album, *Brother Aldo* (1990), by accident, idly thumbing the racks of the only music shop within sixty miles of the family home at that time, perched as I was on the northeast coast of Scotland. I was ready for his subsequent release in 1992, however; I persuaded a friend to drive me to the nearest Virgin Records store to pick up *Balinese Dancer* on release day (such pilgrimages were a ritual for many committed music fans in an era before downloads and streaming). I can still recall the intense musical curiosity and range of emotions it sparked in me the first time I heard it. Although I lacked the knowledge and vocabulary to articulate it with any precision at the time, I knew that I had never heard electric guitar played that way before. And something about the intersection of guitar style, vocals (a little bit Petty, a little Dylan, a little Lou Reed), and the songs themselves touched a musical nerve. Soon after, I had the opportunity to experience it all at first hand when Prophet and his band The Creatures Of Habit played a gig in Edinburgh. Half a lifetime later, moments from that night are still etched in my memory. And so began something of a musical obsession.

By 1993 I was living in the south of England. There was a fiery, fractious Chuck Prophet band show in Portsmouth in 1995 (twenty-five years later, I would find a 'thumbs down' entered in the date in his diary, May 31). In 1997, behind the *Homemade Blood* album, the venue was the Monarch in Chalk Farm, London, for one of the most intense nights of live music I have experienced, before or since. Maybe just to sublimate the energy I couldn't dissipate any other way, I wrote a review of the show and, without overthinking it, emailed it to Henning Ejnefjäll, who ran Prophet's nascent website at the time. A few days later, it appeared on the site, and a couple of days after that, an email from Chuck arrived, thanking me for the review, saying it had made him proud and he'd shown it to some friends.

Over the next couple of years, we exchanged occasional emails. The first time we spoke in person, I broke the ice with a couple of CD-Rs of out-of-print albums by 70s country singer Don Williams. As the years went by, we would hang out after shows. I got to know Stephanie Finch a little better: Chuck's wife and musical partner is a gifted songwriter, singer, and keyboard player in her own right. Chuck, Stephie, and I would chat while the crowds thinned from the merchandise table and the band loaded out. We would meet for dinner before shows. I would do my bit for Team Prophet whenever I could; in 2010, I wrote a preview of Stephie's *Cry Tomorrow* album, and a few weeks later it was reproduced, piecemeal and anonymously, all over the press release for the album. ('I only steal from the best,' Chuck assured me.) When touring to promote that album, the date scheduled for the night after the show in my hometown of Winchester got snowed out; Chuck came over and we hung out for the day. We talked a lot. We listened to Petty's *Damn The Torpedoes* album in 5.1 surround sound. And we talked some more.

It was around the time of the release of the *Temple Beautiful* album (2012) that my friend, part-time music writer and full-time *mensch* Charles Pitter, asked me if I had ever thought of writing a book about Prophet's music. When we broached it with Chuck, perhaps predictably, there was initial reluctance.

To him, it sounded like someone was looking to sum up a career that he felt very strongly was not over yet. He was more interested in a short book to be co-written with Charles focusing on *Temple Beautiful* because it was current, but that project stalled. Still, I kept talking to him about a full-scale study of his career, biding my time, and gradually reluctance modulated into something more noncommittal, and finally, almost out of the blue (as is often the way with him), enthusiasm. I booked the first of what would be four trips to San Francisco for January 2016; there were some last-minute tenterhooks for me (a few days before the trip, Chuck confessed he hadn't even told Stephie yet; 'she's just gonna roll her eyes,' he sighed), but fortunately it all went ahead as planned, and so the project began in earnest.

Over five days, we sat and talked in Chuck's office space while two Zoom H1 recorders listened in. Occasionally he would open his laptop to look up an old email, an article, or a recording. At other times, as we dug deep into the music, he would pick up a guitar to make a point rather than attempt to put it into words. Hours of recordings stacked up. Interviews with friends and associates. With Stephanie (gracious, open, funny), bandmates such as guitarist James DePrato (dry, modest, coolly enthusiastic), long-time friend Patrick Winningham (every story shot through with love and admiration), co-writer Kurt Lipschutz (cerebral, laconic, lurching from guarded to painfully honest), and Dan Stuart (a little scary at first meeting; scalpel-sharp, irreverent, hilarious). One afternoon, as Chuck and I walked along Howard Street, we bumped into fiddle player Brian Godchaux, whom Chuck had played with in the late 1980s but had not seen since.

The story drifted into focus. There were Skype chats with Chuck, producers, former bandmates and associates. Almost without exception, every person I contacted got back to me within minutes or hours. When they heard about the book project, the response was almost always a variation on one or both of the themes: 'It's about time' and 'What can I do to help?' Dan Stuart, always generous with his time and attention, said he 'saluted my efforts' and confessed to finding it 'very strange' reading a history of Green On Red, by then twenty-five years or so distant in the rear-view mirror. Chuck and I emailed back and forth over the four years leading up to completion of the book; at one point I found myself apologising for treating his life story like a novel. How to make sense of the colour and the shape of a life that, like any other, is lived largely at random and at the mercy of circumstance? But a gripping narrative of an artist struggling to carve something out of nothing in an often hostile or indifferent environment gradually emerged.

And so to this book. I think it tells a story. Stories are one of the ways we try and impose order on a world that too often refuses to make sense. And maybe one of the advantages of a biography over an autobiography is that an outsider can bring a sense of perspective, to provide the necessary distance to put the pieces of a life into something that *does* make sense, even if it's illusory. Nevertheless, my hope is that what comes through more powerfully than anything is Chuck's own voice. Wherever I can, I let *him* tell the story … because no one tells a story quite like Chuck Prophet. And although I have sometimes despaired as I have battled to capture his tone, his humour, warmth, his unusually angled—and hence often revelatory—perspectives, his occasional crankiness and hard-won wisdom, I have persevered. If the reader occasionally catches a sense of what it must be like to sit and listen to him talk, then I've achieved something. It would also be true to say that, as I have hinted in this preface already, Chuck's music has woven itself into the fabric of my life; writing this book has as well, and, where it's appropriate, I have shared parts of those tapestries too.

The picture would have been woefully incomplete without the generosity of all those who given up their time to share their thoughts and memories, not always warm and fuzzy ones: there is, as Chuck would say, a lot of blood on the floor. So, my thanks to those who have helped show me where all the bodies are buried: Stephanie Finch, Dan Stuart, Kurt Lipschutz, James DePrato, Patrick Winningham, Max Butler, Roly Salley, Kevin T. White, Paul Q. Kolderie, Eric Westfall, Kara Johnson, Dan Kennedy, Chris Metzler, Chris von Sneidern, Tommy Dunbar, John Murry, Kelly Willis, Kim Richey, James Walbourne, Tom Heyman, Steve Gardner, Mike Rychlik, Chris Cacavas, Pat Thomas, Steven Drace, Darrell Flowers, Scott Compton, and Mike Brook. Above all, Chuck has been generous with his time and attention throughout the process. I will always be grateful.

My thanks also to those who have shared memories, live recordings, or given invaluable feedback along the way: Roland Maguire, Brian Woolland,

Peter Kramer, Oliver Gray, and Charles Pitter (who also compiled the discographies). A special mention is due to Pete Long and Paul Bradshaw for their work preserving archive recordings. Others have kindly donated visual materials: Cliff Green (www.cliffs-photos.com), Giulio Molfese, Andy Diffee, Hugh O'Connor, Billy Douglas, Darrell Flowers, Mike Brook, Chris Metzler, Paul Dominy, Martin Dudley, Rosco Weber, and Shea Ribblett. A special thank you to Tom Erikson and his brother John. Rob Rynski (thanks for the title, Rob!) has always gone above and beyond the call of duty working on the digital archive, organising live recordings and keeping Chuck's laptop functional.

I gratefully acknowledge the support of the research centre at the University of Winchester, which helped fund the time and the travel that has made this book possible.

My editor at Jawbone Press, Tom Seabrook, has been a joy to work with throughout: wise, patient, always ready to talk things through to find solutions, and always focused on producing the best book we possibly can. Thank you also to Nigel Osborne for his outstanding work on visual design, and his patience with both me and Chuck as we worked on the photographic plates.

Finally, I owe my greatest debt to Aileen for holding the fort at home during my trips to the West Coast and allowing me the space to chase this thing down.

In the chapters that follow, I provide references for anything I have quoted from other writers, interviewers, and reporters, and they are listed in a scholarly-style bibliography; the use of endnotes as a referencing system should make it easy for anyone who simply wishes to follow the narrative to skip past them. Chiefly because it would interrupt the flow too much to reference everything I have gathered from the hundreds of hours of interviews with Chuck and his friends and associates, these are contained in quotation marks but not given citations.

Unless otherwise noted, all of the photographs used in this book are from the author's collection, or from Chuck Prophet's personal archive. Every effort has been made to trace copyright holders, but if you feel there is a missing or mistaken attribution, please contact the publishers.

ARE WE ALL PRESENT AND ACCOUNTED FOR?

*How do you define success? If you let somebody
else define what success is, you're a sucker.
I'm no sucker. – Chuck Prophet*

WHO DID? *YOU* DID ...

There comes a moment in every Chuck Prophet gig when he steps up to the microphone and delivers a mock-serious speech about the next song on the setlist. 'Ladies and gentlemen, we got one more thing on our minds we have to share with you and I really don't know how you're gonna take this,' he begins. Over an ominous rumbling chord, he tells the audience he's about to address one of the world's deepest philosophical questions. 'I know we got some old-timers here, and I just wanna warn you fellas, if you've got a heart condition, this song can be dangerous to your *health*,' he intones, as the band builds a wall of noise behind him. Finally, with regulars in the audience worked up into a frenzy of anticipation (and newcomers presumably increasingly bemused), he cries, preacher-style, 'Who put the bomp in the bomp shooby dooby bomp? Who put the ram in the ramalama-ding dong?' And, with that, he's off, launching into 'You Did', complete with extended guitar workouts that can stretch the song out to ten minutes or more.

'You Did' is an intriguing but relatively low-key bluesy number from

Age Of Miracles (2004) that has evolved to become a centrepiece in concert, shifting from tour to tour between a mid-set slot and encore. The original recording works with keyboards, loops, and Stephanie Finch's plaintive, pure voice an octave above Prophet's on the chorus, and the guitar just provides subtle flourishes. Onstage, Prophet will put the pedal to the metal and let rip on his 1984 Japanese-made Squier Telecaster. Perched at the stage edge, as the threaded notes cascade, he looks transported. Dipping back into a verse, the call-and-response structure of the lyric allows him to switch rhythmically back and forth between his vocal mic and the distortion-laden bullet mic that he makes judicious use of throughout a show. Meanwhile, the band circles maddeningly, obsessively around the chord sequence, framing the repeated lyric 'I got a letter this morning', the contents of which are never revealed. The song repeatedly rises and breaks like a wave, sweeping the audience along with it, and, as Prophet reels off those profound philosophical questions ('Who put the boom in the boom-boom-shakalaka?'), with each one, he invites the crowd to shout back in unison ('*You did*').

The in-concert rendition of 'You Did' that has become familiar to Chuck Prophet's regular audiences is a useful starting point for a book about his career and his work. The song itself epitomises his skill as a songwriter with a melody that digs deep and catches, an infectious beat that grooves and a mysterious, witty lyric; it is at the same time an ironic reflection on, and blissed out celebration of, the frivolity of classic pop lyrics reaching as far back as 'Be-Bop-A-Lula' and 'Tutti Frutti'. It displays his rootedness in traditional forms of rock music (in this case, the blues) while remaining effortlessly contemporary: the studio version of the song fuses its loops, drum programmes, keyboards, and treated vocals with traditional guitar, bass, and drums. It also demonstrates how Prophet's recorded repertoire tends to operate merely as a blueprint for the nightly reinventions of those songs onstage. The solos are reminders of why Prophet is held in such high regard as a virtuoso guitarist, while the ensemble performance courtesy of The Mission Express shows off the individual skills of each band member, and the way they function as a supremely tight unit.

Finally, the live performance of the song tells us something else; there are dozens of versions on YouTube but I would recommend seeking out the recording from the Sweetwater in Mill Valley, California, on January 8 2016 (and not just because I was there). The video captures some of the joyous interaction between Prophet and the crowd and is a good indicator of how the band has built a reputation as a fearsome live act. It distils what the writer Christopher Small calls 'the back-and-forth passing of energy from performers to listeners and back again ... that can approach and even cross the threshold of possession'.[2] One day I put it to Chuck that, when the audience calls back 'you did', they're really saying 'we love you'. He nodded but immediately pointed out that he always bounces the ball back, each time responding, 'No, *you* did'—the love is never less than mutual.

THE MUSIC BIOGRAPHY

This book is an account—substantially in his own words, but with contributions from many of his friends and associates—of Chuck Prophet's career, and a study of his music—substantially in my own words, with contributions from other critics and music journalists. The first three chapters cover the career of Green On Red, including the years before Prophet joined the band. This introduction will explain first how the book fits on the groaning shelves of the rock biography genre before I seek to place Chuck Prophet in the context of the industry he has been a part of for more than thirty-five years. My aim is to suggest why this book might be worth the reader's investment of time and effort, even if they may be unfamiliar or only on casual acquaintance terms with Prophet's music.

The majority of rock biographies, unsurprisingly, are written about the most famous and commercially successful artists, from The Beatles and Elvis Presley to Ed Sheeran and Taylor Swift. Economic logic would seem to dictate that books about the most popular singers and bands will attract the most readers. However, it's not necessarily that straightforward. Not every pop music fan is going to be an avid reader, after all. And if the singer in question tends to drag an undertow of serious artistry along with them, they may be more likely to attract Amazon searches in the Book and Kindle stores: the likes of Bob Dylan, Joni Mitchell, and Bruce Springsteen, for instance, invite dedicated study not only of their lives but of *The Work*: both Dylan and Springsteen have had their lyrics published more than once each as collections akin to books of poetry, even though both have questioned in interview the value of divorcing the words from their music. More on this in a moment.

The other well-established category of rock biography is the book devoted to a cult band or singer (if by cult we mean an artist with a relatively small but very devoted fan base). The biographer of the cult artist is most likely to be a serious fan of the music and less likely to be a professional writer than the typical author of, say, a Madonna or Rolling Stones book. A specific pool of publishing houses understands the marketability of a book that is likely to be bought by a sizeable proportion of the subject's fan base, even if that fan base is not very large: a good example would be Paul Drummond's *Eye Mind: Roky Erickson & The 13th Floor Elevators* (2007), published by Process Media.

In the case of both the 'serious' rock musician and the cult artist, there is usually an assumption—not always clearly articulated—that the work being written about has value exceeding what is commonly associated with a popular art form. Bob Dylan is the only popular singer to have won the Nobel Prize for Literature—an award that sparked lengthy and mostly futile debate about (among many other things) the relation of high art to popular culture. Entire, lengthy tomes have been devoted to specific eras in Dylan's career, some only spanning a couple of years. Literature professor Christopher Ricks has described Dylan as 'the greatest living user of the English language' and compared him to Milton, Wordsworth, and Shakespeare.[3] Lyrics are pored over; alternate versions discussed; live performances dissected; interviews parsed for hidden truths.

Chuck Prophet is not a rock superstar. The occasional festival gig or support slot aside, he has never operated on the scales of stadia, arenas, or even theatres. On the other hand, to describe him as a cult artist is probably not entirely accurate either, if we apply the definition cited above—the relatively small but very committed fan base. He has had his songs performed and recorded by Solomon Burke, Heart, and Bruce Springsteen; he has co-written with Alejandro Escovedo, Dan Penn, Kim Carnes, and Kim Richey; he has worked with Lucinda Williams, Cake, Warren Zevon, Kelly Willis, Jonathan Richman, Jim Dickinson, and Tony Visconti. His songs have featured in popular TV shows such as *Sons Of Anarchy*, *Californication*, *The L Word*, and *True Blood*. But none of this alters the fact that Prophet is not and has never been a household name. I've seen him recognised by fans in local restaurants in the Castro and in San Francisco's Museum Of Modern Art as we visited the Bruce Conner exhibition there in 2017. And I've stood beside him while we checked in at the

BBC radio studios in London, he gave his name to the man at reception, and he murmured to me, deadpan, 'He's gonna spell it *P-R-O-F-I-T*.'

Prophet's album sales number in the tens of thousands, not millions: his top hit on Spotify at the time of writing was 'Summertime Thing' (released 2002), with something north of 1.4 million listens, followed by 'No Other Love' (also 2002)—the latter bumped by prominent placements in the romantic movie *PS I Love You* and the TV show *The L Word*—at just over a million (it's a song that one way or another caught the attention of Miley Cyrus, who has tweeted its lyrics). By contrast, Ryan Adams, an artist ten years younger but who would tend to be filed in the same genre as Prophet (the much contested Americana genre—one that Prophet himself is sceptical of as a category), scores over sixty-seven million for his cover of Oasis's 'Wonderwall', and nearly twenty-seven million for his highest scoring self-penned song 'When The Stars Go Blue' (2001)—boosted, no doubt, by cover versions courtesy of The Corrs and country superstar Tim McGraw, and inclusion on the *American Idol* TV show in 2007.

However, being a gifted artist does not necessarily go hand in hand with being a successful one. The fact that Ed Sheeran's hit 'Shape Of You' has been played billions of times on Spotify does not make it a great song; all we can tell from that mind-blowing statistic is that it is a popular one. As Thomas Carlyle once wrote, 'Fame, we may understand, is no sure test of merit, but only a probability of such; it is an accident, not a property of man.'[4] Or as Prophet puts it, more straightforwardly, 'What people don't realise about music is that, while talent helps, you also need some other intangible stuff that can't always be defined.'

Alan B. Krueger, in his fascinating study *Rockonomics*, suggests there are two essential elements in the development of a market dominated by a few superstars: the first requirement is scale economies ('meaning that someone can apply his or her talents to a large audience with little additional cost per audience member'); the second is that the players need to be 'imperfect substitutes', meaning that their work is 'differentiated and unique'. Krueger also acknowledges the significance of blind luck: 'The right artist might arrive at the wrong time, or at the right time with the wrong song, or at the right time and with the right song but with the wrong manager or label.'[5] Charles Pitter points out in his review of Prophet's *Night Surfer* album (2014), 'So-called cult artists almost always have a loyal, sometimes rabid, following of fans, an audience that will stick with them through thick or thin beyond the realms of trend. Artists with bigger commercial clout are more likely to be subject to the perilous sway of popular taste and run the greater risk of suddenly finding themselves dumped unceremoniously at the bottom of the heap, remaindered in the bargain bin.'[6]

This book may be just another entry in the overstuffed music biography market. However, I would like to propose that it is (in the strictest sense of the word) extra-ordinary because Chuck Prophet's *material* status as a performing artist is, in many respects, so ordinary—even if, as I hope to show, the body of work he has created *is* remarkable. While there are countless studies of the most popular bands and singers, and many books about less commercially successful 'cult' performers, there is a large sector of the music industry left largely unexplored: for instance, while quite a few pop and rock stars and bands write their own material, there are also professional writers turning out songs for others to transform into chart hits; there are session musicians and producers, happily plugging away in the service of others to help in that transformative process. Other moderately successful artists might eke out a living until retirement working at something they love to do for little financial return—although it must be said that retirement and careers in music seldom go together, even for those who achieve fame and fortune. And many artists chip away at the foot of the mountain for a few years, a decade, or more, before finally admitting defeat and laying their dreams of a professional music career aside.

Chuck Prophet has done his fair share of songwriting for others; he has undertaken numerous studio sessions and is an accomplished producer. However, his chief pursuit for over thirty-five years now has been his own music—writing, recording, and touring, first with Green On Red and then, since around 1988, as a solo artist. It is something he has pursued with a relentless determination and a refusal to compromise that has left a lot of blood on the floor. He has waged righteous wars with label heads and producers, but friends and collaborators have suffered too. Making things work at Prophet's level of commercial success, keeping the wheels rotating in an unforgiving, psychotically amnesiac trade like the music business, has required self-sacrifice sometimes, and ruthless self-interest at others. As one former bandmate put it to me with a good-natured chuckle, 'He may be an asshole sometimes, but he's *our* asshole.' At times, it has simply been about survival, by which I mean the ability to sustain a music career on a marginal track that has at times worn so narrow that it has cut to the bone.

This, then, is a study of a middling-successful practitioner making a living in an industry—popular music—that is predicated on, and values above all else, massive commercial success (hence the 'popular'). It is an industry built upon monumental dollar figures: the IFPI's Global Music report gives a figure of $15.7 billion in global sales for 2016 and also notes record companies spent $4.5 billion (approximately 27 percent of their revenues) finding and nurturing new talent.[7] The tension between art and commerce in popular music is summed up in this pronouncement from Ed Bicknell, manager of the hugely successful 80s band Dire Straits: 'To me what management is about is: you take the art, if that's what it is, and you turn it into commerce.'[8] There is a lot to unpack here (the 'if that's what it is' is particularly intriguing), but at this point it is worth simply bowing our heads for a moment in remembrance of the many who have fallen into the crevasse between the creation of the work and the selling of it to an audience large enough to enable its creator to keep a roof over their head and food on the table. It is a yawning gap that has swallowed the dreams and aspirations of too many men and women to count.

'HERE COMES SUCCESS, OVER MY HILL'

Chuck Prophet, we might say, is located on a more human plane than a Tom Petty or a Bruce Springsteen. He is a recording artist who might have to worry about the decline of physical media and the rise of streaming services, and the impact it has on his efforts to get his music heard, even though he may insist that the music he creates is his concern and the medium for the message is beyond his remit. He is someone who will fret over how to raise the funds to record the next album, while holding out against the crowd-funding model that has become increasingly popular among some of his peers (he expresses considerable reluctance to 'use the fans as an ATM'). As a touring musician, he will have to work with his managers to plan and budget a tour carefully. And, as a human being, he will like most of us worry about the economic implications of the day to day (rent, groceries, fuel) and the future (pensions, health care).

As a musician who has always commanded a lot of respect from critics and his peers, but who has never seen that translate into major commercial impact, it is not surprising that Prophet has had to field questions about 'success' on a regular basis. This response, thirty-three years after he joined Green On Red, is typical: 'I don't even know if I have a career. I'm still trying to break into the music business.'[9] And yet, a few aberrant months aside, he has managed to make a living (of sorts) ever since his teenage years by writing, recording, producing, singing, and playing music for a limited (but, crucially, faithful) audience. In this respect, perhaps it is a story worth the telling for music fans, for aspiring musicians, for those who have tried and failed, as well as for scholars who might want to understand how one particular musician's life and work has intersected, often at painfully awkward angles, with the industry.

Still, quite apart from sales figures and head counts on the door, Prophet has always been on a trajectory that has mapped a curious path in relation to 'success', and this is another strand in his career that makes him unusual. Green On Red had their moments when they flirted with something closer to fame in the traditional sense of the word. At their peak, they made appearances on the covers of UK music weekly magazines and on popular TV shows in Europe—*The Old Grey Whistle Test* in Britain, *Rockpalast* in Germany. Stuart and Prophet were never able to maintain enough stability or momentum to take Green On Red to 'the next level', whatever that might have meant to them or, more pertinently, their record label; several years before they called it a day, Prophet had already embarked on a parallel solo career that found him beating a retreat from the European festival stages that had become staple fare for the band. He found his musical mojo instead playing to dozens rather than thousands, shoehorned into the smoky firetrap environs of the Albion Bar in the Mission district of San Francisco. Still, his long-term, on-again, off-again co-writer Kurt Lipschutz notes that Chuck was the only one in their circle who didn't have a day job, as he would slyly acknowledge every time he tacked Waylon Jennings's song 'Waymore's Blues' onto the end of his own 'Look Both Ways': 'I got it written on the back of my shirt,' the song brags, 'I ain't no ordinary dude, I don't have to work.'

Try grilling Prophet on the issue of career decisions and he will routinely divert the conversation to a discussion of the artistic process. When I tried to press the issue with him once, his email reply was stark: 'After I spend so much time writing songs and getting those songs to behave and then getting those songs to stick to the tape ... riding around in a van with your friends playing music is like some kind of vacation.' He concludes, 'As for the "industry at large"? I don't have an opinion on that.'

With all due respect to Chuck, there is something disingenuous here. As the following chapters will show, he may have been frequently working at odds with managers, label heads and promoters, but he has still had to inhabit the industry. He still writes and deals with song publishers; he still records and deals with fellow musicians, producers, and studio staff; he still puts out albums and deals with publicists, radio DJs, and journalists; he still tours and deals with booking agents, promoters, and stage and sound crew; he still does his bit at the merch table after almost every gig. And yet ... pushing him to reflect on his career choices is a little like asking a monk what attracted him to a career defined by celibacy and dedication to God. As Chuck would say, he never really had a choice. If one of his defining characteristics is what is often referred to as an addictive personality, he is fortunate that music has been his abiding obsession, a habit he could never break, and the one thing that he says has never let him down.

Once, asked by a label's marketing team how he thought they should promote his new album, Prophet replied, 'I find it's best to stand in a circle, hold hands, and pray.' Part of the problem for a publicity manager looking to promote a new Chuck Prophet album has to do with the troublesome issue of *genre*. Since the emergence of the category 'Americana', he has often found himself tagged with that label—what the Americana Music Association defines as 'contemporary music that incorporates elements of various American roots music styles, including country, roots-rock, folk, bluegrass, R&B and blues, resulting in a distinctive roots-oriented sound that lives in a world apart from the pure forms of the genres upon which it may draw'.[10] While it's possible to understand why one might be tempted to categorise Prophet as Americana—the definition certainly covers a lot of the most important reference points in his music—the straightforward bottom line is that Chuck Prophet makes rock'n'roll music. As he said in a press release promoting the album *Bobby Fuller Died For Your Sins*, 'I just haven't found anything that hits me the same way: that two guitar, bass and drums feeling.'[11] His own wariness about the Americana label—despite the fact that Green On Red were one of the bands essentially credited with the birth of the closely-related genre of alt-country music—has to do in part with the dangers of ghettoization, a particular, Venus flytrap–style fate for a musician with a limited regular audience. But it is also important to recognise that, over three and a half decades of music, Prophet's restless creative spirit has taken him all over the musical map: accepting the limiting factor again of genre-labelling, the 1990s alone saw him move from folk-inflected rock (*Brother Aldo*, 1990) to more overt country-rock (*Balinese Dancer*, 1992), to 'balls to the wall' rock'n'roll (*Homemade Blood*, 1997) and rock music enriched by beats, loops, and electronica (*The Hurting Business*, 1999).

THE INDUSTRY AND THE MEDIUM

All this needs to be put into the wider context of changes in the music industry as a whole, and along the way, as the chapters chronicle each stage of this musical pilgrim's progress, I will return to that frame, not least because for many years Prophet's relationship with the business—managers, label heads, lawyers—has been such a fractious one.

The major revenue streams for most working musicians can be narrowed down to the following categories: live performance; sound recording (technically termed 'mechanical') royalties from physical format sales, digital downloads, and streaming; public performance royalties, including songs being broadcast on the radio, on TV, and in clubs and other public spaces; songwriting, via publishing royalties; other work such as production and session work; synchronization rights (licensing of songs for use in film, TV shows, video games, ads, et cetera); and merchandise. Over the years that Prophet has been making music, the relative significance of these streams has shifted considerably. Furthermore, those changes have been brought about by a wide variety of different factors, cultural, technological, and economic. In the era of streaming services, with Spotify paying out around $0.00437 per stream and Amazon $0.00402, in order to reach monthly minimum wage in the USA, an artist would need 366,169 total streams.[12] Singer/songwriter Jeffrey Foucault offered an insightful snapshot of the state of play in 2019, with social media platforms having collapsed the traditional practices of the industry in terms of publicity and distribution: 'The indie songwriter finds himself paying Facebook to exploit the metadata of his fans so he can talk to them at all, essentially helping a corporation to pick the pocket of the very people whose hearts he meant to break. . . . There's no reason to assume that someone who can write a great song and play it also happens to combine the skill sets of real estate agent, brand manager, and enthusiastic pimp.'[13]

Green On Red's recruitment of Prophet in the mid-80s came at a prosperous period for the music industry and predated by a few years the emergence of the compact disc as a mass medium—an innovation that would fuel a bonanza for the major labels MCA (later Universal), Warner, EMI, Sony, BMG, and Polygram. Music sales steadily climbed through the 1990s, fuelled in part by the allure of a shiny silver disc—today largely a signifier of middle age and obsolescence, but thirty years ago a harbinger of the future. The record companies were high on the hog, their profits boosted by drastic reductions in production costs: toward the end of the decade, the per-unit cost of manufacturing a CD was less than a dollar, while retail prices remained unchanged at $16.98.[14] The 90s was the decade that saw rap and hip-hop flood the mainstream, and grunge take off, take over, and flame out; and it was the era of the mega-deal, with artists such as Prince ($100 million in 1992) and U2 ($200 million in 1993) benefiting, and bidding wars breaking out over artists as diverse as Superchunk and 50 Cent.

'In a lot of ways,' Prophet would opine, 'the money ruined everything in the 90s. Money makes people stupid. I think there were these unrealistic expectations, and there were a lot of bands that ended up signed to major labels in the wake of all that, when the music business model was just massive. I didn't think of that as an inspired time.'[15] For Prophet himself, the first half of the 1990s, as chapters 4 and 5 show, were in some respects simply bewildering, with his own musical antennae attuned to the music of the 60s and 70s, while the record label was demanding he create music for 'the kind of people who played CDs in their cars'.

The turn of the millennium saw the beginning of a huge shift which would realign the decimal place on the annual turnover in the music industry, and a series of mergers followed that reduced the big six record labels of the pre-millennium era to just three (Sony, Universal, and Warner). The development of the MP3 format, and the rise of illegal file-sharing via Napster and similar sites, as well as other kinds of piracy (facilitated by the availability of cheap CD burners), meant that after peaking in 2000, CD sales began to fall off a cliff, dropping by 30 percent in the first couple of years of the new century; in April 2002, one of the media titans, AOL Time Warner, announced a $54 billion loss, detonating profound shock waves. Two years later, Warner Music Group would be dropped from the conglomerate in an attempt to rationalize the business. By the end of 2007, CD sales were half of what they had been at their peak in 2000.

For Prophet, the beginning of the new millennium delivered a double whammy; not only would he suffer the fallout from the contraction of the music industry, but all around him—based as he was in San Francisco, the epicentre of the dot-com boom in the USA—friends and associates who had been eking out a living as musicians, music engineers, and producers were being swallowed into the belly of the tech beast. Talking to both Chuck and Stephanie, it was this that defined the turn of the millennium for them more starkly than anything else.

In 2005, around the time Prophet was dropped from the label New West, CDs still represented 98 percent of legal album sales, but it was essentially a dying format, as the iPod became increasingly ubiquitous.[16] The key term in the previous sentence is 'legal': the 99-cents-per-song format of the iTunes store was not proving to be the saviour of the industry that Apple founder Steve Jobs had promised it would be when he was knocking on the doors of the major labels touting his innovation: for young, avid music lovers, the iPod was the thing they had been waiting for to make their thousands of illicitly downloaded songs portable. The impact of file sharing may be impossible to gauge with any degree of accuracy but is difficult to underestimate. It may have been leaks of the top chart releases that made up the bulk of the files being shared, but the economic impact reverberated down through every level of the business. Sales of digital music overtook their physical counterparts in 2011, the year Prophet was writing and recording *Temple Beautiful*.[17] When Yep Roc released that album, every song was uploaded by the company to YouTube, free to listen. You could say that the battle had been well and truly lost.

And in 2020? The vinyl revival notwithstanding, the average consumer of music no longer requires a physical format or even a digital file. The most important (and often the only) criterion is convenience, and they will find what they are looking for via a relatively low-cost streaming music service such as Spotify, iTunes, Amazon Prime, or listen for free via Soundcloud or YouTube. Downloads are now going the way of CDs. If you are not going to have your music in tangible form, why pay for a single digital file when one song costs more than a day's subscription to a service that gives you access to that song and thirty or forty million more? Streaming revenue was $2.4 billion in 2015, and CD sales a mere $1.5 billion: compare this with $13.36 billion in CD sales in 2000 and you begin to get a sense of the scale of the downsizing, and how radically the music industry has had to realign itself to survive.[18] Furthermore, it is no surprise that the past few years have witnessed the death of almost all the traditional brick-and-mortar music retailers, such as Tower Records and Virgin, with HMV in the UK hanging on by the tips of its claws, surviving major restructuring exercises in 2013 and 2018.

Prophet's perspective on all this is a stubborn one. As he told one writer while gearing up for his 2018 summer tour of the USA, 'There has been so much moaning about the music business and how Spotify is hurting everybody. I've never been in that part of the business. I'm just a content provider.'[19] It was another revealing comment about Prophet's disinclination to engage too directly with the industry beyond what is strictly necessary. 'The people that seem to have the most opinions on the *industry* are the people who seem to be outside of it,' he told me in 2018. 'I mean, I'm a practitioner.'

What remains of the market for physical media is increasingly moving into the luxury and collector's markets, where super-deluxe editions thrive. Much has been written about the vinyl revival, and the way in which it presses a particular configuration of consumers' buttons, especially in the demographic comprising men (and women, but mostly men) who grew up with vinyl, will often (being middle-aged) theoretically have higher levels of disposable income, and are inclined to revisit the music of their youth in a rather fetishistic fashion (how else to explain the button badges, posters, hardback books, repressed singles, replica concert tickets, and marbles—the latter an essential part of the Pink Floyd 'Immersion' boxed sets?). In an era of 'free culture' ethics, the music is always readily accessible but the paraphernalia, the items that are tangible and seem unique—or, at least, instantly collectible—are not.

Speaking to the *Guardian* newspaper in 2011, Tim Ingham of the industry magazine *Music Week* suggested that the boxed-set phenomenon had a lot to do with the changing economic models for popular music sales. 'Record labels are incredibly keen to make up for the shortfall in CD sales that they're seeing year on year in the digital space. But although digital sales are growing, they're not making up for the loss in physical sales. They've seen a real opportunity to hike up the cost of physical goods and direct them towards a small but incredibly loyal audience. If they sell one [boxed set] over the counter, it makes everyone a hell of a lot more money than if twenty people go to Tesco's and buy the Adele album for a fiver.'[20]

Prophet has been releasing his albums on vinyl as well as CD since *Soap And Water* in 2007, although this has been, for him, about the desire to release his music in the highest possible sound quality, and about everything the Long Playing Record signifies in terms of musical heritage; for the label, it was always a marketing decision. ('Of course, I've always wanted vinyl,' he told me. 'But that was never entirely my call.') In 2015, he even dipped a toe in the special-edition market with a boxed set of the *Night Surfer* album divided up onto seven 7-inch singles, housed in a box with 3-D cover art (and free 3-D glasses), with a couple of previously unreleased tracks on the seventh 45. There were also, quirkily, cassette tapes made available of *Temple Beautiful* and *Night Surfer* in 2014; that peculiar market continues to grow, with sales at least doubling, year on year, in the UK from 2015 to 2018.[21] All these releases are things that Prophet has some personal, cultural investment in.

ON THE ROAD AGAIN

At some point in the early noughties, for many recording artists, the relationship between the album release and the tour flipped. While ostensibly the tour would still be booked to promote the album, in effect the album became an excuse to tour; it was out on the road that the real money was to be made. Prophet's European manager, Chris Metzler, confirms that this is a principle generally agreed by everybody in the business, adding, 'It's also safe to say that the story behind the album has sadly become more important than the actual music for getting the news out there.'

The relevant chapters look at this in greater detail in due course, but it is worth mentioning that, for the first decade of Prophet's solo career, he made no attempt to tour his home country. Having cemented a loyal fan base in Europe during the Green On Red years (they spent most of their career signed primarily to UK-based labels), the vital links with venues and booking agents were already in place. The transition from Green On Red to Chuck Prophet tours in Europe was consequently relatively straightforward. However, given the impossible logistics of touring the vast expanse of the United States without an established audience, Prophet spent the 90s on a well-trodden tour track around the old world, playing the club and pub circuit. In 1999, he began to try to tour the US beyond local gigs and regular appearances in isolated musical mecca locations such as Austin, Texas. After a stuttering start, it would take a support slot for Lucinda Williams and a minor radio hit in 2002 ('Summertime Thing') to give him something more than the most precarious toehold in that market.

In 2011, for the first time, Americans spent more on live music than they did on recorded music.[22] Fabian Holt suggests that the market value for live music rose as the 'value' of recorded music (real and perceived) depleted, with consumers prepared to pay for the 'direct' experience.[23] In an era where recordings can be accessed for free, or next to nothing, the uniqueness of the live experience, it seems, is still worth something. Krueger points out that Paul McCartney, who has been involved in writing more no. 1s than anyone else in history, received 82 percent of his income in 2017 not from royalties but from touring revenue. He adds that, of the top forty-eight musicians who toured in 2017, 'on average they earned 80 percent of their income from touring, 15 per cent from recorded music, and 5 percent from publishing fees'.[24]

The economics of mounting a three-week European trip for an American artist touring at club level are unnerving: some countries pay well, but others are still paying the same rates they were using back in 1994, Chris Metzler informs me. The drives between cities can be anything between two and nine hours. Then there is the load-in, setup, and soundcheck (and, if they're lucky, enough time to eat), followed by a two-hour show, socialising at the merchandise table, breaking down, and loading out. They are fortunate if they can be back to the hotel by 1am—hopefully enough time to get seven hours' sleep before they do it all again. Prophet and his four-piece band will typically play every single night on a European tour: whether they have a gig or not, he will still have to pay the band members their wages plus hotels, management, booking agents, and travel, which draws a fine line between breaking even and going into the red: costs are effectively the same whether it is a day off or a day on. The nitty-gritty, especially in the winter months, can be cruel. One night off sick, a broken-down van, or a missed flight can quickly push the tour thousands into the red.

Currently, Prophet can charge £20 for a ticket on a UK tour and $20–25 in the USA. Meanwhile, prices for established stars playing arenas and stadia have been rocketing for some years and show few signs of slowing down. No doubt the extensive (and controversial) resale market has had a part to play: given the prices 'scalper' tickets can fetch on eBay or sites dedicated to reselling live events, the 'official' prices begin to look relatively reasonable. A BBC report in 2018 noted that, taking inflation into account, concert ticket prices have risen by 27 percent since the late 1990s. But these are just averages: at the 'top' end of the market, it cost £23.50 to see the Spice Girls at Wembley Stadium in 1998 (£39 in today's money). To see Taylor Swift at the same venue in 2018, prices range from £55 to £120; a barely recognisable Fleetwood Mac were charging £75—200 in 2019. Ticket prices for so-called 'grassroots' gigs, by contrast, have hardly risen at all in twenty years, remaining steady at around £8.[25]

It's unusual for an artist in his mid-fifties to be slowly growing an audience, rather than playing simply to a nostalgia crowd and trading on fading glories. Many established artists rely on veteran albums of twenty, thirty, or forty years past; audiences may tolerate the occasional new composition or else go on a beer run until it's time for the next 'classic' song. There is a burgeoning market for these bands to tour offering a complete performance of one of their 'classic' albums (and let's not get started on the perplexing appeal of tribute bands). Prophet will always build a setlist around his most recent release, and, given the fact that as a songwriter he has been finding broader and more powerful wings with each album, the audiences want nothing less. In 2017, Prophet played to bigger crowds than ever before, and even if the growth has been marginal, it is significant. A double-header tour in the United States with alt-country veterans The Bottle Rockets allowed Prophet and his band the opportunity to tread the boards of the 400-seater High Noon Saloon in Madison, Wisconsin, for instance, when in 2012 the Mission Express had played the 180-capacity East Side Club in the same city. Over the years, in London, he has graduated step by step from the Borderline (300) to ULU, even if the latter venue, on his last visit, did not reach its full capacity (800).

However, measuring 'success' by size of venue is a tricky business when assessing an artist like Prophet: when visiting him for interviews for this book in January 2016, I travelled with him to a show staged in the corner of the Crepe Place in Santa Cruz and enjoyed the music with a few dozen fans and casual listeners, some of whom came and went over the course of the school night show; the next night, he played to a capacity, three-hundred-strong crowd hanging on every sweaty note at Sweetwater Music Hall, in affluent Mill Valley, just north of San Francisco. The following evening, he played a private gig at the same venue. It's not hard for even a non-specialist to imagine the relative economics of these three shows, played back-to-back over three nights. But for Prophet, the Crepe Place gig is a matter of loyalty to a kindred spirit: the co-owner, Adam Bergeron, is a friend of the band. 'And,' Chuck adds, 'he's also out there in the community making things happen that I care about. He took over the Vogue Theatre. That was where all the Woody Allen movies were premiered in San Francisco. And he's doing what he can to keep it running.'

WHERE THERE IS NO TEMPLE, THERE WILL BE NO HOMES

Prophet is an active member of a wider artistic community, not just a music one, although his place as a local musician in San Francisco was secured long before he released the song cycle *Temple Beautiful*, which he dubbed a love letter to the city he had called home since his mid-teens. It seemed entirely appropriate that when a special concert was planned to celebrate the centennial of San Francisco's City Hall in 2015, it was Prophet who was invited to curate the event and act as musical director. With The Mission Express as the house band, the free show celebrated decades of popular music in the city: Stephanie Finch sang a Tex-Mex version of the Jefferson Airplane's 'White Rabbit' complete with mariachi trumpets; Roy Loney of The Flamin' Groovies got up to perform 'Slow Death' and 'Teenage Head'; punk legend Jello Biafra of Dead Kennedys, who had run for mayor in 1979, sang 'Let's Lynch The Landlord' to a city whose tech industry has seen real estate values and rents price many San Franciscan natives out of their own communities since the turn of the millennium.

In March 2014, Alex Nieto, a twenty-eight-year-old Latino man born and raised in San Francisco, was eating his dinner in gentrified Bernal Heights Park, not far from where he had lived all his life. After a tech-industry employee walking his dog got into a confrontation with Nieto, he called the police, and as Nieto left the park, he was confronted by SFPD officers and killed in a hail of bullets (fifty-nine shots were fired, fifteen of which struck his body; eleven of them were fired with a downward trajectory, indicating they were discharged as officers stood over his prone body). Nieto was unarmed save for a Taser he wore on his hip as part of his work as a nightclub security guard. Almost exactly two years later, all four officers were cleared of civil suit charges against them, and a few days after that, Chuck Prophet wrote (with Kurt Lipschutz), recorded, mixed, and uploaded a two-chord howl of rage at the injustice of it all. 'Alex Nieto' is the punkiest song Prophet has ever released. It takes him back to witnessing Dead Kennedys at San Francisco's Mabuhay Gardens as a teenager; simultaneously, it brings him into the immediacy of a community, *his* community, riven by capitalism, class, race, and culture, in an environment that over almost forty years has nurtured his musicality, his deep and wide cultural awareness, and his sense of self.

'Bob Neuwirth once told me, it's OK to do some things for money,' Prophet remarked in the course of one of our conversations. 'But, in the end, if you're not true to your school, it doesn't work. People are always selling some kind of short cut to success. For me, that is like kryptonite. It just breaks me down and makes me weak. I avoid it. Explaining why I do what I do and how, when it's grooving, it gets me off? It's like trying to explain sex to someone ... don't even try. When it's grooving. The band. The songs ... one fucking couplet! When it's flowing, it's a buzz. And *that's* the buzz. Do it once and you might spend the rest of your life chasing that dragon.'

What follows is an attempt to map one particular artist's trajectory on that journey. Explaining that? Well, I'm going to try anyway.

CHAPTER ONE

WHAT CAME FIRST?

GREEN ON RED 1.0 & 2.0 (1985)

> *Some people thought we were the saviours of rock'n'roll,*
> *and a lot of other people thought we were pathetic*
> *knuckleheads. I think they were both right. –* Chuck Prophet[1]

IT CAME FROM THE SOUTHWEST

Although Green On Red have historically been associated most closely with the California-centric Paisley Underground movement of the late 1980s (of which more later), their origins snake back to Tucson, Arizona, where, in 1979, Dan Stuart (guitar and vocals), Van Christian (drums), and Jack Waterson (bass) formed a punk band, The Serfers. Chris Cacavas came on board a few months later after keyboard player Sean Nagore dropped out of the original line-up. 'I first met Dan after I started playing with the cover band The Pedestrians,' Cacavas told me. 'I believe he and our drummer, Billy Sedlmayr, knew each other, and that's how we eventually met. I remember jamming/rehearsing with Dan and Jack; Van might have been there too, and suddenly we were Serfers.'

'He knew the songs well enough to vamp along and a din emerged,' Dan recalls in his memoir, *The Deliverance of Marlowe Billings*. 'A frothy cocktail of some Doors and Sir Douglas [Tex-Mex pioneer Doug Sahm], with a splash of Talking Heads.'[2] The Serfers' sound was fast and approximate. 'If you played too long, no one trusted you,' Stuart adds. 'What next, a guitar solo? Better not sound too good either.'[3]

The music scene at the end of the 70s was a landscape littered with guitar solos. 'Album-oriented rock' ruled: Fleetwood Mac's *Rumours* (1977) spent thirty-one weeks at the top of the *Billboard* chart in 1977–78, and the Eagles' *The Long Run* topped the chart through the final two months of 1979. The late 70s also spawned disco: the soundtrack to the movie *Saturday Night Fever* (1977) would go on to sell over forty million copies, on a par with *Rumours* and the Eagles' *Their Greatest Hits 1971–75* (1976). In the UK, *Saturday Night Fever* was the no. 1 hit album of 1978, and while Abba had the best-selling UK albums in the preceding two years, *Rumours* took up residence in the Top 10 for thirty-nine weeks there, too.

However, a new musical spirit was also stirring in the second half of the 1970s. In 1978, *Saturday Night Fever* star John Travolta had a hit with Olivia Newton-John via their *Grease* soundtrack single 'Summer Nights'; it occupied the no. 1 slot on the UK chart for seven straight weeks. I was twelve years old (and quite a Travolta fan) when Irish upstarts The Boomtown Rats finally knocked them off their perch; I vividly remember the band yawning and tearing up pictures of the American star for the cameras on *Top Of The Pops* as the song began. It was a key moment: 'Rat Trap' was the first punk/new wave single to make it to no. 1 in the UK. Listening back now, the song sounds like bargain-basement Bruce Springsteen, but it confirmed the commercial penetration that the genre achieved, almost exactly two years after The Damned released what is often described as the first UK punk song, 'New Rose'.

US punk was something distinct—its roots were buried elsewhere, and in strictly musical terms it actually preceded the UK punk explosion: the Ramones, credited by many as godfathers of the movement, played their first gig in 1974 and released their first album in April 1976—but in some respects punk as a subcultural movement was more significant than the music. Malcolm McLaren and Vivienne Westwood established punk as a fashion style and it did not take long to cross the Atlantic. Constance Commonplace, a native of Tucson, recalled how it took over in the early 80s: 'Black was the only color you were caught dead in, and those hippie locks of the 70s were shorn.'[4] Dan Stuart would later reminisce about local venues Pearl's Hurricane and Tumbleweeds: 'During the day they would have bikers and Vietnam Vets on disability, then the punks would come in at night and one of us would have to draw straws to see who would go around to the regulars and get them to pay the cover.' He continued, 'Some of 'em really got it: "Oh, this is just like The Seeds!" And others were more, "You know what a punk is? A punk is someone in prison who gets butt-fucked!"[5] By the mid-80s, the Tucson scene had adopted the moniker THC (Tucson Hard Core), and Greg Gonzales and Parisa Eshrati, in their fascinating history of punk music in the city, identify the peak of the movement as the night that local heroes U.P.S. (Useless Pieces Of Shit) opened for Dead Kennedys in 1985.[6]

Much has been written about the relationship between the UK and US brands of punk music. The Sex Pistols' 'God Save The Queen' may have lacked genuine anti-establishment conviction, but bands like The Clash and The Jam were rooted in a political moment, amplifying social divisions that would soon split further and crack wide open into class war as Margaret Thatcher's 80s dawned. By contrast, US punk bands and audiences, at least on the East Coast, were just as likely to come from middle-class backgrounds: while politically anarchic, rejecting conventional moral and social values, they never really had the working class-specific rootedness of UK punk, even if the cruel stupidity of the Reaganomics 'trickle-down theory' was a target for some. In San Francisco, it was different. Take Dead Kennedys—even the band's name was a political gauntlet, fifteen years on from the assassination of JFK and only a decade after the death of his brother Bobby; the Mabuhay Gardens, where Chuck Prophet would see bands play as a teenager, and where his earliest bands would also take the stage, witnessed benefit gigs for striking Kentucky miners and striking railroad workers, amongst other political flashpoints.[7]

Nevertheless, more significant for US punks than politics or class antagonism was the individual creativity that punk represented. For Dan Stuart, punk was not simply about guitars, 'It was fucked up *anything*. It had to do with the aesthetic, the intention of celebrating the creativity of every individual.' As Cacavas put it to me, 'I didn't gravitate toward the better players, I gravitated toward the more creative musicians.' It came down to what rock critic Michael Azerrad terms the 'punk ethos of DIY. The equation was simple: if punk was rebellious and DIY was rebellious, then doing it yourself was punk'. He quotes Minutemen bassist Mike Watt: 'It was about starting a label, it was about touring, it was about taking control. It was like songwriting; you just do it.'[8] Nevertheless, US punk music was also generally more studied and less spontaneous. The Ramones may have specialised in fast, short shots of adrenalin, but other regulars at New York City's hotspot venue CBGB in the late 70s were more cerebral: Blondie, Television, Talking Heads. Patti Smith's guitarist Lenny Kaye tellingly described their music as 'rock that had a certain sense of intelligence. We were all theorists to a certain degree'.[9] And when Dan Stuart was asked to list early influences like The Weirdos, The Urinals, Germs, X, and Pere Ubu, he summed it all up as 'a lot of artsy fartsy shit'.[10]

Keyboardist Chris Cacavas would later describe The Serfers as 'primitive, punkish, but not merely three-chord rock ... I guess we were making quirky music, sort of *art-punk*, perhaps?'[11] Chris and his Fender Contempo organ 'really defined our sound until the kid [Prophet] showed up,' Dan writes.[12] Cacavas—classically trained on piano, and with a sense of musical adventure that was still burning brightly when I saw him play a rare London show in December 2019—brought a strong melodic sense to the band that began to mark them out from the pack.

Art-punk they may have been, to deploy Cacavas's term, but The Serfers soon started to pick up regular gigs on their hometown's punk/post-punk circuit. Before long, they were opening for the likes of Black Flag, Fear, DOA, and The Weirdos, as well as headlining their own shows. Still, the home turf was hardly extensive, and prospects of full-time music careers, let alone rock stardom, remained remote. Jack Waterson, enduring nine-to-five drudgery in a warehouse to make ends meet, recalled, 'We had kind of gotten down to the very depths of humanity living gig-to-gig. REAL distraught.' The decision to move to Los Angeles was born in part of 'the intuitive feeling of the band ... to move on and make music for a larger audience.'[13]

However, while the band's relocation to LA in 1980 at first glance seems to have been a straightforward initiative to seek wider exposure and greater commercial success, Stuart had another, more pressing reason to make the move: 'I moved to LA fleeing a triple felony,' he says. 'Smash and grab in a music store.' Stuart and a friend had seized a Fender Twin Reverb (not the wisest choice, given the classic amp's notorious weight) and a Telecaster. Unfortunately, it appears the pair had been spotted *in flagrante*: 'We didn't know it, but an undercover cop had just gotten off duty and watched us do the whole thing.' Trailed by cop cars and, Dan claims, a police helicopter, they made their way back to their house. When the cop knocked on the door,

Stuart covered for his fellow felon hiding on the rooftop, and gave himself up.

David Wiley, vocalist for punk band Human Hands, had already told Stuart, 'You guys should really be in LA.' Now, with the triple felony lighting a fire under him, and, as Cacavas recalls, Dan's girlfriend having recently left for LA to go to fashion school, the bandleader had all the incentive he needed. The Serfers had crossed paths on tour with southern California–based The Alleycats, who were being managed by Marshall Berle at the time (nephew of the comedian Milton Berle). Marshall Berle—a veteran agent and manager for The Beach Boys, Marvin Gaye, and Creedence Clearwater Revival, among many others—was seeking a leg up onto the potentially lucrative punk bandwagon; his secretary, Belinda Carlisle—briefly (and nominally) a member of seminal punk band The Germs under the name Dottie Danger, but by then one of the Go-Go's—helped him book some of the younger bands ('She was like [Berle's] inside spy into what was really going on,' Stuart told me), and The Serfers passed across his radar. Carlisle prompted the band's name change: she had been disturbed by several Orange County surf-punk bands 'coming in acting like Nazis and beating up the punks'. Stuart had recently written a song for The Serfers called 'Green On Red' (just released at the time on a Tucson radio station's compilation of local bands, *KWFM On The Air*), and, somewhat randomly, selected that song title as the band's new name.

Green On Red were soon living the grimy rock'n'roll dream. 'The three of us ended up in a one room apartment in the notorious Villa Elaine—an old apartment complex with a beautiful courtyard in the heart of Hollywood on the corner of Fountain and Vine,' Cacavas told me. 'The complex was well past its heyday and was filled with drug dealers and transvestite prostitutes but we jumped right in as if it was the most normal place to be at that moment.' He recalls midnight 'shopping' adventures, walking through the aisles stuffing their pants with all they needed for their daily meal. 'None of us had jobs at that point and our parents weren't hell bent on financing our dreams so it was simply a survival tactic. Usually we would have scraped together enough coins to buy one or two forty-ouncers of malt liquor, and then we'd go back to the apartment, make beef and bean burritos, drink Colt 45 and watch Benny Hill on a small black-and-white television I had pulled out of the Goodwill bin across the street—good times!'

EARLY RECORDINGS

When Van Christian upped and left in December 1980 (he would later form the Tucson-based Naked Prey with David Seeger), the band went on a temporary hiatus and didn't play any gigs for about a year, but in February 1981 they were able to record their first EP, *2 Bibles*, with $1,200 lent to them by Tucson friend Rich Hopkins, who would go on to form Sidewinders (later renamed Sand Rubies when another band with the same name threatened legal action). Drummer Alex MacNicol was recruited to replace Christian, and the songs were cut 'on borrowed equipment at Doug Moody's old 16-track studio on Vine in LA,' Stuart recalled.[14] Mystic Sound Studio 'was in what seemed to be an otherwise abandoned office building,' Cacavas told me. 'I remember the musty smell and Doug's charming, very British, enthusiasm.' Five hundred copies of the EP were pressed, which the band sleeved themselves. Raw and primitive, the songs do show off the band's distinctiveness: Cacavas's organ and piano dominate most of the songs, and the vocals, some taken by Cacavas, lack the punk snarl of later recordings. The closing track, 'A Tragedy', is probably most indicative of the band's direction at this point.

Released in June 1981, *2 Bibles* may have made it to no. 1 at a small college radio station in Cleveland, but it was hardly their big break. That would come a little later, courtesy of Steve Wynn—a Los Angeles native, leader of the band The Dream Syndicate, and one of the prime movers in an emerging community of likeminded musicians. In the summer of 1981, Green On Red started picking up some more high-profile gigs, opening for X and Lydia Lunch in August, but by November the momentum had faltered again, and MacNicol left for New York.[15] The band reconvened for a gig back in Tucson in February 1982, which seemed to rekindle their spirits; they even cut a rough demo on an 8-track recorder on a budget of $200. At the beginning of May, at a gig in LA, they ran into Steve Wynn and his bandmates again, and, at a barbeque organised at Green On Red's house soon after, Stuart played Wynn the demo tape; Wynn immediately offered to put it out on his own Down There label.

Green On Red undoubtedly betrays its low-budget production. It suffers from a congested mix; Dan Stuart's vocal style, described retrospectively by *No Depression* magazine as 'indie-flat' (2003), had not yet taken on its distinctive, seen it all, sardonic sneer. The vocals—Stuart and Cacavas trading lines on the opening 'Death And Angels'—are pushed too high on just about every track apart from 'Lost World', where Cacavas's seeping, buzzing keyboard lines dominate. Most of the songs are taken at a barely sustainable pace. Best of a fairly mediocre collection of songs is probably the surf-rock 'Black Night', which would remain a live staple for some time, and the propulsive 'Death And Angels', where the faux-naif lyrics are swept away by the surge of guitar and keyboard textures. The album closes with the most experimental track, 'Apartment 6', pushed along by Cacavas's stabbing riffs and stop-starting through its switching rhythms.

The eponymous LP went Top 10 on college radio and started to attract attention from the music press too. Michael Azerrad notes that, at this time, FM radio was tightly controlled and 'mostly programmed by a small group of consulting firms', keeping new music off the airwaves. College radio provided a 'valuable conduit', allowing for promotion of indie gigs and showcasing new single and album releases.[16] Sure enough, in the wake of the album's release, the gigs began to multiply. In the meantime, a movement that would come to be known as the Paisley Underground had begun to coalesce. The name is probably most familiar to music fans today via pop maestro Prince's moniker Paisley Park; after seeing the music video for 'Hero Takes A Fall' (1984) by one of the bands in that circle at the time, The Bangles, he donated 'Manic Monday' to them, which became a worldwide hit. Michael Quercio, later to form The Three O'Clock, first used the term 'Paisley Underground' in an interview for the *LA Weekly*; he claimed it was 'just an off-the-cuff remark', but the name stuck.[17] Matt Piucci of Rain Parade would later describe the name as 'mildly accurate'—'It addresses proximity and similarity of musical influences'—though he never felt it was particularly apposite in musical terms; ironically, he believed only early Green On Red, with their keyboard-drenched sound, showed mild psychedelic influences.[18]

The sense of community that emerged among these bands was fostered in large part by the regular barbecue parties hosted by Green On Red out of their two-storey apartment in Hollywood—'a place to schmooze, drink, and swap musical ideas', according to Steven Roback of Rain Parade. 'It was a surprisingly supportive scene.'[19] Stuart felt the same kinship even though 'we were outsiders', as he put it to me, 'cactus heads from Arizona. Some of the others had known each other since grade school.'

Most of these musicians also shared a consciously retro reverence for the power pop of bands like Big Star. From Green On Red, through The Long Ryders' cowpunk, to the unabashed pop sensibilities evident in Rain Parade and The Bangles, for Wynn, it was 'a movement that happened because of a vacuum produced in a very dead period of music, at least in Los Angeles. Punk rock had come and gone and we were left with synth-pop, new romantics, metal-punk and a bunch of other music that just wasn't any fun.'[20] Wynn, like many musicians of his age with tastes outside the mainstream, sensed a profound need to connect, and he wasn't feeling it in LA at that time. As he explained to Michael Hann, 'The idea that you'd make music with guitars. The idea that you'd make music with long, unscripted and unstructured jams. The idea that you were into 60s garage bands. The idea that you'd play one chord until your arm fell off'—all were deeply unfashionable practices at the time.[21] 'The original punk crowd were approaching thirty and burning out fast,' Stuart writes. 'They generally resented us as did the older power poppers who grew up playing Beatle songs.'[22] The music of the Paisley Underground might have been diverse, but all the artists concerned had lived through the first rush of punk and they had come out the other side wondering what more there might be. Punk had become its own establishment—'an actual requirement that you had to . . . be loud, you had to be fast, you had to be sweating and screaming', according to Matt Piucci.[23]

Chuck Prophet, yet to join Green On Red, was very much aware of these bands and their impact on the LA music scene. He vividly recalls hearing of a gig by The Three O'Clock at On Broadway in North Beach: 'After the gig, the singer was standing at the bottom of the stairs, handing a flower to each person as they filed out into the San Francisco night.' Hardcore punk it certainly was not. Prophet also name-checks Rank & File: 'They had cred because Chip [Kinman] and Tony [Kinman] had been in The Dils, who were a San Francisco punk band. Alejandro [Escovedo] was playing guitar and they were opening for DOA, who were a hardcore punk band from Vancouver. And by the end of their set they had all the punk rockers, in matching leather and bandanas and engineer boots, all dancing to "The Wabash Cannonball", which is a great folk song. And when I saw Green On Red, I had a similar experience.'

'People in the fashion world, they can see where things are going,' he continues. 'It's easy: they look for the absence of something. And there was an absence of narrative songwriting and 60s influenced music at the time. What Green On Red was doing was exciting. Chris was like Garth Hudson [of The Band], just playing through everything. It's hard for me to even articulate what that was like. And at the same time I saw The Dream Syndicate at the Stone [on San Francisco's Broadway], and I met Mark Olson that night.' Olson and Prophet would do some recording together as well as a few impromptu gigs, but nothing came of the session, and Olson would go on to form The Jayhawks around the same time Prophet signed up with Green On Red.

SLASH RECORDS AND *GRAVITY TALKS*

Steve Wynn had put out Green On Red's debut, but the reach of his own, tiny independent label was inevitably limited. However, he was about to help the band take their next step up, opening a line on one of the hippest indie labels of the late 70s and early 80s. Slash Records (Dan Stuart refers to the label as 'Trash records' in his memoir—we shall see why in due course) had begun as an offshoot of the eponymous punk fanzine, initially to release an album by The Germs in 1979. Over the next few years, under the management of Bob Biggs, Slash also put out the debut albums by X and The Blasters, both significant in the development of the wild and fertile LA punk scene. The Dream Syndicate cut their breakthrough album for Slash Records, *The Days Of Wine And Roses*, in a five-hour live jam over the course of one night, and it was Wynn who suggested to the label that they needed to hear Green On Red. According to Steve Berlin—saxophonist in The Blasters in the early 1980s, and a founding member of Los Lobos—Slash signed Los Lobos and Green On Red on the same day. Berlin, who would later produce Prophet's third solo album, *Feast Of Hearts*, reckoned Biggs was 'more excited about signing Green On Red' than he was about Los Lobos, and believed they were going to be 'big stars'. By this time, Slash had a distribution deal in place with Warner Records, which left Biggs in control of a label whose slogan was 'Small enough to know the score, big enough to settle it.'[24]

At the time, Slash Records was for Chuck Prophet (and many others) 'the only label that was making sense'. He explains, 'If you were in guitar band, you didn't understand what was happening, what was on the radio, or what was in the magazines. In terms of pop culture, there was nobody to look to.' Slash seemed to promise something authentic. '*Slash* magazine was a real thing,' Stuart agrees, but he had 'absolutely no respect for' Bob Biggs himself, describing him as 'a dumb jock airhead'. Biggs and his associate Mark Trillen, whom Stuart describes as Biggs's 'little hatchet man', his 'assassin', and his 'Iago', were 'just thieves: *You don't like this band? Then get another one.* He would just sign another band.' Yet because of the label's street cred, rooted in the fanzine and their early, hip signings, 'They all wanted to be on Slash.'

Hindsight can be a beautiful thing. At the time, signing with Slash seemed like a huge opportunity for Stuart, Cacavas, Waterson, and MacNicol, and they went into the studio with the label's house producer, Chris D. of LA punk scenesters The Flesh Eaters, to record *Gravity Talks*. The evolution from the first EP is astounding: not only is the mix far cleaner and better balanced, there is a maturity in the songwriting and a sense of songs being arranged—or at least worked out—rather than simply raced around the track in a frantic loop. There are still some full-pelt rockers, like the tremendous 'Abigail's Ghost' and the opening title track, wherein, as so often, Chris Cacavas's ebullient and inventive keyboards give the band an edge.

Gravity Talks may be the high-water mark of his participation in the band: on the country-tinged, ruminative 'Old Chief', he provides a rudimentary but effective lap-steel line; two songs are co-written by him and Stuart, and he also sings lead on his self-penned 'That's What You're Here For', which owes most to the 60s music that Dan Stuart acknowledges as a vital element in the band's DNA. Layered six- and twelve-string guitars (mostly Cacavas again) fill out the sound; Steve Wynn contributes some guitar, and the spooked rocker 'Snake Bit' features Piucci on lead. Dan Stuart's vocals are fuller than on the two previous releases, and more varied: full bore and indignant on a track like '5 Easy Pieces' and almost tender on 'Old Chief'. The song 'Brave Generation', meanwhile, offered some kind of a manifesto to those, like Stuart, who found themselves caught between the fallout of the collapsing American dream, post-Vietnam, and the Reagan era, which had been ushering in a creeping fetishisation of capitalism.

The album picked up some attention in the mainstream music press. Being on the Slash label had its advantages: there was some tour support, even if it was what Cacavas described as a 'coffee and donuts tour', and they were starting to build an audience outside LA.[25] The critical response to *Gravity Talks* also paved the way for their first European shows and the establishment of a fan base that would in time help sustain solo careers for Stuart, Cacavas, and Prophet beyond the lifespan of Green On Red.

However, the band's experience with Slash was also a bitter one, and while some of the rancour was provoked by the contract ('a cross-collaterized nightmare that raped us of our publishing', according to Stuart)[26] a lot of it had to do with lack of control over artistic decisions. Dan cites the video for the single 'Gravity Talks', a vertigo-inducing promo featuring the band interacting with an actor dressed as Isaac Newton as cameras spin and invert. It's hard to figure out which provokes stronger feelings of nausea—the camera movement or the witless concept—but Stuart looks ready to punch someone (the Isaac Newton impersonator, the director, a camera) as the whole sorry travesty stumbles to a close. Similarly, the band had no say in the design of the album artwork ('I still can't look at the cover of that record without wanting to throw up,' Stuart says). Such 'artistic' decisions can be hard to square with Biggs's assertion that Slash's mission was to make sure the label promoted and presented the true spirit of the bands on its roster.[27] Before too long, Dan Stuart's fiercely independent spirit would come into conflict with Biggs's empire-building agenda and light the fuse on the first of many self-destructive flame-outs.

BILLY THE KID

Chuck Prophet was born in Whittier, California, on June 28 1963. 'I came from a pretty average, non-musical, Catholic family,' he later remarked.[28] The only boy born to Chuck and Avis, Chuck Jr. had two older sisters (Jeanne and Francine) and one younger (Alane). His parents had met at the University Of Southern California in Los Angeles, married immediately after graduation, and lived in Norfolk, Virginia, from 1956 to 1960 during Chuck Sr.'s stint in the navy before returning to the Los Angeles area, where Chuck Jr. was born. There were three years in Cleveland, Ohio (Chuck's elementary school years), before resettlement back in California. Chuck remembers ice-skating and learning to paddle canoes. But motherhood came as a shock to Avis, who had been orphaned at the age of eight or nine. While she was not physically neglectful, Chuck reflects now, 'She didn't know how to be a mother. Or what that meant. And she was depressed and anxious. And you could see she carried all that around. I've come to realise, she needed a mother as much as my sisters and I did.'

Prophet acknowledges a history of depression on his mother's side (her brother was committed to an institution when Chuck was ten). On his father's side, there was a history of alcoholism ('I recall my dad going out to Las Vegas to his sister and taking her off life support. The doctor said her liver was the size of a watermelon'). When they were living in Ohio, Chuck recalls seeing his mother pour a drink and light a cigarette. 'And her personality would change. She would get relaxed … mellow … and I clearly remember thinking, *I don't know what that is, but I definitely plan on doing it.*'

Chuck also remembers a series of parent-teacher conferences stretching back to kindergarten, as well as a history of truancy and several changes of school. He continues, 'From the earliest age I remember carrying around this emotional pain … I don't know if it was fear, guilt, shame, or what … and all this vague free-floating anxiety followed me everywhere. My constant companion. And, as early as eleven or twelve, I remember getting drunk with some kids from the neighbourhood, and I liked it. We would smoke weed and do all those things. Anything we could get our hands on. Of course, I always seemed to get more drunk than the others. And I wouldn't say I discriminated against anything. Diet pills, LSD, beer, coke … whatever. I would have snorted gasoline if I'd thought it would get me high. I've heard people say that their drug of choice is really *more*. That's true with me. In every way. Faster! Louder! More!'

He pauses. 'I was an angry kid. I'd pick fights. And was abusive to those closest to me. And extremely hurtful.' He stops to reflect again before going on. 'I lived in my head. I got kicked out of high school my freshman year … and from there they took me to a social worker, and they ended up committing me to a mental hospital facility. I broke out of that place. Threw a chair through a window, and when that didn't do the trick, I used a desk.

'I hit the streets,' he continues. 'Saw a kid I knew from high school on a motorcycle cruising down Whittier Boulevard and I flagged him down. He took me to the city of Newport Beach and I grabbed my [surf] board. I had a friend whose family had a place in Laguna Beach, so I broke in there and crashed. A couple of days later, my sister Jeanne spotted me walking down the Pacific Coast Highway and pulled over in her VW. She took me in. But I had to go back to the hospital. I remember walking through the doors and all the in-patient teens applauded me: *Look at this badass.* My sister said my dad was freaking as they were going to cut me off the insurance if I spent another day out there AWOL.'

He describes the three-month stay in the mental hospital as a 'giant pause button'; even if it did not address the underlying causes, it was a fresh start. 'I'd hole up in my room listening to records, playing guitar. I even had a girlfriend. And I'd go surfing.' Never one for team sports, the surf became an obsession: 'It made me feel free. It always feels good to catch a wave. Plus, every surfer out there is starring in his own movie. My cousin Richard gave me one his old boards. I would skip school and go to the beach. Or we'd family vacay down at San Clemente and camp. I'd surf all morning and again in the afternoon when the sun was going down and the wind dropped a bit. Later, Jeanne had an apartment in Newport and I could stash my surfboard in her garage. I would take the bus and go surfing. In La Habra, we lived at the corner of Whittier Boulevard and Harbor Boulevard, where they intersect. You could take the bus for a quarter to Newport Beach.'

The way Prophet talks about it, it sounds like therapy, and probably far more effective than whatever the medical facility could offer. 'I was an anxious kid. I was all twisted up inside. But all those things that ate at me would just melt away out there. Surfing is an adventure. And, when you're trying to paddle over an incoming set of waves, at risk of getting *caught inside* and pummelled by walled-up waves? You paddle hard and fast. And when you're in it and the adrenaline is pumping, it's hard to remember what all the anxiety was about.' It was a defining feature of Chuck's teenage years. 'Out with my friends—Mark Gardner, John Ladner, Chris Heilman. Surfing the Huntington pier at night in the summer and then staying up all night. Oh, and I was pretty good at it.' He adds, 'I suppose there was something about the outlaw culture too that attracted me. You don't need any permission. All you need is a surfboard and a wave ... and your wits.'

The period of relative stability did not last. 'My family moved to Danville in Northern California, when I was sixteen. I rode it out at a new school for a few months, and that summer I took the Greyhound Bus back down to Orange County, staying at my friend Mark's house with his family. And we would push lawnmowers during the day to make money and mainline cocaine at night. Shooting cocaine made me feel like I was thirty thousand feet above Fullerton. And we'd go to punk rock shows and get blackout drunk. And chase girls. That was sixteen-year-old Chuck. And it was all working for me. Or so I thought. I put on this attitude. I had a lot of bravado. And constantly tempted fate. Driving drunk. I was abusive, I was contentious. I was a brat.'

Nevertheless, the music remained an anchor point. Non-musical his family may have been, but Prophet does note that his parents 'had some cool records' (he name-checks Charlie Rich). Still, the coolest ones ('Bowie, Mott') came from his sister and her boyfriend. He remembers his girlfriend buying him Bowie's *Hunky Dory* when he was twelve—'a real gateway drug for me'. Prophet often jokes that where he grew up in Orange County, if you shook a tree ('and there were a lot of trees in Orange County'), five guitar players would fall out.

When he was much younger, big sister Jeanne had brought home a guitar after a visit to Catholic youth camp and tried to learn a John Denver song; Chuck would watch, figuring it out for himself, and soon enough got his own guitar. A neighbour showed him a few chords, but when he asked his father for guitar lessons, he got golf lessons instead. He picked up a Pickwick collection of Jeff Beck recordings and 'sat and learned a lot of it—and, to this day, that's my go-to place,' he says, picking up a guitar and peeling off a familiar lick, as we sit in his 'shoebox' office space not far off Market Street. Some of his earliest gig-going memories include trips to the Starwood in LA to catch bands like Quiet Riot (in their definitive Randy Rhoads era), but he also recalls being surprised by appearances from the likes of an embryonic Wall Of Voodoo as the punk/new-wave scene was developing. Prophet's high-school band Peter Accident & The Duck Revolution reflected that musical environment, as commemorated in a vivid blog post by one of his contemporaries: 'I remember the spiky-haired, freakazoid guitarist, sliding across the stage on his knees at the High School Talent Show, shredding away ... to some homemade punk song far in excess of the limited talents of the band around him.'[29]

Chuck's father worked in marketing for the Avery International Corporation and had been transferred to San Francisco in 1979, and, while the children finished the school year, Chuck Sr. settled into a furnished apartment. His son would fly up on occasion, and he recalls his father driving him around the commuter belt—Mill Valley, Walnut Creek, and the East Bay—house-hunting (they would settle in Danville, half an hour east of San Francisco). Prophet remembers, on one visit, walking down Telegraph Avenue and seeing a poster for the band Psychotic Pineapple; he persuaded his Dad to take him to the show. They were 'kinda punk, kinda psychedelic—really just this incredibly colourful art-damaged band that wasn't like anything I had ever seen,' he tells me.

'I remember one night after seeing Gary Numan at the Warfield, I was befriended by some punks my age, and after the show we went to the now defunct Electric Theater on Market Street and climbed up into the projection booth where a friend of theirs was working. And then we went to this warehouse after-hours party until all hours of the morning where some bands were playing. It was glorious. It was romantic. It was another world. KALX'S Maximum Rock And Roll show was a godsend. They would announce all the punk shows. Every weekend I'd be out there.'

KALX radio, coming out of the Berkeley campus, played a lot of under-the-radar music, British imports, and local punk. It was on KALX that Prophet heard the announcement of a gig at the Temple Beautiful on Geary Street, a show featuring Wall Of Voodoo: 'Wildly inventive; the guitar player twanged a Fender Jag through a fat tube reverb tank maxed out. The rhythm section was the beat-box from grandma's organ set to a bossa-nova beat. And they looked like they crawled out of some 50s Mexican horror film.' Other bands on that bill included The Mentors ('hideous'), Black Randy, and No Alternative, but it was The Flamin' Groovies that made the biggest impression on Chuck: 'They were dressed in Beatle boots and Carnaby Street suits, playing vintage Vox guitars with the straps up high and wearing shades.' It was a night he would immortalise on the title track of the *Temple Beautiful* album several decades later.

Another defining experience came when Prophet was sixteen and in the school year following his stay at the mental hospital, and The Rubinoos and

The Greg Kihn Band came to play at his high school. 'In one of the classes they had all of the guitars set up and I picked one up, and this guy who was their guitar roadie said, "Oh, you can play? I'm starting a band." He called me later that summer, and that was Tom Nelson and Bad Attitude.' Both Bad Attitude and Prophet's next band, Wild Game, would feature Nelson on vocals and guitar and Steve Croke on bass. Prophet remembers Nelson 'would borrow strings from The Rubinoos' stash without asking'. He laughs. 'So I think that's why I use 52s,' Chuck remarks, referring to the thickness of the guitar strings. 'Tommy Dunbar strings a 52 on the low E. A 52 on the bottom on a Tele is pretty heavy.' Reflecting on his bandmates at the time, he notes, 'Those guys had great record collections and that came in handy when we started getting booked at the fraternity party circuit in Berkeley. We'd play those gigs and fill up three sets with The Animals ("I'm Crying"), "Shaking All Over", Yardbirds classics. Them's "Here Comes The Night" and "Gloria". "Roadrunner", "Pipeline", "Stepping Stone". Anything we could work up.'

Bad Attitude's adventures included a trip to Calgary, Alberta, in February 1982, where they did twelve dates, playing up to four sets a night (and 'never made a lousy dime', as the song goes); Chuck describes it as their 'Hamburg moment', referencing The Beatles' apprenticeship at places like the Star-Club in 1960–62. A press release from the time notes that they play 'primarily original music with a few select covers thrown in', and that 'they've been tagged as everything from power pop to accessible punk'.

Speaking of genres, Berkeley power-pop outfit The Rubinoos were one of Prophet's key influences at that time, and he saw them play countless times. 'They were a big part of my education,' he says. 'Oftentimes they would open with an a-capella number, like "Mr. Sandman", in perfect four-part harmony,' he recalls. 'And they would come back out for an encore and play "Telstar" [imitates tune]. Or they would do the theme from *The Good, The Bad And The Ugly* [plays guitar]. And just the whole American songbook in between: *Nuggets*, The Troggs, Jackson 5. And The Beach Boys. Sophisticated, deceptively simple songs. And they were kind of grown-up. I mean, they had been on television and had made records, toured the world. I probably saw The Rubinoos fifty times. Probably opened for them at least twenty-five times. Tommy Dunbar was an incredible guitar player.'

The Rubinoos and The Greg Kihn Band were both on Beserkley Records, a label founded in 1973 and most famous for housing the earliest solo recordings of Jonathan Richman after he disbanded the first incarnation of The Modern Lovers. (Richman was another key figure for Prophet—a letter dated March 10 1984 survives, welcoming Chuck to the Jonathan Richman fan club and asking for a donation of five dollars to help toward running costs!) Groomed by Beserkley as a teen pop band, chart success would largely elude The Rubinoos, and the band would go through several reincarnations over the following decades, but it is the classic seventies line-up that is seared in Prophet's memory. In 1977, their version of the Tommy & The Shondells number 'I Think We're Alone Now' took them to no. 45 in the US chart, and in 1978 they had some radio success in the UK with 'I Wanna Be Your Boyfriend'; the following year they were opening for Elvis Costello & The Attractions on the infamous tour when an intoxicated Costello got in an argument with Stephen Stills and Bonnie Bramlett, and Bramlett punched his lights out when, in an effort to shock and offend, Costello fired off random racist slurs aimed at James Brown and Ray Charles.

However, The Rubinoos were still teenagers without a driving licence between them when they started out. In 1974, they opened for The Jefferson Starship at Bill Graham's Winterland Ballroom in San Francisco, on a bill that also included Link Wray and Tommy Dunbar's brother's band Earth Quake. Dunbar remembers playing to an indifferent, half-empty room that began to take notice when they played The Archies' hit 'Sugar Sugar' ('We used to play it because it used to piss off our friends,' Dunbar laughs). When they segued from King Curtis's 'Memphis Soul Stew' into the theme song for the latest, ubiquitous Pepsi TV ad, he continues, 'all hell broke loose'. Prophet describes how, 'People just started shouting abuse and throwing stuff at them. Jonathan Richman was in the crowd and he started doing his jughead dance … up close to people. And he was kinda digging it. Jonathan told me, Bill Graham came out and addressed the audience, and said, "What I just saw here tonight is everything I hate about what's going on in rock music right now." And I said to Jonathan, "Well, thank God he stuck up for The Rubinoos." And Jon says, "No, he was talking about them" [*laughs*]. And Bill Graham goes, "Get the hell off my stage, you'll never play in this town again." But Grace Slick [Jefferson

Starship] followed them out onto the street and said, "Don't let anybody tell you what to do. You guys are cool!"' Tommy recalls, 'It was a bit like having your mom come up and say, "Don't worry, everything's going to be OK!"' In 2018, Prophet would secure a deal for the band with YepRoc and co-write and produce their first album of new material in eight years, *From Home*, released the following year to great critical acclaim.

Back to 1983. Prophet's second semi-professional band, Wild Game, cut an album called *Rhythm Roundup*. The first side, comprising four songs—'Want Too Much', '2000 Miles', 'Won't Happen', and 'Real Girl'—was produced by the band and Matt Wallace; the three songs on side two—'Crying Over You', '(I Want A) Rich Girl Friend', and 'Coulda' Been Somebody'—were produced by Dave Carpender (lead guitarist for The Greg Kihn Band), who also contributed some slide guitar to 'Crying Over You'. The tracks were laid down in primitive fashion: 'We recorded ourselves with a PA mixing board and a tape deck, patching all the cords in ourselves and not knowing what we were doing,' Chuck recalled.[30]

If Bad Attitude and Wild Game didn't exactly set the local scene alight, they did at least begin to establish Prophet's reputation as an emerging local guitar hero, playing venues such as Berkeley Square and the Mabuhay Gardens. In the summer of 1983, when Green On Red 1.0 were recording *Gravity Talks*, Wild Game even opened for R.E.M. at the Keystone in Berkeley.[31] Prophet later recalled, 'There were about seventy-five people there, but there was what people call a buzz in the air. My band played a set that included a cover of the MC5's "High School". After the set, Peter Buck walked up and said, "Hey man, cool set. Great MC5 cover."'[32]

At the time, Chuck was playing a Fender Stratocaster: 'I bought it in LA with my paper route money at the Guitar Center on Sunset when I was twelve. I remember being shocked when my father asked the salesman if he could "do any better on the price". I didn't know you could do that.' Chuck's close friend Patrick Winningham (of whom much more later) remembers it vividly for its decals—the shark's teeth familiar from World War II fighter planes. The guitar would later be stolen out of Prophet's car after a Gun Club show at the I-Beam in Haight-Ashbury.[33]

Prior to that, Prophet had been doing a semi-regular midnight DJ shift at the KSFS radio station at the local campus of California State University, where he was by this time, nominally at least, taking classes, including one run by a professor called John Barsotti, who taught the basic principles of multi-track recording: 'He'd play Beatles tracks on reel-to-reel, and we'd discuss how they were put together. I started paying attention.' The station manager recalls Prophet calling from jail one night—Chuck had used his one phone call to check in and apologise because he was going to miss his shift. Prophet remembers the station receiving copies of the first Green On Red record along with the likes of The Dream Syndicate and The Three O'Clock. Intrigued, he caught a couple of Green On Red shows at the I-Beam and was smitten. 'They looked like they should have been operating rides in a carnival or something,' he told me. 'But Danny was this charismatic guy, mouthing off between songs, and there was always something else going on onstage, besides the music.'

Stuart's songwriting had a major impact on Prophet's sensibilities. Chuck later noted, 'Dan had songs like "Old Chief" and "Brave Generation", which he later disowned as preaching and pretentious, but I was completely blown away.'[34] Musically, too, Prophet was intrigued: 'They were raw and very keyboard-driven and kind of Doors-y,' he notes. 'All of the melody seemed to come from Chis Cacavas ... he played the Garth Hudson/Ray Manzarek role. He'd rock back and forth like an autistic child while racing up and down the major scale ... almost classical. He was the random element and he was turning it into music.' Stuart, meanwhile, 'appeared agitated, like he needed a drink ... I knew that look from home. He'd mouth off, very uptight, but also kind of fearless.' He also remembered watching them play 'Snake Bit' at the end of the night: 'Danny was crawling round on his hands and knees, swallowed the microphone—the chord was hanging out of his mouth—he was barking like a dog and crawling into the crowd. I said, "These guys are GREAT! Do they do this EVERY night?!"'[35]

GREEN ON RED 2.0

Chuck became an instant fan, and in January 1984 Wild Game found themselves on the same bill as Green On Red at Ruthie's Inn. Sitting around drinking after soundcheck, Stuart turned to Prophet: 'Hey, man, if I break a string, can I borrow your guitar? Or, better yet, why don't you just come up and play with us? For the encore or some shit?'

'I don't remember what we played,' Prophet says, 'but I think someone said, "If you're ever down in LA, look us up."' At that time, Prophet used to play in the backing band for a stand-up comedian called Barry Sobel; Sobel would go on to write for *Saturday Night Live* and appear in the Tom Hanks movie *Punchline* (1988), but at that time was working the stand-up clubs, making a name for himself, and getting some attention for the way he would integrate rap into his routines—which was revolutionary at the time. 'He also did a great Mick Jagger,' Chuck enthuses. 'Hanging around the comedy clubs, it was kind of a golden era. I was eighteen when I started playing with him, and it was an education.' Prophet would regularly play with Sobel when he was down in LA, and, in the first half of 1984, 'I was at his place and I noticed they [Green On Red] were playing and I think I called Jack [Waterson] and I said, "I want to come down and see you." He says, "Well, bring your guitar." So I sat in with them at the Music Machine.' Or, as he put it to David Cantwell, 'They just put a guitar in my hands and it ended up being like a five-years-to-life sentence.'[36]

Stuart, who coined the nickname Billy The Kid for Prophet, later recalled, 'There was a point right before Billy joined where I got a thing going, lead-wise, but soon forgot it in a haze of pot smoke.'[37] And, just before Chuck popped up, the band were contemplating recruiting an additional guitarist. Matt Piucci had guested on lead guitar on one track on *Gravity Talks* and sat in on a few shows—a bootleg of one at the Music Machine on March 10 1983, despite the rough quality of the audience tape, reveals the added breadth and depth he brought to the live sound—but when Stuart heard Prophet play, he says, 'I dug it immediately.'

'At the end of the gig,' Prophet says, 'I remember Danny said, "I say he's in the band," in front of everybody—it wasn't like they had a chance to vote! And then they said, "We're going to Scandinavia to do a tour, you're going to need to get a passport."' Piucci was disappointed to be passed over. Chuck remarks, 'I still see Matt all the time. And, I kid you not, he acts like I'm still subbing for him. I guess in the back of his mind he keeps thinking he will return to it!'

Up to this point, Chris Cacavas had effectively been the band's lead instrumentalist, and Dan was anxious that a second guitarist, especially someone with chops to spare, might be encroaching on what had been Chris's territory, but Chris tells me, 'I was excited about us becoming a five-piece. The transition was tricky at first but I didn't see it as a competition, I enjoyed what he brought to the table and I was happy to make room for him'. In his memoir, Stuart asks the rhetorical question, 'Was Billy more talented than Chez? No, but he embraced the canon, stocked his library from the mundane to the rarified and embraced it all.'[38] Prophet suggests the tension was largely in Dan's troubled thoughts. 'I mean, we were all playing; it was a *band*. No one solos on *Blonde On Blonde*. The best music is Dixieland, and people are soloing all over the place. That's where the music is.'

The autumn 1984 Scandinavian tour found the band mixing setlist staples such as 'Cheap Wine', '5 Easy Pieces', and 'Gravity Talks' with quite a few recently rehearsed numbers that would appear on the next LP—'Sixteen Ways', 'Sea Of Cortez', and 'Fading Away'—along with covers of the Stones ('Sympathy For The Devil') and Dylan ('Knockin' On Heaven's Door').

At the tail end of the tour, the band were offered a date in London, and a debut show in the UK, set for September 17 1984, was too tempting to refuse. What happened next offers a snapshot of the smaller-scale touring business at that time. The Swedish team responsible for booking the tour gave the band their directions and added strict instructions that they should buy 'a carton of duty-free Rothman Blues' (cigarettes) on their way through Customs for the UK agent in London. The band—nonplussed, short of cash, or both—failed to secure the merchandise, which did not endear them to their contact. Nevertheless, they were directed to a goth bar called Gossip in Soho for what was called the Alice In Wonderland club night. Backline amps and drum kit were already in place, and, as they loaded in, the band met 'three guys with thick Scottish accents . . . we couldn't understand what they were saying,' Chuck remembers, 'but we put it together that it was their first time in London, and they were gonna open the show.

'So the band got up to play,' he continues, 'and they were trying to get feedback out of those amps, and there was nobody there, and it was extremely noisy and the singer was spinning round on the spot until the cable wrapped around his ankles, and then he just fell, right in front of us. And there was something effortlessly cool about them in their sort of ramshackle way. And after two songs there was a seven-foot-tall transvestite bartender with all this hair and lipstick, pouring pints, watching it go down, and he just came out from behind the bar: "All right, that's it. Let's go, come on. Move along. Come on boys, that's enough." He shooed them off the stage. And that band was The Jesus & Mary Chain.'

The seven-foot-tall bartender Chuck remembers was DJ and singer Clive Jackson, better known as Doctor of Doctor & The Medics (who two years later would score a worldwide hit with their version of Norman Greenbaum's 'Spirit In The Sky'). Jackson remembered The Jesus & Mary Chain's gig as an unmitigated disaster: 'Well, it wasn't even music, it was such a shambles. Green On Red had a lot of gear, and one of the concerns was that the Mary Chain were tottering about on stage and we were thinking, some of the gear's going to go any minute. Murray was trying to hold it together on the drums, but Jim was just kicking his guitar around on the floor. People were complaining. I don't mind art for art's sake, but I'm not into shit for shit's sake.'[39] As Jackson removed the band from the stage, drummer Murray Dalglish reportedly kicked at the kit in frustration, knocking a cymbal to the floor, and then froze, believing it was Green On Red's gear he had attacked. As one of the Americans approached, Dalglish recalls, 'I thought he was going to thump me right in the face, and he just said, "Hey man! You were just like the goddamn fucking Sex Pistols!" I really thought I was going to get my arse kicked!'[40]

Green On Red had played about a dozen shows on that tour, and, despite the sparse crowd at Gossip, several music weeklies took note of their London debut, including *Sounds*, whose reviewer, Edwin Pouncey, raved, 'How does a rock'n'roll nuclear device sound? Like this: big, brave and powerful, with a finger on the creative button.'[41] Despite the low-key nature of the gig, it did feel 'sort of like the beginning of something,' Prophet recalls. The British music press would play an increasingly important role in the band's success in Europe; soon after that London debut, Prophet recalls, they started getting booked by Martin Elbourne, a seminal figure in UK music management who was involved with the Glastonbury festival from its inception, and also co-founded the world music festival WOMAD with Peter Gabriel, first staged in 1980. He now works as an international festival consultant,[42] but at the time he was just establishing himself as an agent and manager, working with the likes of New Order and The Smiths. Elbourne and the company All Trade Bookings would become central to Green On Red's story.

GAS FOOD LODGING

Back in the USA, in the wake of the largely successful first European jaunt, Prophet had been expecting to make a record for Slash, but it was not to be. 'It was kind of funny and kind of sad,' recalls Chris Cacavas. 'Chuck joins this band and we were on Slash. So he's, like, "All right! Here I am with this band, they have a label, everything's great!" Next thing he knows, we're off Slash.'[43] The trouble began with a disagreement between Stuart and the label over who would produce the album. Slash Records wanted Mitchell Froom, a relative unknown, in the control room; this was long before Froom would make his name working with the likes of Crowded House, Richard Thompson, and Suzanne Vega. However, Slash had picked up Froom's soundtrack for cult science fiction porn movie *Cafe Flesh* (1982) and released it under the title *The Key Of Cool*. Prophet recalls that Dan Stuart meanwhile had set his sights on Mitch Easter of the band Let's Active (although Stuart says he doesn't recall this detail, a May 1986 interview with him seems to confirm it[44]); Easter had recorded R.E.M.'s first single, 'Radio Free Europe', and subsequently produced their *Chronic Town* EP (1982) and, alongside Don Dixon, their first two albums.

With Stuart and Slash at an impasse—Dan's response to the suggestion of Froom ('Well, who's that?') was mirrored by the label when Stuart named Easter ('Well, who's he?')—the job fell to Paul B. Cutler, who had played guitar in punk-goth band 45 Grave; Prophet recalls that Cutler had run the sound at the infamous punk venue the Hong Kong Café, 'And I think maybe he was a friend of their pot dealers.' Dan describes Cutler, who would in due course replace Karl Precoda in The Dream Syndicate, as 'one of LA's unsung heroes for his recording skills and overall coolness'. As Stuart remembers it, he already had time booked with Cutler when Slash proposed Froom, and he was outraged when Slash wanted to cancel the session. 'The way I dealt with it was just being extremely rude to people,' he shrugs. The sessions went ahead with Cutler.

'Getting signed by Slash felt great at the time,' Stuart would say in a May

1986 interview. 'It was just like we were in Chicago in the early sixties and got signed to [legendary blues label] Chess records. Then we learned it was *exactly* the same, because Leonard Chess never paid anybody either.'[45] The deal with Slash quickly went south after the falling out over the choice of producer. 'That all happened in a half day,' Dan asserts, 'Meaning, fuck you, to the company.' Green On Red made their first album with Prophet for the Enigma label instead. 'We called up the first record company we could find the number of and said, "Can we make a record?" and they said, "Yeah," and we went and cut it,' Chuck later said, simply.[46] That album would be *Gas Food Lodging*.

Both Stuart and Prophet have a great deal of affection and enthusiasm for the first album they made together. Stuart tells me, 'It was fun and quick to make. The songs were there, we had a good relationship with Paul Cutler and a new label that left us alone. Chuck was a great addition to the band (his Fender Squier Telecaster was bought with the record's equipment budget), and the only stress I had was dividing up the leads between him and Chris, which was no stress at all.' For Prophet, it was 'a really great record on a lot of levels. We were energised,' he recalls, and 'Dan Stuart came up with a great bunch of songs.' It marked a significant musical turning point; in retrospect, it was the album that would begin to mark out Green On Red, for some, as alternative-country pioneers. 'If you keep playing you eventually get around to blues and country as a matter of course,' Stuart believed.[47] 'I was ready to play some cowboy chords,' he reasons. 'I was ready to write some songs and chord progressions that were more in line with FM radio, '72, '73.'

The album was recorded at a vintage studio called Eldorado, which had a distinguished history; Johnny Otis cut 'Willie And The Hand Jive' there in 1958. Eldorado was also used to shoot scenes for the Ritchie Valens biopic *La Bamba* (1987), and Prophet recalls how paper gold stars that the set designers had made were still attached to the doors. More significant was Eldorado's geographical position: though it relocated to Sunset Boulevard not long after *Gas Food Lodging* was cut, and then to Burbank in 1996, at that time it was situated on the corner of Hollywood and Vine, with the Firefly and the Clown Room and other bars close by. ('That was important to us,' Prophet admits.) With almost all the songs already bedded in from the tour, the entire album was recorded swiftly: 'We basically cut it live, real fast, very easy,' Stuart later said.[48] The songs were Stuart's, but the new recruit threw some of his own musical chops into the mix: 'Dan brought songs in, and in the beginning, if there wasn't a bridge or something, or a solo, I'd make suggestions.' Writing for *Blurt* in 2014, Fred Mills believed the guitarist brought 'a measure of musical discipline to a band in the process of shedding its punk skin'. He quoted Prophet: 'There didn't seem to be a lot of communication going on, musically or otherwise, at least not to the naked eye. I remember the first time we got together to play, and Dan presented "Hair Of The Dog". We just fell in and it came right to life, but when we were done I said I thought it seemed to run out of steam after a while and asked if they had a bridge for it. Everyone just looked at their shoes.'[49] As the San Francisco–based magazine *BAM* noted in its review at the time, Prophet's 'fiery playing' not only made a significant contribution to the band's sound, it also helped them 're-define their direction'.[50]

Any concerns about integrating a new lead instrument into the band proved to be unfounded: Cacavas and Prophet meshed effortlessly (a *Sounds* feature from 1985 described how the two would stand onstage and play endlessly together, before and after soundcheck).[51] The young guitarist brought a whole set of other influences into play, and as Stuart reflects, 'I found a way that the band could *evolve*.' As he would later tell Fred Mills, 'As a writer . . . I started hearing arrangements.'[52] 'Fading Away' is a perfect example: the second half of the song develops into an extended workout for Prophet and Cacavas as they take it in turns to play lead, anchored around a lithe and nagging riff, while Prophet and Waterson's vocal harmonies tip a hat to the sixties. 'Sixteen Ways', which would become a live staple, also perfectly counterpoints Cacavas's keys with Prophet's heavy-strung Telecaster. At the mid-point, Prophet cracks the song open with a squalling solo. 'Black River' is classic country-rock, with Cacavas contributing harmonica as well as piano, and Prophet pulling out all the Nashville double-stops.

The album was released in May 1985. Stuart reckons that 'the excellent reviews it got was vindication for standing up to Slash and not "selling out", which now sounds a bit quaint but back then was a very huge deal with everybody'. Nevertheless, it was not plain sailing with Enigma, either, at least in terms of distribution of the new album: the label seemed unwilling to make individual territory deals, instead trying to use their new hot property to foist their whole back catalogue on prospective labels; Stuart reckons, 'That certainly slowed things down and hurt the record.' The album was initially only available as a costly import in Europe, before trickling out via Zippo in the UK and New Rose in France; European distribution of their releases would be a persistent problem, a source of great frustration given the band's level of success there on the live circuit, which seemed to snowball with every tour.

It was in fact a torrid time for several bands in the Paisley Underground. According to Sid Griffin of The Long Ryders, 'By '83/'84, we were all getting sniffs from majors,' but grass roots were key. The Long Ryders' first album, *Native Sons* (1984), 'was written about first by a guy called David Bragg writing for some fanzine,' he recalled. Someone at Zippo saw the fanzines and the interest just mounted from there. 'Not *NME* or *Melody Maker*,' Griffin was at pains to point out, 'fanzines.'[53] Michael Azerrad describes the fanzines as 'the house organs of the indie scene', most of them starting out as 'photocopied rants by people who were frustrated at the way the mainstream music magazines largely ignored this exciting new music'.[54] The fanzine, like so many elements of the underground, was also often a localised phenomenon, encouraging fans to discover not the latest sounds as dictated by a major label, but the bands from their own streets, playing their local clubs. For many, fanzines would provide a stepping-stone to wider exposure and the mainstream music press.

Meanwhile, the sense of a busily revolving door at this level of the music business was indicative of an industry in financial overdrive. The major labels were beginning to investigate the underground scene too. Dan Stuart remarks, 'Those were the days of A&R guys with hubris. We had been on Slash and Enigma, and then a guy at Phonogram [Dave Bates] who had nurtured Tears For Fears signed Green On Red, Tom Verlaine, and Was Not Was in a fit of madness.' Bates is an A&R legend—his other signings over the years include Def Leppard, The Teardrop Explodes, Texas, Wet Wet Wet, and many others. Steve Wynn thinks that 'A&M signed us to be cool'; Sid Griffin remembered being 'feted and courted by Polygram and UK A&M and UK Island and all these other people', and back-to-back meetings with A&R teams.[55] Speaking to the *Guardian* in 2013, Stuart was typically wry: 'It got ugly then. A lot of capitulation. Most of us were raised pretty bourgeois so there you have it.'[56]

However, as Prophet notes, Green On Red and some of their contemporaries were unfortunate in that they narrowly missed the college-radio renaissance—the wave that the likes of R.E.M. would ride from the mid-1980s all the way into superstardom. It was a case of bad timing, poor management, misfortune, or some combination of the above. The fact that Engima started having success with some of their other bands, notably The Smithereens, might have been another reason why Green On Red started to lose momentum. The Smithereens' chart success began with their song 'Blood And Roses', featured on the soundtrack for the action B-movie *Dangerously Close* (1986); Green On Red's contribution (the far less immediate 'Sea Of Cortez') went unnoticed.

Nevertheless, *Gas Food Lodging* had made the major music weeklies, as well as the national papers, prick up their ears. Coverage of the band was stepping up into the big league. Mikal Gilmore for the *Los Angeles Herald* lauded it as 'a beautifully crafted … work of longing' and 'the best work by any LA group so far this year'; the *Los Angeles Times* called it 'a quantum leap by an underrated group, present[ing] the frustration, elation, boredom and excitement of life on the road with a new musical strength and powerful vision.'[57] *Spin* called it 'the audio equivalent of *The Grapes Of Wrath*' and 'Woody Guthrie meets the 1980s'.[58] In the UK, it was 'a work of total mastery', according to *Sounds*; 'a record that has the feel of a finely bound book of illustrated short stories to it, some of which could become classics'.[59] Mat Snow for the *NME* described it as 'amongst the very best' of the records currently redefining the new American rock scene and referenced Creedence, Dylan, and Neil Young.[60] In *Melody Maker*, David Fricke also drew lengthy parallels with Neil Young, describing the band's sound as 'a strange amalgam of Young's cutthroat Crazy Horse punk and his offbeat hillbilly delights'—Young's country-styled *Old Ways* would not be released until a few months later, but he had been touring the material with his International Harvesters since the previous summer. While some reviewers remarked on the synergy between Cacavas and Prophet, Fricke noted, 'There is something very convincing in the crude sting of Prophet's random fills, his chunky abusive chords and Stuart's swaggering barroom confessions that sweeps the rest of this album up behind it.'[61]

Of their version of Pete Seeger's 'We Shall Overcome', Prophet would remark, 'This was at the height of Reagan's rising wave of fascism, and Danny in particular was really interested in a lot of populist rhetoric. We put this version together and the changes were just so beautiful. I don't know of anybody else who plays it that way.'[62] Dan remembers, 'I picked it up from a book of gospel songs I found in a thrift shop; believe it or not, I was only vaguely aware of its historical significance as a protest anthem (I was three years old in 1964 when the Civil Rights Act was enacted) and I didn't realise how pretentious we were being by ending the album with it.' Regardless, it is the perfect coda to a collection of tales of squalor and desperation. It is also a distillation of the politics that have always been fundamental to Stuart. Interviews promoting the album found him presenting a vivid snapshot of tensions between the generations—he referenced the emerging concept of the 'yuppie' and pointed out that their parents were in many cases 'legitimate hippies': 'Now these parents are like forty years old, paying a twenty-year mortgage, doing cocaine freebase and voting for Reagan.' But, he continued, some of his generation 'were *really* influenced by the values of the Sixties which gradually became corrupted. We weren't on drugs at the time, we were just children watching, absorbing and learning.'[63] A 1989 interview found him nominating Gorbachev and Reagan as the people of the decade: 'One represents the future and what we can be—accommodation and living together—and the other represents nostalgia and intolerance and hatred.'[64]

A 2002 reissue of the album allowed a couple of reviewers to consider the album's place and its legacy with the benefit of hindsight. For *Uncut* magazine, 'The album indicted the Reagan era like no other ... bemoan[ing] the loss of innocence of a sepia-tinted era, communities razed to dust in the face of corporate revolution.'[65] In *No Depression*, David Cantwell referenced Springsteen's *Nebraska* (1982) and pointed out that the band had emerged from the LA club scene at a time 'when America's haves waged unapologetic class warfare upon its have-nots'. Noting that 'Stuart's songs conveyed the band's sociopolitical vision in affectingly human terms', he compared the combination of 'austere language and generally working-class themes' with the 'depraved pulp fictions' of writers like Jim Thompson and Charles Willeford.[66]

Many reviewers of the reissue identified Prophet's contribution as crucial to the evolution of the band's sound: Neil Weiss, also writing for *No Depression*, credited his 'sharp and soulful fretwork' for the way it 'pulled the band's sound from the psychedelic ghetto into a greater multi-dimensional vein'.[67] Cantwell likened the album to 'a camp-meeting cross of Crazy Horse and Creedence Clearwater Revival, a rootsy song-centric approach that, along with the music of Los Angeles compatriots Lone Justice, Los Lobos, and The Long Ryders, presaged the rise of alternative country at the end of the decade'.[68]

Such parallels suggest how the album might have opened the door to a wide demographic of music fans still keeping the flame at the altar of classic rock, excited by a band with one foot in an Americana musical legacy and one in post-punk anarchism. It was certainly a blend that found a receptive audience across Europe, where the band's critical kudos and fan base continued to build steadily. There might be a touch of rose-tinted romanticism in Fred Mills's 2014 description of those tours, but he captured the excitement felt on both sides of the lip of the stage: 'When the LA band clambered onto stages with nothing to hide behind but faded jeans, flannel shirts and a we're-gonna-show-you attitude, audiences initially may have been skeptical. Two hours later, however, everyone in the club—crowd and employees alike—would be stamping their feet and hollering for more.'[69]

Rose-tinted or not, one undisputed element of the story is the fact that the band managed to acquire (and, for the most part, maintain) a favoured position amongst the music critics. When I suggested to Dan Stuart that the rumour about Neil Young really digging the song 'Ballad Of Guy Fawkes' must have meant more than press reviews, he demurred, 'Actually, we did care about the critics, because they kept the whole charade going. We were "critics' darlings" at the time, and that's why we kept getting one recording deal after another. It used to drive the other bands nuts. Really the only records that got a lukewarm reception were *The Killer Inside Me* and *This Time Around*. I'm not saying we deserved the positive attention, but we got it.'

February 1985 found Dan Stuart taking a forty-eight-hour detour (collaborator Steve Wynn claims thirty-two) to record a set of songs co-written with Wynn in a single alcohol-fuelled session. The weekend's work, featuring contributions from Chris Cacavas and most of The Long Ryders, was issued as *The Lost Weekend* by Danny & Dusty via A&M Records (Wynn's label at that time). Much of it is as ramshackle as the recording conditions might lead one to expect, but it has a charm and spontaneity that makes it a more enjoyable listen than some of the formal recordings the parent bands would issue in the 1980s. Although a 1986 interview mentions that another Danny & Dusty album 'was in the works',[70] it would take twenty-two years for Stuart and Wynn to reconvene with Cacavas and Stephen McCarthy for a second collaboration, with the enjoyable *Cast Iron Soul*—loose rather than falling down—issued by the German label Blue Rose in 2007.

The March/April 1985 tour to promote the imminent release of *Gas Food Lodging* found Green On Red clocking up ludicrous mileage across the European continent. ('We toured like crazy behind that record,' Prophet recalls, 'across the US as well as Europe.') The six-weeks-plus continental itinerary took them from Norway to Sweden to Holland, Belgium and a sole date in the UK—Dingwalls in London, with a guest appearance by Sid Griffin. Adam Sweeting was bowled over by the 'leaps and bounds' evident in the songwriting and by their performance: it's not often a critic would use terms such as 'cohesion and sense of purpose, a grip on the overall structure of their music' when describing Green On Red.[71]

The road was winding longer all the time, with Martin Elbourne at All Trade Booking occasionally adding dates mid-tour. 'There just seemed to be an endless amount of gigs,' Prophet told me, shaking his head. Their Geordie road manager, Andy Proudfoot, 'would stop sometimes at a phone box, and leave us sitting in the van, he'd go in with his briefcase, and he'd write things down: "Oh, they've just added twelve dates in Italy."' Chuck shrugs. 'It was different times; you couldn't call home. Those early tours, you'd come back and your girlfriend would have moved.' Autumn brought them back to Europe for a comparable tour, and over the summer the band had also appeared at Glastonbury, putting on a show that would earn them a place in the *Daily Telegraph*'s top 100 performances of all time at that storied festival.[72]

However, other reviews confirm that the band were not always in top condition. Maurice Lomas, reporting on a gig in Leeds, found them 'ordinary', 'anchored in the sixties' without having 'transformed their seminal influences into anything new or vital'.[73] An October 1985 show at the Leadmill in Sheffield left another reviewer scratching his head, trying to make sense of the hype: 'More than irritating, the copious accolades they receive are nothing short of irrational.'[74] But for *Melody Maker's* Martin Aston, reviewing the Camden Electric Ballroom show on July 4, the rootedness of the music was essential: 'Instantaneously respecting the past, far from doomed to repeat it, but wishing the values from the golden age were still around to guide us.'[75] The Camden gig—sharing a bill with Jonathan Richman and The Boothill Foot Tappers—is one that Prophet remembers particularly fondly.

Months on the road were not conducive to a healthy lifestyle, however. To some extent, the alcohol and the substance abuse was born of simple, prosaic boredom. 'We were either messed up or we were thinking about getting messed up, or we were taking the night off because we were so hungover,' Prophet reflects. 'Just blackout drinking. When I first met the band, within a couple days there was this incident where Danny had punched Chris in a drunken rage, late at night. And we were in a city and we couldn't find each other. Because people would go off and stay with somebody and there were no cell phones, and we were trying to get to the next city or whatever.' While the drinking—and, later, the drugs—took their toll on life on the road, the studio experience was not unaffected either. 'I can't speak for everybody,' Chuck says, 'But when we were recording for *The Killer Inside Me*, I remember we figured out how much money we were spending on beer, and that it would be cheaper to get a keg. And so we had a keg delivered.' And, while cannabis had been a consistent feature of the scene, 'It was later that Danny and I sort of bonded on the fact that we started to really get into black tar heroin. That was a little bit later, a couple of years later at least.'

CHAPTER TWO

KNOCKING ON THE DRAGON'S DOOR

NO FREE LUNCH, THE KILLER INSIDE ME (1986)

> Green On Red was never an organization for
> sensitive people. Insults were our preferred
> mode of communication. – Chuck Prophet

NO FREE LUNCH

Their star rising in Europe, Green On Red were catching the attention of more record label agents. Prophet remembers, 'We played in London and we were getting in the papers, and I think they sent everybody home except Danny. They marched him from one end of New Bond Street to the other—one meeting after another. At the end of the day we went with a company called Phonogram, and we turned the entire advance over to All Trade Booking.' Elbourne's booking agency had been supporting the band on tour, and had been losing money for some time. Prophet remembers, 'They said, "You need to turn this money over to us. We're not carrying you guys." So we did. And as we left the pub, I just kind of shrugged and may have said out loud, "We couldn't ask for receipts or anything?"'

As mentioned in the previous chapter, All Trade Bookings had brought Green On Red over to Europe in the summer of 1985 for Glastonbury. 'They were industry outsiders,' Chuck says of the company, looking back on that time, and the agency's very individual style. 'They booked James, New Order, The Smiths, and us. They had Bakelite phones! They were indie before there was a word for it.'

In many respects, this brief period was a highpoint for the band, despite the wrangling over contracts. The festival gigs were giving them significant exposure, and an appearance on *Rockpalast* (Zeche Bochum, October 4 1985) found the band playing a tidy set: though Dan begins in characteristic bad-boy mode, showing his ass to a bemused audience, it's one of the best places to hear Prophet and Cacavas playing off each other—check 'Easy Way Out' and 'Gravity Talks'. Stuart is in superb voice, his big orange Gretsch locked in with the rhythm section. Highlights include a fierce 'Sixteen Ways' prefaced by a prescient rap from Dan about the way America treats its black citizens, some intense soloing by Dan on 'The Drifter' and a self-aware, ironic 'No Free Lunch', as well as a rampaging cover of Neil Young's 'Down By The River'. And the performance of 'Time Ain't Nothing' makes one wonder again how the song was never a hit (the Manic Street Preachers would cover it years later, releasing it as a B-side in 2010). 'To Danny's credit, I don't know how he did it,' Prophet marvels. 'That song pretty much includes every chord that he knows. In a certain order! And it really captured that kind of longing.' To which Dan Stuart responds, 'Well, everyone's entitled to rip off "Brown-Eyed Girl" once but never twice.'

It was a happy accident of some rather chaotic booking that led to the band's next major recording session and the EP, *No Free Lunch*, that spawned the single. With Glastonbury and several other European Summer festivals booked, but with a long gap in between, the label decided to carve out some studio time. Wool Hall Studios was ten miles from the ancient, picturesque city of Bath and situated in rolling Somerset countryside. The pop group Tears For Fears, signed by Phonogram's A&R man Dave Bates, had converted the hall into a recording studio to create their hit album *Songs From The Big Chair* (1985). In subsequent years, Wool Hall would host The Smiths, Paul Weller, The Pretenders, and many others before Van Morrison bought it in 1994 (he sold it on in 2002). Stuart recalls that the space was not really set up to track live, but the deal Bates secured was too good to pass up. Dan also remembers that the place he and Chuck stayed in in Bath had no mains hot water supply,

'Just one of those shitty electric shower heaters that didn't really work. So we would go back every night and heat water up in a kettle and have a bird bath.'

Prophet paints a vivid picture of those sessions. 'I think we may have considered what we were doing demos. Danny didn't play guitar. He would show fragments or an outline of a song to me, I would play on acoustic down in the basement and he was upstairs with a hand-held mic and a TV monitor in the control room. And he said, "Well, I'm the producer!" And so then we cut what we could and went back out on tour. I don't even think we were really aware of what we were doing'. He recalls the sessions being tough for drummer Alex MacNicol: 'It was very difficult for him because we started trying to play grooves that were outside of the two beats that he was confident with. One time I was helping him with his drums, with the kick pad, and I was down on the ground, and Danny was up in the booth. And I was saying, "Now, Alex, we can just do it like this ... you know?" [*demonstrates the beat*] and he goes, "OK, OK, I think I get it," and he gets in close and he looks down, and he says to me, "Don't tell Dan!"'

At the end of the tour, Prophet and Stuart went back to London and overdubbed some guitar and vocals. Simon Humphreys, who had worked with The Clash, helped with the mix-down. 'And we didn't think anything of it,' Chuck says. 'We went back to the States and they said they liked it, thought it was cute. And they decided to release it as a mini LP.' The release quickly became complicated, however: for reasons best known to themselves, the label decided on a limited UK release, but it was swiftly picked up by college radio in the States, and it started to take off as an import, so Phonogram gave it a domestic (US) release. Jack Isquith was in charge of working the record to radio, and he worked it hard; it even cracked the *Billboard* Top 200, as well as the UK Top 100. During the band's subsequent tour in Holland, Echo & The Bunnymen's personal videographer, Bill Butt, was commissioned to shoot a video for 'Time Ain't Nothing'.

No Free Lunch was to be a buffer before the 'real' record (*The Killer Inside Me*), but Stuart still believes it could have been a hit if Phonogram had thrown a little money at it. 'So what we did was follow up the most commercial thing we ever did with the most unlistenable,' he muses. 'That's Green On Red for you.' Despite the fact they were now on a major label, Prophet told David

Cantwell, 'Like a lot bands in that period, there really wasn't any place for us on the radio. That was for, you know, Huey Lewis. But trying to get on the radio took a lot of spirit out of us. There was all this talk about getting to the next level, which was nuts. We were typically pretty out of tune, and Dan was like John Candy on Ritalin.'[1]

Furthermore, the US (and global) music industry was shifting into a new phase with the expansion of MTV and other music-dedicated channels. 'Remember,' says Prophet, 'This was a time when you turned on MTV and you didn't see anybody playing a guitar. You saw Paula Abdul doing synchronised dance steps or whatever. But then I remember one time seeing The Georgia Satellites on TV, and they were all [*plays Satellites riff*]. This band that had opened for us one time at Tipitina's in New Orleans. And they were on the back of a pickup truck playing guitars. And I remember thinking, *Well, I've never seen anything like that.* I mean, we just didn't picture ourselves coming out of the television. [*laughs*] We didn't picture ourselves selling lots of records.'

As often happens in conversation with Chuck, his mind makes a sideways leap here and he draws a parallel with R.E.M. It is an instructive comparison: two bands getting off the ground around the same time and heading for very different destinations. 'They basically just rose to whatever was put in front of them. I remember hearing that the first time they tried to make a video, Michael Stipe went out and threw up, he was so nervous. And then, the next thing I know, he's walking through the desert with his shirt sleeves rolled up and he's flagged down an eighteen-wheeler, and he's just looking round straight into the camera [in the video for 'Man On The Moon']. And I remember thinking, *Well, it didn't take them long.* [*laughs*] They mastered the medium. So I totally respect how they were just four guys out of Athens and they just kept getting bigger. We didn't have those kinds of *goals*. We didn't have a plan. Just really self-destructive.'

In the meantime, MacNicol had had enough. Stuart reckons the pressure got to him: 'The *No Free Lunch* album was when things were getting, "Oh, Chuck and Dan are pushing too hard."'[2] 'Yeah, Alex bailed, and God bless him, we must have been driving him crazy!' Prophet reflects, 'Alex was tough—he had definitely been through the wringer. But he was easily the nicest, sweetest, most gentle guy in the band. And he was a bad ass. But on a personal level, for him, the magic was gone. Seen the world, done this, done that.'

MacNicol quit on the eve of a US tour. The band placed a call to Paul B. Cutler, who hooked them up with Keith Mitchell; they took him sight unseen: 'Very typical of the way things worked in Green On Red,' Prophet remarks. According to Jane Simon, reporting on the tour at the time, '[Mitchell] didn't know any of the songs but they paid his airfare to Europe anyway.'[3] 'And, yeah,' Chuck continues, 'he hung in through the next chapter, and he ended up being the drummer in Mazzy Star.'

The autumn of 1985 found the band making more European festival appearances (Pandora's Music Box in the Netherlands; Futurama in Belgium, on a bill that also included The Jesus & Mary Chain and Rain Parade) and regional dates across the continent but concentrated in the UK. The setlists included several tracks from *No Free Lunch*, released in October of that year, and a few others that would never make it to tape.

Many fans rate *No Free Lunch* as one of the band's most consistent efforts. Stuart describes it as 'a listenable little thing, and it had almost, like, *hits* on it'. The fact that it was a seven-track mini-album may have had something to do with this—all killer and no filler, as the saying goes—but the truth is that the recording features a punchy, unfussy mix and some glorious tunes. 'Time Ain't Nothing' is one of the band's most unashamedly pop-oriented songs, driven irresistibly along by the acoustic rhythm track, Cacavas's organ bubbling under, and Prophet's economical, eight-bar electric country-rock solo spiking the centre. It comes as a surprise to find out that the song is actually a travelogue of the band's disastrous first East Coast tour, driving three days straight to get to Boston and being pushed onto the stage ten minutes after they arrived.[4] There are more lovely melodies ('Honest Man'), achingly pretty piano embellishments by Cacavas here and rolling Jerry Lee Lewis style licks there (the title track). Prophet contributes some slashing riffs ('Ballad Of Guy Fawkes') and some pedal-steel-emulating swells on the classic country song '(Ain't It Funny How) Time Slips Away'. Meanwhile, Stuart's sardonic vocals, particularly bitter on the political satire 'Guy Fawkes', are consistently strong and avoid the self-parody that would later become an occasional pitfall.

The album received significant press attention on both sides of the

Atlantic, with reviewers noting the evolution of the band's sound 'from a tilt towards the pseudo-psychedelic pop to the more earthy honky-tonk traditions and r&b rock'.[5] *Rock And Roll Confidential* tagged it 'the music you wish Neil Young still made: tough, aching, accents of country, folk, and psychedelia all at once, singing that drawls and *bites*'.[6] For St. Louis's *Riverfront Times*, it was 'a tasty menu of rockin' country … mastered with a bright, contemporary production'.[7] *Rolling Stone* magazine set aside considerable space for a detailed review that praised the interplay between the musicians and singled out 'the jabbing phrases and careening flights of Prophet's electric-guitar leads'.[8] Indianapolis-based *Steppin' Out* rated the band 'the gutsiest member of a growing subgenre of country-rock bands' and described the mini-LP as 'a warming, nearly spiritual record that bespeaks strong promise for Green On Red'.[9] The *Boston Globe*'s reviewer enjoyed the 'unique, country-inflected sound which continues to evolve', and the *Washington Post* review, ahead of the band's appearance at the 9:30 Club, described it as 'another splendid example of the way country's fatalism and rock's stubbornness can together sum up the contradictions of America's past and present'.[10] Esteemed veteran Robert Christgau, meanwhile, was typically acerbic, if ultimately positive, in his review: '[Stuart's] booze roots aren't ready for the mulch pile quite yet, and after too many plays I was surprised to conclude that his second Americana move was far catchier and more good-humored than number one. B+.'[11]

Others demurred. Ira Robbins reviewed the album for *Creem* and judged it derivative—'like the Burrito Brothers imitating Neil Young', with the acoustic, steel, and electric guitars blending into 'a parody of the boring numbers on *Beggars Banquet*'.[12] Although that could be used as a fair assessment of at least half of the alt-country music that would follow in the early 1990s, it seems unjust as a critique of *No Free Lunch*. The *Michigan Daily* found it too 'slick', the arrangements too 'neat and clean', and the collection as a whole lacking in 'grit'.[13] But then it's all about context and perspective: John Vernon's review in the *Illinois Entertainer* references John Cougar Mellencamp's album *Scarecrow* and notes that Green On Red presents similar rural America themes, but in a '*raw*' way.[14]

In the UK, where the band had become accustomed to favourable reviews, there was a more tepid reaction: the *Sounds* review found the new release 'partly a return to a diner where the food has gone a little stale ... a hors d'oeuvre, not without taste'.[15] Nick Kent was characteristically sour, finding Stuart's voice grating and stylised and the Gram Parsons/Neil Young crossover 'intriguing' on paper but disappointing in practice. 'With Parsons six feet underground and Young a reactionary cowpoke these days, there is a field of opportunity waiting to be ploughed and furrowed,' he suggested. 'Something tells me that one day this group may strike oil, but *No Free Lunch*, unfortunately, is no more than a rusty scythe.'[16]

The October UK promotional tour took them through fourteen dates on the standard club and student union circuit. *NME* was stubbornly unconvinced, dubbing 'these scions of the New Authenticity' as 'about as authentic as Nashville rhinestones' and dismissing Prophet, rather bizarrely, as the Grateful Dead's 'Bob Weir reborn as a stadium rocker', and Stuart as 'a makeweight Meatloaf'. While saving a little praise for the 'teeth-baring slasherama' of 'Hair Of The Dog', the reviewer had a much stronger impression of 'prevalent emptiness and second-handedness'—some perfectly good songs, 'except that they're, well, a lot like Neil Young songs'.[17]

Backlash, perhaps? Prophet's thoughts usefully place it within a wider industry context: 'Well, you learn. You lose your underdog status, and then what have you got? You sign to a major, you make a big expensive record and they want to help you but they'd say, "You've got to give us something to work with." And so we just had to get out of the way to make way for the next busload of scrappy guitar bands. And that's the media, whether it's the British press, or the American. If they're doing their job, oftentimes their role—now more than ever—really is the role of first responders. If a fire breaks out somewhere, they're the first ones on the scene and they need to try and make sense of it. When you're in it, you don't understand that. You think everything's going to go on forever. So ... no hard feelings!'

HITTING THE WALL: *THE KILLER INSIDE ME*

The success of *No Free Lunch* allowed the band to line up some shows back in the USA with some tour support; Alex Chilton opened. 'After we pleasantly surprised everybody with *No Free Lunch*, people started to think there might be something here,' says Prophet. 'Although Dave Bates had kind of a difficult time communicating with us.' He continues, 'We were still drinking, we were still fighting, but we managed to make a little batch of demos.'

The demos were recorded with Paul B. Cutler's help. Chuck recalls, 'I remember Danny getting so frustrated one night with a vocal, he threw the headphones on the ground and he jumped up and down, and he just smashed them until they were like watermelon seeds! And then Danny sheepishly went and hid all the pieces, and he and I got a kick out of it later when there was an invoice for the studio. And it said, *Tape: so many hours … so many days … one pair of headphones …*'

The recordings later appeared on the compilation *What Were We Thinking?*, which was released by an Australian label, Corduroy Records, and in Germany on the label Normal. Unsurprisingly, given their status as demos, some gated reverb on the drums aside, most of them sound rough, ready, immediate, and stripped down—qualities the subsequent release conspicuously lacked. There is also a nice range of tone and pace in the collection, from the driving beat behind 'Broken', 'Can't Drive Texas', and the pedal-to-the-metal 'Illinois Central' to the piano-led country balladry of 'Lonely Nights' and the tongue-in-cheek hoedown 'Paint Your Wagon'.

The label shopped the demos around to a few different candidates for the producer's chair. A revealing letter from Martin Elbourne, typed and photocopied and sent to each band member, displays All Trade Bookings' frustration at the slow progress toward their first full release on Phonogram. Dangling European festival dates, Elbourne writes, 'If for any reason the record doesn't come out before the summer it would be wrong for you to come over.' A PS adds, 'Get a record producer sorted out.' The letter is also a little passive-aggressive in the detail of the position Elbourne had carved out for them (wages guaranteed for at least eighteen months, press attention, radio, established for tours in 'virtually every country in Europe', the promise of a Far East tour); 'I'd also like to remind you that as managers go I'm dead cheap.' Elsewhere, he points out that he has worked for the band for nine months without money, 'indeed putting in my own money'. In that context, he suggests, the fact that he gets nothing but 'I'm really pissed off' calls from members of the band might not be entirely reasonable.[18]

'They had set up these meetings with professional producers, people that had had hit records in LA,' Prophet recalls. One of them was David Kershenbaum, who had signed Joe Jackson to A&M and produced him; a few years later, he would produce Tracy Chapman's first two albums (her debut would sell over seventeen million copies). 'Poor David Kershenbaum,' Chuck grins. 'He was a real gentleman, and he told me, "Well, I'm looking forward to the songs," and he was talking on the phone with me about his theories about producing, and later we had a couple of follow up conversations. And he said, "Well, I listened to the songs on the way back on the plane several times, and I just have to say that I think at this point … I'm just gonna have to remain a fan." [*laughs*] I just stored that one away! That's a good one. And so none of that really went anywhere.'

Whether it was the potential producers' dissatisfaction with what they were hearing, or the band's wariness of the producers, something wasn't clicking. 'There really wasn't anybody that we connected with,' Chuck shrugs. 'And eventually I saw that picture of Jim Dickinson on the back of [Ry Cooder's soundtrack album] *Paris, Texas*. Rolling duct tape across the keys. And I thought, well, that's the guy that produced [Big Star's] *Sister Lovers*, so …'

Jim Dickinson, whom Dan Stuart refers to as 'Bubba' throughout his memoir, was a pianist, guitarist, songwriter, and producer with a formidable history; a big part of the Memphis sound in the 60s, 70s, and beyond, he had worked with The Rolling Stones (that's him on piano on 'Wild Horses') and formed the Atlantic Records house band The Dixie Flyers, who backed Aretha Franklin, Delaney & Bonnie, Ronnie Hawkins, Lulu, and many others during their stints at the Criteria Recording Studio in Miami. He had championed Big Star in the early 70s, but it was Green On Red who effectively nudged him out of a kind of semi-retirement.

It was not a straightforward route to Memphis, however. Prophet recalls heading out to nearby club Wolfgang's to see David Lindley's band El Rayo-X ('just brilliant'); Lindley and Dickinson had worked together on several Ry Cooder soundtracks. When Prophet told Lindley he wanted Dickinson to produce Green On Red, Lindley suggested he get Ry instead. 'Well I would,' Prophet replied, 'but we're not really that kind of band.' Lindley was nonplussed:

'Well, what do you mean?'

'Well, we can't really play.'

'What do you mean you can't play?'

'Well we can play, but we're just like The Velvet Underground or something.'

'Who's that?'

'See? That's why I need to talk to Jim Dickinson!'

Chuck concludes, 'That's pretty much verbatim.'

It was at this point that one of the benefits of being on a major label became evident. 'I called over to England,' Prophet continues. 'I said, "We want to get this guy over to help us with some demos," and they just told me to call the New York office and book him a flight.' Stuart gives Prophet all the credit for bringing Dickinson into the equation: 'He was not easy to find, but Chuck's the one that found the phone number. And Chuck's the one that said, "This guy should produce us." Of course, it was both a brilliant move, and a horrible mistake. It was both.' It would be the birth of a fruitful partnership and personal friendships that would last until the producer's death in 2009.

One of the other potential producers who had been in the frame at that time was occasional Dylan collaborator Al Kooper. 'We all went over to his house,' Prophet remembers. 'It was kinda awkward.' Kooper, who would later produce the band's 1991 album *Scapegoats*, recalls, 'A guy from Phonogram called me and said, "We want you to produce Green On Red," so I said, "OK then." He said, "They are in town now, and I want you to meet with them," so I called them and just told them to come over to my house that night; that was when I lived in LA. And they came over with Jim Dickinson and said, "This is Jim Dickinson, and he is going to produce our album." [*loud laugh*] So I just said, "Okaaay," and I pulled out my Jim Dickinson solo album and got him to sign it. I went out and got a case or two of beer and we just had a great night.'[19]

Prophet and a couple of bandmates met Dickinson at the airport, with session time booked at El Dorado studios. But first, there was a detour via Alvarado Street—Dickinson had requested a supply of weed to get things rolling, as it were. 'There was a place where a kid would run up to your car and you would give him money,' Prophet recalls. 'And then they would lower a basket down on a fishing pole from the rooftop with the bag of weed in it. And so we said, "Give him the money," and the kid runs away, and next thing you know this basket comes down. We told Dickinson, "Here's your weed," and we took off. And Jim didn't say anything at the time. We went and stayed at the Tropicana, because that's what you did back then. We stayed at the Tropicana and ate breakfast at Dukes every morning, and Dickinson later told me, "I didn't know what to make of you guys, but I have to tell ya, when we got that bag of weed, I was very impressed!" [*laughs*] And that's kinda how we hit it off.'

The LA studio days fell into a routine. 'We were going there every morning at like ten, eleven, twelve . . . and if we wanted a pump organ, we'd call the rental company and tell them to bill it to the label. Danny would bang out three chords, then I'd pick up on him and strike up a groove with Keith. We'd take a food break, come back and throw in a bridge or another part, and Danny would start to form some words, working through the verses. And we just kept the tape rolling.'

Although in time Dickinson would become someone Stuart and Prophet would regard as a mentor, the initial sessions together did not run smoothly. Ironically perhaps, given the way the working relationships would blossom in due course, Stuart identifies a lack of trust between the three of them as a major cause of the difficulties. Certainly there seems to have been a degree of the band testing the boundaries in the early days. Chuck recalls, 'I remember one night we were in the studio and we were getting frustrated, and we had that keg of beer, and things were getting out of hand. Danny started prank calling some of these sex-chat places, and they figured out a way to record it. And the woman was just giving it right back and they couldn't really keep up with her . . . and it got kinda pitiful. And then the next day, everybody was a little bit [*pulls a shame-faced expression*]. And Dickinson turned to me and said, "You guys need to know that I'm not gonna tell you to stop. Ever! I'll never tell you to stop." And it was almost like we were testing him. It's just too bad that the record doesn't sound half as dangerous as we thought we were.' Nevertheless, as the band spent more time with Dickinson, it seemed more and more like a natural fit. 'It was Dickinson's approach to capture what's in between the beats or in between the notes,' Prophet explains. 'That random element that most people try to get rid of. I think he was just trying to capture the spirit of what we did.'

Dickinson also encouraged the band to book some studio time on his own stomping ground, the now legendary Ardent Studios in Memphis.

Prophet later noted, 'At the time there weren't a lot of people who really had an awareness or appreciation of the history there and what it meant. We wanted to use the Mellotron that was on Big Star's *Sister Lovers* album, and they were confused as to why we would even be interested in that.'[20] Ardent had begun life in a converted garage off founder John Fry's parents' house, but it officially opened on National Street in 1966. Jim Dickinson was one of the key producers in its early years, before the studio moved to its permanent base on Madison Avenue in 1971. In the years that followed, the likes of Led Zeppelin, Leon Russell, the Allman Brothers Band, Dylan, and ZZ Top would record there; later, another generation would follow: R.E.M., The White Stripes, The Raconteurs, and many more.

Despite the emerging synergy between band and producer, looking and listening back, neither Stuart nor Prophet are pleased with how *Killer* turned out. For Prophet, the album was too bombastic, and Stuart agrees that the record sounds 'a little bit dated sonically. But you have to understand that everybody was making the same mistake at that time,' he told me. In terms of the sonics of the album, it can be hard to distinguish where the creative limitations end and the vagaries of fashion in recorded sound (like gated drums) begin. Prophet's perspective is, 'We didn't want to make a record that sounded good. A good record would be like an Eagles record, engineered by Glyn Johns or whatever. We didn't want it to sound *good*. We wanted it to sound *exciting*. We would have taken excitement over good any day of the week.'

Stuart also points out, 'There was not really a captain of that ship the way there should've been. And it really should have been a double album, if not a triple album. Because there would have been other stuff to ease out the bombastic nature of it. There was humour too, but that didn't show up on the record.' In an interview taped two years after release, Stuart told Ralph Traitor, 'They made me pick ten songs, and I guess I picked the most histrionic, overwrought stuff because it was hard to balance it any other way.'[21] Musically, the album is flawed also. 'It does have this kind of manic-depressive energy,' Stuart conceded in 2014, 'But nothing's in time. It's that old Duke Ellington thing: if it don't swing, it don't mean a thing.'[22] 'The record's a sonic nervous breakdown,' he concludes today.

'Recording dragged on and off for six months, which in those days was seventeen lifetimes,' says Prophet. As far as he is concerned, *Killer* was when the band ran up against their limitations and 'hit a wall'. Musically? In the songwriting? Everything? 'Yeah, everywhere, yeah,' he concurs. 'We recorded so much stuff, and Danny tends to think that there was another record there that could have been more light-hearted. And a lot of that stuff got scrapped. So the scales kinda tipped and ... it got to be a bummer and, ya know, dark is one thing, but nobody likes a *bummer*. Art is in the contrast. And so, yeah, it got a little bleak. We got a little dispirited. Jack [Waterson] had a hard time with Jim Dickinson, and Jim Dickinson had a hard time with Jack's bass playing. And we overdubbed on that stuff for a long time and that's always a problem. When the feeling is gone, it can be hard to reconnect or to get back to what was getting you off viscerally, six months earlier.'

Hindsight may offer the prospect of 20/20 vision, but Prophet has been perhaps unfairly harsh on the album in some interviews. Reflecting back in 2002 in conversation with Canadian DJ John Sekerka, who confessed to being a big fan of *Killer*, Chuck described the performances as 'tired, lackluster' and mocked their ambition at the time: 'We thought that we were so bad-ass, and Danny had so much anti-establishment rhetoric.'[23] As Chuck put it to me, 'In the end, when we tried to make a record that actually rocked, we just weren't that dangerous.'

Listening to it now, exactly where it went wrong is debatable. There are some very strong songs in the set, but the lyrics, taken as a collection, lack light and shade. At times, the production seems overly layered. ('The Mighty Gun', for example, has acoustic and electric guitar tracks, as well as bass, drums, percussion, harmonica, organ and piano. The latter is so far back in the mix it seems to be coming from a distant hilltop.) 'Whispering Wind' is a nice concept on paper, but on record the stacked backing vocals simply overwhelm the slight frame of the song itself, and the reverb makes it sound like Elvis's entire band, male and female backing singers, and entourage are squeezing into the bathroom for a gospel sing-along. The potential delicacy of the Tex-Mex tinged 'Sorry Naomi' is bludgeoned to death by a drum track that seems to have been lifted from Springsteen's 'Born In The USA', while the song itself nods to the same artist's 'Highway Patrolman', borrowing a couple of lines for the chorus. (Stuart confirms that *Nebraska* was his favourite

Springsteen album and that, unlike Prophet, he's not a fan of much of his other work.) 'When we tracked this I actually talked Dickinson into playing guitar,' Chuck recalls. 'Strangely enough, Dickinson, being a keyboardist, was always opposed to keyboards poking out above the guitars. But he loved this solo by Chris. When we were working on this, every time he'd smile—just exhale from the ever-present joint in his mouth and let out an enthusiastic *Yeah!* when that solo would go by.'

Prophet notes that 'Sorry Naomi' was intended as an answer to mother and daughter duo The Judds' Grammy-winning country hit 'Grandpa Tell Me 'Bout The Good Old Days'. He points out how 'Dan lists things about the good old days ... like no Novocaine. Syphilis. The usual.' Bigotry and lynching, too. 'We always listened to country radio,' he notes, without a hint of irony. 'And loved The Judds.' 'Track You Down' sounds like a punk throwback, but given its Bon Jovi–style, mob-handed chorus and stadium-rock production, it collapses in a cloud of confusion over what exactly it's trying to be.

Thankfully, the simple strength of some of the songs in terms of the writing mean they survive the unsympathetic production, notably one of the band's all-time masterpieces, 'We Ain't Free', and the overlooked 'Jamie'. Prophet reserves particular praise for 'Born To Fight': 'it's a beautiful song about a guy who painted flag poles for a living and headed down to El Salvador to enlist as a freedom fighter to 'fight for the right'. Dan had read a story about him in the in-flight magazine. "Free speech and assembly and Honky Tonk Saturday nights" . . . that line is so *great*. And the back and forth with the BVs as well. Brenda Patterson! Great singer. Hell, she sang on "Knockin' On Heaven's Door"!'

However, the more I speak with Chuck about this particular moment in the arc of Green On Red's career, the more the term 'magic'—and the loss if it—recurs. He also refers to rising tensions within the band that might have emerged more starkly as the share of responsibilities began to shift. He recalls Stuart once telling him, 'I guess I was just threatened by music.' He pauses and goes on to explain, 'Because [Stuart] is a very intelligent guy, and there was always a dynamic between Danny and Chris. And Chris and Danny just [*pause*] had that static electricity. And Chris was very musical. *Very* musical.' Prophet remembers Cacavas bringing songs to the band. 'And,' he sighs, 'I just knew it wasn't going to happen. That wasn't going to help Dan. I don't think he felt that he wanted to compete with Chris's songs. And he didn't want to stand in the corner and play tambourine, as John Lennon described his experience on *The White Album*. [*laughs*] Dan didn't wanna be demoted to *that*.'

Cacavas demurs when I ask him about it. Early on, he says, there were opportunities for him to contribute, but 'eventually it became clear that the band was a vehicle for Dan's songs. I didn't have an agenda other than to play what was in the best interest of his songs'. But perhaps neither Prophet nor Stuart had fully recognised or processed Cacavas's talent at the time? 'I thought at the time that he overplayed,' Chuck confesses. 'And Dickinson definitely thought that keyboards shouldn't be prominent. He thought keyboards should be supportive and Chris would really poke out here and there. But I realised later when we did those reunion shows . . . I guess my ears had got bigger. I could take more in. And I realised that Chris was just brilliant. I mean, he was so fluid. And he just kept the thing from being static-y. He could make it happen. And that was just the [Green On Red] sound.'

The Killer Inside Me, with its noir-style PoV, shot-through-a-windscreen sleeve art, was released in March 1987. Robert Christgau, this time, was dismissive: 'Yet another pseudoauthentic unlocks the cellar door of the American psyche, revealing—gasp! horror!—the violence that dwells within each and every one of us. What horse manure. C+.'[24] However, the *New York Times* found much to enjoy, focusing on the title and drawing parallels between Jim Thompson's 1950s pulp thriller and the scenarios Stuart paints in his lyrics. 'All this angst and venting of spleen might well have resulted in difficult listening,' veteran reviewer Robert Palmer noted, 'but the lyricism and intensity of Green On Red's music makes the album uplifting rather than depressing.'[25] In the UK, Robin Denselow, writing for the national paper the *Guardian*, found the album a 'powerful, if sometimes messy, collision of country and rock, with an unexpected line in radical, non-redneck lyrics'; he admired the songwriting style, 'almost like condensed film scripts,' and the way the band turned American myths inside out: 'That's the way the West was really won, plenty of cheap labour and the mighty gun.'[26] On a page that had U2's *The Joshua Tree* splashed as the issue's feature review, *Melody Maker* made similar connections, quipping, 'The record is an anguished howl, a scream of dissent. Sam Peckinpah could have directed it, Oliver Stone probably will.' Allan Jones's review singled out Prophet's 'sabre sharp guitar' as a key feature, summing up the album as 'brilliant, essential listening'.[27] Given a chance to assess the album again on its 1990 reissue, Jones would insist that 'only a handful of the best rock records ever made have sounded so naked and wild', describing the album as 'a raw, purple wound'. His verdict: 'Genuinely awesome.'[28]

TOURING *KILLER* AND THE END OF GREEN ON RED 2.0
The summer of 1986 had found the band being invited to participate in the second Farm Aid benefit. Organised in the wake of Live Aid by Willie Nelson and Neil Young to help struggling American farmers, the first concert took place in Champaign, Illinois, in September 1985, and it has since become an annual event. The 1986 benefit was staged at the Manor Downs Racetrack in Texas; Stevie Ray Vaughan and John Mellencamp were among the headliners, and other acts in the diverse line-up included George Jones and Slash Records veterans X. Green On Red's energetic set featured 'Clarksville', 'Honest Man', and 'Keep On Moving'. At one point, Prophet stood on his guitar cable and it became unplugged. 'It was a cheap guitar, it was ungrounded, and I was trying to plug in to a different rig because it was buzzing so loud,' he explains. 'Threw caution to the wind, I didn't wrap the cable around the strap. I'll never do *that* again! [*laughs*] In fact, after our set I was walking around the backstage reception area and Dave Alvin from the Blasters said to me [*adopts exaggerated drawl*], "Well, son, there's a reason why we wrap that cable around our strap." [*laughs*] Yeah. *Thanks! Thanks, dad!*'

The band's stock was continuing to rise, and the tour behind *Killer* was the biggest so far in terms of scale, money, and profile, but for Jack Waterson, at least, 'the soul was gone, man, and I was just doing a job'.[29] Internal relations were deteriorating. 'Dan was out there every day shadow-boxing with his demons,' says Prophet. 'His own fears. He was constantly fighting off imagined threats. It made things difficult. No one protested when he stopped coming to soundchecks. We all got used to him flying off the handle at the slightest disagreement or hint of criticism. And, to be fair to Dan, he had his own issues pressing down on him beyond the daily grind out there', including the impending break-up of a long-term relationship. 'But he was uncomfortable with the whole parade,' Prophet continues. 'Throwing up before gigs. Come to think of it, he refused to do interviews on that tour. Something about *Killer* he didn't want to answer for, maybe.'

A limited CD release on Belle Sound in 2005 of a bootleg taped at the Manchester International on March 27 1987 documents one of the more successful shows of the tour. Time and time again, the audience joins in, making 'Time Ain't Nothing' in particular a raucous sing-along number where Stuart simply lets them take over. If Keith Mitchell's drums sometimes overwhelm the mix, there are plenty of places where Cacavas's keyboards push through, notably on the opening 'Clarksville'. The show wraps up with a cover of 'Jumpin' Jack Flash', with the guitarist from opening act Steve Earle's band joining in.

Some co-billed dates with Tom Verlaine were booked that same year. 'Long-ass bus tour,' Prophet remarks. 'Back then it was strictly guitars straight into the amps. And we'd pass a tuner around backstage before we ran out there. After that, you were on your own. Things had disintegrated to the point that I knew that if I didn't bring Danny a guitar, he'd just shrug and not play one. So I brought along that blue Strat.' Many years later, Chuck would play the same guitar, fitted with flatwound strings, on the *Bobby Fuller* album.

Without a doubt, there were some exciting shows and great performances on the tour, but at times it felt like the juggernaut was weaving all over the carriageway, and the wheels finally came off toward the end of the European tour. As Chuck recalls, 'When we got as far as Greece, one of the last gigs on the tour, Danny had jumped into the audience with his guitar. We could hear the guitar but we couldn't see him, there was just a sea of people. I remember pulling on his guitar cable and reeling him in like a fish! And when he came up, the neck had snapped.' If Green On Red had any talismanic power, he continues, it was in 'Dan's Gretsch guitar that got broken at that last gig'. Stuart later told him that he took it to a guy on the Sunset Strip to try and get it fixed; the luthier offered him $75 because he could 'probably re-use the pickups'.

'Something about that was kinda final,' Prophet believes. 'It just broke the back of the band, and we ended up staying for a couple of days in Greece and relaxing. Martin Elbourne flew out from London, and there were some whispers. Because the album hadn't been that well received, and neither had the shows. We were using some background singers, and because of that the magic was gone. The presales at [London venue] the Astoria, which was supposed to be the final date of a triumphant tour, were pretty slow. The tour had gone on too long, and at that point, we'd already done a bunch of stuff in the States too.' The solution was a little audacious: they got a doctor to write a sick note for Stuart, suggesting he had had a nervous breakdown. 'Which probably wasn't much of a stretch,' notes Prophet. It enabled them to cancel the Astoria gig and collect the insurance on it. 'And then we never played again'—at least, not in that configuration, until the reunion shows almost twenty years later.

According to Stuart, after the disintegration of the band in the wake of the *Killer* tour, he came home, ended his relationship with his long-term partner, Susie Wrenn, and then, 'I just split and wouldn't talk to anyone.' Prophet concurs: 'Yeah. We stopped talking. Totally stopped talking.' As Dan retreated into self-imposed isolation, Prophet ended up spending a couple of months in Berlin with his girlfriend, Kara.

KARA JOHNSON

Kara was originally from Danville and had moved to San Francisco with Prophet around 1983. They had been high-school sweethearts, and they both enrolled at San Francisco State college. 'We moved into the city together,' Chuck nods. 'We were wild. We were pretty inseparable.' They would be together for seven years before the pressures of Chuck's touring schedule with Green On Red would eventually become impossible to bear. From the earliest stage of their relationship, Prophet was already devoting himself pretty much full-time to music: he was playing in the band Bad Attitude and, Kara remembers, 'He would get, like, $25 a gig, and we were living off of that. I think we lived on alcohol and popcorn. Seriously! Or we would buy one burrito and split it. You know, [when he played], they would count heads, and he would get paid a proportion of that. So he played a *lot*. I mean, *all the time!*' Kara reflects, 'I don't know if he ever planned to graduate ... probably not. It was always about the music. And there was no back-up plan for *anything*.'

While Chuck had been focused on his music career, Kara had her own artistic endeavours. 'Kara is a visual artist,' Prophet says, 'She worked her way up … she went to the San Francisco Art Institute, and when she graduated she decided that she wanted to live in Berlin.' Kara had met someone in school back in San Francisco who offered her somewhere to stay for free, so she and Chuck had the run of a massive flat in the increasingly trendy Kreuzberg area of Berlin. 'But stepping into a new world,' Prophet reflects, 'separated by language and geography, that carries its own kind of loneliness. It was sometimes a challenge to get something to read in English. Days would drift by and I was just in a blur. Burned out. Isolated. But I collected some great records on that trip. Lee Hazlewood, some krautrock. Records I still have to this day.' Kara loved the Berlin sojourn, but she could sense her partner's sense of frustration and isolation. It couldn't last.

Despite the ambivalence, Prophet describes Berlin as 'a wonderful city. We explored it taking the streetcars. We always went in the last car. Never paying. And we got invited to parties … and the bars. We wouldn't show up until midnight. We'd hang out drinking and listening to music. We wouldn't even surface until the sun was well up in the sky.' Their sojourn overlapped with Wim Wenders filming *Wings Of Desire* in the district where they were staying. Nick Cave, who appears in Wenders's movie, was there at the time, as was Blixa Bargeld, of Einstürzende Neubauten. 'We used to go drinking every night, and Blixa was the bartender—he would DJ with two cassette players, and they were into a lot of that countrypolitan, housewife gothic music, so I'd be in that bar and they'd be playing John Denver and Glen Campbell, really loud. And that was kind of exotic to them, and it was just killing me! It was just making me so homesick.'

Green On Red as a project had appeared to be over, but then the call came in: 'Come back to the US. Come to Memphis.' The message from Phonogram was that there was some money if they wanted to make some demos. Prophet confesses, 'I always felt that returning to the States was in some way betraying Kara. I think she felt, *Oh, I was on-board for all your high jinks, and you're not on-board for mine.* Like it was her turn to pursue her dream. Maybe it was a fantasy. But that's enough sometimes.' He pauses. 'We flew back. Kara and I never spoke about it. But … something broke after that. After we got back to

TOP LEFT Chuck and sister Jeanne at the Spokane World's Fair, 1974.

BELOW LEFT Bad Attitude tour, Calgary, February 1982.

BELOW Training at KSFS Radio, c. 1983.

▓ TOP Bad Attitude promo shot, c. 1982. Left to right: Tom Nelson, Leor Beary, Chuck, Steve Croke.

▓ MIDDLE Serfers backstage at Tumbleweeds in Tucson, Arizona: Jack Waterson, Van Christian, Dan, Chris Cacavas. (*Cliff Green*)

▓ BOTTOM Wild Game promo shot, c. 1983: Leor Beary, Steve Croke, Tom Nelson, Chuck.

▌ ABOVE Green On Red with fishing rods, Woolworths, Eugene, Oregon, October 13 1984. Left to right: Chuck, Chris Cacavas, Dan, Jack Waterson, Alex MacNicol. (*Chris Metzler*)

▌ LEFT Green On Red, EMU Dining Hall, University of Oregon, October 12 1984. (*Chris Metzler*)

▌TOP RIGHT Jim Dickinson and Dan Stuart, recording *The Killer Inside Me*, c. 1986.

▌BELOW RIGHT Chris Cacavas, Chuck, Dan, and Jim Dickinson recording *The Killer Inside Me*.

▌BELOW Stephie, Chuck, and Larry Dekker onstage, c. 1988. (*Tom Erikson*)

ABOVE Dan and Chuck in Turin, Italy, 1988. (*Joe Dilworth*)

LEFT Stephie, Chuck, J.C. Hopkins, Jimmy Sweetwater, and Roly Salley at the Albion, c. 1988. (*Tom Erikson*)

▌TOP RIGHT Kurt Lipschutz (aka klipschutz) on a train in the late 1980s.

▌BELOW RIGHT Chuck with his grandfather and father in the studio, c. 1992.

▌BELOW Stephie and Chuck at home, c. 1992. (*Hugh O'Connor*)

▌OPPOSITE *Brother Aldo* promo shot, c. 1990.

▌ABOVE Late-era Green
On Red promo shot, c. 1992.
(*Gilbert Blecken*)

▌RIGHT Master-tape box for
Balinese Dancer, c. 1992.

▌BELOW Roly Salley, c. 1992.
(*Billy Douglas*)

China
Records / Chuck
Prophet

DAT: OF —
· LAST DANCE
· ONE LAST DANCE
· SAVANNAH
· ANGEL
· BATON ROUGE
· BALINESE DANCER
· "   "

Somewhere
· DOWN THE ROAD
· CROSSED MISBEGOTTEN LOVE
= HEART BREAKS JUST LIKE
THE DAWN ." DUET MIX
" HEART BREAKS — SOLO
VOC MX
· IN THE SHADE

Twisted Vocal
Straight Vocal

· AM I
FOOLING
— THEE MX
— DUB SIN
THE HOUSE
MX
— MALCOLM
X MX
— MASSIVE
COMPRESSION
MX

— 151 PS
1/2 INCH

XFR'd to
NOV. DAT.
'92

San Francisco, I turned around and was back on the road. Before too long, as the saying goes, she had plans that didn't include me.'

The call from Phonogram was the outcome of Martin Elbourne trying to pick up the pieces. 'They were gentlemen back then,' says Prophet. 'There was a real kind of formality to it: *We can't just put these kids on the street. We gotta give them one last chance.*' Chuck cannot recall precisely what the offer entailed—'ten thousand dollars, or ten thousand pounds, I don't remember'—but when Dave Bates got in touch with Jim Dickinson, according to Prophet, the producer had a tough ultimatum: 'Well, you can send Chuck and Dan to Memphis, but I don't have time for the rest of that. Don't have time. Or money.'

The dissolution of the band might have happened by default rather than through any kind of decision or discussion, but it was no less traumatic for all that. Indeed, the psychic scars probably run much deeper because of the way in which things were allowed to fall apart without negotiation. Cacavas tells me, 'The hardest part was thinking you're still a member of a band and then finding out *through the grapevine* that your band was in Memphis making a record without you. After the initial denial, anger, bargaining, and depression, there was finally acceptance. There wasn't anything I could change about the situation. In the end, if this hadn't happened, I would not have pursued a solo career. Years later, after I broke up one of my own bands, I believe I had a better understanding of the reasons that might have led Dan to making the decision to move on without the original members.'

Chris would go on to cut a series of albums as a collaborator and solo artist, notably with the band Junkyard Love. He would make his home in Germany, from where he continues to record and tour. Meanwhile, Jack Waterson's debut album, *Whose Dog* (1988), 'blew everyone away', according to Pat Thomas, a friend of the band at the time; Pat notes that Dan was particularly impressed and took to wearing a T-shirt onstage featuring the LP's cover.

Even now, almost thirty years later, Stuart finds it difficult to articulate— and this is a man who does not usually find himself lost for words. 'Yeah. I mean, they found out … we didn't even, I didn't even … I was such a coward. I could make up in my mind all these reasons for why I didn't wanna play … reasons I wanted to do some records without Jack and Chris. But really … it was reprehensible, what I did.' 'Those guys deserved more than a phone-call,' he admitted to Fred Mills. 'And they never got even that. I had tremendous guilt and shame for years, I still do.'[30]

Prophet's perspective is more philosophical. 'As a band, maybe it had all run its course. We were all pretty limited in our musicality. I mean, we didn't really have the chops to take it much further … and in many ways that is the lifespan of a group. It had been a pretty solid run. Most bands barely stay together for three years. I don't remember the other members showing any burning desire to keep carrying the torch. What was in if for them? That camaraderie was gone. Maybe the energy you use to fight the world and claw your way up ultimately gets turned on each other.' He concludes, 'Like so many relationships, things just kind of fizzled out. And nothing was really said.'

Stuart once mused, 'We went for our big "masterpiece" on *Killer* and failed miserably.'[31] Two decades would pass before the 2.0 configuration of the band would reconvene, but, Dan exclaims, 'Thank God in 2006 we could play again and I could sincerely apologise to everybody about that. So now, if we do anything ever, it's always with the original guys. I think Chuck would agree with me that all those "part two" records … that's something else. It ended with *Killer*. But some of them I'm very proud of. Chuck, I think, is a bit more dismissive. He calls them "those UK records" [*laughs*].'

CHAPTER THREE

SNAKE CHARM THAT THING!

GREEN ON RED 3.0 (1988–92)

> *You can impose yourself on the world forever*
> *like a baboon showing his ass but don't expect*
> *people to keep on clapping.* – Dan Stuart

HERE COME THE SNAKES

The Green On Red reunion is another chapter. In the meantime, spurred on by the generous advance for the demos, Stuart ('He was in LA or Tucson or somewhere') and Prophet ('I was in Berlin') reconvened, 'and we ended up meeting in Memphis, at the Holiday Inn,' Chuck reports. He saw it as 'a kind of reprieve. Dave Bates was a real gentleman and gave us the budget to go out there and take one last shot'. It would turn out to be an important stage in the history of Stuart and Prophet's working relationship; Chuck remembers it as 'really the first time we sat in a room together and figured out we could make music . . . somehow. Sitting in the Holiday Inn with an unplugged electric guitar, passing it back and forth'. He reflects, 'I think that's probably what saved us. We were able to keep it going.'

Prophet, Stuart, and Jim Dickinson reunited in the same studio where they had recorded much of *The Killer Inside Me*. Early versions of songs that would eventually make it on to the next album were taped, including 'Morning Blue' and 'Rock'n'roll Disease': 'Basically what we could just work up the night before,' Chuck recalls. 'Danny and I surprised ourselves by having a good time. We went to dog races in West Memphis, just across the river, and we were betting and drinking and we were hanging out with Tav Falco and the Burns guys'—Tav Falco's band Panther Burns, an influential group out of Memphis who brought together roots traditions and performance art. 'And we were exploring the city, just having a good time'—all on that generous advance from Phonogram.

The demos went to the record company, and Prophet was back in San Francisco. 'Kara and I were living in the avenues in a flat with a rotating door of seventeen different roommates,' he recalls, when one morning he was woken at 6am by a call from Dave Bates. 'He said that he'd listened to the demos and, "God bless ya, there's a great guitar solo here and there," and he said a couple of nice things and then he said, "I don't think we can carry on," and I said, "OK, thanks," and I hung up the phone and went back to sleep. I didn't even call anybody to tell them.' Asked why he didn't follow up, Prophet is philosophical. 'Because the heart and soul was gutted from the band anyway, the magic was gone. We never had what some of our peers had ... we never had an *organisation*. Who exactly would you have liked for me to call?'

What they did have was their agency back in London, All Trade Bookings, and it was at this point that Elbourne came into play again. 'After we did those demos and Phonogram passed, Martin Elbourne played them for other people and one of them was Red Rhino out of Leeds which was a goth label owned by Tony Kostrzewa—Tony K. And I think he signed us on a one-page contract. I believe it was something like £20,000.' Red Rhino, like the more famous brands Beggars Banquet and Rough Trade, had started as a record shop before moving into distribution and its own label. One of Red Rhino's early releases was the single 'Spiderman' by ska band Akrylykz, featuring singer Roland Gift, who would in due course hit the big time via Fine Young Cannibals.[1] Red Rhino would become a key player in the development of the goth scene in particular, as well as bands such as Red Lorry Yellow Lorry, The Wedding Present, and Pulp.

Energised by the new signing—and the new advance—Prophet and Stuart got together in Tucson, cut some demos and returned to Memphis. The Tucson demos are a major feature of the two-CD reissue of *Here Come The Snakes*, which features a dozen of them. 'A lot of those songs Danny started on his own in Tucson and he didn't know what to do with them,' Chuck recalls. 'And so I drove out there from San Francisco with Patrick Winningham; we stopped in Las Vegas and went out looking for trouble at night. We got to Tucson, and then Danny and I went into this guy's bedroom and we passed instruments round.'

Randy McReynolds's bedroom studio would become Wavelab, the venue in due course for recordings by Blacky Ranchette, Giant Sand, Naked Prey, and Richard Buckner. For Chuck and Dan, it was a place where they could thrash out the bedrock for the *Snakes* album: 'We would always return to the scene of the crime with Randy,' Prophet would later note, 'because he was a patient guy.'[2]

The demos are a little rough around the edges but there is no doubt about the quality of the songs—both the mellow country blues numbers such as 'Broken Radio' and the rockers like 'Keith Can't Read'. Numbers that never made it to the album include 'Yellow House'—a song about serial killer Richard Ramirez—and the catchy, mid-tempo rocker 'Five 'Til Five', a rollicking version of John Prine's 'That's The Way That The World Goes Round', and a song sketch that gave the album its title, even though the song itself didn't make the cut. Dan plays an unsettling, Middle Eastern–flavoured melody on a child's recorder on the song; Chuck calls out, 'Snake charm that thing!' and Dan replies, 'Here come the snakes!' 'We didn't give it any thought,' Chuck shrugs. 'The best titles always assert themselves. Or just appear.'

With the Red Rhino money behind them, Prophet and Stuart regrouped with Jim Dickinson at Ardent in Memphis, cutting the entire album in six days. Although they both have memories of the recording sessions being relatively relaxed and enjoyable, Chuck also recalls some early teething problems, with something of a 'power struggle' erupting between Dan and Jim; he believes there was some emotional hangover still lingering from the *Killer Inside Me* sessions. 'And maybe they had to wave their dicks at each other, as they say in Hollywood.' At the time, Stuart said of Dickinson, 'He's the kid who, when he gets mad, takes the ball home. He's walked out on a lot of sessions.'[3] Prophet remembers that the producer went through a long process of zipping all his things in his briefcase, packing up his guitar, and leaving, saying, 'I'm not doing it.'

'I huddled with the engineer, Joe Hardy,' Chuck continues. '"What are we gonna do? How can we get Jim back? Shall we just carry on without him?" And then something happened. Joe Hardy negotiated some kind of peace settlement, 'And we went to work. And Jim later said, "Hey, if somebody was gonna throw a shit fit, I was gonna do it first." [*laughs*] And, after that, Danny was pretty mild.'

The sessions included a day at Sam Phillips Recording Services, the studio Phillips built after he sold Elvis Presley's contract for $35,000 (worth nearly ten times that amount today). 'It was Dickinson's idea that we go there and just jam on the songs,' Prophet enthuses. He played electric guitar, Stuart acoustic, Dickinson on drums, no bass. 'Danny was kinda making up stuff in the vocal booth.' Prophet recalls with great fondness and not a little awe that the session was under the supervision of guitarist and engineer Roland Janes, who had played on countless seminal records, including 'Whole Lotta Shakin' Goin' On'. 'Roland didn't judge us,' says Prophet. 'It was one of the first times that we felt uninhibited. This is a place where people can wave their freak flag as high as they want. Anyway, we were pretty lost at that point and there we were just thrashing around, hoping to get lucky and pull something out of the air. And Roland was real patient with us.'

Chuck reflects on what that taught him about working with others. 'Why would you do anything to make them feel inhibited or inadequate? Is that going to get you a better song? Or a better performance? I've worked with people who are buzzkills,' he continues. 'Avoid those people. Here's a guy who witnessed the actual birthing of rock'n'roll: Johnny Cash, Jerry Lee, and scores of greats, lesser greats and total unknowns. He understood that music, that making records—maybe even a hit record—could be created by anybody at any time. And he cared about what you were doing. And that couldn't help but make *you* care about what you were doing. Roland is an inspiration,' he concludes. 'I don't want to come off all new age or whatever. But Roland is the kind of guy who gives you faith in yourself. Nowadays it's hard to find people who are as pure. Some people just want to get in there and fix your mistakes. Some people just don't get it. Why would they? They've never taken a ride on the Flying Saucer of Rock and Roll and they probably never will.'

Stuart writes evocatively in his memoir of the Sam Phillips session: 'Behind an ancient kit, Bubba started beating out a primal swagger. Billy played a fucked-up riff, barbed wire stretched too tight. I let out a yelp, my tail caught in the musical meat grinder.'[4] The music flowed. 'So we ended up filling up a ninety-minute cassette,' Prophet says. 'And then we went into Ardent and we just started racing through it: "How about this right here? [*plays guitar*] Does that sound like something?" And then we'd program the drums, and then we'd program a chorus. [*plays more guitar*] And then I'd overdub the guitar and Dickinson overdubbed some bass, and we built the tracks up that way.'

One track that became something of a bone of contention between Stuart and Dickinson was 'Tenderloin'. Prophet remembers the genesis of the song months before—Dan had broken up with his partner, Susie Wrenn, and spent a short time in San Francisco, with Prophet looking out for him; Stuart was holed up 'in the Tenderloin district and, while he was there, wrote this *noir* prose poem'. It's a part of the city that, even more so now, post-gentrification, feels like the landscape for a typical Dan Stuart hard-up lyric. Once when they were recording at Randy McReynolds's place, circling around a riff, Chuck asked Dan about the poem; Dan pulled out the yellow legal pad he had written it down on and recited it as the music played. Dickinson became obsessed with it. One day, Chuck says, 'He brought in a Jack Kerouac record, and then they went to all this trouble to find a turntable and we sat there and listened to it. And we were asking each other, "Why's he playing us this? Why is this happening?" It was Steve Allen playing piano, Kerouac reading. And Dickinson kept saying, "When's he gonna do the recitation?" And then he turned to me one day and he says, "He's not gonna do the recitation, is he?" And I said, "I don't think he knows what you're *talking* about." Jim goes, "The one on the demo, you know." And I replied, "Well, we don't remember that. You've got to *ask* him!" And so then Danny read that thing at the end of that song. And it was great.' Stuart was extremely reluctant—'He'd say, "I wanna hear the *recitation*," like I was supposed to do "Charge Of The Light Brigade" or something,' he chuckled[5]—but eventually Dickinson bugged him into compliance. It is one of the oddest songs in the Green On Red canon, and one of the best.

When I discussed the song with Prophet and suggested there was something 'quintessentially Danny' about it, Chuck agreed. 'Yeah! Totally, *totally*. Dickinson later said about Danny, there was always some decorum of sadness around him. And it stemmed from the fact that Dan thought it was all a sham. And Dickinson says, *Too bad.* Because it wasn't, you know? But there was this sort of depression about it. A sense of not measuring up. And the irony is that I don't think he could have found anybody that believed in him more than Dickinson did.' In a 2009 blog post reflecting on Dickinson's life, Prophet recalled that, when Jim sensed the band's lack of self-belief, he told them, '"Never let anybody make you feel bad about what you're doing." He offered belief. And made you feel your work was important. It was clearly important to him. What a gift he gave us.'[6]

For the most part, Prophet remembers, the album 'was fun to make, seriously light-hearted'. Dickinson could be blunt when the occasion demanded it. Prophet recalls working on a track and asking Jim for some advice, 'And he says, "I dunno, Chuck, why don't you just play somethin' *cohesive.*" So then I did. *That's* production!' Looking back in 2016, perhaps with one eye blind to the early power struggles between himself and his producer, Stuart mused, 'Everything we did wrong, and all our resistance against Jim . . . that all went away with *Here Come The Snakes*. It was a really easy record to make.'

Although the process of making *Snakes* was a major step forward from the recording of *Killer*, neither of them were at their best physically or mentally. 'Well, we were still getting high. We were doing heroin at that point,' Chuck confirms. 'We'd get it delivered in a cassette tape. You can take a cassette tape apart and you can put stuff inside of it. And I think we had a running bet because [co-producer] Joe Hardy said, "You can't get mail on a Sunday." And Dan said, "I bet you ten bucks." And we got a FedEx package on a Sunday! It's nothing I'm proud of. But yeah, we did that.'

With Green On Red down to a duo, Dickinson brought in some hired hands, but, as Chuck recalls, it was kept mostly in-house: 'The second engineer [Paul Ebersold] played drums. We brought Rene Coman with us on bass—he came up from New Orleans—he had played with Alex [Chilton] and he and I got to be friends.' Chuck recalls Coman being something of a 'musical confidant' during those sessions, someone to bounce ideas off. 'And Dickinson played piano. "Zombie For Love" we cut live in one take. Danny played the guitar solo. And then Danny had said to Jim Dickinson, Have you ever heard this song "We Had It All"? Because I think somebody had played him the Keith Richards bootleg. And Dickinson goes, Yeah, I know that song ... only the saddest fucking song in the *world*! So somebody at the studio went and found a Waylon Jennings cassette, and we sat there and listened to it, wrote the words down, learned the chords, and went out there and played it.' Chuck recalls that Ed Kollis, one of the engineers on *Dusty In Memphis* (1969), played harmonica. 'I think he was emptying the Coke machine. Just a chance meeting. It's amazing. Beautiful player.'

After they finished the mixes, they spooled the tape into a potential sequence for a playback. At that moment, Alex Chilton walked in. The Bangles had recently covered his 'September Gurls', and Prophet believes he was probably dropping by Ardent to pick up a royalty cheque. 'We invited him to sit in and he just rolled a big fat joint and sat there and listened to it all. And at the end he goes, "It's good. It's good." And that said a lot about Alex. Just not an exaggerated guy. Alex was cool. Unlike Green On Red,' Chuck laughs. 'He's the definition of cool. He's understated.'

Chilton has been a seminal figure for Prophet ever since they played with him on a bill at the 688 Club in Atlanta, Georgia, in 1986. In a 2007 blog post, he wrote, 'He took off the shirt he was wearing, shoving it into the back of his Fender Super Reverb amp, and pulled out the one he wore for gigs. He threw a harmonica rack over his head and tuned up his guitar to the harp, all the while looking at his bass player and drummer (Rene Coman and Doug Garrison). He stepped up to the mike and clicked his heels four times. That was it.'[7] 'I remember him hitting those chords in "September Gurls",' Chuck tells me. 'And I didn't have the record. I'm not sure I'd ever heard it before. First time I'd heard it, it was coming out of that Super Reverb amp, with a Telecaster. *Bright*.' The blog continues: 'I don't know who my influences were at the time. Neil Young, Joe Strummer, David Bowie, Tom Verlaine? They all went out the window at that moment; floated up into the ether and stayed put. Alex has remained.'

FAILURE TO LAUNCH: GREEN ON RED 3.0

Here Come The Snakes features the most striking artwork of all the band's releases thanks to the idiosyncratic skills of William Eggleston, widely acknowledged at the time as one of the world's greatest living photographers. Eggleston was born and bred in Memphis, and his candid images of the American South were groundbreaking and controversial, often ignored or denigrated for what some described as their banality. But his focus on the everyday, the often-disconcerting angles and perspectives, and his early interest in colour photography defined his genius. Eggleston had supplied the startling image for the cover of Big Star's *Radio City* LP (1974), and was a long-standing acquaintance of Jim Dickinson's by the time the producer introduced him to Chuck and Dan. 'We spent a fair amount of time with Eggleston,' Prophet confirms, 'And it took him a long time to give us that image. We went to his house several times, into the wee hours of the morning. And then one day he just pulled it out of a stack. *"This is the one right here. This is your cover."* We weren't going to argue with him.'

What *had* caused some dispute was the status of Green On Red as a band. Stuart notes, 'When I went out there, I thought I was making my solo record. And everybody knew that.' Prophet concurs: he remembers Stuart telling him so. 'I didn't argue. We were going into Ardent to record. With Jim Dickinson. I was thrilled.' Prophet remembers playing some gigs, including a show at McCabes in Santa Monica, as 'Dan Stuart And Band', with Coman on bass and Tommy Larkins on drums, before the record came out. 'But then contractually different things happened,' Stuart continues. 'The company that paid for it went out of business ... we were in a publishing deal and they had a record company on the other side and so they saved the day. And there was a huge studio bill by then. And ... that was my second major capitulation. Where I agreed to call it Green On Red. And that caused a lot of distress in my life for many, many years.'

The company felt it wouldn't help sell the album if they had to create a new bin at the record store and wanted it filed under Green On Red, but Prophet also believes that their producer's perspective was telling. 'Dickinson said, "If you're collaborating, then it's a Green On Red record. And that's what you're doing here."' Indeed, it's hard to imagine *Here Come The Snakes* as anything but a collaboration between Stuart and Prophet: it's not just the songs, it's the whole sound of the album, structured as much around Chuck's guitar as it is around Dan's voice. Without Cacavas's keyboards, it was naturally a very different soundscape, but no less distinctive.

Advance chatter about the album, coupled with the band's level of recognition across much of Europe and the rock'n'roll glamour of their spectacular flame-out in the wake of the *Killer* tour, put them on the cover of *Melody Maker* and *Sounds*, two of the three great British weekly music newspapers that ruled supreme across a vast expanse of music fandom in the years before the dawn of the internet. The album drew wide and deep critical acclaim. *Sounds* described it as 'bewitched. It contains a great deal of joy—and pain—and a wealth of instinctive rock'n'roll, the kind you could never force or contrive. It's blood from a wound'.[8] The album made it into an end-of-year Top 20 in the *Guardian*, where Robin Denselow noted how the band had been perched on the brink of a commercial breakthrough for far too long and 'surely deserve to make a bigger impact this time around'. David Sinclair of the *Times* described 'an angry, ragged collection that converts the grit of personal frustration into a loosely threaded string of musical pearls' and declared it 'a timeless display of American rebel rock bravado, deeply rooted in the rich soil of blues and country'.[9] Looking back on the album a couple of years later, the same writer found it a 'glorious antidote to [the] bland musical corporatism' that seemed to go hand in hand with the rise of the CD, citing the end of September 1989 as a particular low point, name-checking Tina Turner, Spandau Ballet, Tears For Fears, Phil Collins, and Wet Wet Wet.[10] Even the generally sceptical *Trouserpress* magazine declared, 'What's left of Green On Red sounds relaxed and confident, a warm and boozy vehicle for Stuart's amusingly wry regrets and social observations. For once, Green On Red has realized its downwardly mobile ambitions.'[11]

For many, *Snakes* is Green On Red's single greatest album; some would argue the toss in favour of *Gas Food Lodging*, but it is a fruitless exercise to attempt to evaluate recordings by two such different incarnations of the band. What is certain is that *Snakes* is an outstanding collection of songs and that it captures the essence of the band's reputation of genius teetering on the edge of substance-fuelled breakdown. It is also expertly sequenced, from the opening 'Keith Can't Read', with its cruelly sardonic final verse:

Get off of your knees right now
You're looking up my nose

Girl that ain't gonna cut no ice
Heaven knows

to the closing tender heartbreak of Seals & Fritts's 'We Had It All'. The album contains some of Prophet's most infectious riffs. As Ralph Traitor wrote in *Sounds*, the 'staccato riff' of 'Change' is 'delivered with cut-and-dried precision by Prophet'; he saw the album's success epitomised in the way it 'synthesises country, rock and blues into a syncopated, drooling robot'.[12] Prophet is also responsible for some of the most startling individual moments on the album, including two beautiful solos on 'Morning Blue', sliding from a baritone register up the neck and back again, and a dirty slide solo on the bluesy 'Zombie For Love'. Dickinson's faith in 'Tenderloin' is repaid—it takes pride of place as the grimy, bleeding heart of the album. *Here Come The Snakes* is a testament to what Stuart and Prophet were able to achieve, given a budget, a supremely talented and *simpatico* producer, and a following wind.

However, in the midst of a promising launch for Green On Red 3.0, music business disaster struck again: Red Rhino collapsed just as *Here Come The Snakes* went into the pressing plant. The result was a small initial batch of albums being released with no immediate prospect of any more being produced. The album was finding limited release in other European countries on a variety of small labels, while in 1989 Restless Records would put out limited quantities in the USA. But the liquidation of Red Rhino was a major setback. Prophet picks up the story: 'So that's when China Records said, "Look, you got a band here, they've got no deal, they're already on the cover of the weeklies with no record out, and they've got this album. How can we get involved here?" And that was the beginning of that chapter.' But nothing is ever straightforward once the lawyers get involved. 'It was hard to say who owned the record, and I think they got it from the liquidators, and then they signed us to an extended seven record deal. But at the same time, I had put my hand up to say, "Well, there's a little bit of a problem ... because I signed a record deal with this label called Fire last week for a solo album."'

China had put a remarkable degree of faith in Green On Red by signing them to a seven year, seven-album deal. But, in the meantime, Prophet had signed with Fire for £500, and he thinks the staff there were shell-shocked that he had done so, and on terms so unfavourable to him, the artist. Fire, it seems, were having second thoughts, whether inspired by a sense of guilt or faltering confidence. 'They were probably concerned that I hadn't shown it to a lawyer, and so the contract might not be valid as a result,' Chuck believes. 'But I was thinking, *Why should I? Why should I pay a lawyer $300 an hour to tell me it's a bad deal?*' Eventually, Fire paid for a lawyer to read it; Barry Simons, Prophet notes, 'went on to become Fire's US attorney. So, what does that tell you? I didn't graduate college, but isn't that a conflict of interest?' But at that point Chuck couldn't have cared less. 'I just wanted to get a record out, and it simplified what I wanted to do. And the fact that there was little or no money ensured that I would have to start from scratch. That I would have to strip it all back to the drywall. Because if you want to break off from a band and have a so-called solo career, if that is going to mean anything, ultimately that's what you have to do.' Prophet had seen too many of his contemporaries leave the bands that had made their names, attempt to strike out on their own, only to fail and return with their tails between their legs. 'You gotta make that climb … one inch at a time.'

Green On Red's lawyer Alexis Grower, however, was extremely unhappy and told Prophet he would have to call off the Fire deal. 'And I said, I don't think I'm going to do that.' Chuck laughs as he tells the story. 'I mean, did I know this was all going to happen? Did I think that maybe if I signed the deal with Phonogram and China that they wouldn't let me do a solo record? Probably. So I just went and did it. And nobody was happy about it. Not Alexis Grower, who I didn't feel was looking after my best interests. Not Martin Elbourne, who was owed a lot of money and was looking for another score. And not Dan Stuart, who was waiting at the Columbia hotel, running up a bill. Danny just wanted to keep the gravy train going. I don't begrudge him for it.'

Stuart concedes this, but points out that Prophet was on salary too; Dan was not the only one riding that train. 'He didn't really talk to me directly about it,' Chuck continues. 'I mean … there was tension, of course there was. And God knows what they were whispering in his ear … *Prophet's fucking this up for you.*' Regardless, Chuck stuck to his guns, and eventually the issue was resolved without him having to back out of the agreement with Fire Records. China built an option into the deal that gave them first dibs on the next Chuck

Prophet recording if they wanted it. That would bring its own problems in due course, but for now Prophet was set free to release his first solo album.

For Chuck, it was a career turning point. 'I was hungry to do it low-key, as cheap as possible. Get it all down to nothing, just dirt and spit. At that point I would rather have made a record in the living room with one microphone. I just wasn't interested in making another *Killer Inside Me*. I just wasn't interested in making a conventional record.' By this time, Prophet was regularly gigging with Stephanie Finch, Patrick Winningham, and others in small local clubs like the Albion and the Paradise Lounge (see the next chapter). But the Green On Red story would not conclude for some time yet: there would be three more albums between 1989 and 1992 before Stuart and Prophet finally called it quits.

RUNNING OUT OF ROAD: THE FINAL THREE ALBUMS

The spring of 1989 found the band touring Europe extensively again. The excess that had led to the band's collapse toward the end of the *Killer Inside Me* tour would colour both announcements of the shows in the music press and the reviews themselves. A report listing upcoming gigs in *Sounds* suggested that if they could lay off the booze during the support act, they could yet shake off 'their tiresome reputation as red-eyed somnambulists on a drown-out death wish'.[13]

However, almost as soon as they arrived, the drummer—ex-James stickman Gavan Whelan—quit, and the line-up was hastily reshuffled, with Brent Newman moving behind the kit, leaving the keyboard station unmanned. The change undoubtedly left the rhythm section fumbling a little, despite Coman's expertise, and live reports including one published in the *NME* contrasting the performance unfavourably with the opening act, an up and coming Blue Aeroplanes.[14] In *Music Week*, a disappointed Duncan Holland noted that Prophet, 'looking like a tired Tom Petty', managed despite it all to 'give the band some purpose where the punches went missing'.[15] David Sinclair of the *Times* felt that 'they just about got away with' the switch in the rhythm section, but set Stuart's failings on the night ('little effort or emotion') against Prophet: 'firing on all cylinders, it was left to him to hold the show together' with his 'charismatic and resourceful soloing'.[16] The *Guardian*'s appraisal of the same show was more positive and equally impressed by Prophet: 'Give him a Grammy, someone,' reviewer Adam Sweeting quipped.[17] In *Melody Maker*, Steve Sutherland noted that one of the consequences of the 'rhythmic disarray' was that Prophet's 'characteristic showmanship' was corralled and curtailed, but he felt that the problems were much more deeply rooted than a line-up change. His uncomfortable suspicion was that Stuart, stiff on his legend as the Bowie song has it, had become so immersed in the role of self-destructive artist that 'he's totally forgotten where fact ends and fantasy festers'. He concluded, 'This was what many had come to see—the chaos, the symbolic carnage. . . . There are dangerous days ahead.'[18]

The band returned for outdoor gigs in the summer, including the Reading Festival, in August, at a time when the festival was associated with hard and heavy rock bands rather than indie music. That gig was preceded by a warm-up show at the Islington Powerhaus on the 23rd, which Andrew Smith for *Melody Maker* declared a 'gloriously open, gloriously free performance'; he contrasted Stuart, chatting to the crowd as if they were guests in his own front room, with Prophet—straight-faced and utterly focused on the music.[19]

Another extensive UK tour in November and early December closed out the year. Without a regular band, however, the tours were becoming chaotic. 'It was a bit fractured,' Prophet admits. 'And from there it was just a series of revolving-door people. Sometimes Danny might meet somebody in Austin, like J.D. Foster, and say, "I want J.D. to be in our band." It just became guys for hire. And a lot of them were great but it wasn't a band.' Some of the musicians who passed through at the time were a better fit than others. Stuart remembers, 'We both loved [keyboardist] Chris Holland [brother of Jools], great musician and a true gentleman. J.D. Foster and I later went on to cut *Can O' Worms* [in 1995], and Tommy [Larkins] found Jonathan Richman, which was a perfect match.'

They did a series of gigs with drummer Greg Elmore of Quicksilver Messenger Service, whom Prophet remembers as 'rather intense'—Elmore had been playing in a local bar, and, Chuck says, 'I thought he was great. Hired him on the spot.' However, the touring—and the performances—could often be painfully erratic. 'You could see it, it was sad; there's stuff on YouTube and it's not really Green On Red anymore,' says Prophet. 'It was hard to stop. We didn't really break up. We just kinda ran out of steam in a lot of ways; people stopped giving us advances. Because we were pretty sick. I dunno. Our heart really wasn't in it.' With the focus on touring the European continent, Prophet later recalled, 'by the time it came do the States, the idea of driving a thousand miles in an Econoline sitting on a twin reverb became less and less appealing. So, we just ignored North America, hoping it would go away.'[20]

Prophet remembers that the label rushed them back into the studio relatively swiftly after *Here Come The Snakes*, and that part of the motivation for China Records was that 'They had thought that they were getting that record [*Snakes*] and they found out that it had already snuck out in all these territories. It was sort of damaged goods. They were understandably frustrated.' There was a meeting at China Records; Derek Green, who had signed them, had an esteemed history—the Sex Pistols, Squeeze—and his partner, Bob Grace, had once been Bowie's publisher in the early 70s. 'They were dudes,' Prophet says. 'They were real record men.'

The agenda for the meeting was to get Green On Red back into the studio, and they wanted to talk about producers. The name Glyn Johns came up in discussions and Johns came to see them play the Town & Country in London. 'I guess we were two songs in and something happened. He just saw us playing and he was in. And we went and met at some sushi bar and he just leaned across the tables and told us, "I'm producing your next record." And then I remember Danny and I were walking back from Holland Park, and we're talking it over, and it's kind of like Alfred Hitchcock or somebody says, "I want to direct your movie." OK. What are you going to say? "No, we're holding out for someone else"? So we did it. And once we agreed to that, it got locked in pretty fast.'

Both of them seemed ready to take a crack at a more conventional rock record. At the time, Prophet talked relatively enthusiastically about the decisions made in preparing to work on the album, pointing out that 'Glyn Johns has made countless classic rock'n'roll records which we all know and love.'[21] Johns's long list of credits as producer and engineer includes work with the Stones, Led Zeppelin, The Who, Eric Clapton, and the Eagles, as well as The Clash on *Combat Rock* (1982). Hiring him was undoubtedly an expression of faith in Stuart and Prophet by China Records. The wheels were rolling.

However, disaster struck at the airport when Stuart flew in from New Orleans and Prophet from San Francisco for a preproduction meeting with Johns: the two of them were picked up by a car service, and the driver left Dan's bags on the curb. 'Danny claimed that he had notebooks full of songs, he had two *albums* written in there! And it just got bigger every day. [*laughs*] And we just didn't have any songs. I think he had "Couldn't Get Arrested", and I sat there with him and squeezed out the lick for "This Time Around", which was something. And we ended up having to go into the studio. Danny checked into this place called the Franklin Suites, where a lot of musicians stayed. And he was just kind of barricaded in there with pizza boxes in the corner stacked up to the ceiling. I remember we had one conversation where I said, "So, I dunno about this record." And he says, "Well, I'm doing it." And it was desperate, because we didn't really have any material.' He shrugs. 'Made sense to the label at the time. Didn't make sense to me. I am not one to put the brakes on anything but I expressed my reservations about it.'

With a legendary producer lined up, however, Stuart and Prophet at least tried to go the extra mile—by their own admittedly erratic standards. 'We did some demos for *This Time Around*,' Chuck confirms. The sessions took place at Radio Tokyo in Venice Beach—a converted house (carpet on the walls and blacked out windows) owned by Ethan James, who had produced and engineered work by Black Flag, The Bangles, Rain Parade, and others. There they met drummer Dave Kemper, whom Glyn Johns had recommended to them. By that point, Kemper had been playing for some time with The Jerry Garcia Band, and he would later do a five-year stint on Dylan's so-called Never Ending Tour.

'We met him at the studio,' Chuck says. 'Danny and I showed up and we had a couple of guitars and we said, "We're just making stuff up. You want to accompany us?" And he goes, "Yeah, sure." And then we asked the engineer, "Do you play bass?" And the guy says, "Yeah, I play a little bass." So he was in the control room, turning the tape machine on and playing bass. Danny and I are playing guitars and kind of struggling to get anything to sound like music. And the engineer was supposed to be with us for a few days, but the very next day there was somebody else: "No, I'm here today." "But what happened to the other guy?" "Oh, he couldn't make it." I think he was just not into it!'

A young Jake Puig ended up engineering the sessions for what would become *This Time Around* (1989), which featured keyboards from veteran Mike Finnigan, who had played on *Electric Ladyland* (1968) and with Janis Joplin's outfit Big Brother & The Holding Company. Although the record has less jagged edges than *Snakes*, it was in some senses less 'produced' than its predecessor, which had found the band using some programming and a Fairlight for some of the drums. 'Glyn Johns wouldn't have gone near that type of shit!' Prophet remarked.[22] Indeed, Johns would later note his distaste for the direction popular music was taking in the UK around that time: 'The synthesizer and the drum machine took over and, to my mind, the standard of songwriting plummeted with people becoming obsessed with beats per minute and electronically created sounds that in the end all sounded the same to me.'[23] Presumably, Stuart and Prophet's contrasting roots-conscious sound and commitment to classic songwriting was in part what excited him that night at the Town & Country Club. For *This Time Around*, Chuck claimed to have played everything live: 'I sat on a chair with my amp right next to the drummer and it was bleeding all over the place!'[24]

This was the first time Prophet met Spooner Oldham, who would play piano on his solo debut, *Brother Aldo* (1990). 'We probably knew Spooner from Dan Penn and Neil Young . . . he was living in LA at the time, and he became a friend of ours.' Less successful was a further collaboration with bassist Rene Coman, who by now was a relatively seasoned veteran of Green On Red's sessions and tours. 'I was at the hotel and I was in a Nyquil kind of a daze, trying to make myself sleep during the day because we were starting at seven at night,' Chuck recalls, 'and Glyn Johns called me and asked me, "The bass player. What do you think of the bass?" And I said, "It's all good, what do you mean?" He goes, "Well, it's not really working out." And I said, "Really? Don't you think right now that's the least of our problems?"'

Johns fired Coman anyway, and brought in a friend: Pat Donaldson was a British bassist who had played with John Cale and Richard Thompson. 'He was a great player,' Prophet concedes, 'and we liked him. But the scales started to tip a little bit toward Glyn and his cronies. And Bernie Leadon [of the Eagles] came in and played. Bernie was cool. And there was really no reason for us to rebel. As I say, we just didn't have the material.' Chuck pauses.

'But we did discover that you could pretty much ask the assistants to get you anything and they would do it. You know, at Ocean Way Studios, they were really trained to not say no. And so we used to say, "We want a fifth of Absolut and some Ocean Spray cranberry." And Danny and I would get to the studios and it was cocktail hour.'

The sessions took place overnight, mostly because the studio rates were so much cheaper. Chuck remembers, 'Michael Jackson was in the other room. While we were there. For real! He was just across the hall.' During the day, Peter Frampton would be in the rooms they had hired. 'We'd stay up all night,' Chuck confirms. 'We'd just be all adrenalined out. It was a ten-day affair. There were overdubs and mixing, and it all went by fast. Everybody got paid, but the whole experience just kind of rolled over us.'

In the middle of recording the album, China Records decided to put out a live set on cassette and 10-inch vinyl. *Live At The Town And Country Club* was recorded on April 7 1989. Prophet explains, 'Well, the problem with that was we were recording at night, working until maybe eleven in the morning. Our body clocks were all turned around . . . and then we got a cassette in a FedEx package and it said, *Green On Red Live At The Town And Country*. I mean, we're trying to make a *record*. We're trying to get up early enough to convene in the hotel, try to invent a couple of things, just a chord pattern or something that we could jam on in the studio, so Dan could improvise words over it. So, did we want to listen to this thing and critique it? Did we want to revisit where we were nine months ago at the Town & Country? Where the drummer had left the band two days earlier and the keyboard player had subbed on drums? And so Danny took the FedEx package and threw it in the trash.' Chuck pauses. 'They put it out anyway.' And he understands why. 'I mean, to their credit, they were just trying to stir things up. And I think the papers gobbled it up. I'm sure it's a great record,' he adds. 'I've never heard it.' The recording featured several songs from *Here Come The Snakes*, along with some setlist staples from the Green On Red back catalogue, but it was far from the peak of what Green On Red 3.0 at their best had achieved onstage.

This Time Around was a disappointment. Stuart would later describe Glyn Johns as 'like an English schoolmaster; it was like going to summer camp. It was a disaster'.[25] While the record sounds like it is trying to be current, it feels like it is going through the motions, the gears grinding metal on metal, with no inspiration to grease the wheels. Lyrics of songs such as 'Cool Million' and 'Rev. Luther' seem half-baked, pushing the customary buttons of sleaze and self-abasement, but with little conviction. 'The Quarter' seems like a half-hearted attempt to recreate the magic of 'Tenderloin'. There are a couple of better moments—'You Couldn't Get Arrested' has a pleasing melody, gently melancholy instrumentation, understated vocal, and an intriguing lyric, and 'Hold The Line' is a convincing, beseeching cry for one more chance; its loping groove is scarred by some of Prophet's most imaginative guitar work on the album. But in essence it bears out Chuck's assessment that the material was not up to snuff. The final two songs sound like bottom-of-the-barrel scraps.

'Fun fact,' says Prophet, 'on the British version of *This Time Around*, we have a picture of an arm and a tattoo that says "born to lose" on the front cover. But the Americans were uncomfortable with that; Polygram had just lost one of their acts, Mother Love Bone, to a heroin overdose. So they flipped the back and made it the front. True story: I was walking down Haight Street and I looked in the window of a used record store and I saw that the inside of the cover was now the cover. News to me!'

The whole process had been an unhappy one, and most reviewers had little difficulty reading between the lines: *NME*'s Stuart Bailie commented that 'the band's been hustled into the studio before they've got some songs that they're fully convinced about' and found the album dominated by too many 'bar room fillers and perfunctory Creedence-style grindings'.[26] *Trouser Press* described the songs as 'by-the-number constructions [rather] than emotional outpourings'. However, Paul Elliott, writing for *Sounds*, was more impressed, awarding the album four stars; he also picked up on the CCR influence, noting Prophet's use of reverb and the prominent Hammond organ.[27] David Sinclair, a committed Green On Red watcher, noted how Prophet compos[ed] his guitar parts with marvellous fluency and a simmering, controlled aggression'.[28] *Sky* magazine gave it four and a half stars, bizarrely describing it as 'their strongest set of songs and best recorded sound to date ... Outstanding'.[29] It's not the first time a music critic has peeled off some clichés instead of taking the time to evaluate the recording properly.

The music press can switch into backlash mode quite swiftly when a formerly favoured band fails to match up to its track record. At other times, the tendency is to keep believing, and some of the UK music weeklies were doing their best to remain enthusiastic about Green On Red even when there were diminishing returns on the tour circuit too. But though Dave Simpson came to the Irish Centre in Leeds ready to place them alongside Dylan and Neil Young, he concluded, 'Green On Red stare greatness in the face and go shoot some pool'; they were retreating into 'safe rockers when they should have drawn blood' and settling for the status of 'a damn good blues band when they could've been gods'.[30]

With hindsight, Stuart was prepared to admit that, in terms of recording at that time, 'the well was dry', but he found it 'interesting clinically, having no material and having to write every day for the session'—an educational experience for sure, but perhaps it should have stayed that way, as he implied in his interview in UK weekly *Sounds* at the time.[31] Prophet's view on *This Time Around* today is a philosophical one: 'There were some albums that probably just shouldn't get made. But I do remember Danny saying to me, "I'm glad *This Time Around* wasn't our last record."'

This Time Around was followed by *Scapegoats* (1991), which Al Kooper produced in Nashville with a supporting cast of very talented musicians, including Spooner Oldham on piano, mandolin virtuoso Sam Bush, southern legend Dan Penn on guitar, and Tony Joe White (writer of Presley's hit 'Polk Salad Annie') on harmonica. 'We just kinda shuffled the cards,' Stuart told interviewer Ralph Traitor. 'Had different people come in playing different things,' claiming, 'We had more fun in Nashville in ten minutes than we did in two weeks in LA with Glyn!'[32]

'*Scapegoats* was fun in a way,' Prophet admits. 'A couple of times, Al Kooper left us to our own devices. He would be off to New York to do the Rock and Roll Hall of Fame, and he'd tell us just to do our thing.' Furthermore, there was a kickback from the studio ('like a dream come true' according to Stuart): they were using the original Jack Clement studio in the house (owned by Roy Clark at the time) while the record company was being charged for the more expensive one next door, and Chuck and Dan were able to pocket the difference. Stuart remembers that at the same time they wrote and recorded some demos with the legendary Dan Penn—'We would play them for producers coming in and out of the studio's office'—and that they cut 'Little Things In Life' in a half hour with what he describes as 'A-Team studio players'—Eddie Bayers and Michael Rhodes—whom Stuart and Prophet grabbed as they left a session in the big studio next door, paying them $100 each to sit in and play. Prophet recalls that Bayers 'literally played brushes on a cardboard box'; the drum kit had already been broken down, 'so we just worked out this little skiffle version of it'. This was when Kooper had left for New York. They played it for him on his return. 'I remember we spent half a day arguing what to put on it. And then Al put on a beautiful little Buddy Holly glockenspiel, and it became a record. Before that, it was just a track.'

Scapegoats might be the best of the final trilogy. If it lacks a sense of adventure, and perhaps begins to run out of steam on side two, there are sturdy songs, a full, broad sound, confident vocals, and plenty of opportunities for Prophet to stretch out. In another band's career, 'Little Things In Life' might have gone Top 10. 'Gold In The Graveyard' has an irresistible riff and some of Dan's best cracking-wise couplets, including 'Trying to beat the daily grind / There's no cure for a brilliant mind.' 'Blowfly', with its horn section, tries too hard, but 'Hector's Out Of Prison', with its strings, is another in a series of attempts to recapture something of the epic, inverted grandeur of Green On Red's heyday, and it comes close.

Although the album was a significant improvement on its predecessor, the sense lingers that the ratio of effort to payoff was tipping unfavourably. Prophet recalls walking into the parking lot at Sound Emporium in Nashville and Stuart remarking to him, *sotto voce* and with a mixed tone of apprehension and relief, 'I only got four more vocals to go!'

The UK-based monthly *Brum Beat* called the album the band's 'finest calling card yet', giving credit to Kooper for his production on the collection of songs 'ploughing the same ol' familiar furrow of arid country infused with heartbreak and despair'.[33] In the *Times*, David Sinclair described the album as 'remarkably mellow . . . for a band which has long been renowned for the sociopathological tendencies of its music',[34] but the rather nebulous notion of rootsiness or authenticity remained an appealing feature for some reviewers: 'In these days of polyunsaturated pop,' Pete Clark of *HiFi News* suggested, 'it is vital you get some meat in your diet. Preferably raw.'[35]

The album/tour cycle rolled on, with the band continuing to comfortably sell out medium-sized club venues and getting booked for European festivals. A China compilation released in the autumn—just a couple of months after *Scapegoats*—was a chance for Stuart and Prophet to stage a few promotional appearances and for the press to take stock: *Select* gave the compilation four stars, suggesting that the band had become 'master exponents' of alcoholic bar-room blues without ever achieving the level of success they deserved.[36] Steve Morris for *Brum Beat* noted Prophet as 'hugely underrated' and the band as the only group apart from the Stones 'capable of such loose rumbling rockin' and rollin".[37]

The 'underrated' label was by now becoming a familiar tag for the band; the sense that the band had never managed to push up to the 'next level' was hard to shake—no doubt amongst promoters, label heads and, not least, Stuart and Prophet themselves. A *Record Collector* feature discussed 'the pitfalls of eternal cult status' and documented the 'idle whim[s] of fate' that had littered the band's career.[38] In his *Northern Echo* report on a show at Newcastle Riverside on the spring tour, reviewer Nigel Vincent mused, 'Why Green On Red has not reached the cult megastar status of fellow Americans and guitar bandits R.E.M. still remains a mystery. The songs are there and the fans refuse to lose faith.'[39]

However, the touring remained hit and miss, and more often the latter. Stuart and Prophet's addictions were inevitably impacting on their performances. Stuart recalls in his memoir that 'the rhythm section hated it when Billy and I were fucked up, there was nothing to hold back. Guitars are usually fighting to get away, a crashing shore break,' he adds, but when they were stoned, that tension would be gone: 'Rock'n'roll is a loaded spring; *it's the potential that matters.* I'd get so far behind the beat I felt like a satellite in an elliptical orbit, edging farther and farther away from radio contact. Unfortunately,' he concludes ruefully, 'We weren't playing jazz, or even the blues.'[40]

'When we finished that record [*Scapegoats*],' Prophet recalls, 'Danny had gone out and purchased one of those Samsonite five-piece luggage collections. They were neatly lined up against the wall, like the von Trapp children. It was a different look for Dan. He was moving to Spain, to give it a go with his wife, Nuria. It felt like the end of something and the beginning of something,

I suppose. And that tour pretty much broke up the band, really. We ended up doing a train tour, and Danny's new bride was with him the whole time and it felt like we had gone a tour too far.'

Stuart is rueful when he looks back: 'I was strung out again after cleaning up and La Española [his wife] was the road manager, since she was the only one who could read a train schedule. On the last show of the tour in Athens, I got burned by a junkie with a syringe tattooed on his palm, and I went back to Tucson and stopped using dope finally. The entropy was palpable.' Of a video recording taped at the Town & Country Club in London in September 1992, just ahead of the release of *Too Much Fun*, Stuart believes, 'The band never sounded worse … the interview is unwatchable. I wish we could scrub it from the net.'

Too Much Fun would be Stuart and Prophet's last album together. Prophet's memory is that Stuart started it without him ('We weren't communicating very well'), and that he travelled down to Tucson to join him there. The album featured eleven Stuart/Prophet co-writes and a cover of Roger Nichols and Paul Williams's 'Rainy Days and Mondays', made famous by The Carpenters in 1971:

> *Talkin' to myself and feelin' old*
> *Sometimes I'd like to quit*
> *Nothin' ever seems to fit*
> *Hangin' around*
> *Nothin' to do but frown*
> *Rainy days and Mondays always get me down*

It was the last song they recorded together. 'Quite fitting, no?' Dan remarked, in his email response to my questions about the band's final sessions. 'It's a good record,' he reckons. 'Cut in Tucson at the old 7n7, which became the famous Wavelab of Calexico/Giant Sand fame. Kinda the last hurrah and we had fun. You could park your car in there and sing behind the wheel. In the alley was a shrine at a dumpster where some poor teenage girl had been cut up and discarded by a serial killer. Trains came by on a regular basis which wound up on tape.' Some of the tour regulars contributed—J.D. Foster on bass (as well as some keys and percussion), Chris Holland, and Tommy Larkins—while guitar prodigy Rainer Ptacek, who had sold Stuart his first Gretsch when working at a guitar workshop back in Tucson, contributed banjo and even their old friend Randy McReynolds added some backing vocals.

Too Much Fun has some imaginative production in places, notably the opening 'Frozen In My Headlights', with greasy slide guitar and some unsettling keyboard textures framing a half-whispered vocal. There are some effective horns in 'The Getaway' and blistering flashes of harmonica in 'I Owe You One' and the otherwise unremarkable shuffle 'Man Needs Woman'. The lyrics have been given more thought and care and are reminiscent of Dan's more inspired moments ('So far down even midgets couldn't look me in the eye'). A mid-tempo groove that is not unpleasing dominates, but there are precious few irresistible hooks of the kind that had blessed albums like *No Free Lunch* and *Here Come The Snakes*. Prophet notes, '"I Owe You One" is a diamond. Dan could still comb through the rubble and pull out something beautiful.' 'The songs are fine,' Stuart insists in his memoir, 'but the moment has passed and my heart is damaged beyond repair.'[41]

Chuck once said, in response to a question about his experience with Green On Red, 'What did I learn? How to drink lying down and how to sleep sitting up.'[42] The liner notes to *Too Much Fun* include the comment, 'Why Do We Play Music? ... We're Too Lazy Too Work and Too Nervous Too Steal'—a typically self-deprecating kiss off. 'You can impose yourself on the world forever like a baboon showing his ass,' Stuart muses on the end of Green On Red, 'but don't expect people to keep on clapping.'[43] Prophet is equally philosophical: 'Whatever it was about us that got us to a certain place wouldn't get us to the next place.'

The two friends speak in almost identical terms about their partnership, and with similar metaphors—this was 'time in the trenches'. 'We went through it,' says Prophet. 'Kind of like army buddies. We're not really bitter toward each other, which is pretty rare actually. People don't really bond as closely with the people that they need the most. It's complicated. But over time, people have time to reflect. We have managed to stay more than friends. Kind of brothers, in a way. But there's a lot of blood on the floor.' Prophet admits that it is difficult to separate out the relationship from the abusive, drugs-and-alcohol lifestyle that was an inescapable part of it. 'The real truth is, we were addicts. And on some level the whole she-bang enabled us to keep the party going. And it enabled us to continue our extended adolescence right into adulthood. And kept us off the streets and more importantly away from straight jobs.' And there were times when they needed to be there for each other in literal life-and-death terms. If Prophet's habit had long since spiralled out of control, Stuart's use was always several shades darker. And a heroin habit, of course, harbours the perpetual risk of overdose. 'Yeah. Danny got a key for my hotel room one time from the desk and came up and took me home. Walked me 'round. Brought me back.'

'The best thing that Chuck taught me is that collaboration is a great thing,' Dan later said. 'You need other people, and if you're collaborating with the right ones, it makes it better. Chuck taught me that what matters is the collaborative effort that's captured on the record, and then people's experience of listening to it.'[44] As I wind up my own conversation with Dan, he tells me, 'Chuck has a great line about Green On Red in general. That we used to do things sixty-five percent. Not a hundred and ten percent. Not five percent. Sixty-five. *Sixty-five percent.*'

Stuart would follow up in the wake of Green On Red's demise with *Retronuevo* in 1993 (collaborating with Al Perry); he would go on to record *Can O' Worms* with J.D. Foster in 1995, before a lengthy break from recording and, indeed, the music business as a whole: 'I became a normal person. I had a kid, worked a normal job, all of that.' By the time Green On Red finally called it a day, Prophet had already released *Brother Aldo* (1990) and *Balinese Dancer* (1992) and had been touring in Europe with a band that included his partner, Stephanie Finch. For Green On Red, there would be a successful touring reunion in 2005, but before that there would be many summits, valleys, and bends in the road of Prophet's long career as a solo artist.

CHAPTER FOUR

STEP RIGHT THIS WAY

BROTHER ALDO (1988–90)

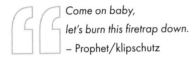

> Come on baby,
> let's burn this firetrap down.
> – Prophet/klipschutz

I COULD MAKE A PRINCETON SING

Up until around 1988, Prophet was living in a warehouse space on Folsom Street that he shared with his partner, Kara Johnson. It was an industrial building that had had some partition walls put in so that it vaguely resembled residential accommodation. There was a sense of communal living among the many people who inhabited this huge, cavernous structure, with different areas partitioned off to form individual living spaces. 'We were all in our mid-twenties, all of us living in kind of marginal circumstances,' Chuck recalls. 'It was tents and cardboard forts.'

'Each artist had built their own room,' says Kara. 'And their own room would be in their own style. And then there was a gallery.' The punk/new wave band The Tubes lived in the same building, which is how Prophet first met Prairie Prince, who would play drums on *Temple Beautiful* and *Night Surfer* decades later. One day, Prophet was up a tall ladder, changing a lightbulb in a dangerous stairwell, as Prairie walked by with Todd Rundgren. 'And they had a couple of blokes with British accents in tow,' Chuck recalls, 'who I realised later were members of XTC. They were joking around—"This guy's gonna make a great roadie someday!"—and Todd was playfully shaking the ladder. I felt like saying, "Shut up, old man!" It was total chaos in that place. But wonderful times. And I could walk to the Albion from there.'

Much more about the Albion shortly. The warehouse cultivated a kind of artistic commune. Prophet recalls that he and some of his friends hatched a plan one year to have a Thanksgiving dinner and recreate *The Last Waltz*— the name given to the 'farewell' gig performed by The Band at Winterland in 1976, featuring guest appearances by Muddy Waters, Joni Mitchell, Neil Young, Clapton, Dylan, and many more. The show, via Martin Scorsese's film of the same name, has passed into rock'n'roll legend. Chuck describes how their recreation of the iconic event came together: 'There were some people there that worked for caterers. Everybody was a freelancer. And so different people pitched in. I think we charged five or ten dollars, and we had a concert in this warehouse. I remember Stephie did the whole Joni Mitchell thing, and we did Neil Young's "Helpless", all that stuff. We all knew the record and we knew the movie and so that's what we did. Out of this kind of Judy Garland spirit of *let's put on a show*. And somebody videotaped it. And I remember we carried this piano up three flights of stairs. Incredible.'

Chuck and Kara had moved back together from Berlin, where they had stayed for several months following the end of the *Killer Inside Me* tour. Their relationship finally began to fracture irreparably when Green On Red 3.0 kicked into gear. 'I think we started growing apart. I was gone and ... and we weren't always very nice to each other, either,' Chuck admits. 'The relationship got pretty volatile, and she decided she didn't want to be with me anymore.' Kara is certain that it was the relentless touring schedule for Green On Red around this time that put intolerable pressure on their relationship. Even when the band were in town to play a show, they would just be passing through.

'He'd be gone for months at a time,' Kara says. 'Back for a day and then gone again.' And in a time before cell phones, staying in touch was a particularly frustrating challenge, especially given the band's European tour commitments. 'I literally just had a list of dates. And countries. And that was it,' she recalls. 'And sometimes there would be a hotel number there, and I'd try to call and I would get someone speaking in a different language. I'd get letters and they'd be like a month old. No email back then. When they were gone, they were just ... *gone.*' At times, with dates being added at a few days' notice, often Kara would not even have any idea which country they were in. 'The hardest part is not knowing that they're OK. I still worry about them flying and driving all over!'

Prophet's voracious appetite for rock'n'roll and his relentless work ethic meant that even Green On Red's often-intense touring schedule was rarely enough to keep him occupied. In 1986, he worked with Eddie Ray Porter on Porter's *When The Morning Falls* LP. Porter, a native of Atlanta, Georgia, had made a name for himself as a songwriter of note in San Francisco in the early 1980s; he and Winningham had met at a Van Morrison concert at the Great American Music Hall in 1983, and they had started a band called State Of Things, which lasted a few years before Patrick left to form his own band, The New Breed. Chuck played guitar on *When The Morning Falls* and worked on the song structures and arrangements. 'Prior to that,' Prophet told Jon Storey for *Bucketfull Of Brains* in 1987, Porter had 'songs that would go on for ten minutes with no arrangements and no breaks'.[1]

The same interview also found Prophet name-checking The Beau Brummels—one of the first Beatles-inspired bands to break out of San Francisco. They had had a handful of hits in 1965, lacing their British Invasion sound with San Franciscan psychedelia, but the flame guttered quickly, and by the mid-80s it had been more than a decade since their last release and twenty years since their zenith. Coming across them playing a regular weekly gig at a local bar, Prophet began to sit in with them: 'They've been playing that bar for like twenty-five years!' he told Storey. 'And there's kids in there from fifteen to, like, fifty-year-old parents dancing! It kept me alive when we [Green On Red] were off.'[2]

However, Prophet was also beginning to explore other musical avenues beyond the sideman role. Given Green On Red's diminishing artistic and commercial returns, it was no surprise when the band eventually folded. Reflecting on the birth of Prophet's solo career, Dan Stuart remarks, 'It was inevitable. I remember getting angry once when there was a schedule conflict or something but, really, I always knew he would go on to his own career and I like to think/remember that I encouraged him more than hindered.' Even as early as 1988, Dan was telling journalist Steve Sutherland—with astonishing foresight—'It's inevitable that little Chuck'll go on. And it's inevitable that I will switch mediums and always be just the fucked up, twisted writer.'[3]

The imperative to keep paying the bills was one thing (as noted in the previous chapter, Stuart and Prophet were in the unusual position at the time of being kept on salary by China Records), but the other side of the story was that Prophet was undergoing a significant change of direction in artistic terms. At this time, he told *Bay Area Magazine*, he was 'really into traditional music ... country, blues, and folk. I like traditional musical structure, but I try to take an unstructured approach to it. To take that music and just set it slightly sideways.'[4] It may have been difficult at the time to define the sound he was busy fashioning, but in hindsight one can trace it in the music of other roots-oriented bands that would soon start to prick up the ears of critics, music fans and, perhaps most importantly, industry types. 'Within a couple years there was Counting Crows, and The Jayhawks were making records that connected with a bigger audience, and by then people were ready for that,' Chuck smiles wryly. 'I mean, I've always been somebody that's had pretty bad timing.'

He continues, 'It wasn't like what we were doing was obscure or anything. We were way off into ... [Bob Dylan's 1975 album] *Desire*, and I was definitely into Richard and Linda [Thompson]. I liked the songs and I liked the guitar breaks. You have to understand that when Stephie and I first started playing together, around '88, every band in this town was just trying to be The Replacements. And people were playing the rock clubs, two electric guitars, it was loud, and ... it just wasn't speaking to me. But when we started playing in the back room of a club, sitting down, playing quieter, and we really got to look into people's eyes ... that was when we started to get this cool thing that got me excited.'

The club in question was the Albion Bar, at the corner of Albion and 16th Street in San Francisco. There was a back room for music ('it was a dive, a firetrap,' Prophet says), and this cramped and smoky space would become the cradle for a new music scene that would be crucial in the evolution of Prophet's career as the end of the 1980s loomed. Patrick Winningham probably had no conception of the seeds he was sowing when he started things off. He was friendly with a waitress called Liz Kastner, a workmate at the comedy club the Other Café—a venue in the Haight that was on the regular circuit for stand-up acts that would graduate in due course to *Saturday Night Live* stardom. Liz (who Chuck notes 'looked after things for me for some time; I'm grateful to her') happened to be on the Albion softball team, and when the owner of the Albion told her he wanted to get some live music happening, she called Winningham. Prophet remembers, 'They said, "For fifty dollars, can you guys keep the music going on?" And we said, "No problem. No *problem!*" So that's what we would do. And Patrick, little by little, started bringing his old band members in. Sometimes we played every Thursday, Friday, Saturday. Sometimes Sunday matinees. I just couldn't get enough of it.' He told David Cantwell it was 'kind of like a poker night. After a while there'd be a line around the block, though since the place only holds about five people that wasn't so impressive. But it was a real magical time.'[5]

'I think we would do three forty-five-minute sets,' Prophet tells me. 'And I could always drink for free. My favourite drink back then was a Vodka Sandwich, two shots of vodka with olives. As I used to say, "A guy's got to get some solid food in there!"'

By 1988, Prophet had split from Kara and had become increasingly close with Stephanie Finch, whom he had known for several years. The figure of the strikingly beautiful blonde with the voice of an angel may sound like a cliché, but then it might just as well have been coined for Stephie. She had first met Chuck in 1984, and, when she moved to San Francisco in 1986, they were soon moving in similar social circles. Unfortunately, she also happened to be the partner of his close friend Patrick Winningham.

LITTLE BOY, LITTLE GIRL

Stephanie Finch is a native of Northridge, California, in the San Fernando Valley. Her childhood musical training was in piano, but more formative was the music echoing through the family home at the time. She recalls, 'At that time, at least for me, music wasn't really as focused on youth culture; it was more about the music on the radio or whatever overlapped.' Stephie's father's particular favourites included Peter, Paul & Mary, Judy Collins, and Aretha Franklin. From there, she says, 'I kind of ventured off on my own. So I would find out that Joni Mitchell wrote "Both Sides Now" and that I preferred her version to Judy Collins's.' Likewise, Peter, Paul & Mary led to Dylan. Stephie looks back on the 1970s as a 'golden age of music' and recalls road trips listening to the great countrypolitan artists, like Glen Campbell. 'That really got under my skin when I was a kid,' she acknowledges.

Inspired by what she heard on the radio and around the house, Finch learned to play a few chords on guitar. She has inherited her father's beautiful Guild electric, which he used to keep under the bed. Although he didn't own an amp, he managed to plug it into the radio ('somehow!') and coaxed a decent sound from it. Stephanie continued with piano lessons through her school years and sang in the high-school choir. She also remembers that although she was 'getting all rebellious by high school', her father 'would rope me in to singing duets at the church with him. He loved to sing'. Her older brother was another considerable influence on her developing musical tastes, and she would take on board everything he brought home from the record store.

Another key musical connection came from Stephie's friendship with Mare Winningham, Patrick's older sister: Mare and Stephie were in the same grade and drama classes in junior high. Around the time Stephie and Patrick started dating, she and Mare would sing as a duo called The Waybacks. Patrick remembers, 'They started singing together at Christmas parties at my house. And the next thing you know, they're doing Everly Brothers songs. And Stephanie was awesome then. Piano, like, *classically trained* piano. And her voice was so *pure*. She sings a lot of background vocals on my first album. She was a *real* musician, just *really* good.'

Mare Winningham had already written quite a few songs, and she and Finch worked out vocal arrangements heavily influenced by the likes of the McGarrigle Sisters and Simon & Garfunkel. Performing Mare's originals and a range of covers, The Waybacks kept going for a couple of years prior to Stephie's move to San Francisco. Mare Winningham was also establishing herself as an actress (she won an Emmy in 1980), appearing alongside many of the so-called 'brat pack' in 1985's *St. Elmo's Fire*, and her celebrity status afforded The Waybacks opportunities for live performances that drew in audiences from the Hollywood set. It didn't harm that as they expanded into a band format, they recruited the youngest of the Carradine clan, Bobby, to play guitar. Finch recalls the likes of Rosanna Arquette and Michelle Pfeiffer being in the audience on occasion. But, the Hollywood dazzle notwithstanding, Stephie says, 'I knew that that wasn't reality. And I guess I wanted to find something that seemed more real. I think even before I moved up here [to San Francisco], I knew that I wanted in some way to be musically collaborating with Chuck.'

They had first met through Patrick. 'I lived in LA at the time, and I was going out with Patrick,' Stephie explains. 'And Chuck would come and play down there with Green On Red.' She would go along to see them with Patrick and her brother Dave. She first met Chuck at a Peter Case solo show at UCLA (Chuck remembers it too, characteristically adding the fine detail that the Pittsburgh band The Rave-Ups were the opening act), but her first impressions of him were not entirely positive. 'He was a kind of arrogant young guy,' she recalls. But Patrick and Chuck were close friends and, along with Kara Johnson, the four of them started to hang out together. Stephie moved to San Francisco to be with Patrick in late 1986. 'We lived in a big flat we rented. It was an era when you could still get these really great deals. The era of eccentric landlords that doesn't exist anymore! I think I was paying ninety dollars a month to live there, in 1987, and it's incredible to think about that now. That was the deal, though: *The rent's low here, but you should never bother the landlord about anything*, so it was a little bit of a neglected building.'

Finch was waitressing at the time at a bustling restaurant called PJ's Oyster Bed on Sunset. 'I remember I had to shuck my own oysters. I still have this scar on my thumb from that!' she laughs. 'And then while I was still dating Patrick, Chuck started thinking too, for whatever reason, I don't think I planted the seed but … that maybe we should try to play together.' At the time, Chuck was living in an apartment on Sunset. 'He had a basement set up with drums, and so we recorded a version of "Dark End Of The Street" where he played drums and overdubbed guitar. I remember when I left there, I was just walking on air, thinking, *This is what I like doing*. I was really excited about it.'

This was around the same time that Chuck and Kara's relationship was beginning to fail. Prophet remembers returning from Memphis, where he had been recording *Here Come The Snakes*, and finding that Kara was gone. 'She'd checked out. And I remember I had that stupid cassette of the record [*Snakes*]. I left it there, and then I went out, and then Kara came back to get her stuff, and she listened to it, and half way through "We Had It All" she just turned it off. [*laughs*] I came back and I hit play on the cassette player, and that's where she'd stopped the tape. Just, like, "Enough!" And she just moved out. Left with some guy that I'd seen around. Well, I was gone so much—months at a time.' All the same, with some inevitable lapses over time, the circle of friendships survived (Chuck and Stephie remain close with Kara and her family, and are godparents to her son, Cash; Chuck describes the circle of friends as 'a real joy'; Patrick was best man at Chuck and Stephie's wedding). 'We were all so young,' Stephie says, 'and we were all friends, so I used to see Kara still. We used to go to the gym together. Just hang out. Anyway, I guess I was really starting to have feelings for Chuck ... and I think he felt the same.'

It was around this time that Prophet suffered a serious accident. 'He was drinking a lot and who knows what else,' Finch remembers. 'Probably doing some drugs. He brought a girl home with him to his warehouse, and he was locked out. So he tells her, "Just stay here, I know another way to get in."' Unfortunately, his alternative entrance was via the roof. Stephie continues the story: 'There was a car body shop right next door. He figured if he went down to that roof he'd be able to get in through the window into his place. And he jumped from his roof to the body shop roof, not knowing that it was glass. And this wasn't just one storey. It was like he had nine lives because I don't know how he survived ... maybe because he was drunk. Because he fell right onto cement. And that set off all these alarms, and the cops came and they thought he was breaking in. And they held him at gunpoint, and he was trying to tell them, "I *live* here." And they say, "Yeah, *right!*"' When they checked his ID and found that he did live in the complex, they let him go. Stephie continues: 'In the meantime, he realised that that girl was still waiting for him. So he went up and I guess he was so drunk he didn't realise how injured he was.'

Chuck called Stephie the next morning and told her what had happened; Stephie called Kara ('they hadn't been broken up for very long'), and the two women went and picked him up. 'He was in really bad shape, bruises all over. His arm was completely scraped up. Didn't have health insurance. We took him to UC [University of California Medical Center]. I think he gave them a fake name and they took him in and did a CAT scan and everything. He was so lucky that he didn't have major injuries. And that was his brief period of being single!'

The line between a professional partnership and a personal relationship began to shift. Prophet is fond of telling the story—or the stories—of how he and Stephie first sang together. It's another point at which myths and facts blur, and probably the deeper truth of their extraordinary musical kinship is more significant than simple chronology. But the story Chuck tells was that he was with a group of friends, swapping songs, and Stephie joined in singing. Chuck turned to her: 'What is that thing you're doing with your voice?' 'I don't know,' Stephie replies. 'Err ... harmony?' 'Yeaaah,' Prophet shoots back. 'We gotta *do* that, man!' However it may have started, and whichever song that first duet might have been (was it Dylan's 'Abandoned Love' or that basement recording of 'Dark End Of The Street'?), even so, many years later, what is unmistakeable is how highly Prophet values what they discovered that time they first sang together. 'Yeah,' he says now. 'I mean, when our voices joined together like that, it was ...' He trails off. 'I always felt like that was a special weapon.'

Meanwhile, it had become obvious to all within range that the spark between Chuck and Stephie was not simply a musical one, and they grew closer as they collaborated more, often working the Albion scene and other local clubs as a trio with Patrick Winningham or with Stephen Yerkey. Stephie had been doing a little songwriting herself at that time, collaborating on a couple of songs with Patrick, and they played for a while with Chuck as a trio. A tape provided by Pat Thomas from that era has them opening with 'Look Both Ways' and Winnningham covering Townes Van Zandt's 'Tecumseh Valley' with Stephie on accordion and Prophet on piercing Telecaster. Stephie distinctly remembers that, at one point, 'We were still trying to play as a trio and Chuck came over to our flat. And Patrick said, "Well, I was thinking we could call ourselves The Miserable Clowns." And I was thinking, *I don't want to romanticise anything like that.* And so ... I didn't voice it, but Chuck stood up and said, "I ain't no miserable clown." And he picked up his guitar and walked out. And I was thinking, *I want to start a band with him.*' Stephie laughs at the memory. '*I don't want to be a miserable clown either ...*'

Finch moved out of the flat she had shared with Patrick, who remembers her being at a point where 'she got sick of a lot of bullshit. A lot of drinking and things like that'. But Winningham could also see what was happening between Chuck and Stephie. 'They were made for each other,' Patrick says now. 'They even looked alike! And they complement each other musically so well. So that was kind of a weird time for a while . . . it was almost like Fleetwood Mac! It became very obvious that they were getting *serious*.' Stephie concurs: 'It was clear that we were kind of falling in love or whatever. So I moved out into a small apartment on Broderick Street. And then I moved again to what was at that time a real crack neighbourhood, and Chuck was coming over there a lot. That's when our relationship was really blossoming. And then that '89 earthquake happened.'

The Loma Prieta quake killed sixty-three, injured thousands, and caused significant damage to the Bay Bridge. Many buildings were damaged—over eighteen thousand dwellings, and thousands more constructions, including the warehouse where Prophet had been living, which was condemned in the wake of what was San Francisco's worst natural disaster since 1906. Finch was feeling increasingly unsafe in the district where she had been living and it was at that point that they moved in together into the apartment they still share on a quiet residential street in the Castro.

Chuck, Stephie, and Patrick continued for a short while doing shows together at the Albion, and Winningham understandably winces at the memories. 'We played two, three nights a week together. And it was intense. They'd go up and do "Dark End Of The Street" and my heart would be just *dying*. And then I'd go up and sing "It Doesn't Matter Anymore" by Buddy Holly or something. And then finally I couldn't take it. So then we didn't see each other for about three or four years, maybe.' Patrick decided to go his own way, as the Fleetwood Mac song goes, and he set up a similar music scene at a place called the Hotel Utah. 'The owner was this guy Paul Gaer. He was a sweetheart. And he wrote the story to *Electric Horseman*, that movie with Robert Redford and Jane Fonda. And with the money he made, he bought this whole dilapidated Hotel Utah. And it was just another dive that we fell into that was playing music. They gave me a weekly gig there and then I started booking for them. And then my wife started bartending—my girlfriend at the time. So then we just took over the whole place.' It would be another vital component of the San Francisco music scene: Winningham would play with, among others, Jeff Trott (who would go on to be a long-term collaborator with Sheryl Crow), and Charlie Gillingham and Dan Vickrey (both of whom would in due course join Counting Crows). Today, the Hotel Utah hosts one of the most popular open-mic nights in the city.

Stephanie Finch had taken some lessons on the accordion. When she was still living with Winningham, she remembers Prophet calling her up and telling her, 'Look, there's a pawnshop on Mission Street. And there's an accordion for sale, you gotta come down here.' She continues, 'So I go, "I'm *there!*"' Admitting she knew nothing about accordions at the time, Finch ended up with a Silvertone that was drastically out of tune. She tracked down a man by the name of Mr. Cirelli who had a workshop specialising in repairing and servicing accordions. 'He lived down in Brisbane. He came from the big-band era.'

Vincent Cirelli, the son of Italian immigrants, set up his accordion business in the North Beach area of San Francisco in 1946 and over the years had established a reputation as a master craftsman. Cirelli let Stephie trade in her Silvertone, 'And I got this beautiful black and white accordion with rhinestone buttons from him. And I took a few lessons from him as well.' It wasn't until it was damaged in transit to SXSW in Austin that Stephie discovered that she had been stuck with a monster of an instrument. 'Someone loaned me this little compact twelve bass accordion—*much* more manageable! Before that it was like trying to drive a Mack truck around a go-kart track.' Just before the first European tour in 1993, she got her own compact accordion, and Cirelli said, 'Well, if you're going to play some shows, you need your name on your accordion.' She continues, 'So he put my name on it in rhinestone lettering. And I forgot about it until, in Belgium, I remember there were people yelling, "Stephie!" And I couldn't figure it out. How did they know my name? And I looked … *Oh, Mr. Cirelli's right, that really works!'*

Cirelli had also tried to give her some career advice, Finch remembers. 'He goes, "You don't want to do this. It's a hard life. But if you're going to do it, the *real* bucks are in retirement and convalescent homes. So I want you to get this yellow accordion"—because my hair was blonder then—"with blue rhinestones. The rhinestones will match your eyes, and if you learn your standards you'll make some big bucks in convalescent homes!"' She pauses and laughs. 'Maybe I should've taken his advice! But I don't think he got very many eager young women visiting his workshop, so whenever I would show up he would have all his cronies there. And then sometimes I would bring Chuck along, and Mr. Cirelli was always really disappointed when Chuck was with me!' she laughs.

THE ALBION SCENE

'It's like the wind was changing direction,' Prophet reflects. 'I had my kite up just at the right time.' Not that it was as obvious to anyone else as it was to him. 'People around me were really underwhelmed by what we were doing there. I was saying, "You guys don't understand; this is *great*. The planets have lined up. And there's all this energy and there's all this music that we can explore."' There was also something competitive brewing in the atmosphere as these talented writers came together, night after night. 'It became a real songwriter's club. And a magical time in many ways. Patrick: great songwriter,' Prophet enthuses. 'And Dan Stuart, Stephen Yerkey ... incredible writers. Steve and I had many arguments about songwriting. He always won.' Pat Thomas, a friend and confidant of Prophet's around this time, recalls Yerkey was 'a bit of a mentor and inspiration to Chuck in those early days, as he was older and had been doing the solo thing longer ... sort of a Johnny Cash figure in some ways, equally as tall and impressive in stature'.

Prophet remembers the period as 'a real creative time', absorbing a lot of roots and specifically country music—Harlan Howard, Waylon Jennings, Jack Clement, and Don Williams. 'All that obscure 70s stuff. Everybody, whether it was Patrick or me or Steve Yerkey, we'd all been in bands that had climbed the mountain, talked to the elephant. And we *found* ourselves,' he says; and, as so often, there is an edge of self-deprecating irony in his voice. 'They say it's lonely at the top, but I can tell you it's *crowded* at the bottom [*laughs*]. Steve had a great band called NonFiction and made one album for Demon that nobody ever heard. Every song on it was just brilliant. And he had a rhythm section, the Campbell brothers, fantastic guys. Lance Campbell, the drummer, impossibly good-looking, James Dean. Lance had a reputation for being able to strip a car in three minutes. And I think he eventually went to jail. And it kind of broke Steve's heart, and NonFiction broke up. And so I sought Steve out and said, "Well, we're doing this thing at the Albion on Friday nights. You should come down."' The picture he paints is of a rapidly evolving musical community. '[Mark] Eitzel used to come down, and I remember [Mark] Kozelek from the Red House Painters would come around and see us play. He got Stephanie to sing on his record.'

The prospect of frequent, regular gigs applied healthy pressure to the songwriting urge. 'When you have a gig on Friday and it's Wednesday and you want to play a new song, you have to finish it. And then, if it doesn't work out, you go back, rotate the tyres and patch the leaks, and then play it the next weekend.' The improvisational spirit was captured by a contemporary reviewer, David Gendelman, who described how the songs would gradually build out from Prophet's guitar as each musician would 'join in and feel each other out'; for him, it was 'proof that the best rock'n'roll ... is spontaneous and never perfected. . . . Prophet, Finch, and The Creatures Of Habit sounded as real as the night itself.'[6]

'The gigs were very low key, not really advertised—just local fans and friends—very family-like—very warm and fuzzy and intimate,' Pat Thomas recalls. 'Chuck probably knew everyone in the audience by name! It was often free to get in or maybe like three dollars. And the beer was cheap and, because we all knew the bartenders, often it was nearly free.'

Winningham reflects, 'It was fun to watch him go from being this guitar player to trying to figure out how to write songs. He figured it out pretty damn *quick*.' It was a culture that meant, before long, Prophet had an impressive 'bag of tricks', as he calls it—a collection of songs that had been kicked around the bandstand enough times to shape up as his first solo album. It would be carved and fashioned as much as a zero-budget release would allow and would be released by Fire Records on that £500 contract as *Brother Aldo* in 1990.

Meanwhile, Prophet and Finch's musical partnership was developing rapidly as they performed regularly, mostly at the Albion, the Paradise Upstairs, and the Shannon Arms in the Outer Sunset. As Pat Thomas recalls, it was 'definitely Chuck *and* Stephanie, side by side ... very much like Richard and Linda Thompson, or Tom Petty and Stevie Nicks'. Stephie was still developing as a guitarist; Thomas remembers Chuck would put a playing card under her guitar strings to mute them while she was learning some of the chord changes. Being relatively cheap and easy to load in and out, they were also, as their reputation grew, able to snag opening slots at venues like the Fillmore. ('Probably before we were ready,' Finch comments. 'I mean, in hindsight. Because I thought we were great at the time. But I don't think Chuck thought we were great!') Among others, the Chuck and Stephie show opened for The Waterboys, Warren Zevon, Nanci Griffith, and Indigo Girls.

Other regular gigs included Winningham's Utah, the Chatterbox (or the Chameleon, as it was at the time), and the I-Beam in the Haight. Prophet notes that one of the reasons why so many music venues opened up around this time was the fallout from the HIV/AIDS crisis, which hit the city so hard in the early 80s: Mayor Dianne Feinstein approved the shutting down of gay bathhouses (located largely in the SoMa district—the gay bars were primarily in the Castro), although it proved largely counterproductive in terms of public health. In any case, the vacancies left cheap spaces open for live music entrepreneurs to move in: for instance, the Music Works, another venue on Prophet and Finch's circuit at the time, had been a leather bar called the Rawhide. 'Oh and the Paradise!' Chuck recalls. 'The Paradise would give you gigs, they'd just fill up the calendar. It was a free bar. And it had three stages. And it was just going seven nights a week. When I was playing with Stephanie and Roly [Salley], and we had a drummer by then, I would always request the small room on Mondays, because on the weekends it was a bridge-and-tunnel crowd—people who'd come into the city to party—and it was noisy, but on a Monday night, it was a good listening room. You'd get the musos out.' One night, as Prophet left the stage, a voice called out from one of the tables: 'Hey, Chuck, great show!' It turned out to be Peter Buck of R.E.M., and they got back up and played some songs together. 'And Stephie says, "Who was that guy?"' Chuck laughs. 'She hates it when I tell that story, but it's true. Totally true!'

Although Prophet and Finch (and, in the early days, Winningham, too) played in various duo and trio configurations, it did not take long for the sound to expand. 'We added what we could afford,' laughs Stephie. 'And I started playing accordion on those shows . . . and then, as the band became more and more electric, I had to keep up. And I wouldn't be heard with an accordion, so I had to step it up to keyboards. Chuck's always happiest when he's playing with bass and drums.' Indeed, recordings from those days reveal not a sensitive singer/songwriter setup but an often raucous and rough-edged sound, pierced by Prophet's single-coil Tele tone, anchored by Roly Salley on bass. Salley was 'around town', says Prophet. 'He was playing with Chris Isaak, who hadn't broken yet. They were a club band, and we just knew him as being the guy who wrote "Killing The Blues".' Salley had released the song originally on a record credited to the Woodstock Mountain Revue, *More Music From Mud Acres* (1977). John Prine recorded it two years later, for his album *Pink Cadillac* (which is where Prophet first heard it); thirty years after its first release, the song would become familiar to millions more via versions by Shawn Colvin (1994), and then Alison Krauss and Robert Plant on their album *Raising Sand* (2007).

Roly Salley recalls first meeting Prophet on the street in his neighbourhood. He noticed Chuck was limping, and, when he asked about it, he heard the story of Chuck's misadventure on the roof of the car body shop. 'Right then,' Roly quips, 'I knew he and I were going to be friends.' His first memories of Stephanie were that 'she was just as graceful and grounded and gorgeous a lady as you'd ever want to meet'. Before long, the three of them were jamming at Chuck's flat; Roly recalls the two of them singing The Crystals' hit 'And Then He Kissed Me': 'Totally charming/disarming,' he remarks.

'Yeah, we invited him [Salley] to play with us one time, and we were surprised when he turned up,' Prophet recalls. 'Well, the truth is, we never seemed that impressive. Kinda scrappy, you know? Some of those older guys who played with us at different times. That whole Albion scene. They couldn't see it. They wanted to know where it was going. They were like, "What *is* this? Is this *it*?"'

With Roly, it was always different. Stephie talks of him as a mentor figure, but the respect was mutual. 'I think they liked that I had written songs and could play the kind of bass that fit with what they were doing at the time,' says Salley. 'In many ways, Chuck taps what I call "the Mississippi River Corridor". So much of our music comes from a hundred miles to both the east and west of the whole length of the Mississippi. I hear it in Chuck's playing a lot. And there's nothing that I don't love about Steph!' When I mention that they both refer to him as a mentor, he replies, 'I must say that they made me feel very welcome and comfortable in their circle. And the fact is that I looked up to them in return. Chuck put me into some musical configurations that are some of my favourite recollections of all time'—notably the session with Spooner Oldham for *Brother Aldo*.

Because Salley's main gig was always with Chris Issak, he didn't tour with Prophet, although he played with them often at places like the Albion and bigger venues as they graduated to the likes of the Great American Music Hall. He would also join The Creatures Of Habit backing Jim Dickinson for a couple of shows at Slim's in June 1992—recordings later released on the album *A Thousand Footprints In The Sand* (1997). 'Chuck is musically fearless,' Roly notes. 'The energy he throws into playing and singing carries him through. He can be unpredictable but since he's schooled in the roots of our music, I find him pretty easy to follow onstage.' He continues, 'Chuck has a fat touch on his Telecaster . . . I love it. The first time I heard it, it reminded me of Ike Turner. His songwriting is fresh, deep, funny, musical and serious. He is the only living person that I truly enjoyed writing with.'

A soundboard recording from this era taped by Pat Thomas at the I-Beam provides a startling insight into how the band sounded at the time. It kicks off with Finch on accordion and Prophet on acoustic for 'Step Right This Way' before he switches to electric for a springy, wiry 'Say It Ain't So'. Before they launch into the Patrick Winningham–penned 'Scarecrow', Prophet alerts stand-in drummer Scott Mathews (of whom more in a moment) that the song is in 6/8 time. The straight-into-the-amp solos are fierce with a bell-like clarity—barely any sustain. The band continues with a lilting 'Killing The Blues' (Stephie sings lead) and a Richard Thompson–channelling 'Look Both Ways'. Chuck calls out harmonica player Jimmy Sweetwater to come up and play on 'Face To The Wall'. They close with a frantic 'Tune Of An Evening'. Despite the occasional touch of distortion, the tape is a gem, capturing as it does the intense musicality, excitement, and spontaneity of what Prophet and Finch were conjuring at this time.

Roly Salley recalls, of the Albion, '120 people barely fit there, but Chuck and Steph always drew about 130 into that room. This is what you call beautifully packed.' He notes, 'In some ways it feels more critical to a musician to play a room like the Albion than it does to play to fifty thousand people in a stadium. There seems to be more on the line in close quarters. The Albion crowd LOVED Chuck and Stephanie. It was like playing the Cavern'—the famed Liverpool venue frequented by The Beatles—'in 1961.' Before long, Kurt Wolf of the *San Francisco Bay Guardian* was describing them as 'the best act currently playing San Francisco's acoustic scene' and 'one of the finest musical teams this city's ever seen'.[7]

It was a time and a place Prophet would commemorate in the song 'Let's Burn This Firetrap Down', released on *Feast Of Hearts*, and revisit again for the track 'I Felt Like Jesus' on *Temple Beautiful*:

On sixteenth street, in the heart of the heart of the city
In the backroom of a bar called the Albion
I could make a Princeton sing
Like a house on fire
For anyone.

For Prophet, at this stage, it was all about starting over from nothing: stripping everything back to the drywall, as he puts it, and building a career as a solo artist without using anything of Green On Red as a reference point. And the Albion scene was the perfect ground-zero venue. 'Chuck said it poignantly,' Pat Thomas recalls in an email to me. '"The Albion: I walked in there one day and stayed for three years."' For a select and diverse group of musicians, he continues, 'journalists, drinkers, misfits, and beautiful people, the bar was home away from home and the back room was "everyman's stage"—anyone who wanted to could play there, the good, the bad, and the ugly'.

BROTHER ALDO—THE ALBUM

The Albion vibe determined the musical direction Prophet felt compelled to take at that point. 'Producer Scott Mathews had converted his Bernal Heights shack into a makeshift studio,' Chuck later recounted in a 1997 blog post. 'He had a funky AM radio console and one good German mic (which we used on EVERYTHING). In order to disguise some of the tape hiss we kept an old tube radio bleeding into the room at all times tuned in between just the right two stations for the optimum static. This approach,' Chuck noted drily, 'was later affectionately, commonly, referred to as "Lo Fi".'

When it came time to play the acoustic guitar tracks on *Brother Aldo*, I had to go and borrow Patrick's Martin,' Chuck remembers. "Cos there was only one Martin between us all. Steve [Yerkey] eventually got a [Martin] D-18. I had this Takamine that I would play—it had a pickup. But as far recording went, we had to share that one guitar. Scott Mathews played drums, I played guitar and we overdubbed ourselves. Stephie came in and Roly played bass.' He continues, 'Scott was a gifted musician. And he could make sense of what we were doing—and point out things like a rub here and there with the harmonies.'

In an interview with *Melody Maker* to promote the album, the inspiration of the community of like-minded musicians glowed: 'Working with friends, just going to people's places and putting it down on tape, that's what I live for. It was exciting and gratifying to write a song and cut it in a day. That was the most rewarding thing about it,' he told Steve Sutherland. Later in the same interview, he emphasised his belief that 'it's not the product, it's the process. You know you've got a record when you can hear something going on'.[8]

It may have been lo-fi in recording terms, but it bears no resemblance to the meandering tones in search of tunes that characterised far too many alt-country lo-fi bands that would follow. If it was designed primarily to highlight Prophet's songwriting chops, then *Brother Aldo* does a fine job. Bluesy, folky, funky (the title track), a little bit country in all the right ways and places, it is probably Chuck's most intimate recording, which inevitably benefits the tender love songs ('Rage And Storm', 'I'll Be Alright') more than it does the epic 'Scarecrow', which was the band's regular showstopper in the early 90s, and showcases the fret-heroism that Green On Red fans were accustomed to, but at the same time strains somewhat against the thin production. The song feels like it belongs on a bigger sounding, more robust album. Generally, though, the guitar work does not draw attention to itself. 'I kept the macho guitar thing up my sleeve because I didn't feel I was auditioning for anyone,' Prophet told Sutherland. *Brother Aldo* is also the album that features Stephanie Finch most prominently; Sutherland's feature described her voice as one that 'instantly reminds impressionably romantic young men of truck-store goddesses soothing lonesome long-distance souls'.[9]

'Step Right This Way' was the perfect show opener, and it would hold that slot in the setlist for Chuck's first visit as a solo artist to the UK. 'We were just trying to get enough songs to fill three sets.' Prophet explains. We were still doing songs like [The Band's] "The Weight". And I said, "We've got to do better. Make our own statements." And so the thinking behind "Step Right This Way" was that everybody had their own verse.' Winningham recalls, 'We were really into Nick Cave at the time. And I said, "Man, this sounds like crazy ass carnival stuff, like *Eraserhead* or something." And we each got characters to sing: "OK, you get to be the geek, the guy that bites the head off the chicken, I'll be the lion tamer that has an alcohol problem. Stephanie's the gypsy who tells fortunes." There was a verse for each one of us.'

Early versions of some of the songs that made up *Brother Aldo* feature some interesting variations. A take of 'Step Right This Way' has a folkier, fingerpicking style, a stiffer vocal, Finch's harmony more prominent, and also features fiddle courtesy of Brian Godchaux, brother of Keith Godchaux of the Grateful Dead. 'Well, it was always a struggle to find the instrumentation we needed,' Prophet explains. 'And the fiddle really worked for us. Later a mandolin, because it stayed out of the way of the guitar. Brian was a street musician ... he came through our circle, and we just liked him. And he kept showing up! If he saw our names somewhere in the papers he would show up and play.'

'When we got a drummer,' Chuck recalls, 'I started playing the Telecaster, and I remember Brian told me, "I did like it better when we played acoustic." And then one time we were playing a gig at the Paradise. Al Kooper was there that night—he was a friend of mine. And I had a few drinks in me, and I just went off the rails and turned way up and was overplaying and just not following any of the arrangements. And soon after we had some kind of rehearsal, and Roly was there and Brian was there, and he was pretty quiet. And then he said, "You know, it pains me to see you doing that. It's like watching somebody on the basketball court who just runs up and down, trying to make all the baskets himself." And he says, "Pass the ball. We're right here." [*laughs*] And he was an older musician we really respected and uh ... it was a sobering moment. And I said, "Yeah, I hear ya. I hear ya. Not proud." [*laughs*] But then he just drifted off but ... cool guy.'

Other songs on a tape labelled *The Cakewalk Demos* include the title track of *Brother Aldo* in a different, strutting time signature. It sounds a little like

The Rolling Stones jamming with Richard Thompson, and is every bit as intriguing as that comparison suggests. 'Yard Man,' which featured in the live set around that time, is one of the bluesiest songs Prophet has recorded. The vocals are deliberately distorted, reminiscent of the bullet mic effect Chuck has featured as part of his stage setup for many years. Another short tape of recordings, labelled *Potomac Demos*, was recorded in Andy Taub's living room on Potomac Street. Prophet remembers these were recorded as an audition tape for Stephanie to play the part of a folk singer in the Mike Myers movie *So I Married An Axe Murderer* (1993). The tape ends with a lovely, intimate version of Salley's 'Killing The Blues'. The acoustic guitar has some beautiful flourishes, with some of those frailing-style trills that Prophet peels off so effortlessly.

He acknowledges that narrowing down the song selection was 'a bit painful': 'That record was hard to make. I just didn't have command of the things I wanted to. And, in any case, records are never finished. They're just abandoned. Eventually they have to grow up and take care of themselves.' He pauses and reflects. 'It tried to capture a time but, I mean, that's a tall order.' On the other hand, in the press release for the 1997 reissue, he admitted, 'If I stand back and squint when I listen to it, I dare say it sounds timeless.... The real test is that when I kick some of those songs around on the bandstand (which I often do) they still manage to stand up for themselves.'[10] Two contrasting examples are 'Tune Of An Evening'—reworked years later as a country ballad—and 'Look Both Ways', which would be rocked up and spliced into a version of Waylon Jennings's 'Waymore's Blues'. Both tracks can be found on the 1997 live album *Homemade Boot*.

The collection of songs moved a step closer to commercial release when independent publicist Chris Carr put the tape in the hands of Clive Solomon, the head of Fire Records in London. Carr had been working as a publicist for Nick Cave, Patti Smith, and John Cale, and Prophet vaguely recalls first meeting him at a Panther Burns concert in London around 1987. They shared similar tastes in music and would stay up listening to records. Carr heard some early versions of the songs and, although they may have been just rough recordings made on a borrowed Fostex 8-track quarter-inch tape machine, he responded immediately. 'The biggest A&R lie in the world is, *Oh, just give me a rough version, I can hear the song,'* Prophet reflects. 'The truth is, not everyone can. People respond equally to the sonics. So the fact that we had these recordings that sounded like someone had placed wet gauze over the speakers and somebody was still hearing it—that was promising. Chris was a big supporter. I owe a lot to him.'

The previous chapter details the trouble Prophet caused China Records by signing with Fire. When the smoke cleared, China had an option on Prophet's future solo releases, and this in turn inevitably impacted on Prophet's relationship with Fire. 'Who can say for sure? But it didn't seem like they were in a hurry to invest in an artist already contracted to another company.' On the one hand, Prophet was philosophical about it ('It's fine with me. I just wanted to do the work. I wasn't really thinking past that'), but on the other it led to some unforeseen fallout, not the least of which was that the label offered no financial support to give Prophet the opportunity to tour behind the release.

The album was adorned with an evocative, sepia-tinted cover using a shot taken in a stolen moment from a session talented photographer Andrew Catlin was doing with Marc Almond; Catlin also designed the artwork. *Brother Aldo* may not have made a significant commercial impact, but it got a considerable amount of critical attention, mostly off the back of Prophet's Green On Red profile. Mat Snow, reviewing the album for *Melody Maker*, was bowled over by the songwriting, the duo's vocals, and Chuck's guitar: 'So gorgeously imperfect, so shuffling, so unexact and goddam REAL, so unembraced by technology, it makes The Waterboys' attempts seem even more laughable.' He concludes, 'As close to the genuine article as a white boy can get.'[11] David Sinclair's review for the *Times* was more mixed but zeroed in on Finch's 'dulcet descant' and the 'fiery eloquence' and 'brooding insolence that lies at the heart of Prophet's playing'.[12] The *Guardian* had no reservations about 'a set of songs which lurch purposefully between country, rock, blues and honky-tonk'.[13] The four-out-of-five review in *Q* noted the expected guitar fireworks but added that Prophet's 'strength as both a singer and writer left to his own devices is an unexpected bonus'.[14] In *Select*, David Cavanagh, like every other reviewer, marvelled at the guitar playing, the voice, and the harmonies—'the most essential twosome in this whole wracked country-rock genre since

Gram Parsons and Emmylou Harris'—and suggested, 'It sounds like a Jim Dickinson brainstorm or the album the Stones went down to Muscle Shoals to make in late '69 ... Brilliant.'[15] UK Music monthly *Vox* also celebrated the vocal harmonies and compared the album ('a surprise and a joy to hear') to Dylan's *Desire* and Neil Young's *Comes A Time*, 'two records which Brother Aldo comes pretty damn close to in the quality stakes'.[16]

When I ask Chuck about how the crossover worked between the solo work and the commitments with Green On Red, and whether by the early 1990s he saw his solo work as his 'main gig', he reasons, 'Well, my main gig was whatever I was doing at that time. My main song was whichever song I was in the middle of performing. And I still feel that way: whatever I'm doing is what I'm doing. It helps to be in the moment.' When I ask him what kind of perspective he had on his developing career at this point, he replies, 'I mean, I know Ry Cooder has referred to the touring and recording cycle as "the treadmill of horror", but even if it was a grind, we were having a lot of fun. It was ... going on a tour, coming home broke, dusting ourselves off, trying to figure out how to make the rent ... we were digging it. But there was no *plan*. Figuring out a way to make a new record. Getting the songs together and then the next thing you know you're in the studio and then back on the road. It's always been ... carving it out of nothing.'

CHAPTER FIVE

CARVING IT OUT OF NOTHING

BALINESE DANCER (1991–92)

> Success to me was as simple as doing what
> I wanted when I wanted on whatever
> terms I wanted. – Chuck Prophet

FLYING SOLO

In March 1992, Prophet made an appearance at Austin's annual South By Southwest Music Festival. In 2017, SXSW logged 2,085 acts, 2,778 total performances and a total attendance of 167,800, but 25 years earlier it was nothing like the arts industry phenomenon it has become; in 1992 there 398 acts and 3,000 registrants.[1] Still, it was an important showcase, and by all accounts Prophet and his band—Stephanie Finch, Roly Salley, and guitarist-mandolin player Rich Brotherton (now Robert Earl Keen's guitarist)—gave a standout performance; for the *Austin Chronicle* reviewer, Jason Cohen, it was 'my "hands-down favorite" SXSW showcase', with the quartet coming off 'like a full-fledged country-rock orchestra' and Prophet adding 'greasy acoustic blues licks, a playful, soulful persona and that distinctive voice'.[2] Peter Blackstock reported that Prophet 'came across as not just a songwriter, but as a fully integrated artist'.[3]

At the time of the SXSW appearance, Prophet was on the ragged tail end of an exhausting process recording his sophomore solo album. A couple of years later, he reflected, 'I wanted to make a record that nobody would be able to tell when it was recorded. I'm a great fan of—and I don't mean to put myself next to these people—albums like *The Basement Tapes*, *Sister Lovers*, or Skip

Spence's *Oar*. What I gathered from those records was that they were records that couldn't have been made if anybody was looking. See, in the process of recording "professionally" so many things get diluted.... To capture the spirit, that's like catching lightning bugs in a jar.'[4]

In terms of tracing the sounds inside his head at that point, Prophet is candid: 'I don't know what I wanted to do,' he admits. 'The music we were soaking in was [Waylon Jennings's] *Dreaming My Dreams*, [Ry Cooder's] *Boomer's Story*, and [Richard and Linda Thompson's] *I Want To See The Bright Lights Tonight*.' With reference points like these, as we shall see shortly, things would not run smoothly between Prophet and the staff at his label, China Records. 'There was nobody who knew what we were even *talking* about. Or had any desire to. The brass at China records said, "We want you to make a record for the kind of people that have CD players in their cars." And I said, "But I've never even *seen* a CD. I don't know what you're talking about!"'

The compact disc first hit the market in 1984, and over the first year, sales jumped by 625 percent to 5.8 million.[5] For the consumer, the exchange of formats may not have been immediate, but for the industry it was momentous. Looking at world sales, 1.2 billion vinyl albums were sold in 1981, and only 126 million by 1992. By 1990, for every vinyl album sold, six CDs and thirteen cassettes were sold. CD sales rose from 260 million in 1987 to 1.152 billion in 1992 (cassettes were still ahead, on 1.551 billion in the same year).[6] While 8-track (which was virtually unknown outside the USA) died in the mid-1980s, in-car CD players had not yet overtaken the standard radio/cassette configuration; still, there was evidently something aspirational in the record company's targeting of that demographic.

It is not difficult to see how Prophet was falling radically out of step with what was happening in the music industry in the first half of the 1990s. In truth, being *in* step had never been a priority. Green On Red, like a number of the Paisley underground bands, may have benefited from a sudden, unexpected spasm of interest in their scene in the mid-1980s that landed the band a deal with a major label, but Stuart and Prophet had nevertheless always meandered along their own, ultimately self-destructive path, commercially, artistically, and personally.

Part of what had driven Prophet to the stripped-down, intimate sounds he had been exploring at the turn of the decade on the Albion scene had been his dissatisfaction with the bombast and production overkill of *The Killer Inside Me*. But while he was immersing himself in roots music, a new genre of guitar-centric rock was just beginning to emerge. Writer Steve Knopper christened it the 'Grunge Gold Rush' and identified a moment at the beginning of 1992, when Nirvana's *Nevermind* knocked Michael Jackson's *Dangerous* off the no. 1 spot on the *Billboard* album chart, as pivotal: it was 'an event that fundamentally restructured the record business in ways still visible to the naked eye'. Attempting to make sense of a particularly unusual period in the history of popular music, Knopper follows the progress of alternative rock band Jawbox, signed to Atlantic in 1994. Three years later, after one minor MTV hit and one song that scored on college radio, Jawbox were dropped and the band split, but not before they had landed a $100,000 advance for their debut album and a $75,000 song-publishing advance from Warner/Chappell. However, despite a publicity blitz, they had failed to sell more than 100,000 copies of the album *For Your Own Special Sweetheart*; Knopper describes this as 'a devastating flop' (although those figures would have sent it straight to no. 1 in today's streaming era). Regardless, the Nirvana phenomenon sent the major labels—Capitol, CBS, MCA, Polygram, RCA, and WEA—into a frenzy; Knopper describes 'platoons of A&R scouts [sent] all over the world, armed with yearly expense budgets for up to $100 000 to wine and dine every half-decent . . . band in flannel shirts making dissonant guitar noise'.[7] The party may have been short-lived, but it was a phenomenon that changed the rules of the game forever.

Prophet reflects back on that era and tries to recapture the sense of bewilderment he felt at the time: 'I had a vague idea of what was going on, but I can't say I really listened to Nirvana or Pearl Jam. I wasn't tuned in. I might have heard it in a grocery store but I didn't hear it in the bars I hung out in. Didn't have TV. I was listening to Fairport Convention and Neil Young. Gram [Parsons] and Emmylou [Harris]. And I was making my little soul music compilations. I guess I just had my head down.'

KURT LIPSCHUTZ

Kurt Lipschutz (aka Klipschutz), a native of Indio, California, spent many of his early adult years travelling. He had settled for a while in Boulder, Colorado, studying with Allen Ginsberg at the Jack Kerouac School of Disembodied Poetics based at Naropa University. Since the mid-80s, Lipschutz has pursued parallel careers as a poet and a songwriter. His first collection of poetry, *The Erection Of Scaffolding For The Re-painting Of Heaven By The Lowest Bidder*, appeared in 1985. Other collections include *Twilight Of The Male Ego* (2002), *This Drawn & Quartered Moon* (2013), and, most recently, *Premeditations* (2019).

The title of each one of Lipschutz's published volumes could be read as a shortcut clue to the kind of poetry he writes; the influence of the Beat poets is unmistakeable, but there is also something of the classical purist about him: alongside Bukowski and 'all the Beats', he lists the likes of Ezra Pound, T.S. Eliot, and Homer, Juvenal, and Catullus as influences.[8] It's also worth saying, if you haven't figured it out yet, that Lipschutz's work can be challenging. While it is often peppered with contemporary and pop-culture references, there is precious little concession in intellectual terms. He does not condescend, but neither will he linger if the reader can't keep up. There is also often an urgent sense of social and political engagement in his work; one of our conversations, a few weeks after the election of Donald Trump, repeatedly jumped back into a locked groove of expressions of despair and vitriol at the state of the nation. In our conversations and emails, and from getting to grips with his poetry, there has always been the sense of an intelligence in constant, restless motion.

Lipschutz moved to San Francisco in the early 1980s, transiting through several administrative jobs (including work for the polling company Gallup) to keep body and soul together. When he met Chuck Prophet for the first time, he was collaborating with a local musician Prophet admired called Bone Cootes; Bone was one of the members of the lively music scene described in the previous chapter. Kurt, co-writing with Bone, was effectively a backroom member of his band The Living Wrecks. Still going through a hothouse process as a budding songwriter in his own right, Prophet invited Cootes and Lipschutz over, and together the three of them wrote 'Savannah', which would appear on Chuck's second album, *Balinese Dancer*.

'Bone and Kurt were joined at the hip,' he recalls. 'And so I carried on trying to help them. I even tried to produce them to no avail. But we did some writing and then I started working just with Kurt.' He has a vivid memory of one particular episode early on in their friendship. 'We had this song ... a song that became "Heart Breaks Like The Dawn"—it was really just couplets and this breezy chord sequence. Not really that great. And there was this moment when we were walking to the Mission from my house, down 24th Street, and Kurt said, "And a heart breaks just like the dawn." And that was it. Pretty small when you lay it down on paper, but it really parted the clouds. And that song just really stood up.'

It was the start of a rich partnership for Prophet and Lipschutz that (with a ten-year hiatus) continues to this day. Discussing their process around the time of the release of *Homemade Blood*, Prophet noted, 'He's not as musical as I am, but he brings other things to it, like structure, and he's got a whole literary background and he's soaked up a whole 'nother world.'[9] 'We're able to sit together in a room, take an idea and play with it,' he noted in one of our conversations. 'We're both pretty good with words. Sometimes our sensibilities with music are a little skewed, but that's all part of it. And he can talk about Greek mythology, and Chekhov or whatever . . . he'll go places. But at the same time,' he adds, 'both of us have a tolerance for pop culture, mainstream films ... we're able to have fun.'

In terms of the relationship between songs and poems, Kurt suggests, with a grin, 'The danger is that the poems are too poetic. And the same goes for the songs. I mean, you don't want *anything* to be poetic really. That's the problem with poetry: the poetic part.' In a *No Depression* interview from 2017, he described the writing process (while also noting how much he dislikes the term—'analysis kills creativity'): 'We sit in a small room and shoot gloomy looks at each other, and listen to obscure legends on Chuck's $40 LP player, then he picks up his guitar and starts to strum, then words come out of my mouth and/ or his, and hopefully the tape is rolling or I'm not too lazy to take notes. Six months later, the song is done. It's just that easy and efficient,' he concluded, with a characteristic dose of irony.[10] The MO may have varied over the years, but it always seems to have been most successful done this way: spending days in a room together, letting the chatter, the words and the music percolate. *Balinese Dancer* would show the first fruits of an enduring partnership.

BEHIND THE BOARD

The formal follow-up to *Brother Aldo* began with St. Louis, Missouri, native Jim Scott. 'Jim later went on to work with Lucinda [Williams] and produced all kinds of great records,' Prophet recalls. 'He was mostly an engineer at the time—he wasn't really doing a lot of producing. But a friend of mine played me something he had done, and I thought, *This guy's really good.*' The LP in question was a Cajun album, *Women In The Room* by Zachary Richard, and Prophet was hooked. 'Just guitar, bass, drums, a lot of accordion. Sonically, just a little bright. Hole in the middle, fat on the bottom. Kind of a roomy sound and clean guitar.' What Prophet heard was enough to convince him to give Scott a try, and he, Roly, and Stephie drove down to LA, inviting along David Kemper, whom Prophet knew from his drum-kit duties on Green On Red's *This Time Around*. Scott engineered and produced. 'The studio was really raw, basically an office building,' Prophet remembers, but the sessions were a success—'Jim knew how to midwife the songs and get a great sound'—and Chuck decided to let the label hear the recordings.

There may have been times when Prophet made a more concerted effort to address industry imperatives; listening back to tapes of demos from this era, he is able to identify the way a handful of tracks seem to have been cut with one eye open to more pop-oriented songwriting. But the fact remains that his heroes were people like Alex Chilton, artists who never conceded an inch that could compromise the work. As he summed it up to me in an email in 2018, 'Success to me was as simple as doing what I wanted when I wanted on whatever terms I wanted. And the long and short of it is, is that when Stephie and I were doing that Gram and Emmylou stuff, they just didn't dig it. China just wanted a rock record. "Well, we just don't really think it's the right thing," the label staff told me. "We think you should do something different." And I said, "That's a pity because we had a good thing going with Jim Scott."' But it was the end of the road for that partnership. 'We just had some demo money and … I think Scott felt a little disappointed that he didn't get the gig. These things can get delicate. I·probably could have fought harder for Jim. But so it goes.'

Some of the songs—and eventually even the versions recorded with Scott—would end up on *Balinese Dancer*, including the album's centrepiece, '110 In

The Shade', along with the opening track, 'Baton Rouge', and 'Who Am I Foolin''—all these tracks feature David Kemper on drums, while Kenneth Blevins would play drums on the later sessions. But in the wake of the Jim Scott demos, it was decreed by China Records that tracking would be overseen by Craig Leon. Leon had an impressive CV that listed the Ramones, Blondie, and The Bangles among many others. 'I can remember I had a meeting with Craig Leon when I was in London. And I just didn't really hit it off with his sensibilities. He's made some great records, and no disrespect to him. I just felt like he hadn't listened to the songs, and I just didn't feel any kind of chemistry with him at all. But [China Records boss] Derek Green was pretty adamant that he was the guy. And I said, "Well, Derek, did you ever notice [Leon's] never worked with the same person twice? Kind of a hit and run. Because I'd like to make another record with Jim Dickinson." But Derek was very persuasive. He says, "Well, see, you're very *old school*. That's not really the way it is now."' It became clear that Green had another deal going down, getting Leon at a lower rate because he had agreed to put out a new-age record Craig had made with his wife. But, Chuck says now, 'I put my best foot forward. I'd certainly worked with some monster egos at that point. Some maniacs. And the reality is, you really can't tell who somebody is or what they're made of until you are in the heat of battle. That kind of speed dating with producers can only go so far.'

Prophet may have set out with good intentions and high hopes, but it didn't last long. 'Leon didn't like what we were recording,' Chuck told me. 'And it kinda got to the point where he put little effort into hiding anything. I do remember thinking he took more interest in the folder with all the takeaway menus than in anything we were doing.' When an artist loses faith in his producer, there is never going to be a happy ending and it did not take very long for Prophet to lose any faith he might have been willing to place in Leon. 'Who knows? Maybe the label had told him, "For God sakes, don't let him make a country record!" But I was just keeping notes about what was happening, and what he was saying no to. And he got wind of that and he bailed. I tried to go talk to him in his hotel and he just went back to England and really trashed me to the label. He told them, "I'm not a clinical psychiatrist or whatever, but I think you ought to know that he's insane."'

The staff at China had been left perplexed by conflicting accounts. Chuck recalls, 'They said, "Well, there's just no credibility here, everybody's saying different things."' The label's solution was to send LA-based rep John Guenarri to meet Prophet and hear some of the recordings for himself. Chuck went to elaborate lengths to prepare for the meeting, borrowing a friend's hi-fi system, lugging huge speakers up to his apartment, and cueing up what he thought were the best tracks they had taped up to that point, including 'Heart Breaks Like The Dawn'. 'I thought [it] was such a lovely track. Greg Leisz was on it, and he was playing this beautiful resonator in an open tuning.' Guenarri sat and listened. When the track finished, he looked at Prophet, and said, baffled, 'What *is* this?' Chuck laughs as he recounts the story. 'He says, "I don't know, I'm not really feeling it. You got anything *snappy*?" I remember he said that word, I'll never forget: *snappy*.' China had been expecting a rock record, and what Guenarri was hearing was country instrumentation over a collection of songs in a folk and singer/songwriter tradition. 'He said, "This isn't what's happening right now; right now, everybody's looking for the next Nirvana." And I replied, "Well, OK, but this isn't it."' After that, Prophet admits, 'I didn't send out any roughs [rough mixes] or anything. I just kinda … went dark.'

Looking back, it is hard to understand how everything could have got so messy so quickly. But, in retrospect, Prophet may have been so laser-focused on the work that he lost track of the business practicalities. 'I mean, honestly, did I have anybody looking after me? Probably not,' he shrugs. 'They had recommended this lawyer and he was so up on another *level* that he just didn't really have much time for me. Derek Green and I had a handshake deal hammered out at his desk in London. But the long-form agreement never materialised. Of course, I wasn't about to put the brakes on going into the studio. Like so many things, it was sandwiched between tours. So, we went into the studio in good faith. And China just adopted a kind of a wait and see attitude. [*sighs*] And then it got messy. They sent a guy over from England. His name was Brian Lane. He had once managed Yes. And he had come on board at China records, and they said, "You need to go to the States and you need to sort this out. It's difficult, and we don't know what's going on."'

A meeting was set up between Brian Lane, Guenarri, and Prophet at the St. James's Club in LA. 'I remember talking to my dad,' Chuck says. 'I go, "I don't know what to do." And my dad says, "Well, you just need to tell them that you're gonna listen to what they have to say."' But it was the same story; Prophet describes Brian Lane as 'real abusive, arrogant, and intimidating: he was waving his arms around and shouting, "If I can get all the members of Yes back together, this is *nothing*!" And I kinda went with his belligerence.' When Lane demanded the tapes, Prophet recalls that he told him, 'I think that a meteor flew over my house and erased it all.' He continues, 'And [studio owner] Dan Alexander tells me, "Chuck, I got a call, and they were very adamant that you were stealing their property. I know you're not doing anything wrong, but this stuff can get ugly real fast." And he said, "I don't know what you're doing but, ya know ... *don't*"!'

The last thing they were able to do before the money ran out was put the pedal steel track on 'Heart Breaks Like The Dawn'. At that point, there seemed no alternative but to pack up and head home, until Dan Alexander stepped in just in time. 'Alex was a true maverick,' Prophet says. 'An outsized character who had been at the forefront of all kinds of analogue resurgence, and at one time owned The Beatles' recording desk. He was a savvy character, and after Leon bailed off the project, he said, "Look, I think you got a raw deal ... if you need more studio time to finish this record, I'll give it to you." He was a believer. So we got another engineer. Greg [Leisz]'s schedule was open, so we just kept working.'

In the end, Prophet recalls, Derek Green's partner, Bob Grace, was a real gentleman: 'He wrote me a note and said, "Hats off to ya for bringing this record in for a landing." And they got behind it.'

GREG LEISZ

Greg Leisz, a linchpin of the sessions, had been a lucky find; the two musicians have been close friends since the recording of *Balinese Dancer*, and have collaborated frequently ever since, notably on the Mexican adventure that resulted in *¡Let Freedom Ring!* (2009), which Leisz co-produced. They originally met through the movie *Border Radio* (1987), a low-budget film made by Alison Anders that features a performance by Green On Red. Prophet recalls, 'It was her first film, and it was just made out of dirt and chewing gum. I was curious about it, and they didn't really have any distribution, so they started playing it at rock clubs. And they played it at the I-Beam, and Dave Alvin performed an acoustic set afterward. And he had Greg Leisz with him, playing Dobro and some lap steel. And I remember thinking, *That guy is amazing*. Because, at that point, roots rock really came out of punk rock. It was Rank & File and Jason & The Scorchers. Nowadays it comes out of Berkeley School Of Music, but back then, The Knitters, Long Ryders ... they all came out of the punk rock scene. We were all kind of self-taught. But Greg was different: he took a solo on a Dobro and there was something *going on*. And then Stephie and I ended up playing a gig with Syd Straw at Slim's. And Greg was on that gig, and he was playing pedal steel, I think. I had an overzealous roadie, and after he packed up my pedals that night, the next time I opened my bag, there was a bunch of extra pedals in there.' Prophet soon figured out they belonged to Leisz and tracked him down. 'He had watched our set with interest,' Chuck recalls, 'and soon we were talking about our mutual love for Sandy Denny and Richard Thompson.' At the time that he met Leisz, Prophet had been hoping to have the luxury of a second guitar player, and Leisz more than fitted the bill.

As Prophet reflects on Greg Leisz's career—working with a vast range of musicians, from Dylan, Brian Wilson, Eric Clapton and Joni Mitchell to the Smashing Pumpkins, Beck, Lucinda Williams, and Matthew Sweet—it is evident that his love and respect for his friend runs very deep. 'He always plays something you want to listen to. Pull up that fader!' He adds, 'The thing about Greg Leisz is that he was always somebody that understood what I was trying to do. And he was always a gentle soul. And it's interesting because oftentimes people equate their importance with how busy they are. And I don't think there's anybody that's more in demand and busier than Greg Leisz, but the whole time I've known him, and it's thirty years or whatever it's been, there's never been a time when he didn't have time for me. He's been a confidant, and he's been a mentor. He was just somebody that I always looked up to and trusted.'

Leisz ended up playing guitar on most of the *Balinese Dancer* album: Fender Jazzmaster on '110 In The Shade' and 'Somewhere Down The Road'; acoustic on several tracks; mandolin on the title track; and pedal steel, mandolin, and National steel on 'Heart Breaks'. Prophet brought a wide range of instrumentation to the table that would enhance some of the new songs with a varied palette of tones; they included a Burns 'Wild Dog' Splitsonic ('stuck through a Vox with everything on 10. It sounded great!'[11]) that Leisz played on 'One Last Dance'. Jim Dickinson would play the same guitar on the *Thousand Footprints In The Sand* live album, and it still pops up from time to time—Chuck recalls using it on *Night Surfer*. Most of the acoustic parts were played on Chuck's Martin D-28, but he also used an old Epiphone acoustic in Nashville (high) tuning, and most of the lead electric lines were played on his Squier Telecaster.

Apart from Leisz, the album features some other intriguing guests, including long-time Jerry Garcia collaborator David Grisman, who plays mandolin on 'Angel'. Prophet himself plays some impressive lap steel—his slide guitar of choice being his Strat with the whammy bar jammed under the strings at the nut to raise the action high enough for a tone bar. The title track also credits Carlos Guitarlos—a familiar character from the Albion days—with 'Mexican guitar'. 'He was in a band called Top Jimmy and the Rhythm Pigs,' Chuck remembers; they had been part of the LA punk scene alongside groups like The Blasters and X. 'Carlos and I have some history. He's just a brilliant guitar player that resembles a pile of dirty laundry,' Prophet jokes. He recalls being hired along with Carlos for a society gig in an art gallery—an event he commemorated in a typically surrealist blog post:

> We'd been busking on the street in Union Square with a generator and Pignose style amps when the curator of the event walked up and hired us on the spot for what at the time was a pretty serious paying gig. We set up in the corner. Carlos had rounded up a street musician who could play drums and bass at the same time without charging double. He was sweating different-sized beads of sweat like crazy. The kind of sweat that you can only get to behave by smoking more crack. ANYWAY: Carlos led us through his songbook. Songs like 'Pigfoot Shuffle'. Before long everyone was dancing: long-legged socialites in pearls, men in tailored suits. In the middle of the solo section to 'Maybellene', the night popped open. Someone overturned the buffet table; Carlos was chasing women around the room lifting their skirts with the headstock of his guitar; secretaries tore open their blouses. [Okay, maybe I made that last part up.] It was beautiful chaos.[12]

BALINESE DANCER

Reflecting on the writing and recording of *Balinese Dancer*, Chuck explains that a lot of it had to do with the musical environment that had grown up around him and those other songwriters on the Albion scene. 'We had our little folk-rock combo. There was a revolving door of whether it was the fiddle guy or the mandolin guy. Stephanie played accordion. I just played a Telecaster into an amp straight in. And so, yeah, our limitations were part of what made things work for us. That's the essence of rock'n'roll: limitations.'

However, Stephanie Finch's memories of working on the album are bittersweet. 'I realised that what we were doing live was maybe not going to happen on the record. We had a lot of duets but I don't think China wanted that. But then it was funny because they didn't know who I was or anything about me but when I met them and we went over to [England to] tour *Balinese Dancer*, they said, "Oh my God, this is great." But they didn't have that vision beforehand, so . . .' She trails off. '*Brother Aldo* was just our own little thing, and no one was really controlling any of it, but you can't keep doing that over and over again. And Chuck just has to keep evolving. And I'm totally *for* that. But I think at the time I was a little heartbroken.' Chuck remembers, 'We had rubbed our rabbit's foot raw on that record. And eventually I made a deal for Jim Scott to come and finish it and mix it. I think he just cashed the cheque and never mixed it. I think he felt like I owed it to him or something. So then Richard Benoit mixed it and eventually we just turned it in to China.'

For many fans of Prophet's music, the album beautifully embodies a very specific sound, deeply rooted in tradition and at the same time more than a little ahead of its time. Although some songs feature layers of guitar, the record still retains a very immediate 'cut live' feel. The opener, 'Baton Rouge', is a good example of Chuck's pop songwriting capabilities: a catchy number that sets the tone for the album—layers of acoustic guitar underneath a stinging electric, and prominent, exuberant harmonies with Stephanie Finch.

Balinese Dancer is his most overtly country-rock-oriented album; this is partly about song structures, with many of them—'Baton Rouge', 'Angel', 'Heart Breaks Like The Dawn'—'all the ones that have that I-IV-I-IV, Keith Richards kind of feel'—having been written in open tunings.[13] The album is also a showcase for torrents of ringing, cascading solos on the likes of 'Star-

Crossed Misbegotten Love', 'Heart Breaks Like The Dawn', and the outro of the epic '110 In The Shade', which, although the song runs just shy of seven minutes, is frustrating for the unwelcome fade-out of Prophet in full flow. There is an overriding sense of melodicism in the solos on *Balinese Dancer* that defines the album's specific sound.

Prophet says this has something to do with the format: 'It wasn't really like the two guitar, Stonesy rock,' he says, which meant that 'that kind of dry, single coil, bent note stuff really popped out'; he cites Robbie Robertson and Richard Thompson as other purveyors of that tone. 'Heart Breaks' might be the album's masterpiece, simultaneously a showcase for Leisz's stacked layers of instrumentation and a launch pad for some of Prophet's most inspired forays on the Telecaster. The song keeps building upon its propulsive, 3/4 time rhythm, and the last of its majestic five minutes features a face-off between Prophet's Tele in the right-hand channel and Leisz's pedal steel in the left. 'I can remember tracking that song,' Chuck recalls, 'and I remember enjoying that back and forth with Greg.' The original version featured Leisz on resonator in open tuning, with the pedal steel overdubbed later.

Balinese Dancer also marks a step up from *Brother Aldo* in terms of its rhythmic development. The title track and 'Savannah', in particular, have a strut and funkiness that will be immediately familiar to anyone who has seen Prophet play live with a band. 'Savannah' smoothly orchestrates its swampy rhythm, wah-wah guitar, Prophet's falsetto 'woo-hoo's, Finch's shadowing backing vocal, and several layers of keys (clavinet, Hammond B-3, and Wurlitzer) while retaining a vibrant, live-in-the-studio feel. Prophet's vocal style is wedded perfectly to the music: shades of Tom Petty, for sure, and a touch of Dylan-esque phrasing here and there, but still distinctively his own. And, like many great vocalists (as opposed to singers), he is never afraid to let the emotion overrule the technically truer note. With Stephanie Finch duetting, there's an even more marked kinship with Gram Parsons and Emmylou Harris, Chuck finding his way around the notes as Stephie chimes in pure and clear. 'Finding our voices and finding ways to make it work,' Prophet says. 'It was a process, but from the first time that we had got together, I knew it was something that felt right. I knew I was good. But something told me with Stephanie I could be great. And I thought maybe other people might feel the same way.'

'Heart Breaks …', 'How Many Angels' (held over for the next album), and 'Starcrossed Misbegotten Love' are what Lipschutz calls a 'kind of a trilogy of high poetic'—in lush, romantic mode, they are some of the most traditional love songs in Prophet's canon, featuring lines such as 'Days waltz by and the night stands still' and vows delivered in prostrate abandon: 'I got a fragile heart, seized by desire / For a taste of your mouth, I would cake-walk through fire.' The music is shaped to match the poetic tone of the songs, both in terms of melody and chord structure and via a series of jewel-like guitar solos.

The outtakes and demos from the *Balinese Dancer* sessions are some of the most fascinating and tantalising in Prophet's archive. There is a country-shuffle version of 'Angel' with Stephie singing lead. There are multiple takes of the epic 'Shreds Of The Truth', some pared down to a trio (Chuck, Stephie, and Scott Mathews) and others more elaborate: with Tex-Mex brushed rhythm, accordion, stabs of guitar, and additional percussion, the song begins to sound like a Sam Peckinpah movie. A version of the album's title track features Chuck playing dobro and harp and Roly Salley on bass, cooking up a brew very reminiscent of Dylan's 'Rainy Day Women #12 & 35'. Some of the recordings feature Derek Ritchie, who had played in Chuck's high-school band Bad Attitude. 'Yeah, it's a shame it didn't work out,' he notes. 'He played a mean shuffle!' However, the highlight is a glorious version of 'Heart Breaks' performed as a duet with Stephie, the two of them trading verses.

There may have been some initial scepticism at China about Prophet's choice of musical direction, but the critical response was enthusiastic across the board. *Guitar Player* described Prophet as a 'storyteller of inward journeys and outward adventures' and 'a masterful player who incorporates threads of country, folk, roots rock and blues'.[14] Venerable rock magazine *Creem* praised his 'stomping acoustic slide work straddled by gruff, barking blues leads and rounded out by soft Hammond organ punctuation' and described his duets with Finch as 'some of the finest duets this side of Richard and Linda Thompson's definitive album *Shoot Out The Lights*'.[15] The reviewer for *Option* would have preferred a few more rockers to balance out the ballads, but loved the production and the instrumentation—'smart, mid-tempo rock'n'roll with a shady edge'.[16] Local publication *BAM* celebrated a variety of influences (Springsteen, Lowell George, Gregg Allman) but insisted that Prophet 'never loses his sense of self . . . the music is nobody's but his own'.[17] In the UK press, *Vox* hailed it as 'album of the month . . . at last a Country Rock album that it's cool to own.'[18] Adam Sweeting for the *Guardian* described it as 'the sort of country record they don't make in Nashville . . . the songs and the performances offer such strength in so much depth that you wonder why Prophet has been lurking bashfully under his bushel for so long'.[19]

TOURING *BALINESE DANCER*

The recording of the album had been far from straightforward. The move to China Records in theory was undoubtedly a step up in many respects, but in some ways maybe it didn't always *feel* like one. However, once the positive reviews started to roll in—and, even more importantly, the label reps got to experience Prophet, Finch, and their band live onstage—there was a noticeable shift. Chuck remembers, 'There was a guy there at the label by the name of Adrian Sear, and he'd worked with Derek [Green] for many years, and he took me under his wing a little bit. And I guess we all made peace. And we came over and played the Mean Fiddler'—on March 5 1993—'and people were responding. The Jesus & Mary Chain were there that night. And the label invited [BBC Radio DJ] Johnnie Walker, and he had become a real supporter and continued to be through the years. Anyway, it felt like something happened and the mood changed at the label. Most people's frame of reference is always something that's already happened but, to their credit, when they saw it live, and they saw people starting to respond, they began to understand it . . . especially Adrian Sear.'

Prophet continues, 'Adrian said, "We're going to put this on vinyl and we're going to price it really low, and chart it." And then we started doing all the Tower and Virgin in-store appearances, all up and down England, lunchtime shows. And I was playing acoustic, and Stephie was playing accordion, and people started to get excited about what we were doing.' Prophet recalls visiting China's offices in London just after *Balinese Dancer* was released, and they told him it had indeed 'charted' in the UK. Chuck didn't ask where exactly. 'The guy said, "I want you to have something." And he pushed a BT phone card across his desk toward me and said, "You'll need this. Try to check in with us when you can. Things are really heating up."'

The label's enthusiasm was gratifying, but, more importantly, there was some financial support for a tour: 'Not like on a Green On Red level, but we started doing a lot of pubs in England, and people were coming out,' Chuck recalls. Booking agents and venues were familiar because of the Green On Red connections, and there was an established audience base. March 1993 found them playing ten shows in the UK and seven more in continental Europe. The live show on the San Francisco circuit had always been built around Prophet as the sole guitarist. 'The thing that made it unique was that it wasn't a two-guitar band,' Chuck notes. 'But there was always somebody else that could take a solo, like a mandolin or a fiddle. So we got this guy, Mike Rychlik. I saw him play at the Albion in a bluegrass band. And I asked him, "Do you have a passport? Do you have a pickup for that thing?"' Having established that Rychlik could play some basic rhythm guitar, too, he was booked for the European jaunt. 'Stephie played accordion and sang,' Chuck notes, 'and then Hank Maninger, who I'd known since high school, played bass. And Tyler Ing played drums—he'd been a drummer around here. An experienced guy. And we did that whole circuit.'

Stephanie Finch recalls vividly the excitement of the prospect of a first tour abroad. 'I wanted to go. So badly, yeah,' she recalls, when I asked her how she felt about it. 'I was very excited and Chuck sat me down and said, "Look: things go on out on the road and you're going to want to keep your own counsel." So I figured he meant "guys away from their loved ones" or something, and I was expecting all this debauchery . . . and just *nothing*. All these years! Just really nice guys who are very loyal to their partners back home.' She pauses. 'Not to say that first tour wasn't weird and hard. It was pretty low to the ground.'

In a 2014 blog post about the tour, Prophet wrote, 'I recall the van on that tour having no heat. But then again, they never do.'[20] 'I remember because I bought Stephanie this parka [coat],' he recalled to me. 'I told her, "You're going to need gloves and you're going to need a parka because you're going to be cold. Your feet will be cold. All the time." Yeah. And we were out there. We didn't hesitate to go out and play. Pretty grimy circumstances. But we did it. And we loved it.'

In London on March 6 1993, the band played on a bill with Thelonious

Monster, a gig Chuck remembers fondly. Thelonious Monster were led by larger-than-life personality Bob Forrest ('a real sweet guy, a character—I really liked him'), who says he was 'one of the worst junkies in Hollywood' through the 80s and 90s. He would later get clean and devote his life to helping others recover but, at the time, 'They were really wild. They were LA scenesters run amok.' Prophet remembers Forrest in the audience during their set. 'He was yelling at somebody: "Hey, listen to these guys, man! This is *real fucking music!*"' Chuck also recalls borrowing a Wurlitzer piano for Stephie from Chris Holland, who had played with Green On Red. The piano wasn't working, and Prophet recalls how, as the audience trooped in, 'I literally had the damn thing apart like, with the top off, and I was looking through the electronics, digging around. It was some kind of out of body experience with 230 volts running through it: my high-school electronic classes were all coming back to me. And then, "There it is, there's a short between here and here. Somebody get me a soldering iron!" And the place started to fill up. And I fixed it while people were coming up to the stage, saying, "What's going on?"'

Few gigs are ever stress-free at club level. But they had paid their dues, and, in terms of their performances, now it was paying off. 'I feel like when we started playing those pub gigs in England, I knew how to connect to the crowd. Because sometimes it would just get really wild in there [at the Paradise]. And you learn how to handle people. And we ended up being a good little pub-rock band, I think. We'd load in, and if there was a calendar on the wall I could guarantee you that Wilko Johnson had either been there, or he was coming! And, when we did those tours, we had a great time. Me and Stephie, just out playing every night with the band.'

The March tour was swiftly followed up with a second one at the end of April that lasted almost six weeks and began with a round of promo, radio, and TV appearances in Spain. The stop at the Fruit Market in Edinburgh, on May 30, was a memorable one for me: it was the first time I had seen Chuck play, and I was floored by the experience, from the opening notes of 'Step Right This Way' to the beautifully orchestrated take on Dylan's 'Abandoned Love'. Mike Rychlik recalls Stephie singing Richard Thompson's 'Withered And Died' at the soundcheck that night, just her and her Wurlitzer. 'Not part of our setlist or anything. She just broke into it. Mesmerizing.'

Stephie's memories of that night are centred around something else entirely: 'We had someone driving at the time who did sound, a really mild-mannered guy. And Chuck is really particular about sound, and he had already been hard on him in previous soundchecks.' When the proprietor of the Edinburgh hotel heard they were in town to play a gig, he urged them to come down to his karaoke bar after the show. 'After a few turns,' Stephie relates, 'Chuck went up there and started singing "By The Time I Get To Phoenix". And this big drunk Scottish guy without warning stood up and went for Chuck.' A fight over the microphone ensued, and Chuck was pushed to the floor. 'Everything felt like it was in slow motion. And the guy was coming back for Chuck, ready to punch him. And I don't know what possessed me but I went up behind the guy and pulled him off Chuck with all my might. And when the guy swung around and realised that I was a woman, he was even more frustrated, because he couldn't punch me! And by that time all the band members had raced up. But this guy had all these friends, big longshoremen. Ready to fight. And a brawl broke out. I remember a chair flew, and that mild-mannered soundman got punched right in the jaw, and he went down. Everyone was just in shock, it all happened so suddenly. All the guys were kind of beat up—except Chuck, of course. Got out unscathed. And then it was all over. We had the next day off, and everyone was just wounded, staying in their rooms. That was my first tour. I should have looked at that and probably run for the hills and not come back!'

The other major non-musical event of the tour Stephie remembers vividly was getting stopped at the French border: 'We got pulled over, early hours of the morning. They searched the van and found some pot, and I didn't know what was going to happen. The border patrol took all the guys away. They were all in one little cell, and they had all been strip-searched. And then it was my turn. This tired, angry woman came in—they'd woken her up, three in the morning . . . all they really wanted was money. They fined us and sent us on our way. The worst part about that was that it was at the very end of the tour. And I didn't pack enough underwear [*laughs*] so I borrowed a pair of Chuck's. And this woman, she gave me such a disdainful look. I remember feeling kind of mortified.'

Chuck later wrote, 'It was painless in the end, but we all agreed it was pretty harrowing looking at those latex gloves sitting on the shelf in there.

Nobody put on the gloves or anything. (They didn't need to!) When I emptied my pockets out I had a massive Chicago roll of cash. This was back when there were twenty-seven different currencies. Small bills. All sweaty. A big roll . . . Obviously there wasn't any internet back then or I would've been snapping away and tweeting live for legal advice.'[21]

Audience tapes that circulate from the first UK tour capture something of the character of those shows, despite the limited fidelity of the recordings. 'Step Right This Way' was usually at the top of the set ('Yeah, did that for a long time. Don't fix it if it's not broken'), and a recording from the Richmond in Brighton (March 14 1993) shows off the dynamic interplay of the musicians; Prophet is working double time, as usual, holding down the rhythm part and squeezing out melodic solos, as on 'Baton Rouge'. The accordion lends this iteration of Prophet's touring band a very distinctive flavour that's particularly evident on 'Who Am I Foolin''. On a gentle 'Heart Breaks Like The Dawn', Mike Rychlik's mandolin and accordion provide a melodic net below Chuck's chiming Tele, and Chuck and Stephie's voices blend seamlessly. '110 In The Shade' is one of the few songs that features Rychlik on electric guitar, and, as he plays the hypnotic, circling, arpeggiated chords of the coda, Prophet extends the song with a frenzied showcase reminiscent of Richard Thompson. Soon after, the show hits a blazing streak with scorching takes on 'Look Both Ways' and 'Brother Aldo', both of them more exciting than the studio recordings; 'Scarecrow' segues into a fiery Irish jig and then a beautiful version of 'Abandoned Love'—a song that would remain a regularly recurring set piece in Prophet's shows, and a highlight of his occasional duo shows with Stephie. 'Yeah,' Chuck enthuses. 'Well, playing songs like "Abandoned Love" keeps a fellow honest. How is anyone ever going to write a song that beautiful?'

Balinese Dancer came out on China Records in the UK but the US release was less than ideal. Licensed to a label called Homestead, a subsidiary of Dutch East India Trading Company, Prophet was left with no tour support once again, and no way of taking the show on the road in his home country. In fact, up until the release of *The Hurting Business* at the turn of the millennium, they did not attempt any tours of the United States. Says Finch, 'The United States is vast, and we just hadn't built a following over here. I mean, we did little things all the time. We would always go to SXSW and stuff like that. We were more of a local band then than we are now. We don't play locally that much anymore, because we travel so much. Now we have the whole West Coast—Portland, Seattle—but we didn't back then.' 'On the bright side,' Prophet adds about the record, 'Homestead kept getting reorders from Austin. Years later, I learned that Alejandro [Escovedo] had worked at Waterloo records and sold one to everyone that came in the door.' Escovedo had been a key figure in the country-punk movement, a member of Rank & File and The True Believers. In 2008, he and Chuck would write the songs for his *Real Animal* album together.

There were still local dates to play—the US release was celebrated with a record release party at the Great American Music Hall in San Francisco on July 19 1993; Prophet was coming straight off the back of a European Green On Red tour, and the week cleared for The Creatures Of Habit to rehearse was disrupted when he went down with flu for three days. ('It always happens; you get sick as soon as you get back. I guess your body knows enough to wait until you get home.') This line-up of the backing band would sadly be relatively short-lived, however. Mike Rychlik would regretfully quit the band in September 1994. That month, Chuck Prophet & The Creatures Of Habit played the Strawberry Music Festival in Camp Mather, California, on the edge of Yosemite National Park. It would be Rychlik's last gig. Two days later, he and his wife drove across the country to start a new life in Bethesda, Maryland, where they still live.

Tyler Ing and Hank Manninger would also move on before Prophet's next tour. In any case, his third solo album would find Prophet moving away from the roots-based, acoustic-centric instrumentation toward a more conventional setup—two guitars, keyboard, and rhythm section—that would be the platform for his most familiar touring line-ups to this day. But despite growing satisfaction at the label, and an increasingly secure grip on the European touring circuit, the transition would be far from straightforward.

CHAPTER SIX

CHOOSING YOUR BATTLES

FEAST OF HEARTS (1993–95)

> Making records has so much voodoo involved;
> trying to get the spirit of the performance onto
> the record is hard … – Chuck Prophet

'THE NEXT LEVEL'

Getting *Balinese Dancer* recorded, released, and promoted had been a struggle, but the turnaround at China had been inspiring, and two European tours had seen the band conquering discerning musical hearts and minds. In the meantime, Prophet had been dividing his attention between working with Dan Stuart and pursuing his own independent muse. Green On Red had released *Too Much Fun* in October 1992, with a European tour to promote it that winter. *Balinese Dancer* came out in the spring of 1993, and hot on the heels of the Creatures Of Habit European tour described at the end of the previous chapter came a final summer European festival trek for Green On Red, including Roskilde, the Heineken Music Festival, Cambridge Folk, and a slot at Glastonbury on the same bill as The Black Crowes, Robert Plant, and Ian Dury & The Blockheads.

By the winter, however, Green On Red were over, and Prophet was writing and demoing for his next solo release. In the meantime, there was a discernible shift in the musical landscape that Prophet was becoming aware of—a change he reflects on in hindsight with a dose of irony. 'After being made to feel that what we were doing was appallingly unfashionable, suddenly here come The Jayhawks. Here come Counting Crows, who took half of Patrick

Winningham's band and went out there and sold eight million records.' Chuck warms to his theme. 'Now, just to give you some perspective, eight million records, that's more than Bob Dylan has sold in his entire career. So what a distorted, messed-up reality *that* was. And I remember playing a gig in that year [1993]. We played the Liberty Lunch at SXSW, and I ran into [producer] David Kershenbaum. He was at our showcase, and we were up there with accordion and everything. We were doing our thing. And afterward he started talking to me about the Counting Crows. He goes, "It's all different now, they have an organ." And I was like, "Yeah." "They're really into The Band." "Uh-huh." Prophet smiles ruefully. 'I just feel like I've always been out of step, you know? But I just don't see how it's ever gonna change.'

A genre that would come to be known as Americana was sinking its roots into the industry. Simultaneously, across the mainstream of pop and rock, there was a corresponding turn toward what could loosely be called 'authenticity', epitomised most visibly, perhaps, in MTV's *Unplugged* series, for which established bands were invited to perform a set of familiar songs in stripped-down arrangements. Jules Shear, who would come into Prophet's life a few years later, conceptualised the show and hosted the early broadcasts. The first episode, from 1989, featured Squeeze, Syd Straw, and Elliot Easton; the likes of Aerosmith, R.E.M., Eric Clapton, and Pearl Jam would follow over the next few years, and by the time Prophet had his conversation with Kershenbaum, the show had hit its peak—1993 witnessed *Unplugged* sets from Rod Stewart, Neil Young, Duran Duran, and, probably most famously, Nirvana (the soundtrack album would top the *Billboard* chart and sell over five million copies in the USA alone). Meanwhile, in the country music genre, neo-traditionalists were starting to establish themselves, rejecting the commercial sheen of pop-country in favour of traditional country, folk, and bluegrass traditions: Dwight Yoakam, Lyle Lovett, Steve Earle, Randy Travis, and Nanci Griffith.

Meanwhile, the moderate success of *Balinese Dancer* had caught China Records on the hop: 'Yeah. It kinda surprised people.' Chuck recalls. 'It charted in England, and China records got in a good mood.' The label felt that there was potential to be nurtured, and they took up another option and finally worked out a proper record deal. Suddenly Prophet found himself talking to rock producers, and while what he calls the speed-dating process was not always comfortable, he did get to meet Sean Slade and Paul Q. Kolderie: 'I enjoyed hanging with them, enjoyed their take on things, and they would play a big part in my future.' Derek Green talked to Prophet about putting in place some proper management, telling him, 'You should talk to this guy Mike Lembo. We think he'd be a good manager for you.' Chuck adds, 'To me, he seemed like an East Coast blowhard. But what else was I going to do? Get a friend from college? And China thought, *He seems to be in all the right places*. So I went out to Tucson and I met with Mike Lembo, and he started representing me. Probably not the smartest thing I ever did. And before long I started getting the feeling he wasn't really in my corner. But, to be fair, I'm not sure he was in his *own* corner. But no one else was clamouring to represent me at that time.' Prophet sums up a whole set of conflicts and contradictions between commerce and his art when he shrugs, 'Something had to change.'

Lembo's career as a manager can be traced back to Florida in the early 70s—his family relocated there from Long Island in 1968, and he worked with Tom Petty's first band, Mudcrutch. Lembo booked the dates and drove the van before the Floridians hooked up with Denny Cordell, changed their name to The Heartbreakers, and recorded their debut album for Shelter Records. More recently, Lembo had managed an Australian alternative rock band called The Church. 'They had a hit record and got on the cover of *Rolling Stone*, but he didn't manage them very long,' Prophet says. 'He had managed Jules Shear; he had some other clients, some producers. I guess I learned pretty fast he was the kind of guy that loved to work his expense account!'

Tales of Lembo's time working with The Church provide further evidence of his management style. Despite the success of their certified-gold 1988 album *Starfish* and its Top 40 hit 'Under The Milky Way', the band members were seeing very little money for their efforts and success. Touring Europe in support of the follow-up album, *Gold Afternoon Fix* (1990), they lost £200,000, rendering their deal with major label Arista worthless. According to the band's lead singer, songwriter, and bassist, Steve Kilbey, Lembo 'was just sitting back at home, commissioning us at twenty percent—of course, twenty percent before any of the bills got paid. If we had commissioned him after the bills had been paid he might have been a bit more careful about not having a cast of thousands and all the rest of it'.[1] The band split from Lembo soon after.

Prophet finds it difficult to articulate the relationship with Lembo, or how his manager's personality distilled something of a toxic cocktail when combined with his own struggles with addictions at the time. 'Mike had some serious personality problems. Not exactly a nurturing guy. And drinking and using wasn't really working for me anymore. But I wasn't ready to give it up. Not yet. And, somewhere along the line, Lembo's poison seeped into me. He'd belittle people. And I began to lose the courage of my convictions.' There is a silence. 'It's difficult for me to look back at that time. It was a struggle. And whatever I was going through in my life, he found his opening. It was a good time for him to work his way in there. I think, maybe, somewhere along the line I didn't believe in myself. But there's also a thing that musicians do. They want to be taken care of. What did I know about running a business? I needed a home office. Simple things, like a fax machine. And so that was it. But you know a relationship is toxic when you just don't want to pick up the phone. I dreaded his calls.' Chuck pauses for a moment, and then continues, 'I probably could have been more proactive in terms of my so-called career. I don't know why I didn't leave sooner. Why I suffered the abuse, or what I was looking for in a manager, or what I was looking for at all . . . but I take full responsibility for all of it.'

Once Prophet started to get clean, he was able to begin to see what had been going on. 'It's actually a pretty classic story in the music business. I grossed so much money playing live just from playing so many shows. But I wasn't taking *home* any money. There was no net, but I was still having to pay a management commission on the gross. And so, on paper, you owe this guy a lot of money, and there's no real way to get out of it except to turn over your publishing. I lost a lot of publishing that he held on to. That hurt.' He continues, 'My biggest fear really wasn't that I was gonna lose money, or not make money. The biggest fear was that I wouldn't be able to do what it was that I loved. And what I loved was making up songs, getting them to behave. Finding a way to get them to stick to the tape, then going out and playing them.

'People often say, "Oh, don't you want to be more successful?" Because they're imposing their own values on you. But I watched my father leave the house at 6am, come home at 6pm exhausted, loosen his tie and have a couple of bourbons, and it was over, man. You know what I mean? He worked *hard*.

You grow up witnessing that and you say to yourself, "Well, I don't know what I want to do, but I don't want to do *that.*" So, if you put me under and gave me the truth serum, my real fear has always been that I would have to stop. Because nothing else in my life was really working except for the music. It was my addiction. And it was probably the healthiest addiction I ever had. And I still have it!' He laughs, pauses, and then continues, 'Yeah, my resentments toward Mike Lembo, at that time they ran so deep; but I've made peace in the sense that I take responsibility for all of it. I still think it's best to choose your battles, in the sense that you're not going to win everything. And what can you do? What's really important to you? And throughout it all I managed to continue to do what's important to me.'

FEAST OF HEARTS

Inevitably, the poor state Prophet was in at this point colours his retrospective on the writing and recording of *Feast Of Hearts*. 'Well,' he reflects, 'a lot of things stopped working for me around that time. And I had discovered smoking crack. [Producer] Steve Berlin and I had a couple of awkward meetings. I wanted Jim Dickinson to do it, but the powers that be were afraid he was wildly uncommercial, and, when it comes down to it, I just wanted the green light.' Prophet admits that, although they never hit it off, Berlin 'certainly put in the hours. And if anything with that record, I felt like there was a disproportionate amount of time spent in the control room. Time spent tweaking things and running signals through boxes and processing. I probably could've used more help with the arrangements on the floor. But then again, that record has a few songs that I really stand by. Dave McNair engineered; Michael Urbano and Davey Farragher, the rhythm section, they were great players. But I suppose what was missing was the camaraderie. The kind that comes with having a real band. And I was hitting a wall. But *Balinese Dancer* had been a breath of fresh air out there on the road. And was ultimately a fun record to work. But it's a classic story: how can we get to the next level? That's where things can go pear shaped.

'You know, it comes down to this with producers,' he reflects. 'Jim Dickinson described Sam Phillips like this—and I've gone on to describe Dickinson the same way. Dickinson would say, "When Sam was on the other side of the glass, I wanted to please him." And Dickinson was such an inspired guy that when he was on the other side of the glass and he said, "That sounds good. Do it one more time. Do it again. I think you got a better one," you'd do it, because you want to please him. But there have been times in my life where it's been somebody on the other side of the glass telling me what to do, and I'll say, "Why?" Or, just, "Not helpful." It's not always about somebody's résumé or whatever ... it's about feeling safe. And that's how I've been able to co-write the way I do; I could make somebody feel *safe*. Because it's *intimate*. It's like sex: "Really? You're going to do *that*? [*laughs*] Is that what you want to do?" Instead, just let them do what they're doing. Let them try it.'

Mike Lembo encouraged Prophet to collaborate with other songwriters and producers, presumably in search of a hit song. 'I went to Woodstock and I wrote with Jules Shear over the course of a few days. I was staying at this weird hotel and I got into some weird stuff. I was a shit-seeking missile. Drinking, doing coke or whatever. Toxically hungover. I was unshackled. But I wrote a bunch of songs with Jules, a couple of really good ones, and he and I later hit it off when I got clean.' (They collaborated on the multi-artist LP *Raisins In The Sun* in 1999.) 'And, with Jules, he can write a song from anything: you could turn on a household appliance. "You hear anything in there, Jules?" "Yeah, yeah, I hear something in there." And he'll pull melodies out. So that was cool but we didn't really write anything that was ... personal. And then I would end up playing with the songs for a long time, trying to personalise them a little bit, though not always to any great effect'. All the same, he adds, 'Going to Woodstock and writing with Jules was actually pretty fun. Despite everything else that was going on, I enjoyed the experience. And I enjoyed tooling around Woodstock, which is a real artistic community.'

When I ask him whether *Feast Of Hearts* is an album he would choose to listen to today, he replies, 'No. I think there's a couple of strong songs on there, and I really liked Jim Dickinson's version of "Hungry Town"'—as released on *Free Beer Tomorrow* in 2002. 'And I think that when Kurt and I wrote "How Many Angels", we really melded and we wrote a beautiful song ... that was kind of struggle-free. I just love that song.'

'How Many Angels', recorded along with a couple of other tracks at a place in Hollywood called Doug Messenger's Recording Service, is notable for an exceptional guitar break. 'Yeah, that's live,' Chuck confirms. 'I felt the demo was going to be hard to beat. And Berlin agreed. In the end, we just went back to it. Oh, and that beautiful pedal steel from Greg Leisz, of course.' '"How Many Angels" is beautiful,' Stephanie Finch concurs. 'I remember doing that vocal. Greg Leisz was there helping me figure out certain notes for that part.'

As we talk more about the album, Prophet agrees, 'There are definitely things that I think are great about it, but the truth is, I wasn't in great shape at the time.' Maybe it was the lack of control that alienated him from the process? Musician friend Chris von Sneidern recalls hearing that, eventually, 'Chuck had resigned to disappearing or sleeping under the piano in passive protest at having been sidelined.'

For Stephanie Finch, *Feast Of Hearts* represented a further step away from where she and Chuck had started as a performing unit. Although the album credits her with vocals and accordion, her memory is that she 'wasn't involved with the tracking of that record'—certainly not in the way she had been on the previous two. Stephanie's perspective on the album is also darkened by what was going on at the time. 'I've always liked all the songs,' she says, 'but that was the record where drugs really entered the picture for Chuck. When he got his hands on crack cocaine … it just changed him.' Stephie pauses. 'You know, it kind of robs people of their soul. Toward the end I think he was feeling really insecure about the record. And maybe the crack was his escape. I remember he failed to show the day they were starting the mixing. And if he didn't turn up for that then something was *really* wrong.'

The version of *Feast Of Hearts* that made it onto the shelves was one that Prophet feels to this day came nowhere near what it might have been. And perhaps its enduring value resides in the songwriting: 'Longshot Lullaby', for instance, remains one of his most affecting ballads. Prophet and Lipschutz have a particular talent for painting miniature portraits of quietly desperate, ordinary lives, and this is one of their best:

Sings to himself a first grader's rhyme
While the snow on the screen dances in time
To a longshot lullaby.

The tone of the guitars is perfectly modulated to the mood of the song, and the rhythm section reins it in, maintaining the focus on Prophet's emotional lead vocal and Stephanie Finch's tender harmony.

Admittedly, *Feast Of Hearts* might be caught in possession of more run-of-the-mill songs than one would expect of an artist who has maintained such fierce quality control. For instance, 'What It Takes' is straightforward country-rock with a 'Positively 4th Street' kiss-off lyric; 'Madam Rosa's' ticks along but only ever really came alive onstage—the recorded version seems battened down, the layers of instrumentation and backing vocals notwithstanding. However, the fair-to-middling songs are outweighed by some slinky, swampy, funky numbers ('Hungry Town', 'Too Tired To Come') that have more of Chuck's irrepressible, instinctive sense of rhythm. Two classic rockers, 'Once Removed' and 'Break The Seal', were re-recorded at a late stage with bandmates recruited for the upcoming tour, Paul Revelli (drums) and Anders Rumblad (bass), because Prophet was dissatisfied with the versions tracked with Urbano and Faragher. David Immergluck, later of Counting Crows, added mandolin to 'Break The Seal' and another guitar track to 'Once Removed'. Finch's accordion on the former, and her harmony, puts us back in *Balinese Dancer* territory for four minutes and eight seconds. Both tracks groove much more easily than the earlier versions.

FEAST OF HEARTS ON THE ROAD

Touring *Feast Of Hearts* was going to require a band, and Prophet wanted to expand his musical palette. Guitarist Max Butler, who would go on to work with Chuck for a decade, had started out in the San Francisco music scene when he was seventeen. Veteran venue manager Dawn Holliday, who would book Chuck frequently for San Francisco shows prior to a feud in the 2000s that would shut him out of a couple of local venues for several years, took Butler on as a monitor engineer at the Fillmore, and it was in that capacity that he first came across Chuck and Stephie, billed as an opening act.

Butler's band, The Sextants, briefly looked to be heading for some commercial success when they secured a major label deal on Imago, the company behind Aimee Mann's breakthrough solo album, *Whatever* (1993); the band's demos had been produced by Scott Mathews, who had worked on *Brother Aldo*. Although Chuck and Max's paths meandered close and occasionally crossed, they had never been properly introduced socially: Butler hung out a lot with Patrick Winningham on the Hotel Utah scene at that time, but this was at a time when Prophet and Winningham were not close. However, Butler remembers seeing Chuck onstage at the Paradise, and the main impression he came away with was, 'This guy can *play*.'

Regrettably, The Sextants' album did not take off, and by 1993 Butler was ready to move on: he did some touring and recording with Tommy Stinson of The Replacements before Stinson signed up to play with Guns N' Roses, and he started another short-lived band that secured some music publishing and got close to recording before folding when the singer gave up to start a family. Butler was making ends meet working at a music store in San Francisco when he got a call from Prophet to come and audition. At that point, Butler had begun his own journey on the uniquely steep learning curve that the pedal steel guitar presents, and pedal steel was an instrument that Chuck was planning to incorporate into his band sound. Max is quite prepared to admit now that he was still an amateur, but when Prophet asked if he played steel, he diplomatically replied, 'Yes, I have one'—and the audition was booked.

Butler packed guitar and pedal steel and rented a car to get to Secret Studios, just south of Mission, and auditioned in the same room where they would later do all the preproduction demos for *Homemade Blood* with Chris von Sneidern. There, Max met Stephanie Finch, as well as recent recruits drummer Paul Revelli and bass player Anders Rumblad. 'Paul had a reputation as being great; could play a shuffle for days,' says Prophet. 'Happy Sanchez recommended him.' The only problem was that Revelli had recently retired from the road, 'having played all over the world for too long with Joe Louis Walker,' says Prophet. 'But I sent Paul a record or two, and he said, "Let's play." We got together and played and, well … I talked him back into the road, I suppose.'

Max already knew Rumblad well—the bassist had put in a good word for him with Prophet—and he remembers Stephie being particularly friendly and kind, but while she and Rumblad helped put him at ease, the bandleader was at first much harder to read: 'Chuck has this way of dealing with people when he meets them for the first time. Sometimes he will say things that are provocative, or kind of edgy, just to see how you're gonna take it.' Prophet had given Butler a few songs from *Feast Of Hearts* to work through before the audition, and that day they played some songs, they jammed, and that was it. Afterward, they all went out for Salvadorian food at one of Prophet's favourite restaurants, Los Panchos in Bernal Heights, which Butler took as a good sign; Chuck and the band were looking for someone who could not only play but who could 'hang'—an important factor for long months on the road. Butler admits that at the time he was still 'a little rough around the edges' as a guitarist, but he got the gig and joined the band for a couple of European tours behind the *Feast Of Hearts* album at the start of 1995.

The European trips found the band in more robust, rocking mode than ever before, with Prophet and Butler forming a two-guitar-attack that was more conventional than the approach Prophet had favoured up until this point. Max would become Chuck's guitar foil onstage and in the studio until the turn of the millennium. 'I don't play rhythm or lead,' Prophet explained at the time, 'I don't play in a traditional way, so I don't want people stepping on me. You get shocked like a monkey when you go up the neck and somebody's sitting there. You gotta develop that telepathy, and Max is very good at that.'[2] Furthermore, Butler's familiarity with a range of instruments widened the palette; he would play mandolin (later mandocello) on certain songs, and was growing increasingly confident on pedal steel, although Stephie notes, 'That's not an instrument you can really fake on—so that was a little rocky!' Stephie's memory of the dozen UK dates was that the new line-up was still gelling. 'But Paul Revelli was always consistent. He was very professional from the get-go.'

James Walbourne—the supremely talented guitarist with the current incarnation of The Pretenders, and one half of duo The Rails with Kami Thompson—was fifteen when he saw the band play a 'hot and sweaty' Borderline on June 2. 'I think he was wearing red velvet trousers but cannot be sure of it,' James tells me. 'Over the last fifteen, twenty years I've seen Chuck play many times. He's a unique musician—one who is always forging ahead with new sounds and experimentation. Oh, and no one can make a Telecaster sing like Chuck. Red velvet trousers or no red velvet trousers.'

Prophet laughs when I quote Walbourne to him. 'Music and clothes are genetically tied, somehow. I like elegance. I pack a very light bag these days. Like the man said, "Style is the answer to everything." Style is not fashion. As for me … for one thing, I've always felt life is too short for ironing. So, if I can hang a shirt in the shower before the gig? Better yet. Style is instinctive. Like Joan Rivers says, "It's like herpes, you either got it or you don't."'

A good quality audience recording from the UK leg, taped at the Leadmill, Sheffield (May 28 1995), gives a flavour of the shows at this time, from a gentle opening ('Baton Rouge' showcasing Butler on mandolin; 'Battered And Bruised' featuring his pedal steel) to a funky 'Hungry Town' (with confident interplay between Rumblad and Revelli). Prophet introduces 'Angel' with the words 'This one's lady's choice', and they play the country arrangement of the song with Stephie singing lead, Max comping and trilling on mandolin, and Chuck's guitar all over the map. It's slightly ramshackle and utterly charming. The second half of the show builds momentum through a fierce run of tunes including 'Savannah' (Max heavy on the wah pedal) and 'Madam Rosa's'. The final encore is what sounds like a seat-of-the-pants 'Balinese Dancer' and a thrilling take on 'Heart Breaks Like The Dawn' with Chuck delivering a tremendous vocal, matched note for note by Stephie's harmony. If there are times when the guitars, or guitar and pedal steel, don't quite mesh in the ways they would on the next tour, the rhythm is never less than rock steady.

There was an acoustic appearance at Glastonbury at the end of June; writer and stand-up comedian Stewart Lee reported on it for *Vox* and, in idiosyncratic style, noted, 'All cheekbones and quicksilver licks, Chuck's drop-dead country cool is only spoiled by the fact that one of his trouser legs is slightly turned up in his cowboy boot heel. Nevertheless, he and accordionist Stephanie Finch enter my Top Three of Glastonbury sex creatures.'[3] The festival gig was slotted around a second European tour, this time opening for smooth blues artist Robert Cray. At that point, Cray was almost a decade on from his crossover success with the album *Strong Persuader* (1986), but he was on the cusp of a run in the US blues album chart that would see him regularly hitting the Top 3 with every subsequent release from 1995's *Some Rainy Morning* up to 2014's chart-topping *In My Soul*.

'Well, Cray was a cool guy,' Prophet reflects, 'and his band were cool guys. He had a history of having great openers. I believe they had taken Joe Ely out, who is one of my all-time heroes. It was cool to play theatres, although we were not really a theatre band at that point—more of a bar band. But I learned to try to reach the back of the room. And I appreciated the label trying something different to get us to the next level, and out of the pub circuit for a little while. It looked good on paper, anyway.' Prophet was already writing for the next album, and at the end of that year and the beginning of the next he took a gig playing guitar for The Silos on a couple of tours, both at home and abroad.

'AND IT JUST WENT AWAY ...'

Feast Of Hearts was supposed to come out on Warner Bros in America. This was at a time when 'people were selling tens of millions of records, and we went down to LA and we did a showcase with this girl, Jen Trynin, who was on Warner Brothers,' Prophet tells me. 'She was managed by the people that managed Nirvana. And we went and played with her at the Roxy.' Trynin's memoir, *Everything That I'm Cracked Up To Be*, published in 2006, offers fascinating insights into the state of the music industry at the time. Courted by multiple labels, Trynin had been seen for a while as the Next Big Thing (before effectively being gazumped by Alanis Morissette). As her book recounts, the tide rises and carries her off with it ('It wasn't that way for me!' Chuck laughs), and then there is this terrible sensation of everything falling away as the label's confidence in her gradually drains, and the hotels become motels, the talk of a European tour stutters, and the dream just curls up in a corner and dies.

'A lot of the Warners people were there,' Prophet says of his own appearance at the Roxy show on August 28 1995, 'and I think that they were underwhelmed. Lembo said, "Well, a lot of it probably has to do with the fact that you're pushing thirty and you're kinda damaged goods." And I believed it. Because—maybe he had a point. I had had a pretty good run. More than most people get. More chances for sure. All those records as a member of Green On Red and now a solo artist, pushing thirty. And in retrospect I have a lot of gratitude towards the guys at China that helped us to crib together just enough tour support to get in a cold van and drive around, because it enabled us to build the audience that we still have today. I got my skinny foot in the door and I feel in a lot of ways grateful that we were able to do that, even if we weren't the object of some bidding war!'

There may have been a measure of enthusiasm behind *Feast Of Hearts*, but the release was once again bungled by the record company. 'We had some

▊ ABOVE With Dave Kusworth of Dogs D'Amour,
Breedon Bar, Birmingham, June 1 1993. (*Martin Dudley*)

▊ RIGHT At the Mean Fiddler, London, March 5 1993.

▊ BELOW Hank Maninger, Stephie, Tyler Ing, Chuck, and
Mike Rychlik at the Great American Music Hall, c. 1993.

▓ ABOVE Chris Von Sneidern, c. 1995.

▓ RIGHT *Feast Of Hearts* promo shot, c. 1995. (*Jeff Smith*)

▓ BELOW Anders Rumblad, Max Butler, Paul Revelli (out of shot), Chuck, Stephie, Great American Music Hall, c. 1995.

▓ OPPOSITE Chuck with Gibson SG, 1997. (*Giulio Molfese*)

■ RIGHT Portrait shot from the
Homemade Blood album cover
shoot, 1997. (*Tom Erikson*)

■ BELOW Chuck and Stephie
onstage in 1999. (*Giulio Molfese*)

■ OPPOSITE PAGE Recording
Homemade Blood, 1996. From
top: Eric Westfall, Max Butler,
Chuck, Paul Revelli; Stephie, Anders
Rumblad, Paul, Max, Eric; Chuck.
(*Tom Erikson*)

TOP *Hurting Business*
tour, 1999. (*Giulio
Molfese*)

▌ MIDDLE The console
at Pigs Head Studio,
c. 1999.

▌ BOTTOM Recording
What I Deserve with
Kelly Willis, c. 1999.

❙ LEFT Go Go Market
promo shot, c. 2002:
Mark Reitman, Vince
Russo, Stephie, Dawn
Richardson, Chuck.
(*Jock McDonald*)

❙ BELOW Recording *Age
Of Miracles* at home,
2003. (*Tom Erikson*)

▌ ABOVE Golden Gate Park, c. 2002:
Chuck, Stephie, Winston Watson,
'Teenage' Rob Douglas, Max Butler.

▌ LEFT Recording *No Other Love* at
home, 2001.

▌ BELOW Driving the Van, *No Other
Love* tour, c. 2002.

bad luck,' Chuck says, philosophically. 'A CD of outtakes and rough mixes was mistakenly pressed up as our promo version and circulated to the press. Ooops! Thanks, Mike Lembo!' Based on the promo, he remembers getting a review that the album was too long. There was also a feature in a major UK daily newspaper. The interviewer, David Sinclair, 'was very business-like,' Prophet notes. 'He's a big Green On Red fan. And the piece came out and it said, "Here's a guy with a great future behind him." And the whole piece kind of worked backwards from that title.' The article is motivated by Sinclair's sense that *Feast Of Hearts* had 'veered towards the middle of the road' and betrays a somewhat romanticised view of Green On Red's celebration of 'the grungier aspects of the human condition'.[4] Inevitably, at the time, it rankled. 'Now I find it pretty hilarious. And I see David Sinclair from time to time and quote it to him. He's a good guy.'

Still, there were some glowing reviews for the album across the UK press, even if most of them seemed incapable of assessing the album without using Tom Petty as a reference point for vocals or general musical style. *Melody Maker* also described him as 'the missing link between Bob Dylan and Paul Westerberg'.[5] The *Top* reviewer enjoyed the album's eclecticism, 'ranging as it does through power pop and rock to the beautiful country ballad "How Many Angels"' and seemed to relish the 'experiments … with weird sounds'— certainly more than Prophet himself had done. A *Glasgow Herald* feature prefacing an appearance at King Tut's Wah-Wah Hut (always one of Chuck's favourite UK venues) described the album as 'a thing of cranky guitars and rockin' retro vibes, located somewhere just off Main Street from which the Rolling Stones were once notable exiles'.[6] *The Big Issue* called it 'a sublime selection of timeless, rootsy blues and country-tinged tunes'.[7]

And, as always, the live shows were a blast and well reviewed: 'a model of fluent grace and economy', according to David Sinclair in that same *Times* feature. Prophet was relishing the additional firepower Max Butler was bringing to the stage. UK monthly *Mojo* caught him on home turf at Slim's, launching the new album. Even if, for this particular reviewer, the 'Telecastery par excellence' sometimes dragged on too long, the report also celebrated his voice ('deep and achingly beautiful'), his stage presence ('Prophet spends much of the time stomping and flailing his way about the stage like a palsied man at a Bill[y] Graham convention'), and the riffs ('razor sharp, sinewy and muscle bound').[8]

Distribution woes had persistently dogged Green On Red. And, despite apparently having support from the label and a manager who made enough noise to convince anyone within earshot that he knew what he was doing, Prophet had returned from Europe to find once again that nothing was moving on the US front. 'We came back home and the record wasn't out. And there was no sign of it coming out. Nobody championed it. It just never found a home here,' Prophet recalls. 'We were supposed to go back to the UK supporting our old friend Chris Isaak, and it didn't happen. As they say in Hollywood, it just . . . went away. And I remember that day Stephanie went out and she scrambled to get to San Francisco State, to sign up for a teaching credential. And they said. "We don't have any openings but if you take the middle school credential programme we'll accept you." She's like, "Yeah, that sounds fine. Whatever you've got!"'

It was not the first time Prophet had felt that the doors of the music business were closing him out. And it would not be the last. But, for now, just when prospects were looking grim, opportunity would come knocking again from the other side of the Atlantic. 'The following year I went to SXSW; I was playing with The Silos,' Chuck says. 'And I ran into Martin Goldschmidt, the guy that owned Cooking Vinyl.' Goldschmidt and Pete Lawrence had founded Cooking Vinyl in 1986 with the release of Michelle Shocked's *Texas Campfire Tapes*. They would go on to build an enviable reputation on the indie-label scene, home in due course to Billy Bragg, Echo & The Bunnymen, and Ryan Adams, among many others.

'Martin said, "Yeah, we'd love to do something with you." And he told my manager, "If Chuck gets a record together, we'll put it out." And I said, "I hope they can do better than that. It would be nice to have a budget." And Mike Lembo, to his credit, said, "Hey, relax, we're *negotiating* here."'

The next album would find Prophet shaking himself free of limitations, frustrations, and unwelcome interference. And, once free, he would never look back.

CHAPTER SEVEN

'BALLS TO THE WALL'

HOMEMADE BLOOD (1996–97)

> Rider won't you pass me by now,
> rider won't you stop for me ...
> – Prophet/klipschutz

HOMEMADE BLOOD AND THE ELECTRIC DEMOS

Homemade Blood would be Chuck Prophet's fourth solo release and his first for the British independent label Cooking Vinyl. Looking back, Prophet concedes, 'We were reaching for something with *Feast Of Hearts*. And maybe we didn't get there. Not that big of a deal. But I did come to realize that we had spent a disproportionate amount of time in the control room. And I made a vow to myself: the next record is going to take place on the floor. Which is a pretty natural way for me to react . . . I mean, it's physics. For every action there's an opposite and equal reaction. Isn't that what they say?' If *Feast Of Hearts* feels a little overproduced, cellophane-wrapped, and reined in, *Homemade Blood* would be Chuck Prophet uncaged.

Prophet credits a lot of the success of the *Homemade Blood* recordings to the amount of time the band had spent playing together. Max Butler had a rehearsal space out by Candlestick Park, and they would play often: 'We just worked those songs out in the rehearsal studio,' Prophet remembers. Thanks to the record deal secured for his previous band, The Sextants, Butler had acquired a stack of equipment, including a Tascam 488 console with a built-in quarter-inch tape recorder. 'We recorded a *lot* that year,' Prophet recalls. 'And some of that stuff ended up carrying over onto [1999 release] *The Hurting Business.*'

Butler says they used to refer to the rehearsals as 'commando sessions', because of the way they would call up bassist Roly Salley and drummer Paul Revelli: 'Quick in, quick out, get the tape rolling, throw up a couple of microphones, and play.' Max believes that the band spirit was a major element in the way the record came together: 'We really did flesh out stuff like a normal band—a hard thing to get when you're a solo artist.' Collaboration has always been at the heart of Prophet's working methods, and it was central to the genesis of *Homemade Blood*. 'Yeah, everything I do is collaborative. You want people to bring love to the process. Where you give them something to work with, and they give something more back.'

The formal sessions, which would eventually be overseen by Eric Westfall at Toast Studios in San Francisco, were preceded by a set of recordings made in a black-box rehearsal space, recorded live on the floor with no headphones and direct to tape by Chris von Sneidern. Von Sneidern was a native of Syracuse, New York, who moved to San Francisco at the age of nineteen and released a series of self-produced albums through the 1990s. He first saw Prophet playing at the Albion in 1988, and then again at the Paradise Lounge the following year, but it was four or five years later that Chuck visited Chris at his home in the Castro and was blown away by a recording of the latter's song 'Annalisa', released on his demos collection *Sight And Sound* in 1993. Around the time of *Feast Of Hearts*, Chuck invited him to audition for the touring band, but von Sneidern did not follow up, and Max Butler got the gig.

Not long after, von Sneidern recalls swapping a VHS bootleg of a Beatles movie back and forth with Prophet and engaging in animated discussions of the band's process at that time. 'I was really into *Let It Be*,' Prophet recalls, 'and I wanted to do the next album as live as possible. Even live vocals and background vocals. Around the time I was working with Steve Berlin on *Feast Of Hearts*, there were a lot of processed records at the time. Records like [Los Lobos's] *Kiko*. So I really wanted to make a record that was live on our feet, and I thought that would be a real challenge. And I said it was going to be more like a play, and less like a film.' He explains, 'Films are made in the editing suite. And plays are made in front of you. And so we were a little bit rehearsed, and then Chris brought in his equipment and captured those demos.'

The same metaphor informed an interview from that time for *Hearsay* magazine, in which Prophet talked about a desire to 'make a record with a group of personalities, like a play, with five people interacting'.[1] And Max Butler is on the same page when talking about the influence of the Beatles documentary on the sessions: 'You see it through the lens of the personal connections of the band members,' he explains. 'The relationship between Chris [von Sneidern] and Chuck, the relationship between Stephanie and Chuck, you became more emotionally aware of all the different things that were at play outside of the music: the egos, the desires, the ambitions … that's all happening in that space, and it's bound to create a different kind of record than it would be if we were all coming in to do overdubs or building up a track or working with session musicians.'

Toward the end of 1995, a studio session was booked. 'I tore apart my whole home studio and set it up at Secret Studios on Army Street,' von Sneidern told me. (The studio was owned by Greg—later Happy—Sanchez.) 'I had twenty-four tracks of ADATs by then, no analogue tape machines, maybe a tape echo. Studiomaster mixing board, various *pro-sumer* outboard gear, and a few mics, including a tube AKG C12a.' By the mid-90s, von Sneidern, though entirely self-taught, had built up a sustainable recording business. 'I think we started the week of November 5 1995,' he told me. 'Secret Studios had a couple of "big" rehearsal rooms, and this one was big enough so the band could set up on the riser. Paul Revelli had his new Ayotte drum set at that time—it sounded good in there. Chuck had his guitar station (he learned that recording at Ocean Way with Glyn Johns, a little guitar hovel to live in) over stage left, Max had a similar bunch of instruments and amps at stage right. Anders had a bass rig somewhere that didn't bleed on everything, and when Stephie could come straight from work, she'd be over crunched in next to Chuck, looking at charts, playing Wurlitzer piano or the Farfisa. We had the PA on, no headphones, just vocals in the PA to guide us.'

There was little isolation, just careful positioning of amps. Von Sneidern's ADAT machines may seem like Stone Age technology to the Pro Tools generation, but it was a 'godsend' to someone like him who would never have had the space or financial resources for 24-track analogue. 'The big problem was that, while they were an innovative digital 8-track modular system, they were built around the transport of the cheapest VCR guts,' he says, and they would cause no end of problems. Occasionally, everything would screw up, and Chris would send the band out for lunch while, as he put it, 'I white-knuckled my way back to being able make music again and not lose what we already had.'

A couple of months later, on January 22 1996, von Sneidern reconvened with the band at Tom Mallon's studio, and another set of demos was recorded. Mallon was the producer who had documented much of the San Francisco art-punk scene, produced the early American Music Club recordings, and provided Prophet with studio time when he cut *Brother Aldo*. In March, Chris mixed them at DCP, a studio within Secret Studios run by Doug Carlson. 'It was nothing special but probably $200 a day if I went in by myself, which was cheap,' he told me. Unfortunately, although it seemed a reasonable assumption at the time that von Sneidern would go on to produce the album, it was not to be. Chris remembers going over 'a few permutations of the budget' with Chuck's 'day-to-day' manager, Dan Kennedy (at that time working for Lembo), and it dawning on him that 'I'd be working for less than free'. As Prophet puts it, 'I guess we just couldn't come to some kind of agreement that made everybody feel good.' Von Sneidern took another gig instead in the fall of 1996, touring with John Wesley Harding. While Prophet stumped up $1,500 from his publishing advance for the initial session, payment for the work on the Mallon recordings was not forthcoming. Von Sneidern says he eventually gave up trying to collect on the outstanding sum, chalking it up to experience.

Back when he had been searching for a producer for *Feast Of Hearts*, Prophet had met with Sean Slade and Paul Q. Kolderie, an enormously influential duo whose Fort Apache Studio in Boston had opened in 1986 and swiftly become a hub for the college-rock scene that was developing at the time. Slade and Kolderie had had considerable success with the likes of Pixies, Throwing Muses, Dinosaur Jr., The Lemonheads, and Radiohead. For Kolderie, part of the magic at the time was down to the fact that bands and producers were developing simultaneously, and the studio grew alongside them: 'The idea was to start a studio that was only about rock . . . no dentist office panelling, no receptionist . . . it was a bare-bones place but you could really get a slammin' sound there and no one felt uncomfortable . . .which is important!'[2]

'To have a place where they could go and record in a sympathetic way was a really important part of it,' Kolderie tells me. He cites London in the 1960s,

Seattle, and Motown as other examples: 'Every place where something musical happens, there's a recording studio that went along with that.' Fort Apache fitted into the same mould. Bill Janovitz of Buffalo Tom would note, 'I don't mean to over-romanticize that period of time, but the Boston music scene at that point was really intense and really vibrant. Fort Apache, to me, really was the binding agent of all of it.'[3]

Neither Kolderie nor Slade was very familiar with Green On Red's music, but Kolderie remembers being flown over to London to meet with Derek Green of China Records with a view to producing one of their bands, and one of the albums he was given by Derek was *Balinese Dancer*, which he liked a lot. He also remembers seeing Prophet live at that point when he came through Boston, and, even though they never met in person, being very impressed by him not simply as a songwriter and as a performer but in terms of his stage persona. However, much as he liked and admired them, Prophet felt at the time, while he was prepping for *Feast Of Hearts*, 'They maybe didn't have an affinity for the kind of music that I was trying to do.' Nevertheless, as he puts it, 'We remained fans … and then later, I didn't have a record deal or anything, but I had this cassette with "Ooh Wee" and "Credit" and some other things [from the sessions with von Sneidern], and that's what Sean Slade and Paul Kolderie heard. And they liked them. So, as demos, they certainly got the job done.' Prophet was aware there was no budget available to him that would stretch to hiring Slade and Kolderie to produce, but the duo clearly wanted to be in on the action. 'We'll do whatever we can to help,' they told him. 'If you want us to just mix it, we can just mix it.' Cooking Vinyl had given Prophet $10,000 when he signed, and they handed over another $10,000 when Slade and Kolderie came on board. 'That was Lembo's doing,' Chuck explains. 'They were his clients. So of course he was double dipping. Commissioning the money coming and going. But, as they say, all to the good.'

RECORDING *HOMEMADE BLOOD*

With Eric Westfall in the control room, the album was recorded in ten days and mixed in three. *Homemade Blood* found Prophet stubbornly swimming against the industry tide. 'We did it in the back room at Toast, Studio A, and they still had that Class A Neve board from when Dan Alexander owned the place, and they still had the two-inch Studer tape machine, although it was starting to collect dust,' he remembers. 'The room was just packed full of gear ... vintage keyboards, vintage amps up to the walls.' As he recalls those sessions, he reaches back to a conversation he had had a few years earlier with Al Kooper. Kooper had been creating some TV soundtrack music, recording to a hard drive on Pro Tools, and he told Prophet, 'In the future all music is going to be recorded like this.'

'I said, "I don't think so,"' Chuck continues. 'And he said, "No, let me rephrase that. There will still be purist weirdos who want to do it this way"—pointing at the two-inch tape machine—"but, by and large, this is going to be the way everybody works on records." And at the time, I couldn't see it, but by the time of *Homemade Blood*, I couldn't miss it. And I wanted to make one last balls-to-the-wall record where there's woodchips flying off the sticks, and the guitars are bouncing off the walls and instruments are bleeding into one another, and everybody is playing standing up in the same room, all at the same time. And that was *Homemade Blood*.'

Undoubtedly, a lot of the ghosts that howl in the bones of the so-called *Electric Demos* from the sessions with von Sneidern would haunt the recording of the album itself, but Eric Westfall would prove to be crucial to the MO and the very distinctive sound that defines *Homemade Blood*. Westfall was already a veteran as engineer and producer, his long list of credits stretching back to work with Christian Death in the mid-1980s, various incarnations of Howe Gelb (Giant Sand, Band Of Blacky Ranchette), The Gin Blossoms on their debut EP *Dusted*, Rainer Ptacek, and former Green On Red keyboard genius Chris Cacavas.

'I had been making records left and right, but always as an engineer/producer, and usually officially just as the engineer,' Westfall says. 'This was the first time somebody of Chuck's stature and talent handed the ball to me. I was really excited about the whole effort, and it was one of the most satisfying experiences I've had in the studio. I was willing to try anything, and Chuck was right there with me, and I with him,' Westfall notes. 'I remember we rehearsed and tracked with drum/percussion loops, and one day Chuck says, "Take out the loop." So we did, and the whole song just opened up. It was ironic: by starting off playing with these loops, we not only tricked the players, we tricked ourselves (fortuitously). So we ditched all the loops, but in their absence we had this rock solid groove and economy that we wouldn't have achieved otherwise.'

Stephanie Finch remembers the sessions as a deeply creative and enjoyable time, in large part facilitated by Eric, whom she describes warmly as 'a really gifted, kind, gentle person'. His experience and his natural musicality were essential elements in the creative process. Prophet recalls a specific illustrative example: 'On "Til You Came Along" we rigged up guitar pickups to Stephanie's accordion, and we were trying to record live, so we had to pump it through an amp because everything was bleeding. And we put this guitar pickup on that accordion there, and we ran it into a Marshall, and we're all in the same room and there was this [*lets out a sharp, high-pitched noise*] as we were cutting the track,' he continues. 'It was so loud in there and everyone had to stop. We were going, "What the heck is that?" And it was her accordion feeding back. And Eric said, "I kinda like it … the song's in F, but the feedback's, like, an E-flat. It's creating this dominant seventh." He had wonderful ears. And he was right. In the track, the sound of the feedback really did work. Eric always sought to understand what was happening as opposed to just fixing things.'

When they were recording 'Ooh Wee', they decided they needed a live take of Prophet singing and playing acoustic, but with isolation between the two, so they could fix any vocals they wanted. 'We built some kind of contraption for Chuck in his booth,' Westfall recalls. 'It was Plexiglas with a hole for his head to stick out, kind of like a guillotine.' Prophet concurs: 'Yes, that's true. That Plexiglas cardboard rig. It worked!' He pauses and reflects. 'It's nice to have somebody in the trenches with you whose ears are that great. Plus you could throw any sonic shapes at Eric, and he embraced all the chaos.'

Part of the appeal of *Homemade Blood* lies in the traces of that sonic chaos coursing through the finished, mixed down tracks. The buzz beneath the opening drum beats of 'Til You Came Along', the stray note on electric guitar as 'Ooh Wee''s acoustic kicks off the riff, the tape hiss like a distant surf beneath the hushed opening bars of 'The Parting Song'. The process of recording almost everything live was undoubtedly a challenge. 'It takes a lot of work to set up live and get five musicians on tape simultaneously,' Prophet reasons. 'But recording is such an elusive thing anyway. It always comes back to capturing that energy and spirit in the room at that time.' Toast Studios was an ideal size for the 'live on the floor' recording Chuck was preoccupied with at the time: 'I like the sound of all the music getting squished together so it's ready to explode,' he told Pete Pawsey in 1997. 'Like Howlin' Wolf records … a record like [The Rolling Stones'] *Some Girls* sounds big, but it doesn't sound open.'

The combination of the room and the specific approach to recording created an exciting and intense atmosphere. 'It was all going on on the floor, it wasn't going on in the control room. They couldn't put tape on the machines fast enough.' The songs were constructed by editing different takes. 'We did it with no digital whatsoever, and all the tape editing was done with a razor blade,' Chuck recalls. 'And Eric Westfall was totally down for it, he didn't sleep. He would do the test edits during the night. Because we were recording live, there were no overdubs; instead, we were editing together the best takes. And there were a *lot* of takes.'

By this time, Max, Stephie, Anders Rundblad, and Paul Revelli had found their feet as a touring unit. 'Kicking songs around onstage every night is like taking your kid out in the backyard every afternoon and hitting grounders to him,' Prophet remarked in 1999. The ways in which the individuals are so tightly locked in—the rhythm section, Chuck and Stephie's voices, Max and Chuck's guitars—is readily apparent from the opening groove of 'Credit', and abundantly evident throughout *Homemade Blood*. Across the album, Max played most of the rhythm parts, while Chuck took care of what he describes as 'the screaming solos'. But Max's skill and versatility were critical to the sound of the recordings. 'Yeah, he could definitely move from the mando family to the guitars,' says Prophet. 'Plus he was a little wilder about running pedals into other pedals into other pedals, which I didn't really do.'

Butler remembers that, at the time he started working with Chuck, he was 'more into the pure tone—just going into an amp'; while he may have had a delay pedal and a distortion pedal, that was it. They both recall attending a Flaming Lips show at Slim's. 'It was just so over-the-top,' says Prophet. 'The guitars had effects going into effects going into effects going into … and it sounded like they were all running on one nine-volt battery that was on its last breath. And I turned to Max and said, "Max, you gotta start doing that!" And so that was pretty influential when we did *Homemade Blood*. We really wanted to push it. Run the guitars, run the amp into another amp, and overdrive that, and ... just pin all the needles, push it.'

Indeed, there are times when the sound seems on the brink of overload—at the end of the solo in 'Ooh Wee', in the full tilt riffing of '22 Fillmore'. Butler added to his standard arsenal of a Boss Overdrive, a Boss Compressor, and an MXR boost a wah pedal that had a defective pot and 'always gave noise and feedback'—another happy accident that gave a particular flavour to the loudest, most manic tracks such as '22 Fillmore'. They were trying to experiment, Butler remembers, and the challenge was to 'rein in the chaos ... we wanted stuff to happen that was singular, that would happen only in that moment ... we knew there was noise that was going be beyond our control, but we could *manipulate* it: generate it and *make* it happen'. Butler also acknowledges that they were listening to a lot of 70s Rolling Stones at that time, and the classic push-pull of Keith Richards and Ron Wood's guitars is a discernible influence. Butler would play his P-90-equipped SG most of the time, but he would have another guitar—either a Les Paul or a Danelectro—permanently in open G (or 'banjo tuning') for slide work.

The music was one element that simply fell into place in a way that it never had for Prophet on any of his previous solo recordings. But the story would be far from complete without acknowledging how crucial the songs are to the success of *Homemade Blood* as a work of art. Kurt Lipschutz was a key player in making the album the high-water mark that it undoubtedly is: when everything else is stripped away, the genius is in the music and the lyrics of the album's twelve tracks, eight of which are co-writes between Chuck and Kurt.

To date, Chuck has recorded seventy or eighty songs co-written with Lipschutz, and the time leading up to *Homemade Blood* was particularly fertile. 'We were just on fire,' Prophet enthuses. 'Had the fax machines going, and we would send things back and forth, and I had that rehearsal studio. We would all get together and play and so songs would get going really fast and we were free. We were *free*.' While Lipschutz was rarely at the studio, Prophet does recall sitting with him there and knocking out the last verse of 'New Year's Day'. Discussing the album almost twenty years later, Kurt also notes, 'I loved all four of the songs that Chuck wrote by himself, and so I thought it was really a home run of a record.'

While this was a fantastically rich period for Prophet in terms of his creativity, on a personal level, he was still struggling to stay clean. Indeed, for long-standing Chuck Prophet fans, part of the mystique of the *Homemade Blood* album has been its status as Chuck's 'rehab album', supposedly documenting his struggles on songs like 'New Year's Day', 'You Been Gone', and the title track. It's a narrative that's far too straightforward to map onto real life, but nevertheless there is something about the album's chiaroscuro of desperate shade and redeeming light that has inspired many listeners in their own dark times. And, for sure, Prophet had his own monsters to feed at the time.

'Hmmm . . . '97?' Chuck muses, looking back almost twenty years later. 'Yeah, I kept trying to get clean. March in '97 was my last drink. I was kinda clean during the making of *Homemade Blood*—I was pretty focused. I wasn't passed out under the piano, like on the last album. But I couldn't keep it together. I'd been trying since '95. I was going to meetings, I was taking suggestions . . . I just wasn't willing to turn my care and my will over to anything other than me. And then I remember I was over in London, doing a promo tour for *Homemade Blood*, and I was playing solo at the club the 12 Bar. And somebody came by with a tray of drinks and said, "Last time we were in Birmingham you bought everybody a round, and we thought you were so cool." And then the guy had a tray of shots or whatever, and I said, "Let's get to work on that." So then I woke up in my hotel room, I couldn't find my plane ticket, and I was in a panic: "Hell, I blacked out." And I was, like, *Man, no more*. You know? *No more*. And that was my last drink.

'The thing is,' he continues, 'I didn't understand total abstinence. I thought I could just drink without smoking crack. I thought I could do heroin without . . . whatever. And eventually it's all the same. The truth is, you're powerless over drugs and alcohol. And then there was the [12 Step] programme, and I took suggestions and I got clean, and I stayed clean. One day at a time. And they tell you, don't change relationships in the first year, or enter a new relationship. Your sobriety is really number one. And so I didn't . . . Stephie and I got married a year later, after I got clean. Went to see a minister, told her the score. I said, "I've been through some things. Smoked a lot of crack and heroin, but I've been clean for a year." And she goes, "Oh, OK. I see you've given this some thought."' Chuck looks away, out of the window, and allows himself a rueful laugh. 'Yeah . . .'

It was Chuck's addiction to crack cocaine that had broken something in Stephanie, who was determined not to be typecast as the long-suffering partner. 'It's like you're always trying to outsmart the person,' she says. 'Hiding keys and things. It's just no fun. I remember saying, "You can't be here; you have to go stay with your parents." And I remember thinking ... I had made a cup of tea, and it struck me, *I don't know where he is, he's not here and not* ... and I said to myself, *Oh my God, he's going to steal their car and take off.* Because, really, there's no conscience, no control. The person's just hollow inside when they're doing that.' Stephanie pauses and then continues. 'His parents never asked. I did tell his sister. I said, "This is happening; I'll leave it up to you if you want to tell your parents."'

Prophet concurs. 'Yeah, it was, "You're not welcome here. You can't just stay out all night, you can't take my ATM card and drain my bank account. You can't *be* here." So then I just drove out to my parents' place. It was brief, but very intense.'

The breathing space allowed Stephanie to take stock. 'That's when I went back to school. I said, I need to get a teaching credential, and so this is what I'm doing and ...' She trails off. 'And you know, the weirdest part is, *that's* when he got better. I didn't have time to deal with him anymore and ... he just found the strength to do it. I mean, he really is a success story with that, because he had a couple of relapses and then he was done. And then he quit drinking. And then it took a few more years for him to quit smoking but ... he quit it all.'

Back to *Homemade Blood*. After listening to the recordings, Slade and Kolderie got straight on the phone to Prophet's manager: 'How about we mix the record? When can Chuck fly out?'

'[That's] what they said to him,' Prophet recalled with a laugh. 'So I headed out to Boston, where we managed to fly well under the radar of normal industry demands. I think I said to them, "Hey, guys, we've only got three days to do this, but don't let that keep you from breaking out your MTV Buzz Bin voodoo fairy dust!"'[4]

Kolderie picks up the story in a Skype interview with me. 'This was the heyday of manual mixing—we did it all by hand, the three of us. There was no automation, there was no Pro Tools, it was a real "hands on the faders" thing. But at the time we were very used to that,' he adds, and because what they had was essentially a 'performance', as Kolderie calls it, with very few overdubs, it was a relatively straightforward task. By this time, Kolderie and Slade had a system: 'We would divide up the console and work together, without talking much: I would sit on the left—we had this big Neve console—I would have the drums and the vocal and maybe some solos, and he would have keyboards and the guitars, and we would very quickly get a hold of it.' Mixing today he compares to 'working on a painting', because the software remembers all the moves you make. Back in the 1990s, he explains, 'Mixing was more like a performance. You would learn your moves and then you would just have to do it in sequence.' While modern technology has many undeniable advantages, Kolderie reckons that part of what is lost in the digital mixing process is the capacity to make mistakes—'some of the better mixing things I ever did were mistakes'—and the sense of an 'active process . . . There were different skills involved, and it was harder to get a good mix'.

HOMEMADE BLOOD—THE ALBUM

Slade and Kolderie knew they had an extraordinary set of songs on their hands as they fired up the console at Fort Apache. 'Credit' could be the best riff Keef never wrote, but the chord progression is also a sly steal from Lou Reed's 'Sweet Jane' (although this particular musical thread winds all the way back to 'Louie Louie' and probably beyond). Prophet says that he thinks part of the motivation for writing such a riff-heavy song ('that chordal thing that just chugs down the road') was having played a lot of more 'precious, delicate' songs onstage over quite a long period of time touring *Balinese Dancer* and *Feast Of Hearts*. For Chuck, it recalls 'Unsatisfied' by The Replacements, or The Who's 'My Generation': songs where 'the *way* that somebody says something says more than words. When I sing "credit" and that place in my voice is so pleading and desperate . . . that's what makes it a *record* and not just something that looks good on paper'.

The opening track, as so often with Prophet's albums (and his shows), is a statement of intent. The guitars, as he describes them, are 'bright, they're full, they're brash'. The interplay of Chuck and Max is at the centre of the album and very evident in the opener. 'It's conversational. And that was really missing from *Feast Of Hearts*.' Featuring a witty, self-deprecating lyric, and some terrific half-throttled guitar solos, 'Credit' is both the perfect opener and a ringer for an encore.

Track two, 'You Been Gone', is another song that greatly benefits from the work done in the rehearsal studio. 'If I hadn't played that with the band early on,' Prophet says, 'then I don't think the call and response thing would have been so prominent. Max's slide figure that answers the vocal ... it's killer.' The song is also a lyrical scene-setter, in some respects, for the album: 'Sweet Lorraine's on SSI.' 'Yeah, everybody down there at the Albion was on SSI,' Prophet remarks. Supplemental Security Income is a form of disability benefit: 'It's, like, seven hundred dollars a month,' he explains. 'There were a lot of people on SSI down there that lived in SROs: single-room occupancy in the Mission. And we just knew a lot of 'em.'

Lorraine is typical of the characters that populate the album, every one of them leading a desperate dance around the cracks of their disintegrating world. 'Inside Track' maps similar terrain. It is perhaps the closest that Prophet and his co-writer, Lipschutz, have come to Dylan's stream-of-consciousness, whacked out, '65–66 lyrical style; or, as Prophet put it, 'just a bunch of post-apocalyptic lines all tied together'[5]:

The money-sniffing dog's barking up a child's skirt
The energizer bunny's lyin' face down in the dirt ...
Laid up with a fever I'm on fire from head to toe
Before my heart bursts into flame there's something you should know ...

The song's penetrating, phased guitar, and a great rock'n'roll scream around 2:20, makes it a highlight on an album that has no lowlights.

'Ooh Wee' is up next. 'I was nine years old in '73 / Strung out Ritalin and colour TV' is a terrific opening couplet, nailing character and situation with a stark immediacy—the kind of thing that Tom Petty at the height of his powers seemed to do effortlessly. One of those funky, swampy numbers defined by Prophet's innate rhythmic sense, 'Ooh Wee' features a Wurlitzer-like guitar figure that Max came up with as they worked on the song, fingerpicked on his Gibson SG, and an extraordinary guitar solo starting at the bridge and flowing into the instrumental verse that pins all the needles into the red in a dramatic crescendo and release, like a wave breaking. One can never be sure how autobiographical this one is (under questioning, Prophet is more likely to start talking to you about the character in the song), but, especially around the solo, it sounds ripped straight from the heart.

'New Year's Day' remains one of the greatest songs Prophet and Lipschutz have ever written. A heartbreaking lyric, haunting slide guitar, beautiful harmonizing from Stephanie Finch, it is a song perfectly poised between despair and hope ('Don't cry, it's New Year's Day again'). Kurt remembers, 'Chuck came up with the thing about the broom ... as soon as you got a guy sweeping a broom in his old high school, you got a story.' The genius is in the detail—as epitomised by the line 'I woke up in my Nissan to the static on the radio'; as Kurt puts it, it's all about 'specifics, as opposed to just gauzy moods and feelings'. '22 Fillmore', meanwhile, is crazed rifferama built around a maddening, obsessive, repetitive lyric. It would remain a regular showstopper in the live set for some years to come.

The title track, which Stephanie describes as a 'Gothic love song', features an appropriately spooky, treated vocal, unspooling mysterious, poetic lyrics ('You've got seven scarlet veils / I got a hammer and I got nails ...'). Lipschutz recalls coming up with the title: 'You just sort of ... turn all the filters off and hope there's something there. To me, once you get that ...' he trails off, nodding. 'That's one of my favourite songs.' While the recording is a superb performance, it is one of those songs always most fully realised onstage, with the arrangement giving Prophet room to unleash extended, squalling solos. The one captured to tape that day really just provides a blueprint for its live incarnations.

'Whole Lot More' is a sunny love song (Kurt confesses it's effectively a rewrite of Dylan's 'She Belongs To Me') that can catch you unawares with a sudden thrown shadow ('Where the dark hall leads to a room full of doors'). The lyrics are set atop a bouncy, mandolin-inflected rhythm, an infectious riff, and some sweet vocal harmonies. 'Textbook Case', meanwhile, may not reach the feedback-drenched heights of '22 Fillmore', but it's just as crazed; an insistent, ascending riff, slashed open by fierce guitar and another desperate vocal.

The album modulates again via 'Kmart Family Portrait', perhaps the definitive 'deep cut' in that Prophet has never played it live. An earlier version built more around a major chord sequence, in effect a very pretty but straightforward country lament, was transformed when Prophet flipped it into a minor key. Muted rhythm track, isolated vocal, a lone electric guitar. The singer of 'Longshot Lullaby', dissecting others' desperation and pain, looks in the mirror and stares into the abyss ('You turn your head, blink your eye, and there's nobody there at all'). Halfway through, the gorgeous melody is opened up by a piercing, weeping solo.

'Til You Came Along' kicks the album back into high gear, another love song. It represents the warmly lit side of the road to counterpoint the album's dangerous shadows, before it drifts into the mists and shades of the closing track, 'The Parting Song' (originally christened 'Resurrection Day'). The track features a repetitive bass line ('like a *TB Sheets* figure' is how Chuck describes it, referring to a pre–*Astral Weeks* Van Morrison track). 'That's Stephie playing the bass on the left hand of the piano,' he says. 'Totally live.' 'Rider won't you pass me by now, rider won't you stop for me?' maybe recalls Keats, 'half in love with easeful death', or Emily Dickinson:

Because I could not stop for Death,
He kindly stopped for me;
The carriage held but just ourselves
And Immortality.

Addiction makes you walk a fine line. Whatever: it signs the album off with an appropriate sense of unease and unresolvedness, as the repeated chorus ('You could be a friend to me / You could be my enemy') and climb-the-wall guitar fade into a gathering, foggy gloom. The original, unedited take runs for over thirteen minutes.

OUTTAKES AND ROAD TAKES

I've already mentioned the fact that this was a hugely productive time for Prophet, for Prophet and Lipschutz as songwriters, and for the band as a recording unit. 'There's a poster of all the outtakes on the wall,' Prophet notes, referring to one of the photos in the original CD booklet. 'I told the art guy, "It'll drive fans crazy, you've got to blur that photo." The photographer who took it [Tom Erikson] was not amused.'

Prophet admits that the von Sneidern–produced *Electric Demos* 'sound better than the record in some ways to me—less processed'. While the record remains definitive, there is certainly a greater sense of space between the instruments, more air, and some instrumentation mixed higher than the released versions, which means that they are almost as intriguing as the previously unheard songs from this period. 'Credit' is a little more laid-back, and the chorus has some 60s-style 'doo-doo-doo's that give it a poppier feel. 'Textbook Case' features some overdubbed backing vocals from von Sneidern, and some Micromoog synthesizer: 'We fiddled with noises mostly, trying to paint some sonic picture of this kid's mind,' says von Sneidern. 'Whole Lot More' (which Chris notes was 'a direct shot at recreating "Maggie May"') has Butler's mandolin much higher in the mix—in some ways, this version seems like a runaway stray from the *Balinese Dancer* album—and Stephanie's backing vocals soar. 'Ooh Wee' is in a different key (B minor, instead of the released version's D minor), which allows Chuck to lift his voice, and the verses give way to a falsetto in the chorus that lends the song a more desperate edge. The early version of 'Kmart Family Portrait' mentioned above features a lilting country-folk arrangement, sweet pedal steel, and some alternate lyrics. In the end, the electric demos are most striking for the fidelity of their recording, captured in a black-box space on home-studio equipment, for which von Sneidern deserves a lot of credit.

There are four outtakes that Slade and Kolderie mixed but that were left off the album, and it is a tribute to the quality of the songs that, listening to them for the first time, I was left wondering why they were omitted—and, at the same time, conceding that there is nothing I would want to remove from the released album to make room for them. But 'Trying To Get Away From It All' (also known as 'Doo Doo Doo') features a sly lyric and an infectious riff (one of Prophet's best) that lodges in your brain and sets up permanent residence. Together with 'Yesterday's Man', 'You're All I Need', and 'Dead and Gone (Get Along)', the full complement of sixteen songs could be re-sequenced to create an album that I would argue deserves to be seen as Prophet's *Blonde On Blonde*: that rare instance of a double album that *needs* to be one. And while both Dylan and Prophet would match or, arguably, best these achievements later in their careers, nevertheless both albums stand as definitive statements of artists at the height of their creative powers.

The album won favourable reviews on both sides of the Atlantic. Major industry weekly *Billboard* described it as 'easily his most accomplished solo album'.[6] *East Coast Rocker* found the album walking 'a secure line down the path of rock'n'roll righteousness',[7] and the *Austin Chronicle* memorably described the sound of *Homemade Blood* as a place 'where the coy but unflinching brutality of the singer/songwriter and the "Hey, where's the volume knob on this amp?" of the rock & roller collide and leave debris strewn about the place'.[8] Denise Sullivan hailed it as one of Prophet's 'finest achievements. . . . The band that backs Prophet's fiery guitar work is a roots-rock unit tightened up from ceaseless European touring, and this live-in-the-studio recording suits their take-no-prisoners delivery'. Two British music journalists who had been watching Chuck's progress over the years noted the album as a highpoint: writing in the *Guardian*, Adam Sweeting found 'evidence of a late developer who may just be reaching his peak'.[9] David Sinclair of the *Times* called it 'brilliant': 'a collection of lovingly crafted, rough-edged songs, steeped in an earthy cocktail of country, blues and Stones-ish rock'n'roll influences';[10] the newspaper's Sunday edition found 'a rare mix of dignified maturity and acerbic viciousness' and cited the album as evidence that 'thirtysomething rock'n'roll for grown-ups doesn't have to mean Clapton-esque flatulence'.[11] *Q* magazine admired its 'passionately ramshackle weavings on suburbia, lost love, life and death and the great beyond', and the 'Blistered Tele strangling amidst wah-wah noodlings'; *Mojo* declared the album 'essential listening for fans of Americana'.[12]

Prophet toured heavily behind the release, especially in Europe, warming up with two shows at the Hotel Utah on March 12 and 13 1997. 'It was fun,' he says, 'because we were sort of unleashed. And that record came out on Cooking Vinyl, and we went and played Glastonbury and Roskilde'—exhaustingly, on consecutive days. 'We played all through Europe, and it was a really big record in Germany. And we just played endless amounts of sweaty, packed shows. It was a really exciting time.'

He continues, 'Max had a period where he got a call to audition for an early version of The Wallflowers'—Jakob Dylan's band, who had a huge hit, 'One Headlight', in November 1996. The tour reached London, 'And The Wallflowers were playing across the street. And we said, "Hey, Max, it's not too late!"' Prophet and the band played two shows at the Monarch in Chalk Farm,

London, and even Sir Bob Geldof came out to hear them play. 'Yeah, I don't know why,' Chuck laughs. 'I remember it being a packed audience, it was wildly enthusiastic.' He broke a string during the encores and hardly skipped a beat. Passing his Telecaster to a willing member of the audience, who swiftly fitted a new string, Chuck urged the band to keep rolling through 'Look Both Ways', improvising verses about Mickey Mouse in Disneyland before grabbing the guitar back and bringing the song home.

The tour was an early peak in the long history of Prophet's live act, and we are fortunate that the regal form of Chuck Prophet & The Bible Dusters was captured in a live broadcast from Roskilde on June 29 1997, released on CD as *Homemade Boot* by the Australian label Corduroy. It is a full-on, powerhouse mix that perfectly frames the band's interplay and the thick, metallic sound Max and Chuck were alchemizing at the time, while also allowing space for Stephie's backing vocals—to particularly breathtaking effect on the gorgeous, slowed down version of 'Tune Of An Evening'. Prophet and the band kick these songs around the stage until they plead for mercy: 'Ooh Wee' stretches out from 5:15 to 6:25, 'Homemade Blood' from 5:54 to 7:55, and there is an extended coda to a gorgeous rendition of 'New Year's Day'.

Homemade Blood is crimson, raw, heart-on-sleeve stuff; it certainly isn't pretty, but it's starkly, often scarily beautiful, and, for better or worse, has remained a yardstick by which subsequent albums would be measured by many for the best part of two decades. It was also the end of an era. From here, Prophet would experiment far more freely with technology and other musical styles (notably loops and rhythm tracks), while keeping them in orbit around his rock, blues, and country roots. Guitar-wise, in the studio, he would start to take his foot off the pedal board—a cause of some distress for his ardent fans. For many who love and know the album well, it still feels like the one solo release where he captured lightning in a bottle, freeze-framing his distinctive sound. The moment when everything seemed to fall into place—the songs, the band, the voice, the inimitable guitar.

'Did it?' Chuck pauses. 'Well, I don't know if I agree. But I know what I was going for. And, in my estimation, we got pretty damn close.'

CHAPTER EIGHT

'JUST START TODAY'

GO GO MARKET, *THE HURTING BUSINESS* (1998–2000)

> 'I'll sleep when I'm dead.'
> Isn't that what Warren Zevon said?
> – Chuck Prophet

ALL ROADS LEAD TO ... NASHVILLE

Around the time Prophet was working on *Homemade Blood*, he received an advance from German music publisher BMG and made the first of several trips to Nashville to team up with a variety of different songwriters. Manager Mike Lembo was losing faith in him; as Chuck puts it, he was 'just never a true believer at all in terms of "Chuck Prophet recording artist". Or as a performer. He thought the only way I would generate income was if I got cuts with other artists as a songwriter'. Prophet believes Lembo was probably inspired by the fat commission he had made on the songwriting of Jules Shear, whose first solo album from 1983 included his song 'All Through The Night', which Cyndi Lauper would take into the Top 10 the following year; Shear had also written 'If She Knew What She Wants', a Top 30 hit for the Bangles in 1986. 'So Lembo told me, "We're going to send you to Nashville." And I don't mean to sound cynical but I thought to myself, *Maybe after I write some hits in Nashville I can go to Hollywood and write screenplays*. I thought it was a bit preposterous. These people writing hits for Garth Brooks? In their own way, they are geniuses.

'Nashville,' Chuck continues. 'So many great singers, so many great songwriters,' he marvels. 'And all those songs of love and redemption and mother and … the South. And girls who wonder why they shaved their legs for some Bubba. I love it. And, really, that's where you would find today's Dusty Springfield. It's a place where John Prine is king. And Waylon Jennings is a god. And all roads lead back to Hank Williams … or at least Don Williams! All to the good. So many great records. And all those raw Fender Telecasters. Soul records, too—Joe Tex. I should mention Jason & The Scorchers as well who, along with Rank & File, made country music safe for punk rockers.'

The Nashville trip also provided a *per diem* (daily allowance), a rental car, and a hotel. And if nothing else, Chuck reasoned, it was going to 'keep me off the streets'. He continues, 'So I flew in there on a rainy night and rented a car, and I had a showcase at the Bluebird.' Of all the legendary venues in Nashville, the Bluebird Cafe is probably the most famous: even casual country-music fans are likely to be familiar with it via the hit TV show *Nashville*, but, in the real world, it helped to launch the careers of Garth Brooks—an open-mic regular back in the day—as well as Kathy Mattea, Keith Urban, and Taylor Swift, among many other lesser stars. Its songwriter circle events remain a fixture to this day.

Prophet's own debut on that hallowed, tiny stage was less auspicious. 'When I got to the Bluebird there was nobody there except for the doorman and the soundman. I did my soundcheck, and then I learned that it was the night of the Country Music Awards. So … it was getting to be 8:30, 8:45, I think I had a 9pm show time. Empty, empty. Dead empty, *dead* empty. There was me, the bartender, the soundman, and the doorman, and we were all huddled together at the bar, just talking.'

As Prophet prepared to take the stage, 'This guy walks through the front door, dressed in overalls, and he comes over and starts talking to us.' That guy was Dan Penn, a legend of the Muscle Shoals scene and a frequent collaborator with Spooner Oldham; the classics they wrote together include 'I'm Your Puppet', 'Do Right Woman', and 'Dark End Of The Street'—the latter the song that Stephie still recalls as the spark that lit the fire of her singing partnership with Chuck. Penn and Prophet had teamed up a few years earlier and written 'Where The Rooster Crows' with Dan Stuart, released on *Scapegoats*.

'I doubt that Dan Penn was even aware the CMAs were on that night,'

Prophet continues. 'Maybe he wanted to come see me before he would commit ... I don't know. But that night at the Bluebird, I got up and played.' They spoke afterward, and Penn invited Prophet over to see what they could do together. 'The time I spent with Dan in his basement in his studio were some of the greatest musical moments of my life,' Chuck recalls. 'And to sit so close to him in that little room knee to knee—we'd put on headphones and he would record his vocal. Thrilling. He had a little drum kit that I would play.' Prophet and Penn wrote 'I Gotta Feeling For Ya', which Kelly Willis would record on her album *What I Deserve* (1998), and they would strike up a productive partnership: soul legend Solomon Burke cut another of their songs ('I Need A Holiday'). Of all the Nashville partnerships, Prophet felt that there was 'great chemistry' with Penn, and a 1999 interview for *Bucketfull Of Brains* found Penn praising Prophet's songwriting skills in return.[1]

On the same trip, Prophet saw Kim Richey play her last gig with legendary Nashville songwriter Angelo in the band. Angelo would in due course co-write for and produce Kings Of Leon; however, he would also write country hits for Trisha Yearwood, Martina McBride, Tim McGraw, and many others. A collaboration between Prophet, Angelo, and Kim ('Bette Davis Eyes') Carnes would give Chuck's *Age Of Miracles* album the sweet-natured pop song 'Just To See You Smile'. Richey would persevere with a solo career that has never broken the way she deserved; however, her songwriting efforts would continue to score regular chart successes—notably a no. 1 hit, co-written with Angelo, for Trisha Yearwood, 'Believe Me Baby (I Lied)'—and several were picked up for the TV show *Nashville*. Chuck ended up forging friendships with both Angelo and Kim Richey and would write with each of them subsequently.

Kim was signed to Bluewater Music—as she put it to me, 'kinda like the outsider, cool Nashville publishing company ... the go-to place if a singer wanted something outside of the mainstream'. (Other Bluewater writers included Bill Anderson, Jim Lauderdale, and Chris Knight.) The songwriting industry in Nashville is predicated in part on a treadmill of blind dates; writers frequently find themselves matched up with someone they have never met before. Richey had heard and loved Prophet's *Homemade Blood* album; she was drawn to it partly because it was so different from anything that was going on Nashville at the time, so when the opportunity to meet him arose, she was delighted. The two of them clicked at once. 'He's really good at lyrics *and* music,' Kim notes. 'Plus we're really different musically and also lyrically, so it's fun to play off of each other.' 'She's just so natural,' Chuck says of Kim. 'Singing, to her, is like breathing.'

Kim remembers that the first time they got together, Chuck had brought a drum machine—very unusual at the time—but he specified that they couldn't use it immediately; it would be a 'reward' once they got a song underway. Their co-write 'I'm Gone' became a Top 40 country hit for Cyndi Thomson in 2002. Further collaborations would include 'You Got Me Where You Want Me' and 'Pin A Rose On Me', both released on Chuck's *Age Of Miracles*; the latter was also recorded for Richey's *Edgeland*, which was released in 2018 and also features their country-rock strummer 'Can't Let You Go' and the gorgeous fingerpicked duet 'Whistle On Occasion'.

Dan Kennedy (much more about him soon) had been tasked with looking after Prophet on the Nashville trips; Lembo had declared that he found his artist too difficult to deal with on a daily basis. When Prophet failed to show up on time for one of his first writing sessions, Lembo was convinced he would be found in a bar or lying face down in a gutter, even though by this time Prophet was firmly embedded in the 12 Step programme. It turned out Chuck had simply lost track of time browsing one of his favourite record stores. Prophet recalls working with Kostas, whose impressive roster of hits includes 'Timber, I'm Falling In Love' (a country no. 1 in 1989 for Patty Loveless) and songs for the likes of the Dixie Chicks, The Mavericks, and Martina McBride, all of whom benefited from his knack for a melody and smart turn of phrase. There would be some unexpected alliances, too: Kentucky native Chris Knight's territory is hard-bitten, authentic tales of rural hardship, so he's not the first artist that would come to mind as a collaborator with urbanite Prophet, and yet one of their songs, 'Banging Away', would be a highlight of Knight's 2003 album *The Jealous Kind*.

Other partnerships would never get off the ground. 'I met tons of people but we didn't always hit it off,' Prophet shrugs. 'But there's a level of professionalism there. Folks like Bill Lloyd have the whole canon of American music under their fingers. I don't really know country music but put me in a room with somebody and all that Green On Red training, and just being in a band since I was twelve years old ... well, it turns out there was a place where all that experience kicking songs around would come in handy. That place was Nashville. And then in the early touring days oftentimes we would stop a tour there and then I would stay to write and drive the van back.'

Two other notable collaborations around this time included a session with Warren Zevon for his 2000 release *Life'll Kill Ya*. 'I really didn't play much on that record,' Prophet would later admit, 'because what he wanted to do was rework his demos. So I was just lurking around in case they needed some guitar replaced or something. I always refer to it as the best paid internship I ever had.'[2] Chuck told me he remembers vividly 'attempting to overdub guitar clueless of the chord changes, with Warren three feet from my face snarling'. Zevon, he said in 2003, was 'one of the sharpest, funniest, wittiest people I've ever been around [but also] one of the most intimidating. . . . I tried to just kinda of blend into the wall when we were in the studio'.[3]

On a more comfortable note, there was a fruitful partnership with Penelope Houston of the pioneering San Francisco punk band The Avengers. Prophet co-wrote three songs for her 1999 release *Tongue*, including the title track, and played most of the guitar on the album, which wrapped fairly straightforward new wave/rock songs in drum loops and Moog synthesizers and layered them with 60s-style stacked harmonies. Chuck and Stephie played a few dates with her as part of her backing band. The invitation came via Penelope's husband, Patrick Roques, who had done some artwork for Prophet, and the collaboration seemed like a natural evolution. Houston had signed a deal with Warners in Germany and, as Chuck puts, it, 'was set to get to the *next level*,' adding, lightly, 'You know how *that* goes ...'

GOING TO A GO GO

The time between wrapping up the *Homemade Blood* tour and gearing up for the next solo album, then, was a period notable for collaborations. Most significant of all was a separate project that centred around Prophet and Finch working more closely together than they had since the Albion days, and at the same time taking the music in a completely new direction, with Stephie as lead vocalist. The initiative seems to have come from Kurt Lipschutz, when he and Finch began to collaborate; Stephie remembers that 'Let's Stay Here' was a song that Kurt started and sent over to her. Chuck came in on the deal, and the three of them finished it together. As the project took off under the moniker Go Go Market, Stephie recalls, 'We were generally in the same room writing the songs. Things were manic, but it was a creative, energized time for me. We would get together with the Go Go Market band members and just improvise—sometimes on one chord, and we would record the rehearsals. And then later we would write stuff over the top of it.'

However, the three-way writing process was not all plain sailing. Finch finds it difficult to put into words what the atmosphere was like at that time, but felt, 'Kurt just always seemed ready for a fight. He and Chuck had had more of that banter already, so for me it was harder and more hurtful. Chuck let things roll off his shoulders more.' In due course, the friction between the two men would lead to a complete breakdown by the time *The Hurting Business* and Go Go Market's *Hotel San Jose* were released, deepening into a rift that would last the best part of a decade. But for now, the Go Go Market project was rolling, gaining added momentum when Prophet played some of Finch's songs for up-and-coming engineer and producer Jason Carmer. Jason loved what Chuck played for him and booked a session, inviting Bay Area DJ Mark 'Ill Media' Reitman to join them. Reitman brought in his turntables, and Prophet was fascinated and intrigued. 'I just hovered over that guy to figure out what he was doing. That night I went home and grabbed a bunch of my records and brought them in.'

Prophet told Finch early on that he thought they should push out of their comfort zone and collaborate with new musicians—'a bunch of personalities who were not set in their ways'. They took out an ad in the *Bay Guardian*; Vince Russo, a former law-enforcement officer in early retirement, was the only one to turn up to audition on bass, so they told him the gig was his if he wanted it. Completing the rhythm section was 4 Non Blondes drummer Dawn Richardson, who also responded to the ad. The novelty of working with new people lent an air of spontaneity that Prophet had missed for some time, and they would open for other bands around the city, including 60s legends ? & The Mysterians ('super-fun!' according to Chuck), Joe Henry, and Jonathan Richman. 'It *was* a lot of fun,' Stephie concurred. 'The live shows were real chaotic. Sometimes we'd just vamp on one chord until it turned into a big wall of noise. We sounded like a challenged version of Booker T.'[4] She also recalls, 'We were so crispy after all the touring behind *Homemade Blood*. And the band was getting set in its ways, so Go Go Market was kind of renegade.'

Finch described the album's genre in interviews as 'housewife goth'; her reference points were Dusty Springfield, Bobbie Gentry, Carole King, and Blondie.[5] 'At first I thought [Go Go Market] would be partly that and partly a kind of great postmillennial frat-party band,' Prophet elaborates, recalling the college parties he played in Berkeley in the days before Green On Red.

'We pulled it off here and there,' Finch muses. 'It was probably our effort to avoid all the trappings of singer/songwriters and Lilith Fair music that was so prevalent at the time.'

'We were up for whatever,' Prophet says, 'and we enjoyed the looseness of being a local band on the scene.'

Some early attempts to record with the band were probably less successful than the gigs, and it wasn't until the live band fell apart that Chuck and Stephie took another run at recording the songs with some of their older friends and associates, notably Sheryl Crow band member Jim Bogios on drums and percussion. Jason Borger (of whom more soon) contributed keyboards and string arrangements, and old friend Roly Salley played upright and six-string bass on one of the album's highlights, 'Talkin' To You'; on the rest of the songs, bass duties were split between Andy Stoller, Frank Swart, and 'Teenage' Rob Douglas. The latter, whose nickname derived from the famed LA sax-playing session musician Teenage Steve Douglas, would become a member of Prophet's touring band for the next five years. Just a couple of tracks survived from the gigging version of Go Go Market: Moses Dillard's song 'Dead' and the closing track, 'Trouble', feature the original Richardson/Russo rhythm section. The former, with its Moog, repetitive Hammond figure, and ghostly traces of Reitman's sounds, gets closest to the sound the band had made onstage.

The opener, 'Channel 9', sets out the Go Go Market stall very efficiently: the opening bars are funky, the rhythm section laying down a groove before some keyboard flourishes bloom and an acoustic guitar picks up the beat. Stephie's vocals are given a push in the centre of the mix—and Chuck, producing, keeps it that way for the rest of the album. The rap comes courtesy of 'Spidey', a friend of Mark Reitman's. 'We recorded his rap over the phone,'

Stephie remembers. 'We knew who he was because he had jumped up onstage at Mick's Lounge while we were playing a show and improvised this whole rap that was pretty impressive.' The post-apocalyptic love song 'Let's Stay Here' is blessed with one of the collection's strongest melodies and recalls the American Sound Studios of 1969-era Elvis. It is built around Jason Borger's piano, a gorgeous string arrangement, and Prophet's own distinctive contributions: some *Elvis In Memphis*–style drama via measured, sparse electric guitar strums and, of all things, kettle drums. 'The strings were samples,' Finch notes. 'A needle drop on a Montovani record or something similar. It just happened to fall on a sympathetic key.'

A distinctively female sensibility ripples through the songs: there are scattered, barbed references throughout to gender differences ('We laughed at the boys / With their shiny red toys' in 'Him'); writer David Cantwell would interpret the lines 'Now I'm taking to you ... For all the good that talking ever does' as a sly dig at the way 'women's desires are ignored by men'.[6] 'Him' shifts unnervingly and unexpectedly between major- and minor-key passages as it explores the deterioration of a close friendship between two women and their rivalry over a male lover. 'I came home one day after tutoring and thought about how girls that age start to hate each other when one of them gets a boyfriend, all the jealousy,' Stephie told Bob Mehr in 2002. Similarly dark is 'Wasn't So Smart', which finds the character in the song lamenting, 'I've got the bruises to prove I'm in need of a kiss.' However, this doesn't sound like a broken-hearted victim: there is a subtle layer of irony, and the Brill Building 'ooh naa naa naa' backup harmonies, along with the string arrangement, warn the listener not to take the story at face value.

Little heard it may have been, but those that did pick up the CD release of *Hotel San Jose* were intrigued and tickled by the album: Bob Mehr characterised the sound as 'deep soul—an album pickled in Southern Comfort, cured in Kool 100s, and oozing with a late-night quality that's undeniably affecting'.[7] The same review singled out Prophet's guitar work, 'judiciously deploying a small army of strangulated riffs and woozy, wobbly fills'. Thom Jurek, writing for *AllMusic*, described the band as 'a cool rock and rhythm project' serving up 'slinky, darkly tinged, street-smart vignettes from the seamy side of modern life in the West', and gave it four stars.[8]

Go Go Market probably suffered more than other Team Prophet projects from a lack of strategic vision and management. It was released on another British label, Evangeline, and then secured a US release a few months later on Berkeley-based Innerstate—home to assorted releases by Prophet associates Chris von Sneidern, Steve Wynn, and Chris Cacavas. 'Those things were poorly planned,' Chuck admits. 'But creatively we were really ... if not hot, we were *something*! We were excited about that stuff.' Years later, playing 'Chuck & Stephie' acoustic duo shows, sometimes with a drum machine, gave Prophet a renewed appreciation for those songs: 'Yeah, songs like "Wasn't So Smart", I'm amazed by them. A lot of chords, a lot of words, and really *refined* songs. It was a creative time.' Stephie notes that 'Let's Stay Here' and 'Talkin' To You' are songs she still returns to: 'They best represented my aesthetic then and now.'

To help promote the album, Finch moved front and centre to open shows on the 2002 European tour. When I asked her if she had been reluctant to come out from behind her familiar stage-right keyboard position, she replied, 'I didn't need persuading, but I didn't have a lot of experience at playing totally on my own, because I didn't feel like my guitar playing was quite good enough to do that. But I did it ... and the audiences were really great. I didn't know what to expect. I remember saying to the guys in the band at the London show, "Anything can happen. If people start talking during my set, I don't want you guys to feel sorry for me." So, I was prepared. But I was lucky, it was very quiet when I played and I was very grateful for that ... it was a lot of fun.' The gamble paid off handsomely and brought more well-deserved attention to Finch's singing and songwriting skills; and it didn't harm that it shifted some Go Go Market CDs from the merch table.

Another collaborative project around this time, Raisins In The Sun, brought together a number of manager Mike Lembo's clients. As Prophet writes in the liner notes to the album, 'Sometimes the planets line up and can induce a spontaneous combustion that defies all logic. In May of 1999, under the influence of a heavy case of premillennial fever, and armed only with yellow legal pads, guitars, sticks, and a portable student piano, Jules Shear, along with Chuck Prophet, Jim Dickinson, Harvey Brooks, Sean Slade, Paul Q. Kolderie, and Winston Watson convened in the Arizona desert with a mission to write and record an album completely from scratch.' The resulting eponymous collection is a rich and enjoyable set of songs that feels, perhaps above all, quintessentially Dickinson-esque (his worn vocal on 'Nobody Loses' is the album's tender spot). The Rounder Records press release compared the sound to 'the rural funk of The Band' as well as Graham Parker outfit The Rumour, or 'the Stones at their loosest'. The band members casually swap lead vocals and riffs and solos between and within songs. 'Candy From A Stranger' is a highlight, Prophet and Shear coolly trading lines over a funky groove.

The album earned praise from the likes of Ken Tucker in *Entertainment Weekly*, *CMJ New Music Monthly* ('gritty, soulful roots rock that's as timeless as it is refreshing'),[9] and especially *No Depression*, which featured the album in a full-page review by Don McLeese, who appreciated all the nuances of rock history in the coming together of these veterans generating 'ten tracks of spontaneously combustive material that sounds less like an sampler of disparate styles than a band firing on all cylinders'. McLeese acknowledged the irony as he hailed them as 'the freshest new band I've heard in ages'. For the Prophet fan, the album is most notable for the way it is rooted in the vibe of his solo albums up to this point in his career, even as his own restless creativity was already leading him in a new direction.

BUSINESS IS GOOD?

The Hurting Business, Prophet recalls, had been in the back of his mind for some time before it started to come together. Even before the idea of recording a 'live on the floor' album, and the triumphant realisation of that dream in *Homemade Blood*, the songs and, more importantly, the modus operandi of what would become his next album, *The Hurting Business*, were taking shape, moulded in large part by the Go Go Market experience. He bought a sampler to supplement his 4-track, he says, 'And I kinda burrowed down.' *The Hurting Business* would represent a clean break from the sound of the previous album, and a different approach. 'Those songs were just not written for two guitars, bass, drums. When we tracked the songs, sometimes it would be just me, some sort of rhythm box, and maybe a drummer playing on top of it with brushes, and that would be the track, and then we would overdub on top of that.'

Prophet's antennae were up, and he had found himself easing into a different music community in the local area. 'There were these guys that took over the studio over here on Mission—it was called Coast, and they changed the name to Toast. And they were doing a lot of dance records and weird stuff ... Phil Steer, Jason Carmer ... and Go Go Market did some stuff over there on spec. There was a cluster of guys and a kind of energy in the room.' It was here that Prophet met Jacquire King, who would engineer and co-produce *The Hurting Business*. Around the time he hooked up with Prophet, King had engineered for Tom Waits on *Mule Variations* (1999); in due course, he would work with Kings Of Leon, before graduating to production duties for them and working with a wide variety of other bands. His collaborations with Prophet began with some session work: 'I went over there and I played guitar on some kind of dance remix or something,' Chuck recalls. 'It might have been a Pete Townshend song. I don't recall. And they had a computer, and they had Pro Tools, and I'd never seen anything like that before. I go into this studio and suddenly I'm recording straight into a computer and there's waveforms on the screen. And the two-inch tape machine is in the corner, and it's collecting dust.'

Prophet admits, 'If I hadn't done the occasional session then I really wouldn't have been exposed. Those guys don't call me very often! I'm not really a session musician: someone who is familiar with counter melody and harmony and transposing and all that stuff at the drop of a hat? That's not me. So, yeah, I knew that [the digital revolution] was gonna happen. And when I had a bunch of these songs together, Jacquire helped me make sense of it all; we did a lot of it on a computer.' Chuck had recorded many of the demos on his own or with Mark Pistel, who had a small home studio. 'I had a drum machine. Put a little bass on. Acoustic. Overdub a little guitar, little wah-wah ...'

Work proceeded at pace once it got properly underway, and the recording process was over in just two or three weeks. 'Everything about it was unconventional. But I like it [the released album]. There's a lot of vintage analogue keyboard textures on that record that are pretty unique. We did some recording at Pigs Head, which was really just American Music Club's rehearsal space. Very primitive. Oftentimes it was so cold in there you could see your breath in front of your face. We put a little mixing console in there, and we would just put a microphone in front of whatever we were recording. But it worked. It was *cinéma vérité*. Just capturing things in a natural environment.'

Another crucial figure in the making of *The Hurting Business*—someone who would become a key collaborator on *Age Of Miracles*, and also provide the beautiful string arrangement for 'No Other Love'—was Jason Borger. 'Borger was just a wonderful arranger,' Chuck confirms. He is a good example of the kind of figure that has become a constant in Prophet's solo work: the trained musician with technical knowledge that Chuck would be the first to agree he never acquired formally himself. Prophet's natural musicality often flourishes most abundantly when he works with collaborators who can fill in the theory.

'By the time that record was finished,' Prophet recalls, 'that's when Mike Lembo and I ended up in that lawsuit.' It is not something that he talks about easily—in contrast to the vast majority of our conversations. In the midst of it all, Lembo destroyed some of Prophet's master tapes—something that only came to light later when Prophet was invited to work on a 5.1 surround sound version of *Homemade Blood* and found the multitracks were missing. 'We had to settle somehow. There was money I owed. We sat down with his lawyer and my lawyer, and Mike was in the room and I was in the room, and we hashed something out: "Well, you'll pay half of this in advance and then we'll go our separate ways, but you're still going to have to pay 10 percent of your income until the debt is paid down" or something. And then that was it. The partnership was dissolved.'

Legal complexities aside, the good news was that the mood at Cooking Vinyl was upbeat over the *Hurting Business* project, following the critical and relative commercial success of *Homemade Blood*, even if actual financial tour support was minimal. But without an agent or manager, when it came to bookings, Prophet was working in the dark, particularly when it came to navigating work permits in the UK. It was at that point he decided to call Dan Kennedy.

Dan Kennedy, over the two decades he worked with Prophet (the partnership came to an end in 2020), was a pivotal, stabilizing figure for him. Though not a practising musician, Kennedy nevertheless always had a deep, abiding passion for music, and as a college kid had developed a sideline promoting gigs at UC Davis, California, earning himself the nickname 'Little Bill Graham'. Kennedy's stepfather from about the age of twelve was Alex Anderson, creator of the iconic American cartoon characters Rocky & Bullwinkle (the TV show originally ran from 1959 to '64, and has been repeatedly revived or rebooted, most recently as an Amazon Prime series in 2018). Anderson had been 'ripped off and taken advantage of' by business partner Jay Ward, according to Kennedy; when the characters his stepfather had created were sold on to TV networks without giving him a credit, Anderson fought an ultimately successful legal battle to have his role as creator of the characters properly credited. Dan believes it is this backstory that explains his deep-rooted desire to protect artists from being exploited: 'He is so hell bent on being fair,' Prophet said in 2012. 'And he is fair. Sometimes to a fault if you ask me. I suppose that explains why we affectionately refer to him around here as "Iowa Boy".'[10]

In the late 1980s and early 90s, while working a day job as a materials manager in Tucson, Kennedy had attempted to get a small recording studio and record label off the ground, and one of the local bands he worked with caught the attention of Mike Lembo. Shortly after that, Dan began working for Lembo, with some of his first assignments being to accompany Prophet on the Nashville songwriting trips. But in between *Homemade Blood* and *The Hurting Business*, Kennedy stepped away from the music industry, switching career paths to train as a high-school teacher. He had eventually found Lembo's business practices and the man himself impossible to work with (not for nothing has Chuck sometimes referred to Dan as the 'anti-Lembo'). However, a year later, Kennedy took a call from Prophet, who announced he was leaving Lembo too, and needed some help booking a European tour to promote *The Hurting Business*. Following that, and some local US shows, Prophet asked Kennedy to consider a co-management arrangement, to help him look after his business. 'I had enough knowledge of what he had been through,' Dan told me, 'and I had the belief that he could be more and I had the desire to make it happen; *and* I could be trusted.' Their partnership, dubbed 'Mummyhead Music', became fundamental and vital to Prophet's career.

The Hurting Business was a record that had come together more gradually than its predecessor but, as Chuck put it with characteristic understatement, 'things bottleneck'. In the blur of activity to finish it, Prophet acknowledges, 'There were some all-nighters. But there always are. If we wanted to come out that year, we needed to meet the deadline. Dan Alexander, the guy that had given me studio time back in the day [for *Balinese Dancer*], had a Neve console and we mixed it in his studio with Justin Phillips assisting, who later became the engineer on *Age Of Miracles*. And Jacquire is a very intense personality. Mixes very quiet and very intensely. It's not a party. And so we were getting the mixes, and I was sending DAT tapes with two or three songs at a time to the label. I would drive to a high-end courier in South San Francisco, and then they would send the tape to England, because they'd already booked the promo tour'—acoustic showcases and radio sessions including a music convention in Munich. 'Back then, we'd get a record out in a matter of weeks,' Chuck reflects. 'They made a five-song sampler from those first few days. And then we finished the record, mastered it, and I was immediately on a plane, went to Germany and the UK.' The former had become a significant pocket in the market: *Homemade Blood* had got the critics' attention, and *The Hurting Business* would be reviewed far and wide there, making the Top 20 in the German edition of *Rolling Stone*'s albums of the year; Prophet's archive features a fat bound book of press coverage compiled for Cooking Vinyl with a scrawled note on the cover: 'They love you in Germany!'

THE HURTING BUSINESS—THE ALBUM

'Rise' is the perfect opener; it immediately establishes the album's predominant medium—dubs and drum loops—but simultaneously the lyrics (and the blues-soaked melody) could date back decades beyond the opening Sam Cooke steal:

> *A change a change is gonna come*
> *Those very words once left me numb*
> *I'll weigh myself when I get home*
> *You can wrap your legs around these bones*
> *Rise, you broken children, rise*

As the novelist Stephen King once remarked about the song in an iTunes playlist of his favourites, 'What does this song mean? I have no idea. But it's lovely, incantatory, and mysterious. God bless Chuck Prophet.'[11] Rooted in a jam session for Go Go Market, with Stephanie Finch singing gospel-style over the top, it just needed the structure to be established. 'I remember I was singing, "Ride! Get on, and ride!"' Chuck recalls. It was Kurt Lipschutz who swapped 'ride' for 'rise', and one simple consonant transformed the song into something that sank its roots deep into musical tradition.

Prophet characterises 'Apology' as 'Randy Newman meets Glen Campbell in a wine bar and they start arguing about the South'.[12] The drama of 'Statehouse (Burning In The Rain)' recalls some of the pulp fiction of which Prophet has always been so fond, while the dark, spooked doom ballad 'It Won't Be Long' is even more mysterious. Chuck's stream-of-consciousness comment on it sheds a little light: 'Jenny Jones nightmare appearance hangover recounted in three verses,' he notes, referencing a daytime tabloid talk show popular in the USA in the 1990s that chased ratings by featuring paternity tests and dysfunctional families; a show ahead of its time, maybe, in all the wrong ways. 'Shore Patrol' heavily features the turntable skills of DJ Rise (of whom more in a moment) and furious, distorted, bullet-mic-style vocals.

Prophet remembers that, with 'La Paloma', he was aiming for 'something electro-rockabilly . . . just improvising a verse, and then looking at it and realising there is a rhyme scheme in there. And then things start pushing the song forward in a line'. 'I Couldn't Be Happier' has an autobiographical element—not something Prophet does very often. 'Having recently gotten hitched,' he remarked, 'I got to thinking someone should write a song for the grooms. Where lovers sway in the key of A minor. The first time I ever sang it is the version you hear.'[13]

One of the most effective songs on the album, 'Dyin' All Young', also has the most fascinating story behind it: Chuck's old high-school friend Parker Gibbs had been working with an urban artist, and one day handed Chuck a stack of records. 'He goes, "I don't know what these are, you might want to check them out." And one of them was a homemade, white label kind of hip hop record.' Chuck was floored by it, and arranged for the artist, known as DJ Rise, to come over to his studio space. 'He brought a box of records and I was playing guitar, and we were just jamming,' Prophet recalls. 'And he had an a-capella record of this guy called O.C. There were all these rhymes. And then it got to that thing, "He never got to see the summer." And he kept doing that line over and over, and then I started playing these two chords on guitar. And then I tape-recorded it and wrote a song over the top of it. I just thought it was great,' Prophet enthuses. 'There was just something about somebody else's voice who had seen ... death. Somebody who had been on the frontlines and came back, expressing himself and what he had seen, and it was all in his voice. There was just something about it that was so more effective than me just saying it, so ... we left it in.'

When it came time to trace O.C. to clear the rights, the problems began. 'Songwriting and record-making is like a pot,' Prophet reflects. 'You throw everything in there. And sometimes you might borrow this bit of melody, or you might borrow this line, and that's the bone that you put in the soup. And then, before you serve it, you take the bone out. Only in this case, we left the bone in.' In the months that followed, as Prophet would admit in a *No Depression* feature in 2002, 'I learned a lot about litigation and sample clearance ... a kind of expensive lesson.'[14]

He explains, 'Mike Lembo had kept a list of people who had at one time shown an interest in me. And so he sent it to this New York label, and the two partners sat down and listened to the record and they really liked it.' But then, when it got to 'Dyin' All Young', they realised what they were hearing was one of their own records. Much as they loved it, the copyright complications were unavoidable. 'Cooking Vinyl let me know that it was up to me to clean up my own mess,' Chuck notes. 'So the guy at the label called me. Pretty nice guy. And he said, "Yeah, well, we're fans. We're not looking here to gouge anybody." He quoted some figure in the multi-thousand dollars, and I said, "I'm sure that's fine, but it would take me a while to raise that kind of money. I could maybe pay you five dollars a month." Just basically approached it the way I would approach the phone company. And he says, "You're a pretty funny guy." Fast-forward: we worked it out for five thousand dollars or something. And, in the end, it was worth it. I think even Martin Goldschmidt agreed. It's a wonderful track.' It remains one of the most powerful songs Prophet ever wrote and recorded, on an album that marked a major evolution in his artistic career.

With the record ready to go in Europe, Cooking Vinyl was looking for distribution in the States and decided to go with Oakland-based High Tone, a label primarily known for its roots and blues roster; founded in 1983, its greatest success was probably with Robert Cray, who released two albums via the label before he moved up to Mercury Records in 1986. Chuck recalls how he took label head Larry Sloven out for lunch: 'He says, "So . . . you think we should do a poster?" And I go, "Well, yeah, the poster's important so the booking agent can send it to the clubs." And he says, "Well, record stores . . . they barely even put the posters up anymore." And I go, "OK . . . I think posters are . . ." and Larry interrupts me: "So . . . you think I should do the poster?" "Yeah, I think you should do the poster." And I'm thinking, *Oh, God. I'm having a hard enough time getting myself motivated, I don't know what it's gonna take to get this guy pumped up!'*

The reviews for *The Hurting Business* were overwhelmingly positive, if sometimes taken aback by the music's sharp left turn. Where a review featured a star rating, the score rarely dipped beneath four stars. The *Des Moines Register* found the combination of 'a divine reverence for roots music with a sense of urgency born of electronic twiddling' and 'a deft mix of old and new'.[15] The *New Times Los Angeles* found 'a talent fully realized, both in performance and songwriting', and an album that 'should have a place on this and other critics' top 10 lists for 2000'.[16] 'Prophet2YK is a man bitten by the cut-and-paste bug,' the *No Depression* magazine reviewer Neal Weiss noted, suggesting connections to Jon Spencer Blues Explosion and Beck. Predicting that established fans might 'quickly return to his earlier works for comfort', Weiss called the album 'Prophet's personal, artistic unshackling. The limitations of genre have been smashed . . . and his inner funk soul brutha has been left to run amok in the rubble'.[17]

The *Boston Phoenix* reviewer loved the 'well-crafted tunes, with lyrics that match' but found Prophet's singing most striking: 'a full, dusky croon . . . that belies his rumpled angel appearance, revealing the devil's glint in his eye'.[18] In the *Austin Chronicle*, reviewer Jim Caliguiri described the album as 'chock-full of songs that are rootsy, inventive, and well matched to finely drawn story lines' and called it 'Prophet's most adventurous work. . . . At times, Prophet strides daringly close to the territory covered by Tom Waits . . . yet where Waits dares to conjure images of a hell on Earth with a clang and a shout, Prophet's vision is easier on the ears and much closer to paradise,' he concluded.[19] *Guitar Player* magazine could see the connections with artists like Beck but felt Prophet had made the transition from 'bona fide traditional skills … without coming across as a bandwagon jumper. . . . Prophet is a triple-threat talent with a sound all his own'.[20] *Cleveland Scene* also made connections with Waits's *Mule Variations* (an obvious reference point, given Jacquire King's involvement), as well as Beck and Joe Henry, declaring, 'Chuck Prophet has once again surpassed the current crop of American songwriters to create a benchmark for others to follow. Maybe this time they will.'[21]

THE TOURING BUSINESS

The turn of the millennium was the beginning of tough times for the music industry. In 1999, the year *The Hurting Business* was released in Europe (it came out at the beginning of 2000 in the USA), music sales reached their peak—approximately $14.5 billion, according to RIAA statistics. From here, for the next fifteen years or more, the only way would be down; by 2013, the total would be less than half the 1999 figure ($7 billion). Some kind of recovery only began in 2016, with a climb to $7.7 billion, as subscription-based streaming services began to show some returns.

More locally, at the dawn of Y2K, the notorious dotcom boom was still swelling, with San Francisco a key territory for the growth of internet start-ups. Mick Sinclair's *San Francisco: A Cultural and Literary History* describes how 'across San Francisco, rents doubled between 1995 and 1999, evictions increased four-fold, and many long-time residents were forced out of the city … while the demolition of low-rent projects drastically reduced the city's affordable-housing stock'. By 2001, the bubble had burst, and areas such as South Of Market would become a wasteland of empty office spaces; Sinclair notes that the only thing booming in SoMa that year were pink-slip parties, 'intended to bring newly unemployed dotcommers into contact with those still able to offer jobs'.[22] However, around the time Prophet was working on *The Hurting Business*, a lot of his friends who had been in the music industry dropped out and started getting jobs with tech companies: a demoralising time for the struggling but fully committed musician. 'It's like a cult,' says Prophet. 'Microsoft took these little companies and they would fly them up to Seattle, and they would have a van pick them up at the airport, and they would take them through the nice neighbourhoods. And the message was: "This is all going to be *you*.' And, yeah, we lost [bassist] Andy Stoller to Microsoft around that time. But the real point is that the fringe scene, that whole art scene that had brought me here in the first place, all our more Bohemian friends, that was all disappearing.'

However, spirits had been high when the album was launched in Europe, and Chuck flew with the band to the continent. UK DJ Mark Radcliffe had picked up on the track 'Dyin' All Young' (an email from the label to Prophet and Kennedy notes how it had set the phones ringing at BBC Radio 1). I caught the show at Underworld, a sweaty basement in London's Camden Town. It was a wild night. Prophet, hunched beneath a low ceiling, took to the stage in a suit one size too small and at least three times as insulated as it should have been, given the kind of venues they were playing. ('Yeah,' Stephie confirms, 'he would sweat so much on that '99 tour—we'd always hang the suit in the back of the van and it would be totally frozen in the morning because of the sweat.') I remember ear-splitting volume and Chuck in irrepressible form. Opening act Steve Wynn, a former Paisley Underground comrade, joined the band for a raucous encore of 'Look Both Ways', which he, Prophet, and Chris Cacavas had written together a decade before. A crowd that seemed one half fanatic and one half just curious was gradually won over, and it felt by the end of the night that if Prophet had intimated that he was the new messiah, they would have carried him bodily into the streets and proclaimed him so to the outside world. At one point he prostrated himself on the stage, shouting into his bullet mic while staring at the ceiling. Talking to me after the gig, he confessed he had been struggling with a sore throat and was probably 'a little high on cough syrup'. Keith Cameron, in a four-star write-up for the *Guardian* newspaper, proclaimed, 'In a perfect world, Chuck Prophet would be inducted to the Rock and Roll Hall of Fame tomorrow.'

In general, Prophet appeared to be in good shape. 'I was drug-free, if not serene,' is how he puts it. But the European tour was extensive and exhausting. 'I remember that tour really well,' reports Stephie. 'I think we flew home Christmas Eve. Eight weeks in Europe. But it was pretty successful. We were a little more dialled-in.'

Stephie recalls one incident on the tour with exceptional clarity. 'Barry Everitt managed us on that tour … he booked the Borderline for a long while.'

For many years, the Borderline was the key London venue for American roots acts including Prophet, and although he would eventually outgrow the venue, for a number of years it was an essential stop, usually playing two consecutive nights. Finch recalls that on the *Hurting Business* tour, Barry Everitt-Marshall started out with some significant health issues: 'Something wrong with his urethra. And the doctor had given him instructions on how to take care of himself, and, well, he didn't.' Barry drank to excess at a gig in Austria, and the next day they were due to drive to the Czech Republic. When he woke up in retention and doubled over in pain, the band drove him to the local hospital, where he had his bladder drained. 'Barry was kind of this warrior,' Stephie laughs. 'It was always, "On with the show!" So he was wearing a bag to pee in.'

The key moneymaking show of the tour, in Belgium, was looming, and 'his fee, everything was on the line'. Prophet hesitated, unsure whether Barry should stay in the hospital, but he insisted he was fine to continue. 'So it's midwinter and we're driving through the Czech Republic,' Stephie continues. 'It just got really dark for a while. Not like, dark outside. Just *dark*. Barry was lying on the back seat and Paul and Max were driving. On the road to Prague, we stop, and Barry goes to use the bathroom. And he was gone a long time. Chuck was getting very anxious, feeling really responsible for letting him come along. None of us had really eaten that day, and Chuck was knocking on the door of the bathroom. No response. So he comes walking back toward the van ... and I see him, he looks kinda weird. And then he just fainted ... out of fear, I guess, and hunger. Anyway, it turned out Barry wasn't in that bathroom, and he came running out when he saw Chuck; lifted him up, back into the van, and then we got back on the road and made it to the show.' From there, it was an all-night drive to Belgium, with Paul Revelli taking the wheel. 'That was the big-paying show,' Stephie remarks, 'so we did that, and Barry retired from touring. I think his health got better, but it took a long time.'

Europe was one thing, but establishing themselves on the circuit back home in the States was another challenge entirely for Chuck Prophet & The Mission Express. It is an object lesson in managing the logistics of touring at this level: so much can depend on diplomacy and the cultivation of loyalties and friendships. On Martin Goldschmidt's recommendation, Prophet and Kennedy had set about repairing the relationships with agents that Lembo had destroyed in his misguided attempt to hook Prophet up with 'the big shots'. For instance, Mongrel Music, whom he had worked with for many years, didn't return Prophet or Kennedy's calls at first. Old compadre and Mongrel-mate Alejandro Escovedo was at least partly responsible for rebuilding that particular bridge: when boss Chris Faville mentioned to Escovedo that Prophet had been calling, looking for a way back in, Alejandro replied, 'I don't know, Chris. I've always just found it's best to forgive.' Chuck laughs ruefully as he recounts the story. He remembers taking Faville out for dinner, 'And he was hurt. He said to me, "Well, we've got this agency and it means a lot to us, and we don't have that many artists, and when something like that happens, it's hard."' Prophet offered a sincere apology for what had happened, and Mongrel Music began booking him again. It was the start of something, and, with Dan Kennedy's help, he was able to buy a touring van. 'We started playing the bottom rung of the ladder,' Prophet grins, 'but it put us on the map. Mongrel did all they could to turn over every rock that might have had a gig under it. So, when New West was looking for new bands, it looked like we were ready to go. You know? And that's really all Dan Kennedy.'

Whatever the territory, the hard truth is that financial support from the label can determine whether or not a feasible itinerary can be built at all. 'It's very difficult to tour from San Francisco. Fifteen hours away in Portland is your first gig,' Prophet explains. 'So we hadn't been touring the States. And when we were going back to England, we were going back for less. Tours started losing money. Settling with Lembo left a debt that I had to pay over time. I was just trying to keep everything rolling.' The US shows would be tough and ultimately spirit-sapping, not to mention bankrupting. 'The economics just don't make sense sometimes,' Prophet shrugs. 'And Paul Revelli's wife had a good business, and he was a homeowner, and eventually he just said, "I can't do this." We lost Paul. And we got Winston [Watson] in there [on drums].'

Oddly enough, it was in Florida that Dan Kennedy first managed to plant a flag that would endure. The radio station WMNF 88.5FM in Tampa Bay was an early strong supporter that has remained a staunch ally, regularly offering Prophet slots at its Tropical Heatwave festival; when the festival closed down and relaunched as a cruise in 2018, Prophet was again a headliner. There was no doubting the commitment and the performances by the members of the four-piece band (reluctantly, the tour was mounted without Max Butler) when they flew out for the first WMNF gig in Ybor City—'packed and sweaty with 300–400 swamp beasts in attendance', as Chuck put it in his Tour Diary blog at the time.[23] And perseverance sometimes reaps its due reward. 'We made a lot of friends we still have to this day,' Prophet says. 'The Beachland Tavern in Cleveland, the Continental Club in Austin. We were always one of those bands that the bartenders and the waitresses liked.'

A review of a show later that year at the Cactus Café in Austin, Texas, noted a starry component in the audience, made up of Prophet's friends and associates—Beaver Nelson, Alejandro Escovedo, and Kevin Carroll, among others—but also that the venue was only half full. Writer Jim Caligiuri praised Prophet's 'sure-handed delivery and dominating stage presence' but also highlighted the perennial problem: 'How do you sell something that truly slides between the cracks, between soul, rock, folk, blues, and country? His music cuts and pastes from such a broad palette that describing it accurately is elusive. Still,' the review concluded, 'his sense of melody and hooks is unmistakable'; sometimes music is best, he suggested, 'when it can't be described'.[24] Perhaps, as Charles Pitter once suggested to me, Prophet's fusion of roots traditions is—not unlike Bruce Springsteen's, for example—a style in and of itself. But it still doesn't make it any easier to sell.

Despite all the hard work, however, Prophet was still only managing to cover isolated pockets of a vast territory. Promises were broken about promotion and advertising for the tour. On one occasion, Chuck and Stephie stopped by the home of High Tone boss Larry Sloven—the one who had been so reluctant to produce a tour poster—to pick up a box of CDs for the merchandise table. As Chuck reached out to pick up the box, Sloven stopped him. 'You didn't think I was just going to let you take those without paying for them?' he demanded. Prophet tried to explain that he needed every spare dollar for the tour and promised he would pay after, but Sloven put his foot down, at which point, Chuck relates, 'Stephanie got so embarrassed, she got her chequebook out. Because she couldn't handle the tension. And we got in the car, and I said playfully, "Don't ever do that again. I was gonna win that. I was gonna get *satisfaction*!" And it was just one box. Thirty CDs. That relationship with High Tone, it just wore me down.' Worse, unable to replenish the financial reservoir from ticket sales, and with no label to provide an advance, there was no money to cut a new album.

'To be fair to Larry Sloven,' Prophet reflects, 'I didn't really understand that Hightone was simply a blues label. And the merchandise table at that point was the whole game. We really were one of those acts selling records from the trunks of our cars. I thought we were swinging for the fences! But it was nice to have Hightone. They had US distribution, and, all my petty gripes aside, having that record out in the States afforded us the opportunity to go out and play with a record that was in the stores, and everything that goes along with that. We planted seeds out there that are still growing.'

The official document of that tour, *Turn The Pigeons Loose*, was, as Prophet admits himself, 'not such a great live album. It has its moments, but it was essentially the equivalent of a contractual obligation'. Prophet handed over the project to Rob Douglas to finish, and it's an oddity—a collection of recordings including soundchecks, not even a facsimile of a real show—and the mix, particularly on some of the tracks, really favours the bottom end. 'It's hardly definitive,' Prophet agrees, 'but then what live album is?' He has no problem with tapers recording and circulating his shows. 'I like that all that stuff's out there—I think it's great,' he enthuses. 'Maybe there shouldn't be an official release. It's all out there, so if somebody wants a live record, they can seek it out.'

Prophet is well aware that many of his fans have been clamouring for an official live album for a long time, but his own ideas are, inevitably, angled slightly differently from the conventional approach. 'I am a little bit more grandiose than that,' he laughs. 'And I'm kind of a victim of that grandiosity, in the sense that if I made a live record I would like to do something like Jackson Browne did with *Running On Empty*, where there's some recording in the living room, some recording in the hotel room, some at a soundcheck. A couple of new songs, and have it tell a story of being on the road. But, in the end, I'm not that interested in looking back. I'd rather just shut the door on it. I would rather just start today.'

CHAPTER NINE

THE NEW WEST YEARS

NO OTHER LOVE, AGE OF MIRACLES (2001–04)

> I think Chuck knows what
> Chuck needs to do ...
> – Dan Kennedy

NEW WEST, NEW DEAL

Following the *Hurting Business* tour, Prophet had the opportunity to do a short tour in a 'songwriter's circle' format with his friend Kim Richey and Ryan Adams, then still six months away from the release of his post-Whiskeytown solo debut, *Heartbreaker* (2000). Adams remembered the tour warmly almost twenty years later: 'When I started to really understand what songs truly were I was lucky enough to be out on a tour with [Chuck] and watching him lay waste to my pathetic paperback pulp writing was a devastating and awesome force in my life. Watching the masters at work is always a humbling thing.'[1]

In 2001, Prophet had again toured long and hard. His 'New Year 2002' blog post was upbeat, but it had been an exhausting year. They had clocked up around thirty-five thousand miles, including a visit to SXSW in March with Max Butler back on board, where they supported Alejandro Escovedo and jammed with Adams. In May, there was a West Coast tour, and at the end of that month Chuck and Stephie travelled to Japan for a handful of shows, deploying a beat box for some of the Go Go Market numbers. The night before they flew, they attended the California Music Awards (Prophet had been nominated for best guitarist and best male vocalist) and played 'Apology' from *The Hurting Business* with backing from Eggs Over Easy keyboardist Austin DeLone. Chuck also presented an award to Green Day: 'They kind of appeared and proceeded to circle around me like uncaged animals. I had to grab one of 'em and press the award into his hands—I remember mumbling something stupid into the microphone like, "cool" or "alright!" and split.'[2]

Looking back from the beginning of a chilly January in 2002 and summing up the preceding year, Prophet was able to be far more philosophical, but as things wound down after *The Hurting Business* promotion and tours, he had had to take stock. The industry as a whole was a couple of years past its peak. Prophet admits he couldn't help but be aware of it, but at the same time, he points out, 'I didn't feel like I was in the belly of the beast so much as I was a fringe artist. Just kind of running a family business, really.' He pauses. 'I'm always amused every time I put out a record and people say, "Well it's just really hard right now." The reality is that I remember people saying that in 1985. I don't ever remember anybody saying, "It's really easy at the moment to put out a record and move loads and loads of units."' He considers this. 'And, anyway, the goal has always been to make a great record. And that's enough. I always felt that if I could make a classic record that it would make sense of all my foolishness and all my mistakes and poor decisions. It's not exactly the dream of writing the great American novel. but it doesn't always come down to money. It's about, how do you define success? If you let somebody else define what success is, you're a sucker. I'm no sucker.'

But the cruel facts were that the business model Prophet and Dan Kennedy were trying to hold together at the time was becoming increasingly fragile. 'We had been signed to small British labels and spent all our energies on the European markets, just ignoring North America. And then American labels maybe licensed it and half-heartedly threw it out into the marketplace, but there wasn't a big push behind it, and North America is a vast place to tour. We weren't getting any traction.' Even today, they frequently have to engage in what Kennedy would call 'deadhead tours', where one band member will drive the van to the first tour stop while the others fly, and they will work their way back home; or else tour out of San Francisco and fly home, leaving one person with the van. In July 2018, for instance, Chuck drove it back from Ohio (twenty-five hundred miles, or thirty-six hours of driving), slotting in a couple of solo dates along the way. 'That part's easy,' Chuck laughs. 'After a long tour I like nothing better than to turn off my mobile phone, throw it on the dashboard, put on some Miles Davis and *drive*. No problem! You don't have to pay me to do *that*.'

Today, they can line up twenty or more dates at a time. In 2002, it was a very different story, and for one of the only times since his teens, Prophet found himself working a day job to make ends meet. 'After *The Hurting Business*, we were so broke: all the touring, and blowing up a van, and trying to keep a band together. So I got a job parking cars. Couple of months. *Man*. Just a mindless job. Sitting in a booth for eight or nine hours a day. But it afforded me the luxury to think. I'd also recently gotten a laptop around that time and did a good deal of writing. I liked the isolation.' Almost casually, Chuck mentions, 'One time I wrote "Summertime Thing" there, just sitting there without a guitar.' It would become the biggest hit of his career.

The music may have still been in the air, but Prophet was currently without a label. The turning point came one night early in 2001. Prophet was attending a party at Adobe Books on 16th Street—poetically, just across the street from the Albion, which had witnessed the birth of his career as a solo artist. Adobe Books was the epicentre of the Mission School art scene at the time, led by urban artists like Margaret Kilgallen, Chris Johanson, and Barry McGee. Mark Eitzel from American Music Club was there, and he happened to introduce Chuck to Peter Jesperson, A&R man for the fledgling New West Records.

'Peter's a kind of a legendary record guy. Signed The Replacements,' explains Chuck. Jesperson had heard the band play in Austin and was keen to follow up. 'We stood there talking on the sidewalk, and he told me that he'd picked up *The Hurting Business* and really enjoyed it.' A meeting was duly arranged. 'He came up here to San Francisco, and we walked around the park to see if we would hit it off. And Peter goes, "Well, we'd like to do something. We're a new company and we think we could do more." And that was music to my ears.'

New West also sent a delegation to a Mission Express gig at the Troubadour, and they liked what they heard. While the touring had gradually wound down into a loss-making exercise, it nevertheless, on the surface at least, looked like a positive when New West was sizing him up. The deal was signed in August, after some protracted negotiation; it guaranteed Chuck two releases and gave

New West the right to option further albums, should they choose. 'We've got a great radio guy,' Jesperson had assured Prophet when they discussed the deal. 'And so I started listening to the radio,' Chuck laughs. 'And when I wrote "Summertime Thing" and we made the demo, I thought, *This could be something. I hear stuff like this on the radio.* I had bottomed out, really, after *The Hurting Business.* I wasn't really writing with Kurt. He had made it clear to me that he was "throwing in the towel". But after "Summertime Thing", I wrote "No Other Love", "That's How Much I Need Your Love", "What Makes The Monkey Dance", just one song after another, and I was energised by it. I flourished, somehow, through that period.'

Prophet may have had the security and the apparent faith of a new label to underpin his next release, but the album that would become *No Other Love* was no easier to make than *The Hurting Business* had been. He confesses that they 'started running through the money pretty fast'. He tried recording a handful of songs, including 'No Other Love' and 'After The Rain', in Tom Waits's studio, with Jacquire King engineering; it was a couple of days' hard graft with Stephie, Rob Douglas on bass, and Jim Bogios on drums; and, although a couple of things emerged from the session, it was 'slow going'. A series of sessions at studio 880 in Oakland, with Jim Waters engineering, was more successful, and they managed to lay down the basic tracks for most of the album. 'Jim was wild,' Chuck says. 'Did everything but put masking tape over the meters. Wasn't afraid to cut things hot. To abuse the tape, to abuse the equipment.' Prophet recalls that Green Day, who later bought the whole studio, were recording next door at the time. In the middle of it all, 9/11 cracked open the American psyche; in a blog post, Prophet noted, 'We pressed on and tried to unglue ourselves from the CNN monitor. Numb enough without the aid of that damn TV screen staring back all night and day.'³

Progress was slow and the money was a constant worry. 'We had to stretch every dollar,' Chuck remarks. 'But what's new?' Waters went back to Tucson, and Chuck and Justin Phelps ('just a young guy, hardworking, punctual, positive energy, talented, game for anything') started working out of another studio closer to home. 'I just walked by a place on Market Street that is now a tiny tattoo parlour. It had been for rent, a ten-by-twelve room. And we moved some equipment in there and did some overdubbing and editing . . .walking distance from my house.' As recording proceeded, however, they were forced to continue downsizing, eventually setting up in Chuck and Stephie's apartment, with Phelps volunteering the use of his own equipment. 'All that stuff, like Greg Leisz playing pedal steel, that was done in our living room, with his amp in my closet with my clothes! And that went on for months.'

In due course, Mark Pistel got involved: 'He had done The Disposable Heroes Of Hiphoprisy, he'd done some Public Enemy–inspired hip-hop and dance music; he was pretty clever.' Pistel eventually mixed five songs, including 'Summertime Thing', with Prophet mixing five more at Waterworks West in Tucson with Jim Waters. 'Just moving tapes around,' Prophet says. 'I was mostly on my own with engineers.' The band had fractured in the wake of the exhausting tours. 'Everybody was a bit burned out,' Prophet admits, even Stephie. 'And I really wasn't working with anybody. And I was just being my hard-headed self. Sometimes it was a grind, but at the same time I was getting better at writing.'

It was a richly creative time, even if, in some respects, it was a less collaborative process than Prophet's typical MO. Still, fingers were drumming tabletops back at New West as deadlines came and went. Then, in the middle of it, Prophet flew to Austin to work on a Kelly Willis record. Jesperson was understandably anxious. 'The company had a lot riding on that record. We all did.' There were expectations from the label, and a feeling that Dan Kennedy should have been more "hands on" as manager, but Dan simply stonewalled: 'I think Chuck knows what Chuck needs to do.'

COUNTRY TIME: KELLY WILLIS

The work with Kelly Willis would be a hugely enjoyable and creative diversion for Prophet, leading to further collaborations with her and culminating in his producing credit for *Translated From Love* in 2007. Willis remembers meeting Prophet briefly on a train in Norway in around 1992. 'I was a fan of Green On Red and was excited to meet him,' she told me, 'but I didn't realize how great he was until this session. The producer [Norm Kerner] hired him.' Kerner had his own studio, Brilliant, in downtown San Francisco. 'Things did not work out between Norm and me,' Kelly continues, 'but I was so enamoured with Chuck's playing and presence and effort invested in my little ol' record.

He understood what I was going for. I had recently left a career in Nashville,' she notes, 'where I spent years bending towards other people's will. So when I started to feel like this producer didn't get me, or my vision, I wasted no time moving on. I had already played that game and wasn't gonna do it again.'

Willis had been signed to MCA after Nanci Griffith had recommended her to the label. Unfortunately, neither her debut, *Well Travelled Love* (1990), nor her follow-up release, *Bang Bang* (1991), were very successful, despite positive reviews. After her Don Was–produced third album failed to make a dent, MCA dropped her, and it was only after she cut an EP with The Jayhawks, *Fading Fast*, that things started to make sense. Willis had always been dissatisfied with MCA's attempts to package her as Nashville product, both musically and visually. The release of *Fading Fast* in 1996 was supplemented by a stunning version of The Byrds' 'Truck Stop Girl' recorded with Son Volt (released on the trucker compilation *Rig Rock Deluxe* the same year), and a duet with Son Volt's Jay Farrar on 'Rex's Blues' for a benefit album called *Red Hot And Bothered* (1995). These recordings allied her more with the emerging genre of alt-country, and finally she signed a deal with the independent Rykodisc. 'Feeling like this next record could be my last record, I really wanted to make something I could hang my hat on,' Kelly told me.

Prophet had not got on well with Norm Kerner either—after a lot of tussling over fees, he had grown tired of the negotiations and told him, 'I'll just come down and give you a day. You're too complicated.' But he loved Willis's demos and was keen to be involved. Chuck and Kelly had a mutual acquaintance in Dave McNair—engineer on *Feast Of Hearts*—whom Willis had hired to take over production after leaving San Francisco. She had also engaged ex–Blood Oranges guitarist and multi-instrumentalist Mark Spencer (brought along as her 'ace in the hole'—someone she knew she could trust). The creative partnership between Spencer and Prophet, she says, ended up being 'a big part of that record. Each day we'd start in the studio and one of them would have an idea they were working on overnight. And the other would also have an idea and then they would work both ideas into the approach. Very little ego about it'.

Here, finally, Kelly was given a degree of creative freedom to establish a sound and identity on a collection of songs that would be aptly titled *What*

I Deserve. It included 'Got A Feelin For Ya', a song Chuck had co-written with Dan Penn (Chuck provides a low harmony) and a superb cover of The Replacements' 'They're Blind', those big open chords translating beautifully into the country genre. In 2002, Kelly would release her follow-up, *Easy*, and Spencer and Prophet would reunite, once again working together on arrangements. Kelly remembers Chuck coming in specifically to hear Faces keyboardist Ian McLagan play his 'Maggie May' organ: in fact, she remarks, 'He and Mark came in no matter what we were doing and threw their two cents (or two hundred) in on everything.' But the approach in the studio was not what Willis had become accustomed to. 'She came from a Nashville background where people would cut two or three songs in a session,' Prophet explains. 'And then suddenly we're in a studio and working on a song all day. She thought something was wrong, or that something was broken! [*laughs*] But she was part of the band, and you could hear that she was working things out herself as we went along.'

For Kelly's third Rykodisc release, Chuck would find himself 'promoted', as he put it, to producer. Kelly concurs: 'Yes! It had been such a collaborative process before but I was eager to record again and wanted someone I could thoroughly trust to take the reins and make the hard decisions,' she says, noting that having four kids under the age of five at the time was a major factor in the extent to which she was able to organise (or not) her working life. The album that would become *Translated From Love* was a departure for Kelly in terms of song choices, but it got off to a rocky start. Chuck bombarded her with playlists until eventually she protested she was 'all comp'd out'. Their respective lists of favourites were '180 degrees apart'. 'I said no a lot,' Willis confirms. 'He was getting tired of hearing no and I was getting tired of saying it!' The breakthrough came when Chuck started recording himself playing through the songs with an acoustic guitar. 'Once we figured out our song choices it was easy sailing,' Kelly says.

Perhaps the most left-field choice of all is the Iggy Pop/David Bowie co-write 'Success'. 'The Gourds made it work, in my opinion, and that was Chuck's idea,' says Kelly. 'He had the creative drive on this record. He has so much energy and curiosity. His pop culture knowledge put me to shame'. The Gourds—a band that one might characterise as new-millennium equivalents of Dylan compadres The Band after too many tequilas—gave the song a South Texas twist: 'They did all that sort of football chanting back and forth, call and response,' Prophet recalls. 'They were funny, and they were such characters. She sang live with them and you can hear her laughing and it's just great.'

Adam Green's 'Teddy Boys' was, Willis explains, 'Chuck's idea of honouring my rockabilly roots and my earlier recordings'—she had started out in the mid-1980s as Kelly & The Fireballs, and Prophet brought in her old guitarist, Michael Hardwick, to play on another track on the album, 'Lucky'. It's the perfect illustration of his approach to production. 'Chuck was so respectful of my career and studied my records and really seemed to care about what kind of record I made,' Willis notes about Prophet's ego-free approach: it is all about drawing out and honouring what is distinctive about the artist. Furthermore, Prophet will often talk about the musical gifts—or otherwise—of producers he has worked with himself: compare his discussion of Jacquire King (*Hurting Business*) and Eric Westfall (*Homemade Blood*) in earlier chapters. Willis notes of Prophet, 'He is a real natural instinctual musician. Some people are gifted. You can do a lot with some talent and hard work. But you know when you are around someone who has a gift.'

Kelly is particularly fond of the title track, a beautiful song by one of Prophet's old partners in crime, Stephen Yerkey. 'Do everything through the prism of love' is how Willis sums it up. And there are other personal notes in some of the co-written songs: 'Losing You', she says, is a 'song about life after my dad died. Chuck wrote the verses. Can you believe how deep they are?' Of Kelly, Chuck would write, 'There's a sadness below Kelly, as if she's been touched by fire a time too many. You can hear it in her voice.'[4]

After this album, Kelly would go on to record more country-oriented albums with her husband, singer/songwriter Bruce Robison, as well as another solo album, *Back Being Blue* (2018). But *Translated From Love* is a unique set for its synthesis of varied songs and imaginative instrumentation—huge rock guitars here, 80s-style synths there—while never losing sight of Kelly's roots, and shot through with some beautiful interaction between Prophet and Greg Leisz on various stringed instruments. Prophet's collaborations with Kelly Willis are remarkable showcases for his skills as a collaborator, whether co-writing, arranging, or producing.

'MOMMA, I'M FLYING'—*NO OTHER LOVE*

Back to the Chuck Prophet business. In contrast to the relatively unpressured sessions with Kelly Willis, progress on his first album for New West remained frustratingly slow for artist and label. Time and time again, as Prophet worked his way through the basic tracks, he would find himself dissatisfied with a part and re-record it himself. On 'After The Rain', for instance, he came up with a figure where the bass answered the guitar's hook, recorded it, and then invited Rob Douglas to come back in and play the part. 'Just a lot of pushing my food around on my plate. And the problem is, the food gets cold. And you can't remember why you ordered it. Six months of it. Just working by myself.' And every time he invited someone back in to re-record a part, he was paying for their time and the studio time.

When I press Chuck further, he explains, as he often does, via a film analogy: 'Well, there's the film you write, there's the film that you shoot, and then there's the film that you edit. Three different movies. You can spend a great deal on preparation and have a shorter execution. Or you can make a record where you do a short amount of preparation but it's gonna be a longer execution. It takes what it takes for the songs to stand up for themselves. And you don't want them overcooked. But you don't want them undercooked either!' By the time they were setting up in his home, Prophet found they had an utterly bewildering set of different versions of the songs. 'And there I was. Trying to figure it all out.'

A peek at Prophet's notebooks shows his obsessive attention to detail: 'off beat chinks are good' . . . 'half as many notes in bridge'. There are directions for engineers ('take out guitar stings at :30 :38 :45 3:17 3:20 3:25 3:58 0:45'), players, about instruments ('string up resonator [sic] heavier'), and, above all, there is a wealth of references to pop history, shorthand notes for Chuck and the other musicians: 'acoustic/bill withers', 'van morrison mariachi guitar', 'finger pick ala james burton, cheap [t]rick pull offs', and 'creedence thompson cluster licks' are just random examples from a couple of pages.

'Summertime Thing' had a drum machine programmed by Jonny Z; the rest of the musicians, Prophet reports, 'played over the top of it. We thought it felt OK but it missed some more *human* feel. And then Michael Urbano overdubbed [drums] on top of that'. Chuck had first met legendary Latino hip-hop pioneer Jonny Z around the time he was putting together *The Hurting Business*, and Jonny ended up providing the beats for both 'Summertime Thing' and 'That's How Much I Need Your Love'. The latter track is also distinguished by Finch's siren-like backing vocal, which I had always assumed must have been pitch-shifted. 'No, no, she sang it,' Chuck tells me. 'And they, like, tripled it, or whatever. It's kind of an homage to the voice that's on "Amanda" by Waylon Jennings.'

A number of songs benefit, apparently, from 'Horns by Mr. Tiny Paws'. 'That was a Tucson guy that I think had alimony issues or issues with the IRS and he used a ton of pseudonyms,' Chuck explains. 'He brought a baritone and a tenor and he stacked his parts really fast and made that little counter melody on "What Can You Tell Me"—all during the mixing.' The mixing itself was done in Tucson, 'on a board that you would use as a PA for a nightclub. It got the job done but … primitive. Super primitive. But Jim Waters threw himself into it—he was great. And we mixed at the board, just like the old days'.

As noted above, Prophet and Lipschutz had ceased working together or even communicating by this time: Kurt had made it clear that the songwriting partnership was over. My conversations with him reveal that the grievances and grudges had been building for a while. He believes that the breakdown in relations was caused at least in part by his sense that he was not getting his due; he confesses he was tired of seeing Chuck, even if by the sin of omission, neglecting to give him the acknowledgement he felt he deserved in promo interviews. Semi-humorously, Lipschutz refers to the bus tour around the city to promote *Temple Beautiful*, years later, when a fan he introduced himself to responded, 'Oh, I thought klipschutz was a figment of Chuck's imagination.' When Kurt told me the story, he was able to take a step back and laugh about it, but in his mind it also epitomised how far off the balance had been, and for how long. 'The question I ask myself,' he says, 'is, "Why am I not supposed to have an ego? Why is that supposed to not matter to me?"'

From a position of hindsight, and with some strong collaborations (such as *Temple Beautiful*) colouring the past rather more warmly, both men are able to be philosophical. Chuck: 'My favourite thing that Kurt says is that we fell out over money. He says there was just … too much of it!' He pauses to consider. 'I dunno. I've been in bands and I've been in other situations where … .we just lost the magic. And you've got to believe in the magic and for me . . .' He trails off and considers again. 'I mean, I'm sure he has . . . a laundry list of resentments. But there was friction . . . you want to feel safe when you get in a room with somebody. It just got unfriendly. And I don't really blame him. I think that I got unfriendly too. And so it came to an end.'

Prophet freely admits that fragments from his collaborations with Lipschutz made their way into songs for the new album, and Kurt chose the litigious route over a song he felt he should have been given a co-writing credit for. He tells me that the record company responded by threatening to take his other co-writes off the album, something he took as a bluff: 'They didn't have enough songs for a record. I mean, *everyone* was bluffing.'

'It didn't hurt that Kurt worked as a paralegal at the time,' Prophet notes. 'And could send things out on legal stationery.' Meanwhile, Chuck recalls this was a time when he felt like he was 'stuck in rush-hour traffic in Chicago trying to get to a soundcheck on time. So I guess I just kind of ignored it. Divorce is messy!'

Legal shenanigans aside, what remains of the co-writes with klipschutz are worth the price of admission: 'Storm Across The Sea' opens with the arresting couplet 'Someone call the ambulance / She's completely nude standing on the fence'; a little later, as the narrator listens to 'a PhD on the radio . . . she grabs the dial, jumps up on my lap / Starts to lick my face like a Persian cat'. It is a beautifully slinky, insinuating number, inspired, Prophet admits, by the Bobby Womack song 'Arkansas State Prison'. 'Run Primo Run', like 'Lucky' on *The Hurting Business*, derives from Prophet's love of pulp fiction and true crime. An email from Lipschutz dating from when the song was still in development (and called 'Run Kilo Run') indicates that Prophet had recommended Kurt take a listen to Dylan's *Highway 61 Revisited* album. The percussion mixed high propels the song along a similar rhythmic road, while the single note Telecaster stings are a tribute to Chicago blues guitarist Hubert Sumlin.[5]

There is some real tenderness on the album, too: apart from the beautiful title track, there is the gentle 'After The Rain', which puts Stephanie Finch's harmony back where it belongs, at the centre of Chuck's ballads. The album plays out with 'Old Friends', one of those songs where what lies beneath in the subtext hints at something far darker than what ripples on the surface: 'Let's talk about old friends / Let's talk about anything except what's really going on.' By stark contrast, there is 'Elouise', which seems like a deliberate attempt to create a dumb rock'n'roll song and then bury it in layers of production, including a guitar that Mark Pistel ran through an Echoplex tape delay. It is one of the most powerfully character-driven songs on the album; if it had been released post-#MeToo, it would have been seen as a precise dissection of toxic masculinity. The voice, Prophet remarks, belongs to 'somebody that doesn't really understand women. . . . It's about a man who has it all and still feels empty: his social interactions go nowhere. No one cares how much he has in his bank account. It's about lack of power in men.'

The liner notes tell us that the title track, simultaneously one of Prophet's greatest and simplest songs, 'was caught surreptitiously': 'Yeah, literally while I'm talking the band through the chord changes. Tim [Mooney] rolled the tape'. Mooney was a longstanding friend of Chuck's—'a wonderful guy'— who played drums for both American Music Club and Mark Kozolek's Sun Kil Moon. As well as his work with Prophet, he produced John Murry's masterpiece *The Graceless Age* (released after Tim's death in 2013), an album Murry believed would never have been made without Mooney.[6] 'I'm totally grateful for Tim,' Chuck continues. 'Because ["No Other Love"], aside from being close to my heart, it's also generated a fair amount of money for me! Definitely paid the utility bills!'

'No Other Love'—first drafts have additional verses that were wisely dropped at an early stage—was first covered by the band Heart (who inexplicably altered the lyric from 'No other love, Mama, I'm flying' to 'Darlin', I'm flying', taking a twenty-word song, changing five percent of it, and immediately robbing the song of its mystical and elemental quality). Further exposure would come through its deployment in the soundtrack for the romantic drama *P.S. I Love You* in 2007, and it was given another lift when 2010 *America's Got Talent* winner Michael Grimm personally picked it out for his debut album, produced by Don Was. Leisz was on the session for Grimm's recording and chased down Bob Ludwig when Ludwig was mastering the album to check that Prophet's song had made the cut. 'That's how sensitive Greg is,' Chuck remarks. 'And what a good friend he is. Because I don't feel particularly lucky when it comes to those kinds of things.'

Despite the change in musical direction, critics were enthusiastic, sometimes wildly so. In the UK, *Q* magazine called it his 'most accomplished and accessible work to date' and gave it four stars out of five; *Time Out London* agreed, adding, 'Throughout, the album drips and burns. Shuffles, prowls, broods, and twangs. Nugget begets nugget. He's on fire.'[7] David Cantwell viewed the album as a continuation of the refashioned sound Prophet had established on *The Hurting Business*. 'There's a good bit of Beck-a-delic Dust Brothers in Prophet's self-produced rhythm tracks,' he suggested, 'except Prophet wants the song to stand out every bit as much as the sound.' Cantwell also accurately captured the fusing of traditional songcraft and technological progress when he wrote that 'That's How Much I Need Your Love' comes off as 'either a great lost Mavericks track or the next Gorillaz single'.[8] Critic Alex Green found a reference point in the Jon Spencer Blues Explosion, notably on 'What Can You Tell Me',[9] while the *Popmatters* reviewer concluded, 'These songs—appealing to the brain, the hips and the heart all at once—are about as pleasant as contemporary music gets.'[10] Edna Gundersen for *USA Today* described Prophet as 'an innovative genre-fusing talent with a wry sense of humor and fearless approach to musical alchemy (especially in mixing alt-country and hip-hop—whoa)'.[11] And for the almighty *AllMusic*, Chris Nickson noted, 'His songwriting continues to grow and his guitar skills … never flashy or grabbing the spotlight, have become mature and sophisticated, a long way from his days in Green On Red. One of America's great underground artists, Prophet's slowly blooming into a major figure.'[12]

'SUMMERTIME THING', SUMMERTIME TOUR

In some respects, Prophet took advantage of the collapse of the traditional business model in the music industry around this time. 'You know,' he reflects, 'we had a place here [in San Francisco] called the Bottom Of The Hill in the 90s that just subsisted on being sold out once a week for a new British band. This was the Britpop era. They had a track that they would put them on. So, Supergrass would fly here, they would play the Bottom Of The Hill and sell it out, and they would try to get the record out to Live 105, and that was the Britpop movement. And clubs got very complacent. Everything's clicking along. The radio station adds the record. People start buying it. It's on MTV.

And then Napster killed all that. Because when there was Napster, that's when Stephanie started having students, little kids, that were saying, "Hey, have you ever heard of the Ramones? Have you ever heard of Joni Mitchell?" And that's when the world opened up because, prior to that, the gatekeepers had the kids. But once the kids could tap into any weird music they wanted, then they checked out of radio. And radio was controlled by the major labels and the fat cats, but all that started to change. And we went out there and found our way in the wake of all that. And when we made *No Other Love*, it caught the ear of Lucinda Williams, thanks to Peter Jesperson, and she invited us to go on tour in the summer of 2002.'

Peter Jesperson had also played Lucinda the new Flatlanders record, but it was Prophet's album that caught her ear. Chuck had met her before; for a while, she had dated his friend Roly Salley. Williams loved what she heard and invited Prophet to open for her on a major US tour, at a time when she was at a peak: *Time* magazine dubbed her the 'Best American Songwriter' that year. All of a sudden, The Mission Express were onstage in front of thousands; there was even a gig in Central Park. 'Not only did we open it but every night,' Chuck noted, 'She said, "I want y'all to go out and buy Chuck Prophet's records, he's a great singer." She really wholeheartedly endorsed us. And there was radio . . . a little bit of fanning the flames. We started to build some momentum.' The admiration between Prophet and Lucinda Williams is mutual: 'There's some kind of mysterious, magnetic, charismatic thing to Lucinda,' Chuck told the *Seattle Weekly*. 'It was just a joy to watch her every night. It was like going to church. Or going to school. Or both.'[13]

The way things opened up for Prophet around this time provides a fascinating glimpse into the way the cogs in some parts of the music industry machine turn. It is also another example of the way in which an artist of Prophet's stature can subsist, working at a middling level of success where, for the most part, he is able to grind out the music sales, the merchandise, and the tour dates in such a way that the columns in the account books remain for the most part on the healthy side between the black and the red. Years of steady commitment to the recording/touring cycle, and slowly building a faithful audience has little in common with the career route of superstardom where the journey from obscurity to chart success can be sudden and dizzyingly rapid.

But chart success can be short-lived and equally precipitous in its descent on the other side of the fame.

However, it was also on the Lucinda tour that Chuck had another hard lesson (as if he needed it) at the sharp end of the business. At around the time Prophet had begun his career as a recording solo artist, Nashville-based lawyer Trip Aldredge had come on board and had been there through the 90s. However, when the relationship with Lembo had fallen apart at the end of the millennium and Prophet was without a deal, management, or even the ability to organise work permits effectively to tour outside the USA, part of the rebuilding process—alongside the key alliance with Dan Kennedy—had been Chuck's decision to go with a new lawyer, Todd Gascon: as the New West deal came together, he felt the need for a 'clean slate, a new start'. However, Prophet had built up a considerable backlog of billable hours with Aldredge that remained unpaid, and when Trip discovered Chuck had signed a new deal without his knowledge, he was understandably hurt. An invoice arrived; Prophet took stock and then asked Dan Kennedy to offer Trip half of what was owed to call it quits. But it took Aldredge over a month to reply, and by the time he agreed to accept the offer, the money Chuck had had in hand (via the New West deal) was gone.

Soon after, during soundcheck at a gig in Nashville, as Prophet bent down to his pedal board, he caught sight of a woman approaching the high stage, clutching one of his CDs. 'Mr. Prophet?' she called. 'Yes I am,' Chuck replied. 'And she handed me an envelope,' Chuck recounts, 'and said, "You've been served." And I looked at it and then just shoved it in my back pocket. And Stephie asks, "What was that?" and I just go, "Ah, nuthin'!"' he laughs.

Prophet did not make his court date; the judge, in his absence, ordered that he should pay Aldredge what he owed and put a lien on his publishing so that BMI paid his royalties directly to Trip until the debt was paid down. 'Presumably that took a while?' I asked Chuck. 'A few statements,' he replies, with a shrug and a laugh. When everything was finally resolved, Prophet wrote to Aldredge. 'I told him, "I got nothing but love for ya; you looked after me when others wouldn't take me on. No hard feelings."' Chuck rounds off the story. 'But I will say this. Some people think Keith Richards is the living embodiment of rock'n'roll. Some people think it's Tommy Stinson.

But on that day I got served onstage, I'd say, it had to be me!'

The Mission Express continued to hit the European tour circuit, in 2002 as a five-piece, and the next year as a four piece. The first go around featured packed houses and full-bore shows. Footage of a show in Vienna from June 10 2002 includes a superb version of 'Abandoned Love' that shows how good this incarnation of the band could be, with Max Butler on mandocello and Chuck reeling off breathtaking solos on his Telecaster (see appendix one). When he had been opening for Lucinda, Prophet took the decision to play almost entirely recent songs, but his own headline shows continued to make room for some old favourites. A typical setlist from the Borderline (May 20) kicks off with a brooding 'La Paloma' and structures the show around songs from *The Hurting Business* and *No Other Love*, but there is a nice surprise in the form of 'Queen Bee' and a final encore of a pacey, funky 'Look Both Ways'. Max Butler's increasingly inventive guitar textures feature throughout and were much missed on the four-piece excursions in 2003.

'That second time around, there was something of a heatwave, plus it was festival season and we were back in the dark black rooms with sticky floors . . . attendance was kind of low,' Chuck reflects. However, there was a memorable date back at the Borderline, June 18 2003, when Prophet's pedal board failed at the top of the show. Undeterred, he declared he would 'play just like I did back in the 60s, before I had any pedals', kicking off a fiery set with 'What Can You Tell Me'. The show was none the worse for the technical hitch; songs like 'Run Primo Run' and 'Elouise' just rocked even harder. The summer of 2003 also found the band being invited to perform on *Austin City Limits*, then hitting its twenty-ninth season. It was a prestigious slot that saw the band open with a tender 'After the Rain' and hit their stride on a fierce 'Diamond Jim'.

In career terms, the next piece in the puzzle would be a successful single. 'I knew when I made *No Other Love* that I couldn't just make an eccentric record,' Prophet told me. 'The label needed something to work with. And there was a precedent: I loved it when the Stones did "Miss You" and when the Clash did "Train In Vain". I loved it when they let their audience know that they knew what time it was.' The song in question would be 'Summertime Thing'. Reflecting on how it came together, Prophet remembers how the mood in the room modulated as they worked on it: he recalls the drummer 'getting up and sort of dancing, mouthing the words. And he was wagging his tail. I mean, he didn't have a tail, but if he'd had one it would've been wagging. And then Rob Douglas on the bass started playing a I–V country pattern over the chorus, so even though the chords didn't change, the verse had a different feel from the chorus, and the chorus had a bounce.' Simply repeating the song title in the chorus worked as a placeholder, and then Prophet realised the song didn't need anything else, 'So I stopped writing.'

Although he was pleased with the song, Greg Leisz's modal riff on pedal steel topping it off, Chuck admits that he was dissatisfied with the final mix, 'So I ended up burying it in the sequencing. But then New West hired a radio guy that had some experience, Jeff Cook, and he heard "Summertime Thing" and he put it on a little sampler, and then there was a radio convention in Maui.' New West reckoned Prophet was in with a shot and flew him and the band out there. 'We went out there and played outside for all the radio programmers in the States.'

'New West got into that dogfight with corporate American radio: "There he goes, Chuck's climbing past The Wallflowers. Past Springsteen. He's climbing . . . oh, he's climbing past Sheryl Crow!" And week after week it was climbing these AAA charts and getting some airplay. And they were also throwing a lot of money at it. I don't pretend to understand how that works but I think it requires a lot of money. But I could tell how anxious they were getting about it. And when all was said and done, the label woke up with just a massive hangover. [*laughs*] And I think they may have resented it a little. Because it didn't really break us as a band. We still had problems, we still needed tour support, we weren't quite self-sufficient yet, and we had some markets where we were strong but many others where we weren't and . . . well, they were impatient. They had sunk a lot of money into it. They got their egos wrapped up in it. And it's possible that led to some resentments. Fair enough.' Even at the time, Prophet was wry about the impact of a 'hit single': 'Instead of seeing five guy with beards,' he told the *Austin American Statesman*, 'we started playing to, like, twenty-five girls in tube tops. And nobody was complaining. Not even Stephanie, my wife.'[14]

AGE OF MIRACLES AND THE END OF THE NEW WEST DEAL

There was still a second guaranteed album under the terms of the contract with New West, but Prophet admits 'it didn't get off to a roaring start. I was working with Justin Phelps again in our apartment. And in the middle of it I just said, "Let's pack it up." So he packed up, we put the furniture back in and . . . that was it. I just stepped away . . . for once! And then I ended up speaking to Eric Drew Feldman'—formerly of Captain Beefheart's Magic Band—'who's my neighbour. I went and talked to him as if he was like a doctor or something. We walked around Duboce Park, and I said, "I've got these songs, but there's a couple more light-hearted songs missing. I think I cut the wrong batch of songs, maybe . . ." And we kept walking around the park, and he just listens and then he says, "Well, it sounds like you've answered your own questions." So we found a deal on a studio and we went and recorded "Smallest Man In The World" and something else on that record that was just a little more light-hearted. And then we went to another studio and did some overdubs and that sort of parted the clouds.' Feldman would end up co-producing: 'Even with all the new technology,' Prophet told one interviewer, 'it's still impossible to be on both sides of the glass at the same time—Jim Dickinson taught me that.'[15]

The album features two top-drawer tracks co-written with Kim Richey, 'Pin A Rose On Me' and the straight ahead, sincere, and relaxed 'You Got Me Where You Want Me', featuring Chuck's warmest baritone. Kim remembers that 'Pin A Rose' was inspired by a line from the TV cop show *Hill Street Blues*: an officer who predicts a tragic outcome in a case of domestic abuse is proven right over the course of the episode, and his response is a bitterly ironic note of self-congratulation ('Well, pin a rose on me'). It was the inspiration for a remarkable song about a doomed relationship where the understated lyric serves only to darken the song's tone to a deeper shade of black.

The album also offers a varied diet: there is the manic, funky 'Monkey In The Middle', and the album kicks off with the heavy riffing of 'Automatic Blues', which is embellished with terrific horns courtesy of San Francisco legend Ralph Carney, whom Prophet eulogised on his untimely death in December 2017: 'He could do the high math and stack those horn parts,' Chuck wrote. 'It would sound like an orchestra. He was a dreamer. He was manic. He was melodic. He was noisy. He was serious, and he was fun, and he was never constrained by anything or anyone.'[16] The album also has a special place in the hearts of many fans because it includes the perennial live favourite 'You Did'—here not the guitar showcase it becomes nightly on tour (see introduction), but instead an imaginatively orchestrated stew of natural and synthesized sounds, with a complex web of interlocking vocal lines.

One of the album's most intriguing songs is 'West Memphis Moon', written after Prophet had seen a documentary about teenagers Damien Echols, Jessie Misskelley Jr., and Jason Baldwin, who were convicted of the 1993 murder of three eight-year-old boys in Arkansas. 'It was something important to me,' Prophet confirms. In five terse verses, he explores the tragedy for both the victims and those accused of the killings: the final lines—'A flicker of hope, a drop of light / Mothers' arms reaching in the night'—expresses the maternal grief expended over all six of the boys caught up in the tragedy, the victims and the accused perpetrators.

Many musicians were engaged in the high-profile campaign to have the verdicts overturned, including Eddie Vedder of Pearl Jam, Natalie Maines of the Dixie Chicks, Patti Smith, Henry Rollins, Tom Waits, Ozzy Osbourne, and Metallica—the latter had even been cited in the case, because the accused had all been fans of the band;[17] there were accusations of Satanism in a lazy but familiar series of moral-panic-style associations in the press. Prophet teamed up with San Franciscan Anje Vela to stage a benefit for the West Memphis Three; Anje recalls how Chuck committed fully to it, despite the fact he was in Europe as it came together. 'He was orchestrating something beautiful while working hard on tour,' she says. 'Chuck lit something in me, trusted me with helping make this and many other events happen until the release of the WM3 in 2011.' One of the artists who got involved through the work Prophet, Vela, and Mark Kozolek did organising benefits was Jello Biafra of Dead Kennedys. About six months after the WM3 were eventually released, Prophet ran into him: 'I said to him, "Can you believe it? Damien Echols and Jason, Jessie, they're all out walking around breathing fresh air. Can you believe that?"'

By now, New West was evolving as a label, focusing much more intently on signing people who were on their way down rather than moving up the food chain—names such as Dwight Yoakam, John Hiatt, and Steve Earle would soon appear on its roster. 'They were all in free-fall from the majors,' Chuck says. 'The majors had basically folded up their tents, and there were all these people that were left homeless.' Meanwhile, for Prophet, relations with the label were becoming increasingly strained. 'I felt like I was driving with the brakes on. Whenever there was an idea from our camp about adding dates or maybe something as inane as a poster, the label would respond with, "I don't know, that sounds kind of expensive." Dan [Kennedy] was buffering me from a lot of that drama thankfully, but I got into an argument over the mastering of *Age Of Miracles*. The label used the mastering engineer Gavin Lurssen. He had a different approach—he attempts to imitate the high-end roll-off of vinyl. And after a long day of gently suggesting he take a different approach—it just wasn't tickling my monkey bone—I told them I really didn't like it. New West said if I wanted to remaster it, I would have to pay for it myself. I said, "OK, but it will take me a while to raise the money. Maybe, like, a year." Was I difficult? Maybe. Hey, it's not a hobby! It seemed so important at the time to take that stand.'

There were other difficulties that contributed to the label's impatience. Dan Kennedy recalls a high degree of frustration on the label's part when the designer, Mike Prosenko, working obsessively over the album cover—the colours, the fonts, the images—would not let it go. But Prosenko was working with another William Eggleston image, and the stakes felt high to him, too. 'Meanwhile,' Chuck sighs, 'the tour support wasn't exactly flowing, and *Age Of Miracles* really suffered as a result of it. It got hard. But we did what we could to give the album the old college try. I think we may have even worked up some money ourselves to go over to London and play some shows and make ourselves available for promotion. But you can feel when the label is ready to move on. They adopted that kind of wait and see attitude. But we still had some fight in us and we did what we could bring it to the people. "The fans in the stands," as Dickinson used to say. It's always a fun time when there's a new record.'

The UK visit was limited to two shows at the Borderline, on November 9 and 10 2004. There was also a US tour with labelmates Old 97's. ('Misguided,' Prophet reflects. 'We may not have even been their first choice for support.') The Mission Express were also struggling to gel. 'We had yet another drummer.

Yet another bass player. And Max was on the way out. He was starting a family. Yeah. Definitely a period of adjustment.'

Constant line-up shifts meant the band was not in great shape, but one positive was the new bass player recruited for the Old 97's tour, who has remained a mainstay of The Mission Express to this day. Kevin T. White had been playing professionally since the age of fourteen, was part of the House Of Blues house band in Cambridge, Massachusetts, and ended up in Shelby Lynne's band after relocating to San Francisco in the late 1990s. Kevin got to know Max Butler, and, having seen Chuck and the band play regularly since 1997, mentioned to Max that he would love to audition if the bass slot ever became free. 'I auditioned twice,' Kevin tells me. 'The first time was when Winston Watson was playing drums. I was pretty nervous, and I didn't get it. About three months later, I got a call asking me if I'd come down and audition again. The guy they'd hired hadn't worked out. So I auditioned a second time, and it went a lot better. I got a call about two weeks later, asking if I'd do a couple gigs, just to see how it felt. No one ever told me I got it. I just kept getting calls until I figured out on my own that I had the gig!' But Kevin could see the stress telling on Chuck, even if he did not know how troubled the relationship had become with New West, which left Prophet very low. There were dark moods and times and bad-tempered soundchecks. 'Yeah, we weren't playing that great,' Chuck admits. 'And it was starting to bear down on me. Everything takes its toll.'

Reviews for *Age Of Miracles* continued the established trend, however. *Paste* magazine described it as a 'genre-bending, musical-adventure show.... Pick a track at random and you might find soul, rock, R&B, pop, funk, electronica, country or even hip-hop. He pulls it off is because he remains unswervingly true to his own vision and themes'.[18] Zeth Lundy for *Popmatters* had a couple of reservations, finding both 'You Did' and 'Heavy Duty' 'nearly ponderous'; still, there were 'plenty of soon-to-be-classic ringers' that warranted a 'wholehearted recommendation'.[19] The *Washington Post* noted how the diverse musical styles were all unified by Prophet's distinctive voice and 'by a creative delight that never seems smug or academic'.[20] *Mojo* magazine gave the LP four out of five and heralded 'the sound of a man in love with his record collection—and that makes it music to the ears'.[21] The *San Francisco Chronicle* admired the way Prophet was able to deliver 'a set of ace tunes ... simply by clamping his hard-luck voice on dreamy, soft-focus melodies that aren't afraid to stretch expectations'.[22] *Billboard* magazine described his songs as 'seriously beautiful, charming and unpredictable' but hit upon a theme that had been familiar in reviews of all of the last three albums: the music is 'difficult to classify', so while his artistic potential is undeniable, the writer noted, 'commercial potential is another story'.[23]

Another story indeed. The New West accountants read it for themselves and concluded that the figures simply weren't there. The *Billboard* review of *Age Of Miracles* had noted that 'some airplay might get Prophet the explosion he deserves', but the success of 'Summertime Thing' was starting to look like an aberration, even to the most optimistic observer. The fateful call may have started to feel inevitable, but, when it came, it was still shattering. 'Chuck took it pretty hard,' Kennedy says.

'I remember when Jesperson called and dropped me,' Prophet nods. 'I was standing in the kitchen when I got the call. Pretty sure I cried, yeah.' When I asked him if it felt like the end of the road at that point, he replies, 'Oh, that was *totally* the end of the road. I mean, I *felt* like it was the end of the road. Felt I had a pretty good run. Made a bunch of records and so ... yeah, for sure. I remember I went out and I ended up walking from my house all the way to North Beach. And I was, like, *What time is it? Where am I?* Just utterly lost.'

It would take time to rebuild. But rebuild he would.

CHAPTER TEN

FROM THE GROUND UP

SOAP AND WATER, ¡LET FREEDOM RING! (2005–09)

> Never quit learning even if you
> have to unlearn everything first.
> – Chuck Prophet

THE TIME BETWEEN

It was time to reassess. Prophet may have been without a label and contemplating the end of the kind of career he had been battling to maintain for two decades, but he was by no means idle. There were more sessions with Kelly Willis (see previous chapter), and he also kick-started his own record label: Belle Sound would be the home for *Fruitvale* (2007), an album by Sonny Smith, and, in due course, Stephie's solo release *Cry Tomorrow* (2010). Prophet would also use it to release a variety of rarities, such as an expanded reissue of *Here Come The Snakes*.

Sonny Smith had opened a couple of shows for Prophet, who admired his songwriting skills. They also had a mutual friend in Kelley Stoltz, an arrestingly original songwriter and part-time member of later touring incarnations of Echo & The Bunnymen. Smith sent Prophet some songs he was working on, and Chuck loved them, sending them out on Sonny's behalf to a variety of record labels where he had connections. 'And, um . . . nothing happened,' Chuck shrugs. 'And I said, "Well, don't worry, son, we'll figure something out. I could always start my own label.'" Encouraged by Mark Kozelek, who hooked him up with a manufacturer, distributor and independent publicist, he did exactly that, and approached it all from a typically oblique angle. 'Yeah, we did some fun stuff, like instead of a one-sheet bio, we did a comic book of Sonny.'

Fruitvale was an appealing, literally characterful set of folk-pop songs set in the Oakland district of San Francisco, and the album was moderately successful, earning a mention in *USA Today*. 'It got out there,' Chuck confirms. 'I think he went and played a fair amount of gigs. He may have opened a tour for Neko Case. And I didn't see it coming, but it turned out to be convenient for me, honestly, because it enabled me to set up shop so that when Stephie made her record, we didn't have to shop it around; we knew that we had a good publicist and a home for it.' Nevertheless, Prophet does not underestimate the challenges of running your own label, notably 'the space between the expectations and the reality: it's filled with drama!' Belle Sound has been the official home of all of Prophet's albums from *Soap And Water* on. 'We fund our own records and license them to other labels, and so we still consider them to be a Belle Sound copyright. Somewhere down the road the copyrights will revert to us.'

Neither did Prophet give up on the road, despite continued trouble keeping the band together—and, more specifically, someone serviceable on the drum kit. The so-called Dress In Layers Or Die tour kicked off in January 2005 and was followed by another European leg in the spring dubbed the Skinny Dogs And Phantom Holidays tour, with Mark Mallman supporting: thirty-three shows in less than five weeks. At this point, Max Butler had, not without some regrets at the time, made the decision to leave the professional side of the music business, chiefly for the sake of his marriage and family relationships. He had played his last gig with Chuck New Year's Eve 2004–05, and, for a couple of years, former Go To Blazes main man Tom Heyman stepped in. 'I enjoyed playing with Tom—we were simpatico,' Prophet notes enthusiastically. 'And shared a lot in common, good lapsed Catholic guitar players that we are.' Like Butler, Heyman could play pedal steel as well as six-string. It was a solid partnership, and Heyman is a superb stylist, but perhaps there was never sufficient time to develop the kind of onstage telepathy that Prophet and Butler had nurtured.

'There were always high points,' Chuck continues. 'And familiar faces at the shows we would see year after year. There was always a lot of love out there, but the touring was getting tougher and tougher all the time. The band wasn't that solid. It was a difficult time keeping that together. We had this drummer, Jeff Anthony, and he could get *belligerent*. Great drummer but ... some personality problems.' Chuck pauses and draws breath. 'I wouldn't describe touring as a day at the beach. But there was a lot to navigate on that tour. After breathing the same air, and the submarine duty like atmosphere of the van, things can get brittle.

'We had one episode in a hotel parking lot in Houston, right after Hurricane Katrina. And there were a lot of people from New Orleans displaced, and they ended up in Houston, and we got to this pretty greasy motel where we thought we had three rooms.' But the motel only had a booking for one; they managed to stretch to a second, but with one for Chuck and Stephie, and the rest of the band having to triple up, there was understandable unhappiness. 'There was an altercation in the parking lot between Jeff Anthony and Kevin [T. White]. Stephie said later, she was surprised Kevin didn't just deck him. And the place was packed, like a refugee centre. And it felt like a chapter was coming to an end. I was thinking, *I don't wanna do this.* Not just *I don't wanna take rooms from people that are displaced,* but *I don't wanna be in a band with these guys. I just don't wanna be out here.* We definitely hit some kind of wall behind *Age Of Miracles.* We had done everything we could. Felt like maybe it was time to fold up the tent.'

Force of circumstance had something to do with Prophet's decision to build the next tour around a solo format. In part, it was in anticipation of a support slot on an upcoming Aimee Mann tour. But it also allowed him and Dan Kennedy to plot an extensive European schedule for January 2006 at a fraction of the cost of traveling with the band. However, rather than adopt the familiar acoustic singer/songwriter mode, he chose instead to go out with a Harmony electric guitar and a Roland 808 drum machine. Of those shows, he confesses, looking back, 'I have no perception of how it came across, no perception at all. People rarely mention it.' He had asked his booking agent to find venues he did not usually play, and the promoter that the agent found in Germany only booked punk-rock venues—perfect, though Chuck adds,

'Some of the fees were incredibly low, playing squats and weird places in towns I'd never been to.' The contract stipulated Prophet would be picked up from the local train station. 'Boy, I was just totally isolated. I mean, the isolation was incredible.' As well as eight UK shows and several in Germany, Prophet covered Spain, Switzerland, and the Netherlands. He then returned to the USA for a string of fourteen dates with Aimee Mann. 'I did Europe, then flew to Chicago in February and went through the Midwest and up into Canada, and down into Florida.' He was a long time gone: 'Yeah. Totally by myself. I'd pretty much go for long stretches without talking to anybody.'

The solo headline show would generally begin with a funky cover of Dylan's 'From A Buick 6' (the arrangement borrowed from Mike Wilhelm), ease into 'Solid Gold' (switching between the standard mic and the bullet mic for the backing vocal part), and then introduce a reinvented, brooding, beat-led take on 'Lucky', picking up the pace for 'Just To See You Smile'. 'Rise' was a perfect choice for this format, Prophet dropping the beats in and out and switching between mics. There was also a tender cover of Lee Hazelwood's 'Houston', a beautiful 'Heart Breaks Like The Dawn', and a climactic, reverb-drenched take on The Surfaris' 'Wipe Out'. Not every song worked quite so well—'Diamond Jim' struggled to find its groove for instance—but 'You Did' sparkled, especially on the occasional European date where Chris Cacavas guested on keys, filling out and embellishing the sound throughout. A typical setlist would close out with a sprightly 'Boogie Shoes' (KC & The Sunshine Band) and 'No Other Love'; often, Prophet would throw in a new song, 'Jesus Was A Social Drinker', at that time a novelty number a long way off the fully developed, hooky song that would finally emerge on the *Bobby Fuller* album in 2016.

Meanwhile, it was tough on the home front. Stephanie had had enough of the touring circuit: 'She was pretty disillusioned with all of it. When we got home and lost the military routine of being on the road, she suffered some deep bouts of anxiety and depression. It became hard for her to shake it. And it made it hard to go out with her in the first place, knowing she would return to that kind of depression,' Chuck reflects. 'Yeah. Things got bleak. I remember standing on a train platform somewhere in Germany. And there was a cold front coming in from Russia. And I just remember . . . [*breathes in sharply*] taking a lungful of bitingly cold air and it was just . . . very intense.'

Around this time, Prophet also made an appearance in a low budget, *vérité* independent movie, *Revolution Summer*, produced by Jonathan Richman and directed by Miles Matthew Montalbano. 'I played the role of a dealer,' Chuck confirms. 'I ended up writing much of my own dialogue.' He told Frank Goodman at the time, 'I wouldn't call what I was doing "acting" or anything; I was really just doing my best Dennis Hopper imitation.'[1] The film may not have had made a dent commercially but it did make some critics' lists; the *San Francisco Chronicle* put it in its Top 10 in an end-of-year review.

GREEN ON RED REUNION

The end of 2005 and the beginning of 2006 also witnessed the somewhat unexpected reunion of Green On Red 2.0; Dan Stuart says the catalyst had been the death of drummer Alex MacNicol in 2004. But it was the manager of Hotel Congress, David Slutes, who engineered it, reaching out to each member saying that the other guys had already committed to the gig to commemorate the club's twentieth anniversary. 'I think he may have bluffed,' Prophet remarks, 'but he pulled us all together.' The first show, staged on September 4 2005 at the Rialto Theater in Tucson, was filmed and released as a DVD, *Valley Fever*. It found the band, including Daren Hess on drums, in remarkably great shape. The next show, with Jim Bogios replacing Hess, was billed as the band's rescheduling of the cancelled Astoria date in 1987. All the UK broadsheet press came out to see it: the *Guardian* thought both Stuart and Prophet looked healthier than they had twenty years earlier, even if the music was frozen in time: 'Beery, bleary anthems of lewd, heavy-drinking men and the damage they do to their women and their livers.'[2] David Sinclair gave the show four stars, noting how the 'more seasoned professionalism' of the band decades on 'meant the songs actually sounded better than ever'. He felt Prophet stole the show 'with a succession of elegant, dramatic and tightly scripted guitar solos'.[3] All involved seemed to have a ball. 'It's like spending a weekend with the kids from your first marriage,' Prophet told *Jambase* interviewer Dennis Cook with a laugh. 'It's a mixed thing.'[4]

A series of reunion shows across Europe followed in the summer, hitting festivals in Greece, Austria, Italy, Norway, and the UK, with a couple of smaller shows slotted in, including Koko in London and the Paradiso in Amsterdam. The Koko gig, included in a series of shows featuring bands playing classic albums, required them to play *Gas Food Lodging* in its entirety; it was undoubtedly more of a challenge, but by that time the band members were locked in, and the gig was a triumph. More dates were added for September, an itinerary Prophet refers to as the 'ceramic hip replacement tour'; it was Dan who had the medical expenses to pay. Prophet's amusing blogged diary shows how much he ended up enjoying at least some of the experience: of the Norwegian Festival performance, he wrote, 'We're well inspired. This gig makes me wish I was still drinking. Insanely good.'[5]

Chris Cacavas admits, 'It wasn't exactly like riding a bicycle, but I think we got our groove together for the most part. I remember when we were rehearsing in London there was a strong dynamic between Dan and Chuck and I think it was difficult for me and Jack to find, or rather redefine, our previous roles as members of the band. It was hard not to feel superfluous, or a bit like a hired gun. But in the end the shows were a lot of fun and there was certainly no lack of respect amongst us.'

'As much as each one of us has evolved,' Prophet remarks, 'it's like families: people revert to roles and routines. Some people are just never gonna do the dishes. And I might be one of them!' he adds with a laugh. Asked recently whether further reunions might be possible, Chuck was noncommittal: 'I'll use the cliché *never say never*,' he told *Classic Rock*. 'We're still brothers, or maybe like army buddies. I suppose it's possible.'[6]

DREAMING WAYLON'S DREAMS

Come 2007, label or no label, new music was brewing, but January brought an unusual diversion, and one that birthed an unexpected gem to the Prophet catalogue. A blog post composed by Prophet's friend and fellow musician John Murry, reproduced in the album's liner notes, tells the story more evocatively than I can re-tell it:

On Friday, January 5th we were all at Closer Recording Studios on Howard Street in San Francisco. Mr. Chuck Prophet and Stephanie Finch were upstairs in their closet-sized office and Tim Mooney, Nate Cavalieri, David Manning and I (John Murry), were downstairs in the main studio control room. JJ Wiesler was in his studio down the hall with Max Butler, Mark Pistel and Robbie [Robi Bean] on drums. Sean Coleman was there, too. He's got a room upstairs where he's constantly building strange electronic shit or tearing strange electronic shit apart. Figuring out which he's doing when is an impossibility. Sean and Tim own the studio. The studio, like every self-respecting establishment, has a high-falutin', fancy smancy alarm system to keep folks out. We didn't know it can keep people in, as well. Sean left, set the code, and went somewhere. We didn't know he'd left for some time. He's like that, all slinky and stuff; like a garden snake in tall grass. Tim, on the other hand, is of a different breed entirely. He writes everything down. Perhaps it's years of drumming that's beaten his capacity for memory into submission, but he can't remember a goddam thing. He writes down phone numbers, atm card pin numbers, addresses (including his own), license plate numbers, prices of combo meals at Burger King along with their corresponding menu numbers, etc. He didn't write down the disarm code for the alarm or the alarm company's phone number. In addition, he'd left his cell phone with Sean's number in his Ranchero . . .

Ridiculous, huh? We were locked in. No two ways about it. No one way about it, really. The fridge contained two chocolate bars and one of those big-ass Costco jars of peanut butter. And beer. We drank, ate peanut butter; tried to figure out what to do. Chuck Prophet was pissed. He and Stephanie wouldn't come downstairs and wouldn't let us come up. Needless to say, after a few hours had passed Chuck got hungry and, food—in particular stale Mr. Goodbar's—holding a certain magical power over him, he and Stephanie came down. They brought with them as a sort of peace offering a battery powered record player and a Waylon Jennings LP. The record was, by mutual agreement among all gathered around the dinky heater eating peanut butter and drinking stale beer, his best: *Dreaming My Dreams With You*. We listened to it once. We listened to it twice. The third time around JJ joked that, since we were temporarily incarcerated until Sean returned, we oughta re-record the album in full. We all laughed half-heartedly. Chuck did not laugh. He had this creepy look in his eye. It kinda grew into a 'hey man, I got this really good shit to smoke' whole face thing and then he started talking. He started talking really damn fast. Yes, this crazy alpha-dog son of a bitch was saying. We would do the fucking thing. We would re-record the record with all new interpretations of the songs. We had no power. We were half drunk, didn't want to argue because peanut butter makes your mouth REALLY sticky and it kinda starts to hurt if you try to talk too much, and so we gave in. JJ had all the gear up and running in no time. Guitars, amps, mandolins, basses, drums, a Casiotone key-tar thing, and assorted crap was gathered together. We started recording, beginning with 'Are You Sure Hank Done It This Way' and going straight on through to 'Bob Wills Is Still The King'. Sean came back late Saturday night. We scared him; not looking so good and all: smelling like peanut butter, cigarettes, and beer and what not. The rest is history. Recorded history.[7]

The resulting album, *Dreaming Waylon's Dreams*, is many times over a better set of recordings than it has any right to be, given the circumstances. *Nashville Scene* described it as 'a loose, lively document that sounds neither country nor pop. Prophet's humorous baritone holds notes and inflects lines with a sort of pathos that never gets out of hand'.[8]

The whole recording is a delight, partly due to its spontaneity: at the beginning of 'I Recall A Gypsy Woman', Prophet sings the first line at Don Williams's pitch, quickly realizes that it's too low for him, and shifts up an octave and although he strains a little in the chorus, the effect is bewitching. It's a beautiful performance. 'Waymore's Blues' is slinky, if not sleazy. The vocal—punctuated with 'woo's and chuckles—is so laidback it's starting to angle toward horizontal, and it's a perfect fit: 'Sweet Jesus,' Chuck croons, sounding half awake and half surprised, 'I don't have to work.' On 'High Time', several guitars battle it out with David Manning's fiddle until the song finally breaks down. It's followed by two ballads: 'I've Been A Long Time Leaving' is carried on a wash of Casio textures and organ, while Stephanie Finch lends a mellifluous lead to 'Let's All Help The Cowboys', with the band in well-disciplined Nashville session mode. Stephanie flips the song on its head with a cool layer of irony. This is followed by the most experimental take on the whole album, a keyboard and drum machine-orchestrated version of 'The Door Is

Always Open' with Prophet's treated vocal buried deep in the mix.

Dreaming Waylon's Dreams was released on Evangeline Records, initially in a limited release of one thousand copies—hand-numbered, packaged in a 7.5x5-inch chapbook with artwork by Bruce Licher. A standard version would later be reissued by Décor Records to coincide with a 2010 tour. It remains a favourite among the Chuck Prophet cognoscenti.

SOAP AND WATER

With the future of his own music career in doubt after being dropped by New West, Prophet had also sketched out a book proposal and struck a deal with Chronicle Books to publish it. Reflecting on the time when he was starting to pick up the pieces, Chuck says, 'I thought, *Well, this is OK, I'll write for other people, I'll produce, I'll do this book. It's not so bad.*' The proposal Prophet worked up with the help of a journalist friend, *Shoulda Stayed In School—Road Diaries From The Rock'n'roll Trenches*, would be an edited compendium of life on the road, a collection of 'prose, poetry, photos, doodles, artefacts, scrawled lyrics and diatribes', as the outline put it. This was a time before the idea of blogging had really taken off, but that is essentially what the collection was intended to be. Prophet had pencilled in potential contributors including Nikki Sudden, Amy Rigby, Peter Case, Dan Stuart, and Steve Earle. The outline makes for tantalising reading, but the project would never take flight.

'It's not like I didn't want to do it, but I kept putting it off,' Prophet shrugs. 'I had written some songs and I went down and did some recording with JJ [Wiesler],' he recalls, 'And then JJ said, "We'll make an album." And then John Murry started working on *World Without End* down there. And so one day I just looked myself in the mirror and realised I wasn't going to do the book. I told Dan [Kennedy], and he figured out a way for us to give the money back.' And they did. Chuck Prophet—possibly the first author in history to have returned an advance for failing to deliver the book he signed up to write. 'It was the right thing to do,' Kennedy says simply, when I ask him about it.

JJ Wiesler, who had played bass at a Go Go Market trio gig, owned Closer studios, where the Waylon Jennings album had been recorded. Prophet recalls doing some demos there with some help from Aidan Hawken, whose debut album, *Pillows And Records* (2005), had made something of a splash, named

'Best of iTunes Independent Music' that year. 'I'd played on his record, and so Aidan volunteered to play on some recordings with me. That's when JJ just said to me, "This sounds like a good solid start of a record."' Guitarist Tom Ayres helped out; Prophet described him as 'a real find … just a guitar wizard, a real resource'.[9] But Chuck felt they were still 'missing one person on the team' and Brad Jones's name came up. Jones was a multi-instrumentalist who had worked with a variety of artists, notably Over The Rhine and Prophet's friend the part-time musician, full-time writer, and former Del Fuego Warren Zanes; Jones had also produced Josh Rouse's albums *Nashville* (2005) and *Subtitulo* (2006).

'I must have played some stuff for Brad, and he said, "This is solid; this could be a great record."' So he came out here, and he was totally willing to sleep on the floor and do whatever it took.' At the time, Prophet described Jones as 'the perfect complement to my manic energies—a pretty cool, calm, and collected, and very Midwestern, no-nonsense kinda guy'.[10] He continues, 'And I remember, as I was showing him some songs, I kept getting phone calls. And he could hear me. There were problems with the budget. And Brad just said, "If you're worried about money, I just want to let you know that we're going to make this record. And we're going to finish it. You can just forget about the finance. I've got a studio, I've got the means, I've got the skills … I just thought I'd share that with you." And I thought, *I like this guy!*' Brad was what Chuck calls 'a true believer' from the very beginning, and, after what he had been through, it was precisely what he needed to hear, at exactly the right time.

Soap And Water ended up being recorded chiefly in San Francisco and finished off at Brad's studio, Alex The Great in Nashville. In some respects, it represented a step away from the layered sound that had characterised his previous two albums. The songs seem less cluttered, although the arrangements remain refreshingly off-kilter, with Aidan Hawken's keyboards often counterpointing the guitars, once again routinely upending expectations of an Americana artist. There were also innovations of a different kind. Prophet told Brad Jones he wanted some choral singing on the album, but he wanted to avoid 'people who sound like they're singers'. Brad's suggestion was typically left-field: 'He got this children's choir to come in [the Vine Street Christian Church Children's Choir], and one of the kids came right up to me and he said, "My dad produces records, he produced Madonna. And he produced

Prince." And I said OK. And I turned to Brad: "Brad, can we get this kid a little closer to the mic?"' He also recalled, in a blog post, 'One little girl was listening to the first song we pumped through big speakers out into the studio. With a concerned look, she asked her teacher, "When is he going to start singing? He's just talking." That's not talking, kid, that's IT.'[11]

Prophet and Jones had been going through countermelodies the night before the session, and the song 'Let's Do Something Stupid' popped out. 'It's a character-driven song about a guy that always does the right thing and it doesn't get him anywhere,' Chuck explains, drawing an analogy with a character from the TV show *The Sopranos*: '"I always do the right thing, what good did it do me?" I just thought that the lyric with these innocent voices would make a great record.' A rep from one label they were courting at the time clearly disagreed. 'I went out and got some refreshments,' Prophet recalls. 'I got some wine and beer, made him feel comfortable, we played him that, and I was watching his expression, and he was all, "What *is* this?"'

'Would You Love Me?' may be one of the best songs Prophet has ever written. 'I love that song, yeah,' Chuck affirms. I muse aloud about what it is that might make a great song a classic. 'Unrequited love,' Chuck shoots back. 'Bam. There you go. Elvis. Jesus. Anna Nicole Smith. It just came to me, one situation after another.' Originally inspired by watching the Mel Gibson movie *The Passion Of The Christ* ('Sitting in a movie, staring at the screen / They're dragging Jesus through the town, don't look good to me'), the song is, among other things, a profound meditation on the tragedy of the King's final years, distilling all the sadness of Peter Guralnick's tremendous biography *Careless Love: The Unmaking Of Elvis Presley* (2000) into a few heartbreaking lines. 'Elvis had a recurring nightmare, that he would come out onstage and the crowd would be gone,' Prophet says. 'I'd seen a documentary on cable TV in a hotel when one of those Memphis Mafia guys said, "Women would still throw their underwear, but it just wasn't the same any more." People were just going through the motions.' As Prophet's song goes, 'Elvis hung his head and said, "They'll forget me when I'm gone … when I'm gone."'

'Downtime' features an odd fade, the song simply disappearing in the middle of a verse. 'Yeah, it's kind of a demo,' Prophet says. 'It had an off-the-cuff thing, and I wanted to preserve that. And when you fade out in the middle of a verse, there's something also not very precious about it. You're not going to hear that on a Robbie Robertson solo album!' he grins. 'Those fades are five minutes of just, like, *sounds* ... right?' In the end, it's not an unpleasing effect on 'Downtime', almost as if a conversation is petering out as someone walks away down a corridor: 'What was that? What did you say?' 'Freckle Song' is a classic riff-driven opener, with a wonderful throwaway, half-spoken line, 'Throw me overboard, captain, would ya please / I just can't stand myself.' Chuck laughs and admits, 'I like it when people repeat that one to me.'

There were also two songs drawn from writing sessions with Kurt Lipschutz, 'Heartbeat' and 'Doubter Out Of Jesus', a song that intrigues both lyrically and musically. It wasn't recorded until almost everyone had already gone home: Chuck was alone in the basement studio with Brad and guitarist Tom Ayres; the drums were being broken down, so they grabbed a drum machine. Brad played the bass line on a keyboard. 'On the album, it's just this little thing, shades of electro, kind of like [the band] Suicide. And then we started doing it live, oh *man* ... Kevin adapted that keyboard to the bass and it just got ... really spacious live.' Honourable mention should also be made of 'New Kingdom' and its tremendous guitar breaks dropping out of the sky and igniting the song.

Soap And Water was the first time Prophet was licensing out music he owned himself; the deal was arranged with some financial help from Dan Kennedy. Kennedy remembers the finalising of the artwork was made tortuous again by the designer. ('Working with genius can be exhausting,' he remarks. 'The guy's brilliant—but he has such *baggage*! And he couldn't ever sign off on anything.') However, the album garnered more press attention than Prophet had enjoyed for some time. The *Houston Chronicle* declared, 'If the ongoing Maroon 5-ization of rock disturbs you, Chuck Prophet is your hope for the future ... from the nitty to the gritty, there's nothing else out there quite like this.'[12] Steve Almond, writing for the *Miami New Times*, picked up on 'Something Stupid', remarking how Prophet turns it into 'a kind of mini symphony, summoning a wall of sound that includes strings, keyboards, assorted background voices, and his own sinuous work on the Stratocaster. Radio might not want to risk this kind of majesty,' he concludes, 'but you should.'[13] It got strong notices too in *USA Today*, the *New York Daily News* (which compared the sound to Petty's Heartbreakers and the Stones), and the *Washington Post*.[14] *Entertainment Weekly* scored it an A-. In the UK, high-circulation rock and pop magazine *Q* judged it 'the best work of his career',[15] awarding it—as did *Mojo* and *Uncut*—four stars out of five. The *Irish Times* gave it a five, calling it 'a monumental album of constant surprise, chilled intelligence and quietly assured song writing skill, singing, playing and production'.[16] Critically speaking, at least, Prophet's stock had never been higher.

STRUNG OUT ON COLOUR TV

'Doubter Out Of Jesus' was the song Prophet chose when invited to play with the band on *Late Night With David Letterman*—a major promotional coup. Chuck prepared carefully, making sure everyone (including the house band's leader, Paul Shaffer), had a part to play. In Shaffer's case, that would be the tubular bells. 'They rolled in these tubular bells from their rental company. And even Paul came in and was looking at it, like, *What?* [*laughs*] And then all the sound guys were arguing. "No, you mic it here, dumbass." These New Yorker union guys. "You don't tell me how to mic a tubular bell!" "Put it down here!" And they couldn't configure the camera because it was in front of him [Shaffer]. It was just comedy. I was thinking, *What have I done? Me and my ego!* But then Paul Shaffer was over there with the tubular bells really enjoying it.'

When they had been rehearsing for the show, Chuck recalls, he had looked around and thought, *We look like a bunch of janitors.* He trooped the band off to Barney's department store to suit them up. 'I must've put five thousand dollars' worth of clothes on a credit card. Stephie wore her own clothes but the rest of us … We put tape on the bottom of the shoes. So that when you take the tape off they still look brand new. I learned that trick from Kara. I got them to leave the tags on. And so after the show we were able to return it all.' Kevin T. White remembers feeling intensely nervous as they waited to go on. 'Then I looked over and saw James [DePrato] had a goofy smile on his face, and I just relaxed and realised I was just about to play music with a bunch of friends,' he says. For Prophet, as he wrote in his entertaining blog post about the event, the performance was a blur: 'As soon as it starts, it's over. Handshakes all around from The Dave. Afterwards, Paul [Shaffer] hovers around the Farfisa, talking to Andy and Stephie. On the way out, he says, "See ya next time, Chuck."'[17]

It was a remarkably self-assured and breezily confident performance. I recall congratulating Chuck when it popped up on YouTube soon after broadcast. 'It was great,' I told him, 'but it's not my favourite song of yours.' 'My Mom said exactly the same thing,' Chuck replied.

Rival TV host Carson Daly had caught the Letterman appearance, and the band were invited to play his show in February, performing 'Would You Love Me?' and 'Freckle Song'. A third appearance came via the relatively new web-based TV show *Live From Daryl's House*, hosted by Philadelphia white-soul legend Daryl Hall of Hall & Oates. Prophet was on a surfing trip to Costa Rica when the call came (you can see a bandaged knee in the footage from an injury sustained in the surf), and he headed home, then did the twenty-five-hour drive with Kevin T. White to Austin, Texas. Prophet had negotiated with Hall's musical director, T-Bone Wolk, which songs they would perform, deciding on 'Summertime Thing', 'You Did', and Alan Toussaint's 'Soul Sister' after Wolk vetoed Chuck's suggestion 'Golden Years.' ('I wouldn't mention that to Daryl,' Wolk told him. 'Daryl's got problems with Bowie.' Maybe there's only so much room for white, blue-eyed soul boys.) Then, while Kevin drove, Chuck went over the songs in the back of the van.

As soon as he jumped out of the van at the studios, Prophet was unnerved to find a camera crew following him up to the room where they were due to rehearse and tape the performance. 'Daryl didn't really address me directly,' he remembers. 'I would talk to T-Bone and T-Bone would talk to Daryl. I wasn't offended by it, it's just one of those things. He's got his musical director. Anyway, I had been listening to Hall & Oates on the drive, and I noticed that every song ends with Daryl just kinda going off, doing what I called Darylisms. *Woo, woo*, you know. OK, you laugh, but they're all different! And he's an incredible musician. And it all comes out in his singing. And so we played "Summertime Thing", and then it just kinda falls apart. And T-Bone says, "So how do you want to end it?" And I said, "I want some Darylisms. We'll go out with some Darylisms." And I was looking at Daryl, like, *if he's up for it*. And then there's this silence. And then Daryl goes, "See? See, this guy *gets* it. I like this guy, this guy gets me!"' All three performances are outstanding; it's a pleasure to hear Prophet's songs being given a white soul lilt. The joy of jamming on such top-drawer material is lit up across the faces of everyone, not least Daryl Hall himself.

THE MISSION EXPRESS REMIXED: JAMES DEPRATO

Back in the autumn of 2006, the band had reconvened—'kind of reinvented one more time'—with Kevin T. White back on bass, Tom Heyman on guitars, and Todd Roper of the band Cake on drums (except for a few shows that were covered by Jim Bogios). White admits the Green On Red reunion had been a nervous time for the band: 'I hardly heard from him at all; I figured he might go back to Green On Red or just start a new band, start afresh.' There were dates around northern California, and a string of shows with Alejandro Escovedo; as Chuck notes, 'We were always happy to play gigs together.' He remembers that Al's keyboard player, Bruce Salmon, had his young son on tour with him at the time: Ellar Coltrane, who played the lead role of Mason in Richard Linklater's extraordinary film *Boyhood* (2014), which documents Mason's coming-of-age and was filmed over eleven years. Chuck remembers, 'He and Stephie were palling around. She would take him shopping!' It was on this tour that Escovedo pulled Prophet aside and asked him if he would be interested in writing his next album together. The writing would take a year, on and off, but it would be another watershed for Prophet. Meanwhile, in between recording *Soap And Water*, he kept up a tough schedule of dates: the spring of 2007 found him opening with the band for Mofro, as well as solo for Escovedo. There were also a couple of 'in the round' songwriter gigs with Kelly Willis, Bluebird Cafe style, and some Mission Express headline dates in Colorado in June.

The following year found Prophet and a new line-up of The Mission Express hitting the road hard: Europe in April, then May to August across North America. Kevin T. White by this time was firmly settled upstage left, anchoring everything with his instinctive, forever-in-the-pocket playing, and always looking like the happiest bass player on the planet. Kevin laughs when I put this to him. 'Sometimes there are nights where I just think I'm in the best fucking band in the world,' he tells me. 'And then there are nights were I'm tired and beat up and stressed from the road and am smiling just to hide it all. But for the most part, when I'm playing, I feel safe and happy.'

Those stresses on the road can become unbearable. And the drum seat continued to rotate. In 2008, guitarist Tom Heyman would leave the band too and be replaced by James DePrato, a native of Norco, California, from a

AUTOMATIC BLUES

Automatic blue edit 10/12/03

CLAUS

Tossin' / *throwin' matches*

flyin'

Hidin' *Kippin'* *all the while the sandman*
Starin' down *the sandman's flyin'* *never sleeps* *he lives up on the roof*

Sitting in the kitchen, boiling up some eggs
The morning sun is crawling up my leg
The sandman sleeping, crashed out on the roof
swoops down out of nowhere with the automatic blues — *can't face another morning w/ the automatic*

Here the rooster crowing out the automatic blues, blues

Well the TV preachers preaching and the sinners bow their heads *(The way it* *like he used to do)*
Rats are in the alley and the dogs are breaking bread
You might be on your back somewhere or leaning up in your pew *The sandman don't deliver*
When Sunday draws the curtain on the automatic blues *somewhere a rooster's crowing*
the sandman's running loose

The conductor has a face no one's ever seen
Brakeman's staring at an empty screen
It's a prerecorded service with a prerecorded view *BEST*
Hear the brakeman blowing out the automatic blues *am I here with you, or did you here with me*

STATIONMASTER *call me sentimental but I always*
The whistle sounds the flight of the bumble bee *miss the ol' trains*
One thing is for certain nothing's what it seems
The switchman out the window's staring back at you *who says there's no such thing*
When his lantern disappears inside the automatic blues *says as the good ol days*

vague so hard to read

At the bottom of the ocean lives a beast with 7 fins
A And every seventh year, it rises up again — *like the 7th samurai hill rise back up again*
Sure as the sun dances with the moon
You can bet the tide is stirring up some automatic blues

when it's stinking up the kitchen
It's stinking up with kitchen filling up your mouth *who's gonna throw it out?*
B It's a serious stain, and it aint coming out
Go on and take a bite boy, don't forget to chew
Wind up choking on the gristle of the automatic blues

The elevators calling like it knows my name *GOOD* *call me sentimental*
I'm singing Louie Louie to a funky chambermaid *but I've got a thing for trains* *BEST*
I think I'll take the stairs if that's alright with you *BEST*
Can't stand another measure of the automatic blues

The sheets are made of cardboard, the pillows filled with lead *just been fed for we red*
Thought I'd sleep like baby but I cried instead *GOOD*
The thermostat was frozen, woke up with the flu *I tried the slick kill and razor bow*
Wrapped up in a blanket with the automatic blues *put away that ukulele*

When they terminate the power we'll make out own fun
You play your ukulele, I'll play my laser gun — *pick up that ukulele / put away that*
When nothing functions like it's programmed to *hung up at the turnstiles*
We can always count upon the automatic blues

Cross my heart and hope to die I poured it down the sink *GOOD* *piped in music*
FOCUSED The tears I'm crying, they aren't what you think *+ filtered air*
I'm firing on all cylinders, just need a little juice
It's last call at the clown room with the automatic blues

```
The conductor has a faced that's never been seen
Brakeman staring at an empty screen   looks right
The switchman out the window stares right back at you
When his lantern disappears inside the automatic blues   refused

Call me sentimental but I miss the old trains
Don't tell there's no such thing as the good ol days
A pre recorded service with a prerecorded view
Hear the stationmaster blowing out the automatic blues
```

looks right through you
filtered air
SIMULATED
perfect

▊ ABOVE With Brad Jones at Ring Mountain Day School, Mill Valley, California, November 23 2013. (*Darrell Flowers*)

▊ LEFT With Alejandro Escovedo, St. Claire Studio, Lexington, Kentucky, 2007. (*Rosco Weber*)

▊ BELOW Green On Red reunion, Spain, July 9 2006: Jack, Dan, Chuck, Chris.

❚ TOP Greg Leisz and Tom
Ayres, Mexico City, during
the recording of ¡Let Freedom
Ring!, 2009.

❚ MIDDLE ¡Let Freedom Ring!
cover shoot, Mexico City,
2009. (Suzy Poling)

❚ BOTTOM With James
DePrato and Peter Buck,
Ginger Man Pub, Austin,
March 16 2012. (Paul Dominy)

RIGHT With Dan Kennedy, backstage at *Late Show With David Letterman*, January 9 2008. (*Shea Ribblett*)

BELOW On the solo tour promoting *¡Let Freedom Ring!*, Belgrade, Serbia, February 25 2009. (*Stanislav Milojkovic*)

▌TOP LEFT With Garland Jeffreys, Lobero Theatre, Santa Barbara, April 23 2016. (*David Bazemore*)

▌BELOW LEFT With Jello Biafra, outside City Hall, San Francisco, June 19 2015. (*John Margaretten*)

▌BELOW With The Rubinoos: Al Chan, Tommy Dunbar, Jon Rubin, Donn Spindt. (*Paul Chinn*)

■ BELOW LEFT Among the benches at Golden Gate Park, *Soap And Water* shoot, 2009. (*George Westcot*)

■ BELOW With Charlie Sexton on the East River Truckers Tour, Spain, January 2019. (*Mike Brook*)

■ OPPOSITE TOP With reward note for stolen guitar, August 24 2012.

■ OPPOSITE MIDDLE *Strings In The Temple* show, Great American Music Hall, November 24 2013. (*Darrell Flowers*)

■ OPPOSITE BOTTOM Hardly Strictly Bluegrass Festival, San Francisco, October 4 2019. (*Chris Metzler*)

TOP With James DePrato, recording *Bobby Fuller*, Nashville, 2016. (*Andy Diffee*)

MIDDLE 2020 portrait. (*Sloane Kanter*)

BOTTOM The Mission Express—Vicente Rodriguez, James De Prato, Kevin T. White, Stephanie Finch, Chuck Prophet—Hardly Strictly Bluegrass Festival, San Francisco, October 4 2019. (*Chris Metzler*) district where, as Prophet once put it, tongue in cheek, 'If you don't have at least one car in the driveway and a couple more on blocks on the lawn, folks start to question your sexuality.' DePrato says he grew up in the MTV era, 'when guitar players were the coolest people on Earth'. At a swap meet in nearby Ontario, James's rock-music-loving father bought his seven-year-old son a $40 electric guitar, and James was hooked. 'I guess I was lucky enough to be raised in a house where they were listening to The Allman Brothers and Lynyrd Skynyrd, ZZ Top, Van Halen, and Cream,' he told me. He recalls regretfully that when he got his second guitar, he smashed the first in the back yard: 'I was obsessed with that Woodstock tape of The Who.' By the time he was twelve, DePrato was being home-schooled and playing in several bands 'with thirty-five-year-old potheads'. He used to call in regularly to a talk programme on LA radio station KLOS, where they would interview some of James's contemporary guitar heroes, and once ended up jamming live on air with Bay Area guitarist Marc Bonilla over the phone. James was invited to come in and play at the station, and Bonilla gave him a Yamaha Pacifica guitar and invited him to help cut a track for his next album; he is credited on 'Under The Gun' on the LP *American Matador* (1993). He was thirteen years old.

DePrato continued to spend most of his time playing guitar—both live and session work—and very little time pursuing his studies. He was also picked up by a couple of gear manufacturers after he was taken along to the annual NAMM music convention in 1993; you can find him demonstrating pedals for the likes of MXR on YouTube. 'I got a bunch of endorsements,' he says. 'I guess I peaked around fourteen. [*laughs*] And then I got older, I got acne, and just was a regular ugly-ass teenager after that!'

He ended up settled in the Bay Area after playing the circuit with a hippie band for a while. A couple of years later, he got the call to try out for Chuck Prophet via bassist Kevin T. White, who had known James for years. 'I met him when he was just twenty-two, and he made an immediate impression on me,' Kevin tells me. 'His playing was so far advanced for someone his age.' They played together occasionally and would come across each other on the road as the years went by. After Heyman left, White says, 'I asked Chuck if James could audition, and he said he had a guy from Florida in mind he was pretty much sold on, but he would let James come in and play, as kind of an afterthought.

So the day comes, and we play with this guy from Florida, and it goes OK. And then I asked Chuck about James. I'm pretty sure he had forgotten that he said he could come down and audition. But James comes up, and the first song we play is "Age Of Miracles." James had learned it in the key it was in on the record, but we had been playing it in a different key. So James on the spot transposed it and played it flawlessly, and I could see the look on Chuck's face, like, *Oh, he's the guy. But I've already told this other guy that he has the gig.* We play a few more songs. It goes great. James leaves, and then John Murry pokes his head around the door and says, "That's your fucking guy, Chuck.'"

'It was super easy,' says James. 'I mean . . . they worked like a rock'n'roll band.' For DePrato, that key shift on 'Age Of Miracles' was elementary. 'It's not like a piano, where all the shapes change as you move up—you just kinda slide your hand up the fret board four more frets.' James laughs. 'That's the first time I've ever impressed anybody doing something that simple!' There was one kink to be ironed out, however. James had come to the audition playing his favourite guitar at that point, a blonde Telecaster—almost identical to the only electric guitar Prophet ever plays onstage. 'You got the gig,' Prophet told him on the phone, 'but you can't play a blonde Telecaster!'

In a scenario a little reminiscent of Prophet's recruitment to Green On Red, DePrato had never been out of the country—he didn't even have a passport—and all of a sudden he had thirty days to learn the songs and get ready for his first European tour. He remembers being taken aback that so much of the 'heroic guitar stuff' on the records was played by Prophet himself, not by an ancillary guitarist. 'I was surprised to find he could really play the guitar . . . I mean, he could really, *really* play the guitar.' The education went both ways. 'We would listen to records as we were driving across the United States,' says James. 'And I'd put on a Thin Lizzy record and he would listen to it and go, "I never really checked these guys out. Maybe *that's* why you have two guitar players. We could do this stuff and it wouldn't be lame!"' Prophet recalls hearing 'Long Distance Turnaround' by Yes and mentioning it to James, who promptly showed him how the harmony worked; from there, they swiftly figured out a twin lead solo for *Temple Beautiful*'s 'Willie Mays Is Up At Bat'. 'Amazing,' Chuck shakes his head. 'You've got to drag it out of him, though.'

The twin-lead jams that have become central to the Mission Express live experience may come from DePrato, but there are all kinds of highlights when they lock into each other. 'Some people say, "You're not playing as much," and I go, "Yeah, I like to listen to James,"' says Chuck. Similarly, it was a while before DePrato started singing harmony onstage; James says it was a case of, 'Well, you never asked.' 'He could hit the notes too,' Chuck says. 'He understands the harmony, he can go right to the interval.' James says he has had to experiment to find the right guitar to play in The Mission Express. 'I toured with Chuck a long time before I realised that you have to have single coil pickups if you're going to play next to him. Because his tone is so loud and bright that if your tone is not also loud and super bright then no one's going to hear a damn thing you're doing.'

'I have such a deep appreciation of everything about James,' Chuck reflects. 'His playing, his personality, his quiet wisdom. Oftentimes, when there's some kind of incident out there on the road, I won't do anything or cast any judgement or make a move until I hear James's take on it. He can be very insightful. He's like what the Italians might call a *consigliore* out there for me. Such a gifted guitarist. His playing is so in tune. And so is his personality.' Prophet and DePrato have also developed a sideline in instrumental music recorded under the name El Depravo: 'Artesian jams,' Chuck calls them, 'gap-toothed guitar noir, Link Wray riffage, blues jams ... indie rock.' They have built up a library of recordings that have been licensed for film and TV soundtracks, and they released a cute one-off single, 'Tulare Kiss' / 'Revolution Casino', as a limited 7-inch in 2012, complete with suitably depraved artwork by Michael Gabriel.

It is not an overstatement to say that this configuration of the band— which stabilised properly when Vicente Rodriguez took up residency behind the drum kit in 2013—ushered in a new era of live performance for The Mission Express. Vicente is proud to have had the chair longest: 'I don't know what the chemistry is, but it just works,' he smiles. 'Onstage we are one,' is how Kevin puts it, simply. 'We move together, listening to each other and reacting to what each other is playing. It's a rare and beautiful thing. Offstage, it can get more complicated when you work with people for years on end. But what always brings me back is the songs, and just how fucking good this band is. And, at the end of the day, I want to be a part of a great band.' As an afterthought, he adds, 'James, Vicente, and I are all happy drunks. That seems like a small thing, but you don't want some mean bastard to come out when we hit the bar!'

Soap And Water was launched in the UK with a tour comprising ten back-to-back dates in the autumn of 2007, including two at the Kilburn in London for the American Music Festival. All the shows were supported by Bob Frank and John Murry. 'How'd Bob Frank and John Murry end up on tour with us?' Prophet asked, rhetorically, in a blog post announcing the tour. 'Well, John Murry moved into the recording studio we all share. He slept on the couch. He LIVED on the couch. He wouldn't go home. He wouldn't bathe. It became a problem. He got on my computer, hacked his way into my web site posing as me and posted random self-aggrandizing messages about himself. He stole my pin numbers and ordered out for pizza. Then he didn't touch it. When the pizza was cold I confronted him about it, he shrugged and said he was depressed …'[18]

Murry is an immensely gifted singer/songwriter with an unfortunate talent for self-destruction ('I get in my own way and often wonder why' is one characteristically understated self-reflection).[19] Adopted into a family descended from the novelist William Faulkner, Murry was brought up in Tupelo, Mississippi, Elvis Presley's birthplace. As his website bio puts it, having been institutionalised for mental health issues and addiction at an early age, Murry discovered salvation in music. However, 'Memphis led to San Francisco and San Francisco led to heroin and heroin led to a near fatal overdose on the corner of 16th and Mission.'[20] The incident is narrated in shattering detail in his masterpiece, 'Little Colored Balloons'. It was Chuck Prophet who took Murry into detox for the first time; he did what he could to set him straight. There is a lot of love between these two, evident in my individual interviews whenever they talk about each other. 'Chuck and I are friends and would be whether either of us played an instrument or not,' is how Murry put it in an *Uncut* interview in 2012,[21] while Chuck says, 'I immediately liked him. Felt like I'd known him my whole life.' John recounts for me stories of the pair of them loitering in high-end fashion shops in San Francisco pretending to be slumming-it millionaires and enjoying the free cappuccinos. Murry onstage— and in formal interviews—can be an unnervingly intense presence. Off duty, he is personable and hilarious and there is a dose of healthy ridiculousness and fun about their misadventures.

Murry's stunning LP *The Graceless Age* would follow six or seven years after the first opportunity John had to support Chuck on tour. Tim Mooney produced it. 'Tim Mooney and Chuck Prophet,' Murry told one interviewer, 'you get those two mentors and that's all you need.'[22] At the time Prophet was set to tour *Soap And Water*, Murry had recorded *World Without End*, a collection of murder ballads written with Bob Frank, something of an unknown legend who had released his first album on Vanguard in 1972 and not released a follow-up until thirty years later. Murry and Frank's collaboration, also produced by Mooney, is a melodic, atmospheric, but (unsurprisingly) mournful set of songs.

The autumn 2007 European tour went relatively smoothly, and Frank and Murry's opening set was well received by audiences gripped by the duo's grim tales, wrapped in deep-soaked Americana. However, when the tour hit Southampton that October, there was a blowout between Murry and the soundman when they overran their allotted time. The result was an ugly scene that flattered no one. Prophet demanded that Murry apologise or go home, and John did what was required: 'I said, "I'm sorry I tried to hit you, but I still hate you,"' John recounts, 'and for the rest of the tour we just kept our distance.' The final dates of the run were completed without further incident. In the spring of 2008, there was yet another European tour, including a dozen UK dates and a US tour that stretched through most of May to August.

REAL ANIMAL

It took a while for *Real Animal*, the songwriting collaboration with Alejandro Escovedo, to come together, with songs being written in fits and starts over the course of many months. 'We would go back and forth between here in San Francisco and Wimberley, Texas, where he was living, in the hill country. We just hit it off. We never ran out of stuff to talk about. And, if we did, we would just put on a Mott The Hoople record and lie on the carpet. We did a lot of that. And Al's attitude was always, like, "Oh yeah, man. This is all part of it."'

The scheduling was made tougher by Escovedo's management, who would repeatedly put him out on the road despite ongoing health issues related to hepatitis C. When dates had to be rescheduled because he was too unwell to play, they would be done haphazardly, resulting in some 'insane' drives. 'He did that final tour,' Prophet asserts, 'and it just destroyed him and after that the management was gone and the booking agent was gone.' Still, the songs gradually came together for an album that would in due course take Escovedo to another level of exposure. Prophet wrote in a blog post that it felt like they had a concept for an album, 'all chronicling a life in music through life, death, loss and the promise of Rock and Roll deliverance'.[23] There was some preproduction with Glyn Johns at his chateau in France; Prophet flew into Paris to meet with Escovedo and his manager. 'Al didn't click with Glyn,' Chuck remembers, and it was at this point that Tony Visconti came on board to produce.

Both musicians were thrilled at the prospect of working with the man famous for his long association with David Bowie, as well as Marc Bolan and T. Rex, Wings, The Moody Blues, and Morrissey. Booking St. Claire Studio in Lexington, Kentucky, for two weeks just prior to Christmas 2007, they arrived with Escovedo's touring band (including a string section) in tow. And as Chuck put it, 'Alejandro, with his $800 shoes and near encyclopedic knowledge of the Stooges, brought the perfect marriage of the regal and the street. Visconti brought disorder of the highest order.'[24]

'We hit the pavement running with that record, and I'd written all the songs with Alejandro,' Chuck says. 'Thing was, I don't even know if Tony Visconti knew that. Suddenly he's got someone correcting other people on the chords and things (who *is* this guy?) and I could see how that would be a little bit awkward.' Occasionally, Chuck and Al would huddle over a flight case as they figured out which verse to use. Prophet has nothing but admiration for the veteran producer. 'Visconti really did have the ability to take a track that seemed a little out of control, and he'd make it into a *record*,' Chuck told me. 'By putting his hands on the faders and really shaping it into something. And there were times when we would be working a song, I thought it was getting better, and he'd lean into the talkback and just say, "It's getting too polite." And he was right. So, he's kind of a master of that, in many ways.'

The admiration was evidently mutual. An interview with Visconti six months later revealed that he was indeed aware of Prophet's significance in the *Real Animal* project. 'Alejandro was writing lyrics up until the very last minute,' he told the *Austin Chronicle*. 'Alejandro and Chuck were often sitting on the couch right until the vocal, changing some words, changing some lines. Even when Alejandro was on mic, singing, Chuck would interject and said, "No, no, you have to change this word, it's not working." So it was always a work in progress.' Visconti declared the lyrics 'worthy of a Bowie or Dylan. These are some of the best lyrics I've ever had to work with and it's easy to produce an album when you have lyrics that good'.[25]

Real Animal might be Escovedo's best collection of songs, and his most impressive album. There are superb hooks in 'Always A Friend' and 'Sister Lost Soul', both first-class pop songs. Darker hues are added via the likes of 'Chelsea Hotel '78', with its drones and off-kilter strings, while harder edges come via the heavy riffs of 'Smoke'. At the other end of the scale is the tender, gently satirical 'Sensitive Boys' (beautifully covered by Stephanie Finch on 2009's *Cry Tomorrow*, where the female vocal sharpens the irony). Musically, 'Golden Bear' simultaneously recalls Chris Isaak's hit 'Wicked Game' and cheekily borrows from the Visconti-produced Bowie song 'Ashes To Ashes' with its keyboard tones, but the lyrical content is something else again, addressing the ticking clock of a terminal disease.

Following the recording of *Real Animal*, Springsteen associate Dave Marsh, who had always been a major supporter of Escovedo's, stepped up, and Springsteen's manager Jon Landau agreed to manage Al. Out on tour in Europe, one evening Prophet opened up his laptop to find a message from Peter Blackstock, the editor of *No Depression* magazine. 'And I click on a link, and there's Alejandro and Bruce Springsteen in Houston, Texas. In front of twenty thousand people, mouth to mouth, singing "Always A Friend." Yeah, it's kind of a thrill to have Bruce singing your words!'

LETTING FREEDOM RING

By February of 2009, Prophet already had another record brewing, and a solo acoustic European tour previewed a few of the songs that would appear on his next release, *¡Let Freedom Ring!* The title track was originally just a scrap left over from many years earlier, a co-write with Kurt Lipschutz, but it would prove to be the perfect fit for the collection of songs Chuck was writing. 'Almost all those songs were written during the summer of 2008,' he told me.

'We had come back from Europe after one of those long tours. And my body clock was turned around and I kept waking up at three or four in the morning. So I would get up and walk to my office in the dark and play with the songs. It was an easy, inspired time. There was a heatwave and I had the window open and it all just kind of blew in there. It was the summer when the bottom fell out of the wet sack of the American economy.'

Of the title track, Chuck says, 'I think that was just me riffing on the one-percenters of the world. And then there was "Holding On", "What Would A Mother Do", "American Man", and "Barely Exist".' It was a deeply unsettling collection of snapshots of contemporary North America, I suggest. 'Yeah,' he nods. '"Barely Exist" is a photograph of people just trying to make their way. I have friends who could speak Spanish before they could speak English, because of a Mexican nanny. So,' he continues, quoting the lyrics, '*Who's gonna rock her to sleep? Who's gonna hold her when she cries?* That doesn't seem like a villain to me. And the irony is that we spend a billion dollars a year keeping people out of this country—people who want to come here and clean our toilets and change our babies' diapers. It makes no sense. The rise, the fall, the death, and the rebirth, and subsequent complete obliteration of the American Dream—that was my sandbox for the album.'

'Sonny Liston's Blues' was inspired by footage of the press conference preceding the match Liston would lose to Muhammad Ali: 'They were picking on Sonny Liston and really enjoying Ali,' he recalls. '"He's so ugly. I feel sorry for him. I'm so pretty." And the press were just eating it up, and then one said, "Sonny, do you have anything to add to that?" And that's when he lifted himself up and he goes, "I'm a man of few words, and I think you heard most of them today." And just walked off. And I loved that as an opening; blues couplets: "I'm a man of few words, baby / I think by now you've heard 'em all."' Prophet also points out that the song is completely live. 'Three guitars on the floor. Me, Greg [Leisz], and Tom Ayres, and Rusty [Miller] on bass. There were four people playing Fenders. At the same time. In the same room. And not one overdub. Not one background vocal. Not one tambourine. You're listening to exactly what it sounded like in that room in Mexico. I can hear it. I can *smell* it!' he laughs.

Part of the magic of *¡Let Freedom Ring!* came from the specific recording environment Prophet chose in which to create it. 'I had written some songs,' he recalls, 'and I was asking Greg for some advice about other situations and engineers and he expressed an interest in producing for me. And I got a call from an old friend of mine, Jason Carmer.' Carmer had been part of the Toast Studios crowd and had been involved in the recording of the Go Go Market LP. He had relocated to Mexico City with his wife and young child. 'And he said, "It's like the 60s down here. This place is alive, people are making music, it's bustling." And that just appealed to me. I was in Nashville, and I took a detour and went to Mexico City. We went looking for studios.'

At the end of a three-day scouting trip, they walked into Estudio 19, and Prophet knew he had found what he was looking for: 'It's like I tell people, I was looking at a studio that was completely state of the art … around the time of the Eisenhower administration!' Prophet got straight on the phone to Leisz, who was already on board to produce: 'I told him, "I've got these songs that are all about what's going on in this country right now. And I've found the perfect studio … in Mexico City!" There was a long pause, and then Greg said, "That could work." And when he was in, I was thrilled. He drove up here from LA, we rehearsed the band, and we went down to Mexico City and just threw caution to the wind.'

As things turned out, the quirks of Estudio 19 were the least of their problems. The equipment was temperamental—'It's really difficult to keep old gear maintained and running, and it's moody. That's part of the sound of it'—but a few days into recording, a 6.4 earthquake hit the area, and there were periodic power outages. Then, on the third day, a swine-flu epidemic and resultant media-whipped panic hit the city. 'The CNN paranoia, if you crank that stuff up to 11, makes everybody start to feel a little off,' Chuck said at the time. 'People got itchy. We put on blue masks and had a driver take us to the studio.'[26]

'There were tanks going up and down the street and they were tossing boxes of blue masks,' he adds. 'Everywhere we went there were no restaurants open. But we would just go and knock on the door and they would quietly let us in and cook for us. And it was apocalyptic. Poor Greg had a little bit of a faint cold, and maybe allergies, and the whole time he was thinking he might be coming down with the flu. But he didn't say anything at the time.

And we cranked that record out in eight days. The paint was still wet on the songs when we got there. But after having made *Age Of Miracles* and *Soap And Water* with strings and horns and children's choirs, I just really wanted to make a two-guitar/bass/drums kind of record.'

Carmer, engineering, noted how the bleed and leakage between voices and instruments was turned to their advantage in recording: 'People think isolation is the way to go,' he told *EQ*. 'But getting the bleed reinforces the stereo imagery. You can hear the guitars from the perspectives of all the mics in the room. The bleed gives you great depth of field.' What emerged, after a few minor overdubs back in LA, was a terrific, live-sounding album that has a similar urgency and presence to *Homemade Blood*. The overdubs, done in a single day, were primarily backing vocals provided by Stephanie Finch and Kelley Stoltz (the 60s-style 'shooby-dooby's on 'Good Time Crowd' are particularly fine), pedal steel (Greg Leisz), and fiddle (Sara Watkins), which provides a heart-tugging, country lilt to 'What Can A Mother Do'. Kevin T. White plugged in to provide a new bass line to the feverish, wryly humorous 'Hot Talk'. James DePrato overdubbed some guitar, most notably a slide part that lifts the title track into another dimension. 'Where The Hell Is Henry?' is a chaotic tangle of guitar and vocals, punctuated by laughs and calls, squeezed into the final day of tracking when Greg told Chuck the night before that they had time for only one or two more and that he might want to 'talk to his heart' and decide what he wanted to prioritise. The spontaneity makes the song one of the most enjoyable on the album.

The sessions were also distinguished by the involvement of Ernest 'Boom' Carter, a veteran best known for playing in Springsteen's E-Street Band for a few months in 1974 (he can be heard on 'Born To Run'). 'Boom is a real stylist,' says Prophet. He figured out very quickly not to direct Carter, but instead invited him to 'do his thing. That's really what I wanted rather than trying to shape it into something it wasn't. I wanted to be able to hear the personality of the individuals'. He reflects for a moment. 'Dickinson used to talk about arrangements being the enemy of rock'n'roll. And I wasn't quite sure what he meant. But an arrangement is a producer or some other person's vision of the song. And it's nothing compared to the sound of a band, the sound of personalities fighting it out.'

There are a couple of particularly striking love songs on the album. 'Love Won't Keep Us Apart' is another co-write with Lipschutz that features Leisz's beautiful pedal steel adorning what is already one of the LP's best melodies. This song and especially the closing 'Leave The Window Open' feel more nakedly autobiographical. 'I don't know if that was a particularly happy time for me,' Chuck confesses. 'Lots of isolation that year. And our marriage was in the doldrums ... I certainly was not running with the good-time crowd.' Of 'Leave The Window Open,' he confirms, 'Yeah, the decline of our marriage is in there .... not sure what pulled us back. Next!' The song is disarming in its lyrical simplicity, but the gaucheness is carefully deployed, conversational. The beautiful melody sits atop two distinct guitar tracks that layer over each other and help lift the song higher and higher in waves of emotion. And Prophet's voice soars. It is one of the best vocal performances he has ever committed to tape.

Reviews of the new album usually mentioned Green On Red in passing, and still tended to refer to Prophet as 'underrated'. The reference points were familiar—Dylan, Petty, the Stones. For *City Pages*, the album was 'bar-band rock of a high order: smart, loud, funny, simple, pissed off, but also sentimental in that last-call sort of way' and also 'attuned to Great Recession anxiety and passionately pro-underdog'.[27] And most reviewers did pick up on the darker undertow of the album—what Chuck himself has called, a little coyly, 'political songs for non-political people'. For the *Shepherd Express*, it was 'a sensible, rollicking, perhaps important look at the hard times of the moment'.[28] The *KC Free Press* noted how the songs 'illuminate the current American predicament, wryly capturing the woes of the workaday and the marginalized'.[29] According to *Popmatters*, it was 'hands down his best work', and the reviewer, Cody Miller, captured its precise political trajectory, describing it as 'an album that speaks to the masses of disenfranchised people who felt the Bush Administration let them down, even if they couldn't exactly articulate that emotion in anything other than rage and questions that remained unanswered'. Miller reckoned it was the album Green Day were trying to make when they cut *21st Century Breakdown*, released just a few months prior, the difference being: 'Prophet doesn't try to be the voice of a movement; he's just a guy writing songs that reflect the emotion of a large group of people, making him the less-apparent heir to the likes of Dylan and Guthrie.'[30] The *East Bay Express* compared the album to Springsteen's dissection of Reagan's America on *Nebraska* (and the same artist's failure to recapture and update that analysis with 2009's *Working On A Dream*), 'weaving together the failures of this American dream with its fraying cords of hope'.[31] In a similar vein, the heavy-hitting paper the *Village Voice* called it 'a *Born In The USA* for our time' for the way both albums 'manifest patriotism through disenchantment, and both rely heavily on marginalized characters to expose socioeconomic woe'.[32]

Across the board, the album found reviewers reaching for superlatives: *No Depression* proclaimed it 'vintage Prophet songwriterly rock'n'roll';[33] *Mojo* called it 'unrestrained, uninhibited, alive' in a four-star review;[34] according to *Blurt*, it was 'the sound of an artist at the top of his game'.[35] 'Is this the best Chuck Prophet album ever?' asked the *Cleveland Scene*. 'Sure, why not? They all get to wear that medal for a while.'[36] The London *Times* called it a 'beautifully realised slice of soulful rock'n'roll and exquisite songwriting'.[37]

TOURING ¡LET FREEDOM RING!

There had been a short solo acoustic tour in Europe to begin promotion for the album. Two band tours of Europe would follow, in autumn 2009 and spring 2010, with a North American tour during the winter months between, which gives a sense of how firmly Prophet and Kennedy had managed to establish a far wider territory over years of patiently building audiences: Ohio, Kentucky, Tennessee, West Virginia, Philadelphia, Massachusetts, New York, Virginia, Maryland, Georgia, and ending up in Florida. After a fortnight's break, there were further shows in Washington and Oregon, and finally back to California. After the second leg in Europe there was another set of US dates in July and August, including some solo gigs.

Prophet is one of the few artists of his vintage that will still routinely structure his setlists around the new release. His shows make few if any concessions to nostalgia—the exceptions being the familiar guitar showcases 'You Did' (now stretching out to a distinctly prog-rock eleven minutes plus) and 'Summertime Thing'. The ¡Let Freedom Ring! show would usually open with 'Sonny Liston's Blues' and draw heavily on the most recent two albums, often including the infectious, Springsteen-endorsed 'Always A Friend' in the opening salvo, and 'I Bow Down And Pray To Every Woman I See' restructured as a fleet-footed shuffle. One welcome surprise in rotation for the European tour was 'We Had It All', sung as a duet with Stephanie Finch. Forever restlessly reinventing, Prophet also revisited 'Queen Bee', electrified it, and performed it in double time. Other covers included a spirited take on Springsteen's 'For You' (featuring a piercing, intricate twin lead solo), and an old favourite, Alex Chilton's 'Bangkok' (Chilton having died a few days before the band played SXSW in March 2010). Topping them all was a breathtaking, full-pelt 'I'm Not Talking' (Yardbirds), often played as a final encore.

Some gigs also featured a guitar history lesson that included snatches of canonical riffs and solos from the early 60s through the 1970s. It was a pleasing reminder of Prophet and DePrato as connoisseurs of the whole history of rock'n'roll. 'It was an excuse to keep things spontaneous between me and James,' Chuck remarks. 'It never happened the same way twice. James could always stump me, especially going into TV theme songs. I'd jog my memory—try to harness the subconscious mind for some forgotten Frat Party riffs buried in there somewhere. But James? He's so quick on his feet. Going from Ozzy to the theme from *Gilligan's Island* into Bach or something. Just crazy, hare-brained stuff. We'd always end up laughing hysterically.' Equally, Kevin T. White is in awe of Prophet as 'a student of rock'n'roll'. He explains, 'The history and the depth of his knowledge about music is staggering. Not too long ago we were driving to LA, and Chuck started talking about the southern California early punk scene and didn't stop for two solid hours. I wish I had a tape rolling on it.'

The *¡Let Freedom Ring!* UK tour included a show in a village hall in Tingewick in May 2010—a sleepy settlement in rural Buckinghamshire with ancient Roman roots, one shop, and one pub, and a personal aside here shines a light on Kevin's character. I had taken my teenage boys along to the show, together with my eldest son's bandmates. At the end of the show, as Chuck discussed footwear fashions with them, Kevin approached, inviting the young drummer and bassist up to the stage to try out the gear before loading out. After a brief jam, and as I said my goodbyes and prepared to take the starstruck boys home, Kevin appeared with the instrument he had been

CHAPTER ELEVEN

SOMEDAY THIS IS ALL GONNA BE GONE

CRY TOMORROW, TEMPLE BEAUTIFUL (2010–13)

> *I somehow think if I could make a classic—a real classic record—then everything would come together in my life, and that's probably a lie. But in terms of the lies we tell ourselves, it's not the worst.* – Chuck Prophet

CRY TOMORROW

In the midst of his own triumphant return to the album/tour cycle, Prophet had participated in the Green On Red reunion and also written and recorded with Alejandro Escovedo. Five years on from the low point of the end of the New West deal, he was in an increasingly secure position, building a comfortably habitable perch somewhere on the escarpment of an industry still suffering the subsidence caused by the digital revolution on all fronts: not only distribution but recording, mixing, and producing. The development of the digital audio workstation had kicked off a generation of successful bedroom pop artists, and the proliferation of the internet and the rise of video blogging in particular was disrupting traditional models of promotion. Prophet and Dan Kennedy, however, were navigating their own path: there was now a successful licensing deal with a simpatico label, increasingly diverse projects (more co-writing, production duties, and adventures such as the Green On Red reunion), and a substantial, loyal fan base on the live circuit for Chuck's own music.

By 2009, Stephanie Finch was ready to follow up on the artistic success of the Go Go Market project with another album centred around her voice and her songs, almost a decade on. Finch found herself collaborating chiefly with her old friend Randall Homan, who for a while would come over regularly on a Friday night for informal writing sessions. As Stephie put it, it all happened 'a little more organically' than the Go Go Market process. 'Chuck stepped in at the end of a couple of the songs, but it was mostly me and Randall.' Prophet recalls that Finch had been wanting to make another record of her own for a while, 'And then one day she just had those great songs.'

The album has a cohesive and integrated band sound. Rusty Miller, whom Prophet had got to know around the time of *No Other Love*, played bass. Prophet gives a nod to the way Stephanie's rhythm guitar and Kelley Stoltz's drumming 'marry' so convincingly. As producer, he was adamant that their partnership would remain at the heart of the recording, and he remarks how, if the singer is not a polished guitarist, sometimes a producer will routinely remove those parts and replace them with slicker performances. 'And then, little by little, you start giving up the person's feel. Stephanie found somebody that had just the same sort of sway or wobble that she has . . . I liked the fact that it was Kelley, because he's not really a professional drummer. The first day we recorded "Tina Goodbye", and everybody was really surprised. I remember Kelley, who had made a few records and had run his band into the ground touring, being really energised: "I want to do *my* record here!"'

Infectious hooks and melodies abound. The album opens with the irrepressible energy of 'Tina Goodbye', the sound coloured by melodic bass and stabs of 80s synth; 'Don't Back Out Now' epitomises the eclectic style, layering guitar and piano over a Kinks-inflected riff. 'Transmission' manages to evoke both a contemporary feel and the 60s musical landscape of Sandi Shaw and Dusty Springfield, and is distinguished by a heart-meltingly beautiful bridge.

Of the covers on the album, the Prophet/Escovedo track 'Sensitive Boys' (from *Real Animal*) sounds in its original form like a man describing the burden of emotional vulnerability, but, as Ken Tucker of NPR's *Fresh Air* notes, Finch 'takes the song and makes it a sharp-eyed, tough-minded critique of boys who fancy themselves to be sensitive'.[1] 'Count The Days' is another great vehicle for her skills as an interpreter; she toughens up the persona in the song, making it sound more like a threat than a lament: 'If you don't believe I'm leaving, count the days I'm gone.' The Randy Newman cover has its roots in an unusual connection back to Finch's own past: Chuck recalls early in their relationship a trip to Monterey to visit her former singing partner, Patrick Winningham's sister Mare, who had recently auditioned for a TV series called *Cop Rock*. Sitting at the piano for that audition had been none other than Randy Newman. A cassette of the audition had ended up in Chuck's hands: 'I used to listen to it in the car,' he enthuses, 'I used to listen to it at home. I used to listen to it for pleasure. *All* the time.' When it came up in conversation in the studio, Chuck brought the tape in, and they ended up cutting 'She's The One' for *Cry Tomorrow*.

As on the Go Go Market album, there is often a coolness to Finch's delivery that places an ironic distance between voice and lyric. This is not to say the performances lack passion, but there is always a controlling intelligence that is evident in all the songs. 'She's a believable singer,' Chuck reflects. 'She's kind of an actress in that respect, I think.' One of the real coups was getting the album reviewed on national radio via NPR's show *Fresh Air*, an arts-feature programme with considerable reach and prestige. The release was previewed by a double bill of Chuck Prophet & The Mission Express and Stephanie Finch & The Company Men at the Great American Music Hall, and a fall US tour with Finch opening. At the end of November there was a short UK tour for The Company Men that brought Stephie and the band to my local venue, the Railway Inn in Winchester. It found Finch in fine voice, confidence boosted by a backlog of shows. A highlight was an encore of Stephie and Chuck duetting on Tom Petty's 'The Waiting'. It was a warm, intimate show made all the more magical when we stepped outside into several inches of snow that had fallen unnoticed in the meantime.

THE SPANISH BOMBS

The end of 2010 brought an unexpected opportunity. A Spain-based promoter called the Houston Party had established a lucrative pattern of inviting performers to revisit classic albums by other artists and bands. Prophet was at first reluctant until he began to think about The Clash's 1979 double-LP *London Calling*, a keystone of his own late teens—and ever since. The band that would come to be known as The Spanish Bombs coalesced around a collaboration with old sparring partner Chris von Sneidern: the two of them had bonded over *London Calling* back when *Homemade Blood* had been at the demo stage. 'Chris and I had a lot of history and it wasn't all good,' Chuck admits, conceding that his friend had a right to feel he had been passed over as potential producer for that album. 'He and I remained cordial but it took some doing to convince him that it would be a cool thing to do. We did an unannounced show at the Make-Out Room, which is our neighbourhood bar, playing *London Calling*, and word got out and people were showing up.' Stephanie talked to Chris after the show and asked if he was excited about going to Spain; he replied, a little sceptically, 'Yeah, if it happens.' She looked at him and said, 'You don't really know Chuck very well do you? I wouldn't underestimate his will, because it *is* going to happen.' Probably the scepticism was at least in part due to what had happened all those years ago. Chuck just shrugs: 'Anybody can be a pessimist and I guess they'll be right a fair amount of the time.'

But Prophet's commitment to the project was never in doubt. He and von Sneidern spent a considerable amount of time early in the process working out arrangements, with Chuck taking the Joe Strummer role and Chris covering Mick Jones's parts: 'I remember cycling in the morning down to CVS's apartment, where we worked out the chords and the lyrics with two acoustic guitars, sitting knee to knee, and we figured out who would be singing which parts. And then we let the rhythm section work things out on their own.' The band was made up of Josh Lippy on bass, Derek Taylor on drums, and Ben Frederick on keys. As Prophet told *SF Gate* at the time, 'We're not changing one comma. But we have changed the grooves under the songs' feet.'[2] Prophet also remembers von Sneidern rewiring the speakers to put the left and right channels out of phase with each other: 'And then suddenly instruments started popping out and he was able to isolate some of the lead guitar lines and stuff.' In the same interview with *SF Gate*, Prophet proclaimed it 'the Rosetta stone of the punk apocalypse'; when we spoke, he compared it to the Stones' definitive 1972 double album *Exile On Main St.*: 'There's rockabilly on there, there's ska, there's folk music, there's these jazzy excursions. There's the straight-up disco of "Train In Vain", there's kind of a glam rock thing. It's all in there.'

The setlist replicated the album in its entirety, in order, with 'Bank Robber' thrown in as an encore, and the shows in Spain were a huge success: packed venues and wild crowds. 'It was incredible,' Prophet remarks. 'The atmosphere was totally electric. The national newspaper gave it some coverage. There was some dumb luck, and the planets just kind of lined up. Hard to say why. But it helps that it's just a great record. It took us by surprise, because we thought it was going to be just this summer holiday gig. And then they had us back to play some festivals.' Prophet admits that by the time they got to London, they were 'a little bored; probably a few gigs too far'—although it did not seem that way from the audience side of the monitors. The Garage show on July 23 2011 opened with Johnny Green, The Clash's tour manager, reading from his autobiography, *A Riot Of Our Own* (1999), and another figure from the era, DJ Scratchy, played a set of the band's vinyl favourites before The Spanish Bombs' set, which was received with wild enthusiasm.

For von Sneidern, there were aspects that made it more bittersweet. He clearly enjoyed the onstage experience immensely, and he was also given the support slot to open every show with a solo set. But he had reservations about the way the tour was promoted, with posters naming the band Chuck Prophet & The Spanish Bombs. While he understood the move in business terms, it rankled. However, the tour ended on a high with a massively oversold homecoming show at the Great American Music Hall. 'And by the time we got there,' Prophet notes, 'Chris had a wireless rig on his guitar and was completely untethered. That got interesting.' In reflecting on it all, Prophet says simply, 'It made sense at the time. It takes the pressure off a little bit. It's like driving somebody else's car.' Just over seven years later, there would be a new kind of joyride plotted, again with a specifically Spanish set of destinations. The East River Truckers tour at the beginning of 2019 would see Chuck team up with Charlie Sexton to play a show based around The Rolling Stones' 1978 album *Some Girls*.

LET'S TALK ABOUT OLD FRIENDS
Prophet and Kurt Lipschutz had not spoken in a long time. Their last direct collaboration had been on *The Hurting Business*, although songs they had worked on together were revived, finished off, or reworked by Prophet, and

something had appeared on each album since their working relationship (and their friendship) had ended in 1999. Re-acquaintance came about when Finch and Lipschutz re-established contact. 'I don't think I had talked to him for a while,' Finch remembers, 'but Klip and I started having coffee together. So it was really my suggestion that they start writing again after all those years.'

It had been ten years since the two old friends had exchanged a word. 'He said at one point he could write a book of all the reasons why,' Prophet says. 'And I'm sure I could as well. But like Dan Penn told me, if you are lucky enough to find someone you can perform the miracle with, don't take it lightly. So, you either honour it or you don't.

'Stephanie kinda brokered it,' he confirms. 'And then I said, "Well, here's the date, here's the place. We can get together, try to write, and if we don't … if we can't … that's OK too." And then, two days before the date, I was on the train platform and I turned, and he was standing right there. And I said, "Oh, hey. Guess I'll see you in a couple-a days!"' The fact that the song chosen for the high-profile *Letterman* appearance in January 2008, 'Doubter Out Of Jesus', had been co-written with Kurt, may also have been a factor in the reconciliation. Prophet had made a point of singling out Lipschutz's contribution to the song when he blogged about it, and Kurt had taken note. 'All the best lines are his,' Chuck wrote at the time. 'We've written tons of songs, among my favorites in my song bag.'[3]

In a ruminative mood during one of our conversations, Prophet reflected back on the reunion. 'Kurt is an American Original. Believe me, I wouldn't have tangled with the dude as long and hard if he wasn't. I just feel like, having him come into my life, seeing that Bone Cootes thing that afternoon in that bar, through the drunken haze, I *saw* something, and I'm really glad I did. And I'm really glad that we took a break. It all makes sense.' I had spent some time with Kurt the day before, and I mentioned to Chuck the restless energy that he emits, even before that third cup of coffee at the Olympic Café. 'Oh yeah. I'm so lucky to know him. Kurt and I, we never run out of things to talk about … whether it's pop culture or whether it's some kind of newsworthy event in the air, I always look forward to hearing Klippy's take on it!'

At the time of the reunion, Prophet had just finished working on *Real Animal*, and he was hardly overflowing with musical ideas. 'But when Kurt and I got in a room, we immediately started kicking songs around. We fell into a pattern of knocking out a verse or something and then arguing for two hours about where to eat for lunch. Those were really happy times. We get all worked up into a froth when it's flowing. And Kurt gets really excited when we're onto something. There's poetry in melody. I appreciate all of that. So many songs might never have gotten off the ground without his enthusiasm when we're bouncing ideas off of the walls.'

The San Francisco theme that would eventually define the album took a while to emerge. 'We had a lot of what we might call boy/girl songs, relationship songs. She- done-me-wrong stuff.' A list of songs for the album dated April 26 2011 has thirty-six titles, including 'One More Night With You', 'Lonesome Me, Lonesome You', 'Gotta Get Back To You', 'Go Easy, Baby', 'I Miss You So Much', 'True Love', and 'Give The Boy A Kiss'. A handful would eventually surface as B-sides ('I Call Your Name') or on the next album, *Night Surfer*. Prophet continues, 'We were getting together on a regular basis and the songs were piling up. And then at some point I went and made a bunch of demos so I could hear the songs coming through big speakers.' The demos were recorded swiftly at Tim Mooney's studio Closer, with Prairie Prince, Rusty Miller, and James DePrato. Chuck had known Prairie from the days in the warehouse space on Folsom Street; coming across him at a local session, Prophet invited him to join them to record the demos—about a dozen tracks. He had met Rusty when he was invited to produce an album by Rusty's band Jackpot, *Shiny Things* (2002), and the association had continued with the Company Men project and ¡*Let Freedom Ring!*

'I thought three of the songs had some sort of San Francisco connection. And at that point I realised, if you stand back and squint, if we threw out most of this stuff except for a couple of songs, I think we could have the start of a great San Francisco record. I said to Kurt, "We could do it, but it might take us a year." And he was suffering; he had hepatitis C, and it was kind of hanging over his head like a death sentence. And he needed to get treatment that was going to put him out of commission for a while. And I said, "Well, why don't we finish writing this record and you go get the treatment?" And he did. But yeah, it took us a year to write the record.'

'One of the things that I've tried to avoid is the trappings of the singer/

songwriter: "Chuck went here, Chuck went there, Chuck got his heart broken,'" Chuck reflects. 'So I was excited when we tapped into the San Francisco thing. And, to Kurt's credit, he embraced it. We thought it should centre around the Temple Beautiful, because that was where, as a fifteen-year-old kid, I saw those bands that really opened my mind to punk rock as a personal expression. There were five bands that night, and they were all completely different in so many ways, musically and even visually. But they all had one thing in common, they were doing what [local punk rock promoter from the 80s] Dirk Dirksen described as "laying it on the line in an effort to express themselves".'

The Temple Beautiful was a former synagogue situated at 1839 Geary Boulevard, next door to the Masonic Temple that would become the Reverend Jim Jones's Peoples Temple—the song 'Willie Mays Is Up At Bat' includes a reference to the cult leader. During his sojourn in San Francisco, Jim Jones forged strong bonds with local politicians including George Moscone and Harvey Milk—of whom more in a moment. Jones's cult moved its base to Guyana in 1977, where the Jonestown mass murder/suicide would claim the lives of over nine hundred cult members. The nomenclature of 1839 Geary Boulevard was fluid through the 60s and 70s, and it was occasionally used for performances; in the fall of 1967, the Grateful Dead rented it as a rehearsal space, and a decade later it was the venue for Hot Tuna's live album *Double Dose* (1978). It was sometimes known as Theatre 1839, sometimes simply as 1839 Geary Boulevard, but to the punks it came to be known as Temple Beautiful. The Clash played their second ever US date there, on February 8 1979, and a poster survives, dated January 25 1980, featuring bands Prophet name-checks from his own memories of the era, includes Wall Of Voodoo, The Go-Go's, and The Mentors. Temple Beautiful—not the song but the place—and everything Prophet had invested in it—historically, emotionally, musically, and culturally—would become the cornerstone of one of the greatest albums of his career.

WRITING *TEMPLE BEAUTIFUL*

Prophet notes that working on *Temple Beautiful* was a fast and focused process, 'very uncomplicated'. It was in some respects his most autobiographical work, but, as noted above, it was a far cry from your typical singer/songwriter confessional. In place of painful dissections of the heart, Prophet offered a deep dive into the geography, the music, the culture, and the mythology of the city that has been his home since his teen years. 'When I moved to San Francisco,' he told *Magnet* magazine, 'I started getting my own kind of self-education in different people of different races and colors and sexes ... punk rock and arty stuff. For me, coming here kind of opened my eyes.'[4] In interviews, Prophet sometimes uses an addiction metaphor to convey the power of the city over him: 'It can suck you under. That first hit. It really does a whammy on you. And if you're like me, you can find yourself chasing the San Francisco dragon for the rest of your life. That's what this record is about.'[5]

'The best stuff is always personal on some level,' he tells me. 'I mean, the bands I saw at the Temple Beautiful just changed the course of my life, really. I think almost everybody that ever played there ... I think they're all gone now.' Except, perhaps, for Roy Loney, founder member of The Flamin' Groovies. Chuck had come across Loney in various contexts since first seeing him perform. 'He used to work in a record store out near San Francisco State when I was going to college. And he also works at Jacks Records in our neighbourhood, which is just one of those dusty, timeless shops where you never know what you're going to find. And Roy often walks down my street. Over the years I'd seen him but we never really had any real interaction, and Brad Jones and I were cranking up a Flamin' Groovies bootleg. And I just decided that we had to have Roy Loney on the album. And of course he played the Temple Beautiful. I sent Roy Loney a note and said, "Hi Roy, this is Chuck Prophet. I don't know if you know me. I feel like I know you." I said, "I'm working on this record and I thought we needed your voice for a song. It's about the Temple Beautiful." And he replies, "Yeah. I'm about twenty minutes away." And he came over. I think he was on the mic within two minutes. And when he got to the bridge, he's just trying to find his pitch, he's like [*sings up and down*], and Brad kept it. And so it was just perfect!'

Prophet and Klipschutz were clicking again, as Chuck's description of writing 'Willie Mays' illustrates: 'As fun as it was, we had lots of villains but every great myth needs a hero. We had gone for a walk and ended up in front of the Willie Mays statue at the ballpark. And we said to each other, "No-brainer." Kurt came up with that: "Three on and two out / Under the lights / Nobody knows who'll make it home tonight." And I just couldn't see that as a chorus. I said, "I don't know what you're thinking ... that's a terrible idea." And he fought me on it. And I remember hitting an E chord and saying, "I hear the church bells ring / Willie Mays is up at bat," and just going from E to A, and then Kurt finishing my sentences: "And all he did was touch his hat." And I said, "Meanwhile Carol Doda stood up and said I won't be ignored." And he said, "She showed him everything she had / And then she showed them all a little more." And we were literally finishing each other's sentences, and probably got halfway through them in one fell swoop. And then I monkeyed with it on my own for a while, and somehow made that chorus work.'

In interviews as well as in stage patter for the tours, Prophet referred to the fact that his 'shoebox-size' office where they were writing had no Wi-Fi, and that their celebration of San Francisco was Google- and Wikipedia-free. 'We ended up relying on the more mythical version of events. Which suited us fine, because it's not journalism. Maybe next time we'll get a fact checker,' Chuck jokes, 'but it really wasn't in our budget.' I put it to Chuck that one of the most striking things about 'Willie Mays' is, oddly, its universalism. The chant in the song is a celebration of a baseball player, but it works just as well as a football (soccer) chant. Prophet will often play on the topic of British versus American sports culture when he introduces the song (he jokes about watching his first soccer game: he sat in the hotel bar for two hours and 'no one scored one fucking point!'). In performance, 'Willie Mays' has become as much of a set piece as 'You Did'. On recent tours, Chuck will make his way out into the crowd and offer up the mic to anyone who looks ready to have a go at singing the 'woah woah's. 'Yeah,' he reflects. 'I like it because it's not about me. That's one of the greatest things about it that I didn't see coming. I felt the same way about the whole album. I really enjoyed promoting that record. Talking about yourself or trying to promote yourself, it's not much fun. But to expose people to all that history there, especially when San Francisco was going through such a tragic period of gentrification, to really celebrate these heroes was a lot of fun.

'Just how San Francisco opened my eyes to so many things,' he continues. 'Not just rock'n'roll, but the arts, and the sexes and politics ... all those art houses, like the Strand and the York, and the Electric and the Bridge and the Vogue. I saw so many French films and so many art movies, not to mention *Mad Max* ... I didn't really grow up in that VCR culture. I saw a lot of those movies in movie theatres. And also the fact that, even before I moved into the city, I was playing with the comedian Barry Sobel from time to time. And that exposed me to ... Dana Carvey, Robin Williams, Mike Pritchard, Bobby Slaton, Paula Poundstone, Jake Johansen. I always perked up when the heckling started. The comedians were brutal: I've seen hecklers reduced to tears. And I slowly became aware that every time any of those comedians got up there and tweaked their act, it was a leap of faith. And these guys were all totally accessible when I used to play with Barry. There was always an after-hours party somewhere, people were doing coke and playing ping-pong ... I saw a lot of stuff like that before it was on TV. I saw a lot of stuff like that before any of those guys could get *arrested*.'

Prophet is on a roll as he recalls what the cultural atmosphere was at that time: 'We used to play these gigs back then and we would get thirty dollars and split it four ways. Dirk Dirksen took over the Mabuhay Gardens, which was a Filipino restaurant and started having bands there, before my time ... Blondie played there, Suicide, Devo. I saw Dead Kennedys there within weeks of moving to the Bay Area with my family. It probably held less than two hundred people ... I remember standing on Broadway in North Beach, which was all strip clubs, with the barkers saying, "Come on in, naked girls!" It was still left over from the 60s. North Beach is still this vibrant neighbourhood. There was the Mabuhay, the On Broadway; across the street was the Stone, next to that was the Chi Chi. And when they all let out at two in the morning, the street would just be filled with people.

'I remember standing on the sidewalk in front of the Mabuhay Gardens on a hot summer night, and across the street at the Stone, which was a bigger, swankier club, somebody was putting the letters on the marquee one at a time, spelling out Dead Kennedys. And Dirk Dirksen turned to me, he pointed at it and he shook his head ... because they were going to play the more lucrative side of the street. "I talked to Jello about it," Dirk told me. "They want to make more money and they want to quit their day jobs." And he said, "Kid, as soon as people quit their day jobs, the scene will be over." And it's hard for people to understand that it was really just art for art's sake. And it was pretty short-lived really. But ... we didn't know *anybody* that made money. It wasn't about that. It was about the adventure and the travelling more than anything.'

Prophet had seen both sides in his years as a working musician. Coffee-and-doughnut tours in the early 1980s; the European festival circuit; the 'hand-to-hand combat', as he terms it, of playing clubs night in, night out; then painstakingly building and maintaining a touring base in the USA. A survey conducted around the time of *Temple Beautiful* by the Future Of Music Coalition canvassed 5,371 American musicians and found that only 6 percent of their aggregated income came from music sales, and 28 percent from live performance.[6] *Temple Beautiful* would yield a set of different marketing approaches—vinyl as well as CD, a cassette tape, a couple of singles backed with outtakes—but the strategy would once again, of necessity, be built around months of touring in the USA and across Europe.

TEMPLE BEAUTIFUL—THE ALBUM

The opening track, 'Play That Song Again', doesn't stake out the album's territory immediately, waiting until the second verse to introduce San Francisco in something approaching stage-musical fashion as 'a city full of animals, a city full of thieves / A city full of lovers trying hard to make believe'. In the *Temple Beautiful* iBook prepared for an abortive deluxe edition of the album, Lipschutz notes, 'The words "San Francisco" never appear on the album, though they were in the chorus to this one for a while. It gave us nothing but trouble till Chuck got frustrated and started to bang away and shout at the walls—and we had a song.' Earlier drafts of the lyrics included direct references to South Of Market, the Lower Haight, Geary Street, and Broadway, all dropped as the song was fashioned into something more mythical.

The *Temple Beautiful* album is peppered with cameos by colourful San Francisco characters: the stripper Carol Doda, the life-size animatronic Laffing Sal (a famous beachside fairground attraction), Fillmore owner and music impresario Bill Graham, the aforementioned suicide-cult leader Jim Jones, and the cartoon characters Bugs Bunny and Daffy Duck. 'The Left Hand And The Right Hand' (featuring a clever promo video directed by Albert Birney and Nick Krill) tells the story of the Mitchell brothers, Jim and Artie, who owned the strip club the O'Farrell Theatre, described by Hunter S. Thompson as 'the Carnegie Hall of public sex in America'.[7] The brothers were responsible for the famous mainstream hardcore porn film *Behind The Green Door* (1972), and the O'Farrell was one of the first establishments to introduce the concept of the lap dance. Prophet refers to the brothers' fate as 'your classic Cain and Abel story'; in 1991, Jim was convicted of manslaughter for shooting Artie dead in 1991 in a dispute over drugs; he served half of a six-year sentence and died of a suspected heart attack in 2007.[8]

Prophet and Lipschutz's song is more of a parable than this detail suggests, and Chuck tends to dedicate it to any number of famous, fraternal rivals in concert, including Ray and Dave Davies of The Kinks, The Everly Brothers, and Noel and Liam Gallagher of Oasis. The song is built around an infectious, loping beat and a melody that's 'catchier than a cold' according to the *Popmatters* reviewer.[9] The verses are models of concision, charting the bond (summed up in the line 'Ah, but no one could harmonize the way those brothers did'), separation ('One day it was separate checks, the next day bodyguards'), and reunion ('Well, now they're back together, still at each other's throats / Breaking strings and dropping beats, singing all of the wrong notes').

'White Night, Big City' was written as a tribute to a very different San Francisco hero, Harvey Milk, who had been elected to the San Francisco Board Of Supervisors in 1977; he was one of the first openly gay men to win political office in the history of the United States. A year later, he was shot and killed by Dan White, a former supervisor who had believed himself snubbed by the mayor, George Moscone. Provoked further by a series of disagreements with Milk—White was a homophobe opposed to Moscone and Milk's liberal agenda—White shot and killed them both in the offices of the City Hall. Tried for first-degree murder, he was convicted of the lesser crime of voluntary manslaughter. The perceived injustice ignited the so-called White Night Riots; the gay community in the city staged a peaceful demonstration that turned violent, causing damage to property and resulting in 140 casualties. It was an event, and a man, ripe for commemoration. There's a powerful tension in the song between the tragic subject matter and the ironic, self-consciously dumb backing vocal that helps to lighten the song. 'The message is heavy and the music's fun,' Chuck acknowledges. 'And I improvised all those "What? Who? Where? Why?" lines in one go. And Brad Jones kept it. He recognised it as a big *some*thing to colour in.'

'Castro Halloween' is another song that references the long, proud history of the LGBT community in San Francisco. The tradition of the Halloween street party in the Castro district goes back to 1946, but it took on 'a decidedly adult air' in the 1980s.[10] Prophet would remark that the 'party and a half' every Halloween would 'last 'til dawn. I live four or five blocks away, leading my quiet married existence, watching reruns of *The Wire* while the biggest dress-up party west of Berlin was in full swing'.[11] Unfortunately, as the years passed, it also became increasingly unruly, with gang violence and muggings commonplace. In 2006, nine people were shot, although there were no fatalities (the song references two people being shot and killed—proof, one could say, of Prophet's 'Google-pure' claim). The incident led to the closing down of the Halloween tradition, something the song mourns: 'Halloween was here but now it's gone / Men in skirts and heels are marching on.' The song is powered along by James DePrato's slide guitar and features a classic Prophet solo framed by layered vocal harmonies. Prairie Prince and Rusty Miller's propulsive rhythm is another key element. 'Prairie has the ability to overplay, but with taste,' Chuck notes.

The song 'Who Shot John', which lyrically and musically recalls 'Hey Joe', benefits from another in the album's unbroken series of strong melodies and an effortlessly cool vocal. The lyrics were inspired by John Murry's intervention: 'He popped his head in one day and said, "If you're thinking of writing about San Francisco you need to write a song about all the people that crossed each other." And that's what the streets [in the song] are named after': among others, Eddy Street in the Tenderloin, Van Ness, and Cyril Magnin Street, just off Market Street.[12] The idea of characters facing off in a series of duels is built on the metaphor of one street crossing another.

The album moves into deeper mythical territory with its closing track, 'Emperor Norton In The Last Year Of His Life (1880)'. Joshua A. Norton was a character described by the *San Francisco Chronicle* as 'the greatest, and most beloved, nut in the history of San Francisco'.[13] A British native, he emigrated to the city in 1849, bringing with him a $40,000 inheritance.

Making a swift fortune—the *Chronicle* reported that by 1853 he was worth a quarter of a million dollars—Norton was riding high on property investments and commodities before losing everything in a sequence of rapid reversals of fortune. Driven insane by his sudden, calamitous downfall, Norton came to believe he was the emperor of the country, making his announcement in the *San Francisco Bulletin* in 1859. He lived this way for over twenty years, cossetted in his delusion by the people of the city; he enjoyed the privilege of a free meal at almost any restaurant in the city and he attended theatres, churches, public gatherings and places of business to bless them with his imperial presence. In the *Temple Beautiful* iBook, Prophet notes, 'The day after he died over 30,000 people lined the streets of the city to pay homage to their adopted prodigal son.' He also describes how the song was born: 'One morning klipschutz burst into my workspace holding up the keys I'd given him and said, "Every set of keys is an original!" I strummed an A minor chord and *Bam!* we were off and running. That was the opening line that led us into this song.'

MARKETING THE TEMPLE

The album's thematic hook in publicity terms was a gift; it too provided a key, a way into the album that could give it an edge in a market that had become increasingly difficult for an artist working at Chuck Prophet's level. Having continued to establish a reputation via an impressive string of releases, one after another, Prophet was becoming a regular for some print-based music journalists, at home and abroad. At the same time, the significance and influence of printed press and music magazines from the newsagent's shelf was continuing to decline; in the second half of 2011, for example, the UK magazines *Uncut* and *NME* shed around 14 percent of their circulation year-on-year (to 62,305 and 27,650 respectively); *Q* fell 12.1 percent to 77,522.[14] At its peak, the *NME*, as a weekly, had been selling around 300,000.

One of the consequences of this decline was that a story—something to hang the album upon beyond the quality of the music itself—was becoming indispensable for a publicist trying to find a way in with an editor awash with submissions. Prophet pushed the narrative hard in interviews, and every reviewer took note, often responding in kind with the idea of the album as a map of the city's cultural history. 'Prophet makes San Francisco come to life in all its enduring, freaky glory' declared the *Tucson Weekly*, hailing it as 'a city of unhinged expression that holds in permanent thrall those lucky enough to get it.'[15] *NPR*'s Ken Tucker, who had also given *Cry Tomorrow* a glowing review, summed up the album as 'one man's alternative history of three decades of West Coast culture and politics', adding, 'All that, plus a few awfully good songs about having your heart broken.' Like many reviewers, Tucker noted the distinctive appeal of Prophet's 'searching, keening vocals,' and his gifts as a guitarist and songwriter.[16]

The *Washington Post* reviewer declared, 'If this isn't the best album of Prophet's career, it's definitely one of the most invigorating.'[17] 'Another glittering accomplishment from a hell of a consistent artist' was the *Austin Chronicle*'s conclusion.[18] In the UK, *Mojo* proclaimed it 'a hooky, memorable album', and *Uncut* called it 'mythological in scope, soulful in execution', singling out the title song and 'Castro Halloween' as the stand-out tracks while concluding that 'the whole lot is first rate'.[19]

Paste magazine was one of many that compared the project to Lou Reed's *New York* (1989), in a review that also praised the album for its 'core immediacy', its 'thump, churn and ferocity', and its 'punk aggression, the unadorned arrangements that slice to the core, the voice that tears through layers of guitars, bass and drums'.[20] *Classic Rock* magazine called the album 'A heroic all round smash and grab raised on rebel rock across the generations.'[21] *Popmatters* noted how Prophet wore his influences on his sleeve, and how a lot of the record sounded like 'some rock'n'roll gem recorded in 1978 (just for fun let's say with Nick Lowe producing) and then cryogenically frozen to be listened to in some dark, dystopian future desperately short of good tunes (i.e. 2012)'.[22] For *The Line Of Best Fit*, the album represented Prophet's 'most focused and concise work in years' and felt like a 'return to form' in the way it harked back to 'the raw pomp and swagger' of *Homemade Blood*.[23]

Temple Beautiful would be the launch pad for some of Prophet's biggest tours to date, but Prophet, Kennedy, and the Yep Roc marketing team also experimented with strategies designed to capture attention: one-offs that could cause a stir with alerts via social media. The album hit stores—what was left of them—on February 7 2012, and was celebrated with a release party that included a bus tour for forty fans around the city hosted by local DJ Peter Finch and ended with a private concert at the Catacombs, featuring special guests Kelley Stoltz and John Doe, formerly of the San Francisco punk band X. There was a string of shows in February, followed by a set of solo dates in Europe supporting The Jayhawks, which gave Prophet some useful promotion ahead of a full band European tour in April and May: five of the seven songs he played at the Barbican, London, on March 8, were from *Temple Beautiful*. Fighting off a recent bout of ill health, he delivered a set that somehow managed to make an impact in a cavernous auditorium and draw the audience in. The full-band European jaunt was followed almost as soon as they returned home by a full US tour that took them across the country from May to August.

The *Temple Beautiful* songs rapidly populated the setlists. The strong thematic cohesion of the album, the abundance of hook-laden songs, and the guitar-bass-drums foundation that most of them shared meant that they translated naturally to the stage, although early dates tended to kick off with some older songs, notably 'Storm Across The Sea', now restructured around a riff lifted from The Flamin' Groovies' 'Slow Death'. The same band's classic 'Shake Some Action' appropriately, swiftly established itself as a regular encore.

THE SWORD IN THE STONE

On August 23 2012, Prophet posted an announcement on his website: 'My 1984 Fender Squire [sic] Telecaster is Gone. I'm Offering a Reward of $500.00.'[24] Breaking the cardinal rule of touring musicians (he was not the first to do so, and will not be the last), Prophet had left the guitar in his van overnight, parked outside his apartment, along with Kevin T. White's Harmony bass. It wasn't until they started loading up for a gig in Portland that Prophet realised the guitar was missing. Someone had broken the side window of the van, reached in, and taken the two instruments. The loss was devastating. The guitar had, over the years, taken on a kind of talismanic aura. 'People talk about that guitar. It was one of the first Squiers to come off the line, out of Japan, and it doesn't have a serial number. And that was kind of a problem when it came to finding it. I got a call from Rick Nielsen [of the band Cheap Trick]. He said, "I got a bunch of those. They give 'em to me. I'd be happy to give you one." And I said, "Well, that's nice but … but I want *mine*. And I'm hoping that I'll get it back." And he goes, "OK, well, let me know." I was like a child: "I want my own!"'

When I ask Prophet how he felt at the moment he realised it was gone, his answer is unexpected: 'Well, part of it was, *Oh, finally I'll get that thing out of my life*. Because so much of my attachment to it is irrational. Walker Percy talks about how people develop irrational attachments to inanimate objects. But it's not coming out of the guitar. It's coming out of *you*. It's the Excalibur sword, it's like the one guy that can pull it out of the rock—he has the power. But what he doesn't realise is the power is in *him*, not the sword!' In truth, of course, Chuck was heartbroken. 'Over the years, I've had some others that were made from parts of different Squiers, and they were supposed to replicate the one I had. But I've never learned to love them.'

Tweeting the sad news, the band set off for the gig, and when Prophet got back online, the story had gone viral, as they say—at least, within the local music community. 'People were outraged!' he exclaims. Across Twitter, Facebook, and internet forums, the call went out to find the guitar. In the meantime, Prophet's faithful friend Patrick Winningham was on the case. 'Kara [Johnson] and I just stopped our lives for a couple of days,' Winningham tells me. 'She made the flyers, and then I went around putting them out everywhere. I know what that guitar meant, and so did Kara. The universe wasn't gonna be right until it was back in his hands!' Patrick believes the fact that Chuck's profile in the city was that much higher because of the recent release of *Temple Beautiful* was fortuitous, too. 'It was an ode to San Francisco, right? So the whole town kinda said, "We're gonna find this thing." And writers like Joel Selvin and Leah Garchik were all putting stuff up. So these crack-heads, they had nowhere to hide. I talked to him on the phone and I remember telling him, "Chuck, I promise you you'll get your guitar back. I promise you we'll find it."'

When a call came through from someone responding to the reward offer, a meeting was brokered to recover the guitar and hand over the reward—or the ransom. But Winningham's wife, Marion, was adamant he should not go alone. Prophet picks up the story. 'Patrick had the reward money, and his wife said, "You're not going down there with that money, they're just gonna roll you. You're gonna get jacked." So I called Tom Heyman, my old guitar player. And I said, "You need to go down there; Patrick needs some backup." He goes, "No problem, I have a belt buckle, it's the size of a turkey platter." Nobody was going to mess with this guy. A guy with a belt buckle that big has got nothing to lose, and you know he's *gotta* be packing heat! Meanwhile, Patrick told Marion, "Look, I'll take this Bible with me. Nobody's gonna roll a man with a Bible!"' Between them, Winningham and Heyman seemed ready for anything. They set off for the appointed rendezvous point: a Starbucks on 8th and Market.

As Prophet's blog post put it at the time: 'No one took Bin Laden to the ground, but some true blue heroism went down all the same. . . . After a few pleasantries were exchanged, another guy wheeled around the corner on roller blades—with both instruments strapped to his back! Where's the film crew when we need 'em?' Patrick notes, 'The thing about Chuck's guitar is, it has a banjo tuner for the low E string. Very distinctive. And so, the second he opened up the case . . . I saw that tuner, and I knew straightaway.' There was an argument when it emerged that Kevin's bass was no longer the guitar it had been. As the blog post recounted, 'Patrick and Tom docked these two fine citizens two C-notes (or was it three?) for spray painting the bass lime green (fair is fair) and drove off with the guitars. Hey, if "Mike" and the Roller Blade Man are high as fuck right now, God bless 'em anyway, they did the right thing.' For Patrick, it was 'one of the happiest days of my life'. Prophet wanted to celebrate the safe return of his precious Squier with the fans. 'So I went up to Healdsburg for the show,' Winningham continues, 'And I said, "King Arthur's sword is back in his little hands again!"' Patrick fixes me with a look, and there is a dramatic pause before he adds, quietly, 'So now if he ever loses it again, I'll kill him!'

STRINGS IN THE TEMPLE

On November 24 2012, Chuck Prophet & The Mission Express performed the *Temple Beautiful* album in full and in sequence, 'like a novel', with a string octet at the Great American Music Hall, a venue geographically and culturally at the heart of San Francisco (its long history includes time served as a bordello, as well as a venue for burlesque, jazz, and folk). Prophet refers to the venture as 'Plan B' after the original idea of turning the album into a fully fledged stage musical hit the rocks. (The project would never go away—see this book's conclusion for more.)

Prophet tapped Brad Jones to work out the string arrangements, and the musicians were local; the rehearsals began the morning before the gig, with one more rehearsal onstage the day of the show. The film's director, Darrell Flowers, had first met Prophet at a gig at the Make-Out Room in San Francisco in 2008. Seeing them load in, Darrell offered to help, and they got talking. Flowers's background was in lighting for film and video; being familiar with a few of Prophet's promos, he politely suggested Chuck could do with some help in that department, and offered to help out in the future. In a follow-up correspondence, Chuck asked Darrell if he knew any video editors, and Darrell put him in touch with his friend Scott Compton, an editor and director with his own editing company—coincidentally located just across the street from Chuck's office space. It led to the idea to document the making of the ¡Let Freedom Ring! album—the footage Scott shot in Mexico is a treasure trove, and we can only hope it will make its way out to the fans one day. Flowers helped out with some of the camera work and subsequently directed and put together the travelogue promos for *Temple Beautiful*. From there, he graduated (with honours) to directing duties for the film of the performance with the string octet.

The film that emerged, *Strings In The Temple*, is a faithful document of an extraordinary gig. While it is hardly a documentary—the concert taping is simply preceded by a montage of rehearsal footage and some brief interview snippets—the film is nevertheless a valuable record of a remarkable musical event, one of the most memorable highlights of Prophet's career. Flowers somehow managed to pull together a crew of a dozen people, including seven camera operators, all willing to work for free. The editing is beautifully handled, resisting the temptation for too many swift cuts, providing crystal clear close-ups of a bow on a cello, DePrato's slide gliding down the guitar neck, a beaming Kevin T. White, the familiar sidelong glances exchanged between Prophet and Finch, Prophet going nose to nose with the front row of the string section in the furious finale to 'White Night, Big City'. Brad Jones looks like he is having a ball at the conductor's stand, and high angle shots reveal a stage littered with discarded pages of musical notation, testimony to the seat-of-their-pants nature of it all. There is an additional charm in the fact that, probably for budgetary reasons, there are no overdubs or fixes. The occasional bum note or hesitation is preserved for posterity.

As one might expect, the string arrangements bring a sense of delicacy to many of the songs—not a mood one often associates with Chuck Prophet in a live context. But on the opening 'Play That Song Again', for example, guitar solos give way to pizzicato strings and some subtle keys from Stephanie Finch, or restrained guitar lines from James DePrato. Mission Express regulars Vicente Rodriguez and Kevin T. White hold the rhythm down on a stripped-down drum kit and, for most of the set, an upright double bass. Stephanie Finch played a celeste, contributing to the delicacy of some of the arrangements. 'Castro Halloween' is positively orchestral, the wall of overdriven guitar replaced by a lush chorus of strings and muted harmony vocals. Prophet solos on his Martin D-28; DePrato's electric slide is barely audible. While the original version, as well as the live electric incarnation, plays out with an extended coda, the stringed version is far more elegiac, coming in for a soft landing soon after the final chorus.

The start of the show is a little subdued, but it builds swiftly. The title track is graced with a guest appearance by Roy Loney. Prophet straps on a Silvertone 1446 hollowbody, a model made famous by Chris Isaak in his 'Blue Hotel' video—this one was a gift from Jack Waterson; there is some overdrive dialled in, but throughout the show the string section is left to do most of the heavy lifting. 'Temple Beautiful' is a song that is more difficult for band and octet to hold together, and, once or twice, the joins show. 'Who Shot John', shorn of its overdriven guitars, drags a little until James is given the space to let rip. On the other hand, the new arrangements really open some of the songs up: 'Museum Of Broken Hearts' becomes the deeply moving elegy the album strives for, and the sparse version of 'He Came From So Far Away' beautifully showcases Stephie's plaintive backing vocal. 'Willie Mays' is a highlight, Prophet switching from acoustic to electric before the coda, the delay requiring Brad to improvise new signals to keep the strings going, suspending the chord until Prophet comes swooping back in for the final solo; as he bounces on his toes like a boxer, the song lifts off, and there's even room for some of Prophet and DePrato's trademark harmonizing leads. It's a perfect example of what Brad Jones refers to as Prophet's 'planned chaos' blooming into a transcendent moment.

The performance ends with two contrasting numbers: first, the celebratory 'Shake Some Action', with White switching to electric bass and the classic riff translating easily to violins and violas; and finally a gorgeous rendition of 'No Other Love' that Chuck dedicates to his mother. It was a hugely ambitious gamble, and the serene beauty of much of the music belied the frantic hard work that had gone into staging the whole production, which was overseen by Prophet and long-time friend Linda Champagne. As an event, it was majestic: the all-seated audience were in tuxes, and there was a glorious sense of celebration about the whole concert.

While a deluxe reissue of *Temple Beautiful* bundled with a DVD of the film was originally mooted and even announced, tentatively, on Prophet's website, the decision was made to enter it instead for a number of film festivals; it won the best documentary direction prize at Amsterdam in 2015. In March 2020, the entire movie was uploaded to YouTube and pristine audio made available as a download.

There would be more strings shows over the next couple of years, routinely performed with musicians brought in with minimal preparation. A special one-off appearance was arranged in the UK, at Gateshead's Summertyne Americana Festival, in July 2014. The pick-up band there included an old acquaintance of Prophet's, former Dogs D'Amour guitarist Darrell Bath. Chuck and Stephanie met the string octet—the Summertyne Strings—for the first time at 10:30 the morning before the show, and, by the next evening, they were almost note perfect. In the beautiful, timbered, in-the-round setting of the Sage 2 at Gateshead, the show was the triumph of the festival (and that included Hollywood action man Steven Segal's blues bluster in the main room of the venue later that evening). On the Sunday, before they flew home, I drove them down for a one-off duo show at the Cellars in Eastney, Portsmouth, on the south coast of England. A relaxed and intimate set was distinctive for the way it featured Stephie's songs more heavily than usual. There was a heart-stopping rendition of 'Different Drum', as well as familiar duets such as 'Abandoned Love' and a new addition that would become a staple of the Chuck and Stephie show: a perfectly weighted rendition of The McCoys' 'Sorrow' (made famous by David Bowie on his 1973 covers album *Pin-Ups*).

Moving into his fourth decade as a performing artist, Prophet was still picking up speed. A new approach to collaboration with Stephanie Finch had resulted in the *Cry Tomorrow* album, and the establishing of a format for another kind of live performance that was a double whammy: creatively rewarding but also providing an economical model for touring in a different way. Duo shows would begin to appear with increasing regularity in subsequent years, including a set of shows in the Republic of Ireland in the Summer of 2015 that featured a wild and raucous gig at the upstairs room of Whelan's in Dublin, while, in the larger venue below, Ed Sheeran played a 'secret' gig to a significantly younger demographic. In the autumn of 2018, they would do a full set of tour dates across the UK and the Netherlands. The Chuck & Stephie show was deeply satisfying for both of them on an artistic level, but there was more to it than this. With distressing family matters back home impinging on the day-to-day reality of a tough schedule, every night seemed a kind of catharsis for them both. At times, the intensity seemed palpable.

The first show of the autumn 2018 tour had been staged as a birthday party for Oliver Gray who had for many years promoted Chuck's shows around the south of England. John Murry drove from his adopted home in the Republic of Ireland to play between the headline and the openers (talented local duo Lucas & King). It was a celebratory gig with many long-term fans in attendance. As the show bedded in over the next few nights of the tour, however, a bout of flu took a swipe. On the kind of schedule Prophet is required to maintain in order to make such tours add up financially and logistically, there is no margin for sickness, and ill health kept Stephie from singing on a couple of dates, though she still played. Back in London for a sold-out gig, it was Chuck's turn. Having shouted his way through the pain in Bristol the night before, he was left without a voice, and, although he kept believing until the last possible moment it might come back, the announcement had to be made from the stage as the lights went down that he was unable to perform. With refunds offered, opening act Jesse Malin stepped up to deliver a full ninety-minute set. The audible disappointment soon gave way to powerful waves of appreciation both for Jesse and for Chuck and Stephanie as Malin whipped up repeated ovations from the audience for the missing headliners. The love in the room was unmistakable. The tour resumed the next night in Bury, and another week of shows followed, finishing with a packed house and an intense, joyous show at Brighton's Komedia.

Looking back over this period, The Spanish Bombs excursion had given Prophet a break from the typical album/tour cycle and allowed him to celebrate a seminal LP that meant a great deal to him. His musical antennae always up, in the summer of 2014 he had also accepted an invitation to play four shows with Mexican rock'n'rollers The Twin Tones ('Way off into Mexican surf and Ennio Morricone—pretty wild'), including several massive outdoor festivals in the north of the country. And while the *Strings In The Temple* project was essentially a plan B after the idea of a stage musical was put on ice, it was itself another adventurous departure that would provide another outlet, varying the format when it came to booking gigs. Furthermore, the recording of Stephanie's *Cry Tomorrow* had helped create the impetus for the two of them to plot duo acoustic tours. And the 'real classic record' of Prophet's highest aspirations? There are many who would say that that is exactly what he achieved with *Temple Beautiful*. Few would argue that, fifteen years on from the peak of *Homemade Blood*, the album represents another artistic highpoint. It had certainly brought him some of the best reviews of his career. It had also brought a level of exposure that, while not exactly a revolution, was still a significant step up. It was a momentum that would continue to build.

CHAPTER TWELVE

OPEN YOUR HYMNALS

**NIGHT SURFER, BOBBY FULLER
DIED FOR YOUR SINS (2014–18)**

> Wish me luck—
> even if I don't need it.
> – Prophet/klipschutz/DePrato

NIGHT SURFER

Chuck Prophet & The Mission Express toured long and hard behind *Temple Beautiful*. On top of the standard band tours, there were the strings shows and the occasional duo gigs with Stephanie Finch. Furthermore, there were ongoing efforts to stage a musical version of the album, something into which both Prophet and Kurt Lipschutz invested tremendous amounts of intellectual and emotional energy. But, as always, Prophet had a full plate. 'So many gigs,' Chuck recalls. 'So much travelling. Outside production jobs ... I spent a lot of time not in San Francisco.'

What is more, *Night Surfer*—for which Chuck wrote several songs on his own—followed much harder on the heels of the previous release than was customary. It was recorded at Decibelle in San Francisco, with further work done at Alex The Great in Nashville. At this point, Bill Wesemann came on board as part of the production team—he would be there for the next album too—and Paul Q. Kolderie took care of the mix. The album was released on September 22 2014, once again licensed to Yep Roc. Persuading the label to put the album out without an extended lead-in time was not easy, and the difficulties are probably indicative of the relationship between an artist of his stature and the label, even when that relationship is generally speaking one that both sides are comfortable with. Prophet had talked to Yep Roc in March and told them he wanted to put a record out in the fall so that he could tour behind it; Yep Roc quoted the standard six-month window they needed to prepare a release. 'I get it,' Prophet said at the time. 'They're running a company and they only have so many open spots in their release schedule. But there are some things more important than campaigns for records. For me, this is who I am and maybe it is not the smartest thing but I needed to be out there in the fall playing and we need to figure out a way to do it—and Yep Roc somehow made it work.'[1]

Reviewing the album at the time for the *Zouch* website, I took a metaphorical step back to try to capture a wider perspective on its place in the span of Prophet's career. Picking up on three key American singer/songwriters that have come up frequently in our conversations, I found a neat symmetry. Discounting live albums, *Night Surfer* was Prophet's twelfth album in a twenty-four-year solo ride from 1990's *Brother Aldo*. A quarter of a century on from his own debut, Bob Dylan had been in the writer's block alcohol blackout of *Knocked Out Loaded* (twice as prolific: this was studio album no. 23, 1986). At the equivalent point in his career, Springsteen was also in a drought-ridden place, two years on from *The Ghost Of Tom Joad* (1995) and five years away from *The Rising* (his own album no. 12, 2002). Tom Petty was perched between two of his least well-regarded albums, *Echo* (his twelfth LP, 1999) and *The Last DJ* (2002). In all three cases, while there were some later, isolated epiphanies (not least Springsteen's remarkable *Western Stars* in 2019), their best work was behind them. Prophet—admittedly twenty-three years younger than Dylan and fourteen years younger than Springsteen and Petty—was still on the rise at an equivalent career point, as a songwriter, singer, and musician. His own take on this is to wisecrack, 'I'm a late bloomer.' Stephanie Finch thinks there are a number of circumstances that might explain it: while established, successful artists may get comfortable and distracted by fame or success, she points out, Chuck has never had the option. Without a doubt, he has been driven by an unfailing work ethic, but every album and every tour has required an immense amount of effort and self-belief to make it happen. 'And you know,' Stephie adds, summing up so much of her husband's character in a single word, 'he's still *hungry.*'

Night Surfer was pieced together in part from leftovers from the previous albums—songs that did not fit with the San Francisco theme. Pitching the album as dystopian, as Prophet tried to in promo interviews around the time, was perhaps something of a stretch. But there was a recognition of the success they had had by hanging a narrative on *Temple Beautiful*, and it was inevitable that a similar marketing strategy would be mooted. Still, if it doesn't fully convince as a contemporary *Diamond Dogs* project, *Night Surfer* is nevertheless an album with an anxious and sometimes despairing eye on the future, and it certainly informed Prophet's thinking as it was gelling, as this entertaining extract from an email to drummer Vicente Rodriguez indicates:

So, we're still playing with the Futuristic LP concept. And the music leans on the Glam. Similar to the classical in *Clockwork Orange*. There will be some kind of hero. Clint Eastwood's tight-lipped 'Man With No Name' meets Mel Gibson meets the Artful Dodger. He wears a plastic poncho with some kind of sports franchise on it. He surfs. And he does the cutbacks around the skyscrapers that are jutting out of the water.

It's raining ALL THE TIME.

There's been a big disaster. I don't know exactly what. A big nuke, a climate change, disease ... Not sure it matters. Al Gore will know.

And the record takes place in the civilization after such a disaster. It's all classic sci-fi stuff. Except, I really don't know much about that genre. So in a way, it's like we're making a record that's a Lars von Trier version of *Rise Of The Planet Of The Apes* ...

Prophet outlines the scenario in a little more detail before concluding, 'My point is what? Oh yeah, I found this mix tape of rare glam junk. There were countless singles out of Australia and Holland. And they all tried to cash in on the Ballroom Blitz. It was a gold rush. And this is kind of like the *Nuggets* of that era. So, if you're feeling it, listen to this stuff. Soak it up. Get it in you. It can't hurt nobody.'

Prophet would in due time admit that he had second thoughts about making a dystopian concept album but added that 'it was enough to get me excited about writing songs'.[2] Fragments survived: it's there in the cover art, and, from the 'Countrified Inner City Technological Man' of the opening track, via the teenage billionaires of Silicon Valley ('They Don't Know About Me And You'), to the monstrous consumer of 'Felony Glamor', the album conjures up a vivid array of characters to populate these twelve songs, with the lyrics characteristically catching details of the real world from unexpected angles. Laconic lyric perfectly matches wry vocal, and the Prophet/klipschutz axis continued to skewer an unexpected truth from fifty paces. The *Consequence Of Sound* review perceptively described the record as one 'bent on salvaging— or at least recognizing—what's still worth clinging to in our lives', concluding, '*Night Surfer* remains that rare record that elucidates how dysfunctional our world has become while somehow leaving us thankful that we get to trudge ahead through the mess.'[3] Or, as Prophet puts it, even more succinctly, 'The future might just save us. But we have to get there first.'

Musically, the album was in some respects Prophet's most adventurous to date. Glam rock is traceable via the stacked heel stomp of 'Love Is The Only Thing', but throughout there are echoes in the intricate vocal harmonies, the arrangements, and in the touches of Mick Ronson–toned guitar. Brad Jones's assignment writing strings parts for the revamp of *Temple Beautiful* seems to have carried over into the making of *Night Surfer*, too: several songs benefit from rich, intricate arrangements. If Prophet was continuing to ease off on the pedal board a little (there's plenty of guitar here, but fewer 'just watch me now' solos), it may have been in the interest of pursuing something more subtle, and a more varied musical palette. Particularly vivid is the pizzicato violin on the semi-autobiographical 'Lonely Desolation', where a sunny pop tune is subverted by the dark lyrical undertow; the song documents a mental health crisis in Chuck's teenage years. 'Wish Me Luck', which Prophet occasionally refers to as their 'show tune' (it's a co-write with DePrato and Lipschutz), is particularly lush. The strings also draw attention to the album's melodicism and showcase Prophet's voice in many places: the sly 'Guilty As A Saint' is blessed with some beautiful falsetto swoops. There may be less rock'n'roll hollering, but by pulling back a little on the throttle, many of the songs ended up featuring a sweeter and fuller vocal tone. *Popmatters* hailed Prophet's singing on the album as 'the strongest it's ever been'.[4]

'Wish Me Luck' was one of several tracks that Prophet chose to augment with a promo video. It's a song with a strong hook and an opening line brimming with caustic wit: 'My life is an experiment that doesn't prove a thing.' Prophet's willingness to put himself on the line to appear in his promo videos in acting roles, rather than simply a music performance context, lends them a specific kind of charm. 'Wish Me Luck' casts him as a PA carefully setting up an ironically low rent hotel room with his employer's complex, precise, sugar-loaded rider. The song follows the progress (or the deterioration) of the narcissistic monster who is singing the song ('Look out all you losers, here I come!') up to the point where he attempts to persuade Prophet's character to dig a hole in the ground in the desert and then pile the earth on top of him. It's a comic, ironic take on MTV storytelling, directed with flair by Ryan Browne, and with the role of the client performed with camp gusto by Robert Longstreet, who would go on to star in the popular Netflix drama *The Haunting Of Hill House* (2018) and the *Shining* sequel *Doctor Sleep* (2019). Prophet admits that the portrait is based on a real person but has always refused to reveal their identity.

A promo for the melodic pop of 'Tell Me Anything (Turn To Gold)' indulged Prophet's love of true crime and pulp fiction with a narrative that cast him as a private eye tracking a character played with dry insouciance by Stephanie Finch. A more straightforward (but slickly shot and edited) live performance style video was made with the band for 'Ford Econoline', featuring Prophet wielding his Silvertone. The song is a flat-out, punk-edged rocker that transfers naturally to the stage. The Prophet promo would reach its zenith on 'Your Skin' from the next album. Chuck plays the part of a put-upon office worker given his pink slip. As the story progresses, he gets drunk at a farewell party and suffers increasingly nightmarish, paranoid visions of his co-workers. The story ends (with a nod to Petty's famous *Alice In Wonderland* video for 'Don't Come Around Here No More') in a frenzy of violence as Prophet's character is cut open and the partygoers eat his internal organs.

'Truth Will Out (Ballad Of Melissa And Remy)' is one of the most intriguing songs on the album. It recasts the story of Amanda Knox by flipping between murder, arrest and trial, and an imagined future some years down the line. Knox was an American student accused of killing her British flatmate

Meredith Kercher in Perugia, Italy, in 2007; after four years in prison, she was released and returned to the USA; however, it was not until 2015, after a lengthy appeals process, that she was finally acquitted. Chuck and I had independently become fascinated with the case and would keep each other up to date with developments. Eventually I would include a long chapter about 'Foxy Knoxy', as the media called her, in a book about 'real life' *femme fatales.*[5] Fittingly, considering the spectacle that the press made of Knox, the song is structured in part around looking, being looked at, or avoiding the gaze: Melissa faints at the sight of the murder; she 'didn't look at him once' as her lover/accomplice gives his statement; and the character called the Greek 'faced the camera—didn't utter a word'. Melissa is apparently acquitted and tries to establish a normal life but lies awake at night 'wondering how long this fairy tale can last'.

Lipschutz notes that 'the song was already "done" when I came up with the last verse, and it's always a hard sell to get Chuck to lengthen a song once the structure and shape has been established'. But the addition is vital to the impact of the song; in that final verse, the perspective suddenly shifts as the Greek reflects back: 'Sometimes I think I'll give Melissa a call,' he muses, 'But I wouldn't know where to begin.' The bone-dry, semi-spoken verses alternate with an increasingly desperate vocal in the chorus, while a rising, keening bridge leaves the drama cliff-hanging beautifully.

'They Don't Know About Me And You' is one of the album's musical highlights. From a low-key opening, the song takes wing and becomes a soaring anthem. The harmonic structure and instrumentation keep building through the first half of the song, laying a platform for the point at which it shifts key and takes off, backing vocals and guitars framing a melody that Tom Petty would have killed for, thirty-five years on from 'Even The Losers'. 'I always thought that arrangement was like Bad Company,' Prophet tells me. 'Took me right back to when I was eleven years old, playing guitar.' Lyrically, it comes closest to the dystopian *Diamond Dogs* vision that he presented so eloquently to Vicente Rodriguez.

The sound emanating from the studio continued to reap the harvest of James DePrato's closer involvement. 'If I say, "I need a Maestro-Fuzz Tone approach to this tune," he knows I'm talking about an effects pedal made in the 60s that's all fuzz and no sustain. It's helpful to know these things and allows us to pass the guitar back and forth when we're recording,' Prophet told the *San Francisco Chronicle* in 2014. In addition, special guest Peter Buck of R.E.M., whom Chuck had first met in the Green On Red days and remained friendly with, lit up several songs with a sparkling jangle of electric guitar. 'He's a real hook machine,' Prophet continued. 'He can come up with a simple part that really lifts the song up and takes it to unexpected places.'[6] Brad Jones took care of the bass, and some piano and sitar parts were contributed by Matt Winegar, with Rusty Miller on piano. The drum stool was once again occupied by Tubes man Prairie Prince, his playing often complex, never fussy, and always propulsive: blowout closer 'Love Is The Only Thing', with its warped 'Jean Genie' riff and glam rock mob-handed vocals, is the best example. Given a cheerier lyric, it could have been the UK's Christmas no. 1 if someone had turned the clock back forty years. Even though the album does not have the tightly coherent band sound that would emerge on the next album—the first time Prophet decided to bring The Mission Express into the studio at the same time—nevertheless, as the *Popmatters* review noted, 'The playing is outstanding, with a real sense of the band as a unit, kicking out, having fun.'[7]

When the band did hit the road in the fall, they began with the regular fixture of Hardly Strictly Bluegrass in Golden Gate Park and the two associated gigs at the Make-Out Room, before heading for Europe: France, Germany, all areas of the UK, Spain, the Netherlands, Ireland, and Belgium. As usual, the schedule was tightly packed: twenty-seven shows in twenty-eight days. Often opening with Lou Reed's 'Rock'n'Roll Heart', the setlist included a good proportion of the new batch of songs from day one. Indeed, a typical European show was made up of seven *Temple Beautiful* songs, five from *Night Surfer*, and only four from earlier albums. As the tour progressed, more *Night Surfer* songs showed up, including 'Truth Will Out' and, when Prophet had figured out an arrangement that worked, 'They Don't Know About Me And You'.

Blurt awarded *Night Surfer* the now standard issue four-star review; as so often, there was a tendency to detail reference points for Chuck's style (here, Dylan, Lou Reed, Bowie, and Elvis Costello) but the reviewer suggested that Prophet was 'in many ways . . . every bit their equal—a response that raises questions about how and when an artist rooted as deeply in tradition as

Prophet is can be seen to have emerged from the shadow of their influences.[8] For *Louder Than War*, the reviewer provided a more nuanced perspective on Prophet and his musical roots: 'Prophet is a singularly personal writer, aware of his lineage in the roots of modern American music and whose grasp of the pop, punk, country, and rock'n'roll influences that brought him to this place means that he's comfortably able to straddle the old and the new.'[9] British print magazines called the album 'one of his best . . . a perfect entry point for anyone who might be intrigued' (*Q*) and wrote approvingly of its 'swashbuckling set of blasted guitars and rootsy grooves' *(Uncut)*; *Mojo* called it 'one of the grandest statements Prophet has made as a solo artist, filled with horns, strings and arena rock guitars'. *Off The Tracks* summed up *Night Surfer* as 'close to perfect, almost his very best; the only reason I can't quite call this his best album is because his discography is an embarrassment of riches'.[10]

Meanwhile, Prophet continued to clock up the miles. The year 2016 was structured largely around continuing touring commitments, chiefly with The Mission Express. A North American tour spanned March to May and included a run of half a dozen shows in California with Garland Jeffreys. Jeffreys had started out on the New York folk circuit in the 1960s, releasing a series of solo albums through the following decades, and he had a hit with a cover of the ? & The Mysterians song '96 Tears' in 1981 (a perennial reference point for Chuck in our conversations about songwriting). Jeffreys's own song 'Wild In The Streets' was covered by the punk band Circle Jerks around the same time, but he never really broke into the mainstream himself. Like Prophet, he often finds profiles of his career prefaced with phrases such as, 'By any artistic standard, Garland Jeffreys ought to be a household name.'[11] Half black and half Puerto Rican, he was a roommate of Lou Reed's at Syracuse University, and in his early years he worked with another Velvet Underground lynchpin, John Cale, who used Garland's roots-rock collective Grinder's Switch as the basis of his band for the solo release *Vintage Violence* (1969), an album that Prophet notes as an influence on his own early solo work. Jeffreys had come out to see Prophet and The Mission Express at the Bell House in New York City in August 2013. They had worked up some encores together, and from that came the idea of a set of double-header shows with The Mission Express backing Garland for his songs, Dylan/Petty style. The rehearsal process did not prove to be an easy one—Garland had some problems recalling the lyrics to a few of his old songs—but the shows were joyful.

On one of the UK legs of the tour, Prophet was approached by a fan by the name of Steve Gardner, a Yorkshire-born Brit who had been writing songs in his spare time for several years. Frustrated by the gap between the songs in their raw form and the sounds inside his head, he had taken the audacious step—or, rather, giant, zero gravity leap—of emailing the professional musician he admired the most, attaching the lyrics of a song about a faded rock star, and asking said musician whether he would be interested in bringing these songs to life. A year later, Gardner found himself in San Francisco, preparing for what would be the first of two weeks over the course of a year in the studio with Chuck Prophet & The Mission Express.

The album is worth more than a passing mention for a couple of reasons. It is impossible to cover in detail all of Prophet's production credits. For instance, in 2014 he was in the chair for Peter Mulvey's album *Silver Ladder*, which Mulvey had crowd-funded; the result was an album Mulvey considered his best to date, and he described working with Chuck as 'Fantastic. He's amazing, utterly contrary, like a crocodile on Ritalin'.[12] The album is tighter and harder-edged than Mulvey's customary sound, with a broader musical palette that complements an impressive set of songs.

The Gardner project was a different prospect entirely from cutting an album with a seasoned professional like Mulvey. Quite apart from his generosity of spirit in taking on the project, it is a tribute to Prophet's genius as a musician, arranger, and producer that he was able to fashion a genuinely intriguing, quirky, fun rock'n'roll album out of Gardner's raw material. The album, *Bathed In Comfort* (2017), moves between vintage-sounding shuffles, bigger production numbers and piano-led excursions (murder ballad 'The Miller's Daughter' is graced with haunting, spectral backing vocals from Stephanie Finch). Highlight 'The Day The Aliens Saved The World' was recorded in two different arrangements, and the superior take sounds like Kraftwerk jamming with a garage band in one of the trapezoidal echo chambers Les Paul had built beneath Capitol Records in LA: it rocks. To produce Gardner's album, Chuck decided to bring The Mission Express into the studio with him for the first time, along with his friend Matt Winegar, of whom more in a moment. The project seemed to provide an impetus for Prophet to record with the band as a complete unit for the first time in the studio on his next album.

THE NEEDLE SKIPS AND JUMPS: *BOBBY FULLER DIED FOR YOUR SINS*

The studio time for tracking *Bobby Fuller Died For Your Sins* came straight off the back of workshops for the *Temple Beautiful* musical. Of the songwriting process for *Bobby Fuller*, Prophet remarks, 'It was relaxed. Kurt and I mixed it up and just by honouring our time together we started to collect a handful of interesting songs.' One or two Prophet had written on tour (Including 'We Got Up And Played'), which was 'unusual for me'. Paul Q. Kolderie took care of the tracking and the mix. Bill Wesemann had an 'executive producer' credit ('It was great to have him on the team, to have him bless it,' Prophet notes); Matt Winegar, Chuck, and Brad Jones were listed as co-producers. When I ask Chuck about the latter's particular qualities, he replies, 'He's just really nimble. He's an incredibly capable guy and then on top of all that, on top of his musical ability, and the breadth of his knowledge, and his work ethic ... I'd say the *worst* part is his efficiency. We say, "Brad, we're just gonna have to slow the heck down." And our playful nickname for him when he's out of the room has always been *Fast Brain*.'

Chuck goes on to discuss Jones's egoless production style, and I am reminded of Kelly Willis describing Prophet in almost exactly the same terms. 'He's into whatever you're into,' Prophet says. 'And he's got an understanding, cool style. He's very Midwestern and honest. If he has a concern about a song, he'll tell you. He cues off my voice too. That's what he listens to when he hears the music; he just loves the information coming at him. And he likes my phrasing and my natural rhythm.' Chuck singles out 'If I Were Connie Britton' as an example: 'He really fought for that one. Because he thought it was very graphic. I guess it just really hit his Chuck Prophet sweet spot! [*laughs*] So you know. I trust him. I totally trust him. If you work with Brad, I can guarantee he's got your back.'

The opening three tracks of *Bobby Fuller Died For Your Sins* establish what Prophet refers to as 'the major food groups'—some harmonies with Stephanie Finch, some prominent riffs, and what he calls a little 'psychedelic surf guitar' on 'Your Skin'. It sets a reverb-heavy, chiming guitar from James DePrato against Chuck's gloriously nasty tone: 'Yeah, I'm playing a fuzz guitar that was sitting in the studio; a broken Ibanez that barely stayed in tune, I just picked it up. We did the trade-offs and it just worked. We cut the song the first week and nothing came of it. Then, a different key, different feel, rhythm, instrumentation . . . just a different approach. At one time I was gonna make a kind of electro-pop record, like Suicide or Gary Numan but with guitars— maybe like ZZ Top. And that was because I got together with Matt Winegar, who's an old friend of mine. I mean, both of us have done our bodyweight in drugs together but that's another story.'

Winegar spent his early years as a musician in the Bay Area, was a founding member of The Spent Poets and Slider, and later moved to LA and then Salt Lake City, where he has his own studio, Secret Sidewalk. He has worked with the likes of Primus, Megan Joy, and Royal Bliss, and more recently mixed Fantastic Negrito's astounding *The Last Days Of Oakland* (2016), as well as the follow-up *Please Don't Be Dead* (2018), both albums Grammy-winners. When Winegar moved back to San Francisco, he and Prophet got in touch, and they ended up working together on a tribute song for a compilation, *While No One Was Looking: Toasting 20 Years Of Bloodshot Records* (2014). The song was 'Dirt' by R&B legend Andre Williams.

'I've always appreciated Matt's musicality,' says Prophet. 'And I got excited about writing songs, thinking, *I can't wait to take this over to Matt's house.* We enjoy each other's company and it helped me avoid falling into clichés, into places that are too comfortable. People do that. If you're a piano player, your fingers go certain places. If you're a guitar player, your hands go certain places. And sometimes you need to take the guitar out of your hands or do whatever you can to mix it up. And so I started going to his garage and recording. And instead of just making demos with a band out of habit, I started doing these kind of electro-pop 80s demos. And I thought at one point the record might be an electro-pop album, just Matt and me, but then when the band came in and we started playing it . . . it's just always better. Because machine music can really give you a thrill. It can give you an injection of excitement. But the problem is it can never sustain it. And the songs better be really *short*, or else they just get static. They're not dynamic, and you don't find yourself returning to them.'

Of 'In The Mausoleum', Chuck notes, 'I think I might have lost my nerve and put a bridge in there. I think originally it was one chord.' He recalls that it was a song from the reject pile that Lipschutz pitched to him, originally titled 'In The Colosseum'. Prophet also acknowledges that 'there's definitely hints of "Frankie Teardrop" in there'—the song by Alan Vega's band Suicide, produced by Craig Leon and cited by Springsteen as a major influence on his *Nebraska* album. Prophet includes his own acknowledgement by subtitling the song '(For Alan Vega)'. Vega had died around this time, and his music was very much in the air. 'He was a real hero of mine. I've always liked his kind of post-apocalyptic rockabilly. He just had different ways of creating. He wasn't an acoustic guitar/ harmonica kind of guy, but he was a singer-songwriter all the same. It's always cleansing for me to listen to Alan Vega at high volume. Any time in my life he's never let me down.'

Chiming guitars, 60s-style, underpin a lot of the songs on the album, notably 'Bad Year For Rock And Roll' and the glorious, anthemic title track that kicks off the album and would become the perfect opening number on tour. 'Well, you know, it's that Bobby Fuller, Buddy Holly Fender guitar, single coils,' Chuck confirms. 'That's definitely what I was going for on this record. And that's why we were at Hyde Street [where Chuck had made his first professional recordings]—they had an echo chamber and we were able to get all those things down the line.' Prophet claims that the song was conceived when he and Lipschutz were in his office space, listening to a Bobby Fuller record; Chuck turned to Kurt and quipped, 'Do you hear the record crackle and the needle skips and jumps? I never saw a movie that moved me half as much.' And Kurt shot back, 'Bobby Fuller died for your sins.' With that, Chuck says, 'We were off and running.'

Bobby Fuller was a figure Prophet felt he could identify with. 'I relate to him on so many levels, including that he was hopelessly out of time,' Chuck told *Billboard* magazine.[13] 'As a kid in 1960s El Paso,' he explains, 'Fuller was so obsessed with Buddy Holly, he and his brother drove to the New Mexico studio where Holly recorded, studied it, then constructed a replica in their parents' living room. But by the time the Bobby Fuller Four made it out to California to chase the Golden Dream, they were 50s greasers in a world of Beach Boys bangs, Beatle boots, and The Byrds. Then, sadly, Fuller was murdered at twenty-three. So, much of my record is California *noir*: people who came to California chasing a golden dream, with the *noir* being the difference between dream and reality.'

'Bad Year For Rock And Roll'—for a time earmarked as the title track— would become the target song in the never-ending quest for airplay and its streaming equivalents. 'You could say it's about the musical heroes that we lost in 2016, when the record was written,' Prophet asserted, 'but it's also about losing any faith or illusion we may have had about democracy in this country as well. I think the election year is embedded in the DNA of the whole record, really. It's about losing faith and getting it back.'[14]

Prophet notes how difficult it was to capture the sound on songs like 'Coming Out In Code', tracking it live with The Mission Express. 'I think there was probably six people playing at the same time. Yeah. It was hard to get. Because we wanted to get a take where everybody had a great performance. It probably took thirty takes for it to sound that way … and then, once we played it live, it was even better, it was even greasier … when you bake something it's even better the second day,' he laughs.

The poignant 'Open Up Your Heart' begins with a lonely acoustic guitar and some gentle harmonics before modulating to a full band sound complemented by subtle strings and spectral vocal harmonies. The song was originally called 'Go Easy Baby', rewritten after being discarded at the *Night Surfer* sessions. 'Basically the resolve was, "Go easy baby, go easy on me,"' Lipschutz recalls. 'And we thought it wouldn't go over very well—like it's your job: "Go easy. Put my dinner on the table and fix me a drink." So we opened it up into being more vulnerable so the resolve is now, "When you gonna open up your heart for me?" And it's like the injured party standing under her window with a rose. It's a little bit more of a winning stance!'

Of the hilarious, shameless pop of 'If I Were Connie Britton', Prophet tells me, 'I was at an industry party in Nashville, where she lives, and there was a group of people comparing Connie Britton sightings. And I just had too much fun writing it. It just kept coming!' I wonder aloud if the subject of the song might get to hear it one day. 'I hope so,' Chuck replies. 'I don't know. I don't know anything about her! I just know that she's … just got all that *hair*.' Exploring the album further, he remembers the solo on 'Post-War

Cinematic Dead Man Blues' as particularly unusual in that he took the time to do five solos and picked the best one. The lyrics were inspired by the movie *The Third Man*. Prophet says of the backing vocals: 'Whenever something like that happens, I'm really happy, and I always do my best to protect it. Anytime you can get a background vocal—I don't mean harmony, I'm talking about call and response—anytime you can get that, you're on your way to a hit record. [*laughs*] It's Motown. It's David Bowie. If I ever stumble into anything like that—that isn't just straight blues turnaround Dylan—I get very happy because it doesn't come naturally to me. Good choruses are such a rare thing around here!'

I mention how the backing vocals are central to another of the song's highlights, 'Jesus Was A Social Drinker', and he responds, 'Yeah, the doo-wop thing to keep it light. The Lou Reed ability to really contrast it with something. Give it some sense of irony. Otherwise it's just a downer!' I tell Chuck the song feels like having a conversation with him. 'That's nice . . . it needs to sound effortless for it to work'. It is a song that he had returned to several times since he first wrote it. On his solo electric tour around Europe in 2006 (see chapter ten), it was an unexpected treat, but it had remained something of a novelty song—a category of songwriting that Prophet has never had much time for. 'Well, it's not enough for a song to be just a bunch of couplets to pay off. There's got to be something more to it. Otherwise it's overcooked, and you see it coming. Just not something you return to.' The keyboard part, which reminds me of Gary Numan, Chuck says was a deliberate nod toward Roxy Music. 'Everybody's got their own take,' he laughs. 'That's fine!'

'Alex Nieto' is the last song on the CD version of the album, and on streaming sites. It is a protest song, directly inspired by the death of nightclub bouncer Alex Nieto in a San Francisco park on March 21 2014 at the hands of San Francisco police (see introduction). The full, heartbreaking, enraging story can be read in Rebecca Solnit's report for the *Guardian*, 'Death By Gentrification: The Killing That Shamed San Francisco'.[15] Lipschutz knew people who were very involved in the case. 'The family sued the police for wrongful death and lost in federal court,' Kurt explains. 'And I brought that into the room, and then it happened very fast.' It was partly about the name itself, which fitted so well rhythmically. 'And it was the refrain: Chuck was able to put it into a kind of a real hard-charging aggressive rhythm. "Alex Nieto was a pacifist, a 49ers fan"—that was part of a one-page lyric sheet that I had. You don't really know all the detail from the song itself because we kept it oblique in the song. But the guy was wrongfully killed: he was a martyr. But we resisted the extra twist of the knife to say, you know, the SFPD shot him down and black lives matter, and all that.... There's the song ... and that's it.'

Prophet told one interviewer, 'People have listened to me rant about Tech City USA and how I believe San Francisco is under siege by techie man-children and billionaires. But still, I never dreamed I'd be in the middle of a culture war with real bodies. Alex Nieto was born and raised in the city. Alex Nieto was on his way to work as a security guard when he ended up with fifty-nine bullets in and around him, all fired by the police.... The song is a two-chord homage to a good man who should still be alive.'[16] It is possibly the heaviest, punkiest track Prophet has ever released, a howl of dignified rage hooked on a suspended B chord played in snarling overdrive.

BROTHER BOBBY'S TRAVELING SALVATION SHOW

The new album dropped on February 10 2017, and once again the press reviews were enthusiastic. There were fewer paragraphs, too, about Chuck's perennial underdog status, suggesting his profile was becoming more distinct. The *Independent*, one of the quality papers on the UK newsstands, described him as a 'master guitarist and accomplished songwriter', as well as 'an encyclopaedic master of musical form'.[17] For *Record Collector*, the album was 'a reminder of how potent straightforward melodic pop/rock can be', describing the band's sound as 'garage rock with a clean sophistication'.[18] Both reviewers scored the album four out of five, as did Hal Horowitz, for *American Songwriter*, who celebrated the album's 'memorable melodies, exuberant playing, detailed lyrics and unflinching honesty'.[19] Mark Deming praised the songwriting ('smart, honest, and thoughtful') and Prophet's ability to strike the ideal balance between his musicianship and 'real gift for spinning tales'.[20] *Spill* concluded that Prophet 'has created a masterpiece'.[21]

The release of the new album triggered the usual cycle of live dates that was preceded by a set of solo appearances in folk venues in New York and New Jersey in January. On February 8, the band kicked off the European leg of the tour in Hamburg; a week later, they were in Oxford for a high-energy show on Valentine's night. Seven UK dates were followed by five more on the continent, then back home for a ten-day layoff before three shows in two days at a regular haunt in Austin, Texas, the Continental Club. The pace remained relentless; a long North American tour followed that stretched into the summer. In July, a return invitation to the Summertyne Festival in Gateshead, which had previously witnessed the sole Strings In The Temple outside of the USA, afforded the opportunity of a week of UK/Ireland dates, before they returned stateside for regular festival slots. At the end of October, two dozen more dates across Germany, Italy, France, Spain, and the UK included their biggest audience ever in the British capital at the University Of London Union—a triumphant show that found Chuck in particularly exuberant form. The year was rounded off with another visit to Austin, and three local dates between Christmas and New Year.

In February 2017, in the middle of the first UK tour behind *Bobby Fuller*, Prophet was offered a slot on the BBC1 politics programme *The Andrew Marr Show*, which often plays out with a live performance by a current band. It was a challenge selecting the right song and working out an arrangement that would fit the one minute and fifty second slot they were shoehorned into. They turned in a breezy version of 'Bad Year For Rock And Roll' that resolved at the end of the bridge, and the Sunday morning TV spot was indicative of the fact that Chuck Prophet was on an upward curve in terms of his visibility, marketability, and the crowds turning out for the shows. *Bobby Fuller* broke into the *Billboard* chart—no. 123, Chuck noted in a blog post. 'I'm not quite ready to call my mom and ask her where she wants them to drop off her new yacht,' he quipped, 'but it's still pretty cool. You can't see me, but my head is swelling up pretty good.' The album also debuted at no. 6 on *Billboard*'s Heatseekers albums chart. Asked in an interview with *CityBeat* about his ability to keep growing an audience as a 'fifty-plus-year-old rock musician', he replied, 'I honestly don't know why (it's happening).' He continued, 'I hope I'm getting better at what I do. I feel things have built in a slow way. I guess that's the way things need to build, if they're going to build in any meaningful way.'[22]

KEEP ON MOVING

THE RUBINOOS AND *THE LAND THAT TIME FORGOT* (2019–20)

> The past is never dead.
> It's not even past.
> —William Faulkner

THE MUSICAL, THE RUBINOOS, *SOME GIRLS*

As another decade approached, Prophet continued to pick up speed. He and Kurt Lipschutz had spent intense periods of time over several years developing a stage musical version of the *Temple Beautiful* album with Kurt as lead librettist. Initially commissioned by FOGG Theatre in February 2014, a series of workshops in August 2016 followed intense work on the libretto with contributions from Jim Lewis (co-writer of *Fela!*, the musical about the life of Fela Kuti) and Emilie Whelan. By 2018, the libretto had evolved again; award-winning director Clay David took on the producer role and Whelan direction, with local guitar protégé Matt Jaffe as musical director. November 2018 witnessed an exciting showcase performance for a packed house at PianoFight, a trendy arts venue in the Tenderloin.

While the production is currently on hold, a video recording of the showcase, and the full libretto (which features material as old as 'Let's Burn This Firetrap Down' and brand new songs alongside the repertoire from *Temple Beautiful* itself) testify to its potential as a fully fledged stage musical, its dramatic power derived from a set of fertile contrasts and conflicts: 'Punks vs. Tech Titans, Age and Experience against Youth and Power, all to a backdrop of competing styles of urban living amongst the City's greats and not-so-greats, wannabes and has-beens,' as the PianoFight programme put it. Emilie Whelan describes it best on the musical's website when she dubs it 'a kind of punk-rock love letter to [the city] at a time of identity crisis' and 'a wild ride: part a tour of today's San Francisco, and part a patched jean jacket of anarchic memory'.

If the stage musical project represented unfamiliar and sometimes bewildering territory for Prophet and Lipschutz, ostensibly more familiar ground for Chuck came via an invitation to follow up on the *London Calling* adventure of 2011 with a Spanish tour built around The Rolling Stones' 1978 album *Some Girls*, which Jagger and company had never toured outside of the United States.

Chuck and Charlie Sexton had been friends for many years, and Charlie would regularly get up onstage and jam with The Mission Express when the band swung through Austin. Sexton has been Bob Dylan's guitarist (with one brief hiatus) since 1999, but his career stretches back to teenage years on the Austin blues scene and a solo deal at the tender age of sixteen, later teaming up with Stevie Ray Vaughan's former rhythm section and Doyle Bramhall II for the band Arc Angels. Spain, the *Some Girls* album, and playing with Chuck—Charlie didn't need any more incentive than that to get on board.

I caught the Barcelona gig on the eight-show tour at the end of January 2019, and by that time the band members (including Vicente Rodriguez on drums and Steve Adams on bass) were locked in. The crowd was wild, dancing from the opening number and singing along (most enthusiastically on deep cuts such as 'Far Away Eyes' and 'Before They Make Me Run'). The show mostly consisted of the *Some Girls* album re-sequenced, with a few expected extras, like 'Brown Sugar' and 'Jumpin' Jack Flash', and the occasional nugget, including a soulful 'Love In Vain'. It was a very high-energy show, and the whole band seemed to be having the time of their lives. Chuck and Charlie shared vocals throughout each song, with Charlie doing high harmonies when required. The baton was passed back and forth on the solos, too, and there were some exploratory jams (soundchecks found the duo sharing riffs and licks with comfortable, laidback enthusiasm). Between them, the two master guitarists, rooted in quite different traditions, summoned up a beautifully meshed sound, listening to and playing off each other, revelling in each other's lines. If the Stones could still play like this, I found myself thinking, I might actually go and see them. Stripped of tiresome stadium trappings, the songs flashed again like jewels in the stage lights.

During the second half of 2018, Prophet had immersed himself in a new co-writing project with a figure from his earliest years as a gigging musician: Tommy Dunbar of The Rubinoos. Dunbar remembers seeing a Temple with strings show at the Palms in Winters, California, in June 2014, and then meeting up with Chuck again at one of the Garland Jeffreys shows two years later. Informal conversations morphed into something more concrete. Prophet was the driving force behind the project from the start, and it began, as it always must, with the songs: Chuck would take the train up to Dunbar's place in Sacramento, and they would spend the day throwing around ideas. 'Writing that record was one of the happiest times of my life,' he says, and before long the music was cooking: in one five-hour session, they wrote three songs, including the beautiful ballad 'Heart For Sale'.

The Rubinoos had for some time been maintaining a presence on the touring circuit, notably in Spain (fourteen tours in almost as many years since 2002), but it had been almost ten years since they had made an album together. It was what Tommy refers to as Chuck's 'boundless energy' that got all the members of the band (Dunbar, Jon Rubin, Al Chan, and Donno Spindt) committed to working on a new set of recordings, to be tracked at Hyde Street Studios, where they had cut their first albums forty years earlier. There was another boost when Prophet hooked them up with his label, Yep Roc. Dunbar admits that it was the first time since about 1980 that they seemed to be recording as a real band, and Prophet's enthusiasm was infectious. The result was a sparkling collection of garage-band power-pop that retained the spirit of the band from their late-70s heyday.

That enthusiasm was evident when Chuck shared some early mixes with me in January 2019, eight months before release. As always when he is in the producer's chair, Prophet's key aim was to be true to the essence of the band—and few people know The Rubinoos as well as he does. The album *From Home* is rooted in everything that made the band great in the first place, while at the same time the sound is utterly contemporary in the context of the underground garage world. 'It's still gotta sound teenage,' Prophet explains. 'It's gotta be rock'n'roll, it's gotta be soul music—music that's authentic to *them*.' The production and arrangements are all stripped back, leaving the emphasis on the harmonies: 'One guitar, drums, bass,' Chuck points out as we listen back to one of the new songs. 'It's just vocal . . . with rhythm accompaniment.'

Lyrically, too, there is nothing multi-layered or ironic. A song that apparently began as an ode to the *Mad Men* actress January Jones ended up as a song about . . . the month of January. 'Rocking In Spain' is a paean to exactly that. 'Honey From The Honeycombs' pays tribute to the drummer of the British beat group The Honeycombs, Honey Lantree. What is most remarkable about the album is how youthful it sounds—the twin lead vocals of Jon Rubin and Tommy Dunbar, swapping back and forth and then in unison; the stacked harmonies with Al and Donno betray next to nothing of the passing of four decades. 'I think we share a lot of the same frames of reference,' Prophet says by way of summary. 'We all believe in WWJD: What Would Jonathan Do? As in Jonathan Richman . . .'

THE LAND THAT TIME FORGOT

If The Rubinoos project brought Prophet full circle in some respects, revisiting the music of his teens, his own 2020 album, *The Land That Time Forgot* also marked a return of sorts: across the twelve tracks, it features Stephanie Finch more prominently than any of his solo releases since *Balinese Dancer* in 1993, and her involvement, track after track, lights up the recordings. When we spoke in January 2019, Chuck had been writing on and off with Kurt Lipschutz over several months. At that time, he talked about the idea of recording a more acoustic-based album and mentioned in passing that the label had perked up at the idea, primarily because of the commercial potential—there are plenty of opportunities to get placed on playlists on Spotify and Apple with this particular brand of music. However, what Yep Roc had in mind may not be what inspired Prophet as he was preparing to record. 'Out of all the acoustic music I listen to for pleasure, almost all of it is acoustic music . . . with a rhythm section!' he quips, referencing the Stones' *Beggars Banquet* ('it's pretty acoustic but it rocks') and then cueing up Richard & Linda Thompson's 'When I Get To The Border' to make the point. In the end, however, Chuck is sceptical of the idea of letting an approach to recording dictate very much at all. As he puts it, 'The songs are going to tell you what they need.'

The songs themselves were in place, but initial tracking with Matt Winegar at familiar studios Secret Sidewalk in Oakland and Decibelle in San Francisco did not go smoothly; when Prophet felt they were hitting a wall, he took a timeout and embarked on a solo tour. Working with Kenny Siegal at Siegal's own Old Soul Studio in Socrates, New York, offered a fresh start; Kenny introduced Chuck to 'a great bunch of musicians', and the studio, situated in a large Greek Revival, Italianate-style mansion on the riverbank in Catskill, was big enough for them to track live. 'We fought like cats and dogs,' Chuck laughs about the collaboration with Siegal, 'but to good advantage.' Over two four-day sessions, Chuck stayed in the house; he would get up in the morning and do rewrites, and the band would stroll in around 11am; they would record late into the night.

Three songs were retained from the earlier sessions with Winegar, who earned himself a special mention in the credits, 'The A and B the C of D Award' (above and beyond the call of duty), for his ceaseless patience and enthusiasm. Bill Wesemann was on board again as executive producer, Greg Calbi mastered the recordings, and Paul Q. Kolderie ended up remixing the entire album when it became clear to everyone that the two sets of songs from New York and San Francisco were very different beasts. 'The San Francisco tracks that Matt cut were explosive, three-dimensional,' Prophet explains. 'Shiny. In a different way. We had some catching up to do with the tracks we recorded in that dilapidated old mansion in Catskill. But we got there.'

Eleven of the twelve songs were co-written with Kurt Lipschutz, and Kurt's presence is felt nowhere more obviously than on the album's closer, a frank and funny takedown of the 45th US President, which was accompanied by a hilarious Claymation video created by Kendra Morris and Julia Haltigan. Chuck admits that he discarded the song multiple times, but Kurt believed in it and Chuck kept returning to it, eventually managing to make it work. Comparing his own life as a touring musician with Trump's, the song figures out who belongs and who doesn't, and concludes with the request to Trump to 'Get Off The Stage'. The song also features the lines:

Now me, I spent half of my life
In an Econoline van
With my band and my wife
And when she steps up to the mic
I've seen grown men burst out crying.

It's a verse some long-term fans might say has been waiting thirty years to be written.

It's early days as I absorb a new collection of twelve songs and write the final pages of this book, the end (for me) of a four-year journey. My overriding impression is of a pop album rather than a rock album; possibly a reflection of the fact that the majority of the songs are built primarily around acoustic architecture (but never without that rhythm section). It certainly possesses a gentler groove than any of his recent releases. Upright bass is a feature across the album. Even the songs that lean less heavily on acoustic guitars have been layered with various keyboard arrays, saxophone, even sitar ('Fast Kid'), rather than conspicuous electric tones. The notable exception is the epic 'Nixonland', which features some widescreen electric guitar from James DePrato but is still underpinned by layers of strummed acoustics. The guitars on the pacey 'Marathon' bring to mind the irrepressible energy of 'Queen Of Hearts'–era Dave Edmunds, but there is also what Chuck calls 'krautrock bass' and 'all my rockabilly, space-age Roxy Music tricks in there'; it is reminiscent of 'Jesus Was A Social Drinker' in its intoxicating blend of diverse styles. The song— ostensibly about the dance marathons that became a popular spectacle during the Great Depression—is structured as a duet between Chuck and Stephie, her vocal chiming like a bell, unaged over the thirty years since the *Brother Aldo* LP.

They say that the personal is always political. *The Land That Time Forgot*, partly because of Stephie's closer involvement, feels at times like a very personal and intimate album; the back cover features a shot of Chuck's parents in his Dad's Chevy. There is a deep tenderness in the tale of two beautiful losers, 'Willie And Nilli', in 'Love Doesn't Come From The Barrel Of A Gun', and on 'Meet Me At The Roundabout'. But the politics feel pressing, too: not only the Trump-baiting 'Get Off The Stage' but also 'Paying My Respects To The Train' (referencing the procession of Abraham Lincoln's coffin by train from Washington to Springfield, Illinois, in 1865) and the brooding meditation 'Nixonland' (Chuck was born where Richard Nixon grew up, in Whittier, California).

The album also contains some of the most starkly beautiful melodies Prophet has ever written, notably on the open-G-plucked 'Meet Me At The Roundabout' and the piano-led 'Waving Goodbye'. The latter focuses on

WHAT MAKES THE MONKEY DANCE **301**

the experience of a young woman from girlhood to adulthood, discovering her identity, and it does so with heart-tugging poignancy. Meanwhile, 'Womankind' is another example of Chuck's tendency 'always to empathise with the woman's place—just out of habit', as he put it to me once; it is a tendency that sings across the years since 'Longshot Lullaby'. The more didactic verses of 'Womankind' modulate into the chorus, a gentle celebration of a long-term intimacy ('I'll be yours and you'll be mine / We've got nothing left to prove').

Listening to *The Land That Time Forgot*—about four months away from release as I write this—I am reminded of what Chuck said to me in one of several impassioned diatribes about The Rubinoos (Tommy Dunbar, incidentally, features on background vocals throughout, in some beautiful harmonies with Stephie, worked out and recorded at Tommy's studio in Sacramento): 'They were out of step with the times and they didn't care— they knew what they liked it and they loved it, and their convictions carried them.' The same principle has sustained Prophet over his long career. As he told *Billboard*, when discussing Bobby Fuller, 'I've always felt out of time. And I embrace it now.'[1] It might be a cliché to invoke the famous line Elvis used to describe himself ('I don't sound like nobody'), but, to these seasoned ears, *The Land That Time Forgot* finds Prophet leaving his influences far behind. It is, simply and distinctly, a Chuck Prophet album.

WE GOT UP AND PLAYED

One of the defining features of Prophet's career has been his knack for keeping himself interested in what he is doing. Back at the turn of the millennium, discussing his sharp left turn with *The Hurting Business*, Prophet had explained to the *San Francisco Chronicle*, 'I've already tried everything else on the menu.' Reeling off a list of traditional instruments, he added, 'When you bring in a DJ, they'll give you something that you could have never imagined. It's always been about making it fresh.'[2] Whether it is switching things up with his decision to record ¡*Let Freedom Ring!* in Mexico City, or 'writing concept albums [such as *Temple Beautiful*], or whatever it takes,' Chuck tells me. 'Whatever it takes to wake up excited about what I'm doing, that's about as good as it gets for me.'

This gift has a lot to do with his own restless creativity and curiosity, but it may also be one of the backhanded benefits of his marginal place in the industry. There are, inevitably, economic challenges in sourcing the funds to record a new album and plotting yet another tour around the States or Europe; on the other hand, Prophet's hard-won position allows him a relative degree of freedom from the kind of demands a major label imposes on its artists in terms of material and scheduling. His status as a so-called 'fringe artist'—'just kind of running a family business'—has helped him maintain that creative independence. From swimming against the industry tide with his first solo albums; contrarily plugging into the digital revolution as the roots movement he had pre-empted shifted into high gear; and finally forging a distinct place both in the music critics' consensus and in a faithful community of music fans, Prophet has thrived on the instability that his marginal status in the industry has given him.

In the end, however, every time, the album is simply the conduit that connects Prophet back to his audience. At this time of writing, the siren call of the road is in the air again: Chuck is on a 'Solo, No Chaser' tour with a full schedule of live dates to follow later in 2020. The vinyl sequencing of Prophet's 2017 album *Bobby Fuller Died For Your Sins* closes with 'We Got Up And Played', a song that is in a sense an answer to that siren. The road has been Prophet's home for a good part of every year since Green On Red first put that Squier Telecaster in his hands and offered him his 'five-years-to-life sentence'.

'That was Brad [Jones]'s vision,' Prophet notes of 'We Got Up And Played'. 'To make it sound like a band doing a soundcheck to an empty room.' It is a starkly beautiful track. You can almost hear the paint peeling off the basement walls. 'It's totally honest. You know, it's amazing how the road can hold so much promise,' he continues. 'Whether it was my home life, just craving independence and then playing in crappy bands and having bike messenger jobs, dishwasher jobs, the road really was so *great* early on for me. So much of an escape from where I came from. But you get to a place where it can also become a curse. Because as dark as the place is that you are trying to escape, an empty motel room can be a pretty dark place too. So that's what that song's all about. And it's Cleveland, Ohio. Wednesday night. And when the light gets scarce, you're not getting up 'til noon. You're getting in the van, you're loading in, it's dark at five. And it's a big, empty, cold room. That's the feeling of that song. It's bleak and it's desperate because it can be a very alone place.'

'And yet you still get up and play,' I remark.

'Yeah,' Chuck replies, thoughtful. 'That's right. No matter what the circumstances, you always manage to get up and play. It comes down to this: "Don't you honour anything?" And that's been my argument through the years: "Look: you've been given this life. Honour it. Don't waste it. It's a beautiful thing. Don't throw it away." For me, music is the only thing that ever worked. "There's seven people here that paid money to see us tonight." [*laughs*] "We've got to go *out* there." You still do it. And it's awesome. Because ... *because*. You don't know. You might have a great gig.'

And the music moves the air. From the widescreen festival stages with Green On Red to the close-up, hand-to-hand combat in basement bars, and on through hundreds of venues across the continents as the years have rolled by. There's always that half-sung, half-spoken, warm drawl wrapped around a single coil, chiming Telecaster, unspooling another yearning melody.

We got up and played
We got up and sang
We plugged in our guitars
Tried to make it rain.

Keep bringing the rain, Chuck. It nourishes the soul.

GREEN ON RED AND CHUCK PROPHET: TWENTY HISTORIC PERFORMANCES

One can never predict when videos might disappear from the ether, but I hope that at least the majority of these recordings will linger as long as this book does. Key words will lead you to the clips. Thanks to those who sent suggestions as this list was being compiled.

'SEA OF CORTEZ'—GREEN ON RED ON *WHISTLE TEST*, 1985
Recorded 1985; uploaded November 27 2011
Showcasing the band's classic line-up. The BBC even provided a cactus to make the band feel at home.

'HAIR OF THE DOG'—GREEN ON RED AT ROSKILDE FESTIVAL, 1993
Recorded July 4 1993; uploaded July 7 2009
Not long before they finally called it quits, this festival footage finds Stuart having a ball, and Prophet in rock god mode.

'LONGSHOT LULLABY' AND 'STEP RIGHT THIS WAY' AT GLASTONBURY, 1995
Recorded June 1995; uploaded April 13 2012
Rare footage of Chuck, Stephie, and Max Butler performing for the BBC cameras at Glastonbury in 1995, the year they played the acoustic stage. Use keywords 'Prophet liveGlastonbury'.

'HOMEMADE BLOOD' LIVE IN VIENNA, 1999
Recorded December 20 1999; uploaded November 24 2009
There is not enough pre-millennium footage of Chuck on YouTube; this is from the *Hurting Business* tour. This intense performance captures the thick, metallic sound Prophet and Max Butler were alchemizing onstage around 1997–99.

'ABANDONED LOVE' LIVE IN VIENNA, 2002
Recorded June 10 2002; uploaded December 14 2009
A second clip from Vienna, Austria, this time from the *No Other Love* tour. A song that remains a highlight of the repertoire, thirty years after Chuck and Stephie first played it together; here, it features Max Butler on mandocello.

GREEN ON RED REUNION SHOW, ROCKPALAST, 2006
Recorded August 7 2006; uploaded January 16 2019
A pro-shot recording of the band's reunion show recorded at Harmonie in Bonn, Germany. It opens with a raging 'Cheap Wine' and just keeps building.

'DOUBTER OUT OF JESUS (ALL OVER YOU)' LIVE ON *LETTERMAN*, 2008
Recorded January 9 2008; uploaded January 10 2008
One of Prophet's most high-profile gigs, and a story for the ages. Featuring Paul Shaffer on the tubular bells! (see chapter ten).

'COUNT THE DAYS' STEPHANIE FINCH & THE MISSION EXPRESS, ALBUQUERQUE, 2008
Recorded January 2008; uploaded December 29 2012
The Company Men band that made the *Cry Tomorrow* album and with whom Stephie toured at this time may have had a lighter touch, but this is an exciting, powerhouse performance, and features a rare instance of Prophet using a looper for the song's siren-like riff. Todd Roper on drums.

'SUMMERTIME THING' LIVE AT *DARYL'S HOUSE*, 2008
Recorded 2008; first aired May 15 2008; uploaded December 30 2011
Chuck's biggest hit played with the biggest-selling artist Prophet has ever performed alongside, except maybe Peter Buck? (Let's check those sales figures, R.E.M. vs. Hall & Oates.) Complete with Daryl-isms on the outro (see chapter ten).

'WE HAD IT ALL'—BACKSTAGE AT MANCHESTER ACADEMY, 2009
Recorded September 27 2009; uploaded May 8 2010
This Chuck and Stephie rendition of what Jim Dickinson called 'the saddest song in the world' (see chapter three) was recorded in a stairwell before the show.

'LET FREEDOM RING' LIVE IN LONDON, 2009
Recorded October 1 2009; uploaded October 23 2009
A nicely shot performance courtesy of Luke Haskard and Mark Waller, with soundboard audio. This show was taped for a live album that ended up in the bin.

'NO OTHER LOVE' AT A HOUSE CONCERT, WINNIPEG, 2011
Recorded July 11 2011; uploaded July 12 2011
As Chuck says, he does not get a chance to perform 'No Other Love' very often. This is a tender rendition of one of his most beautiful and best-known songs in front of forty-five fortunate people in Winnipeg, Canada.

'STORM ACROSS THE SEA' AND 'BALINESE DANCER' AT THE GREAT AMERICAN MUSICAL HALL, SAN FRANCISCO, 2012
Recorded March 30 2012; uploaded April 5 2012
Fans of Prophet's live performances owe a debt to dedicated fan and taper Marty Lefkowitz. This is not pro-shot footage, but the quality of the recording (a soundboard and microphone matrix) is excellent, and finds the band reinventing this *No Other Love* sleeper via The Flamin' Groovies' 'Slow Death' and then reviving the title track of Prophet's second solo LP almost twenty years on.

'SISTER LOST SOUL' SOLO ACOUSTIC 2015
Recorded August 26 2015; uploaded August 31 2015
This beautiful track, co-written with Alejandro Escovedo for the *Real Animal* album, is performed

here at a regular haunt, Armondo's in Martinez, California. It is a good representation of the Chuck Prophet solo acoustic show.

'TEMPLE BEAUTIFUL' AT THE STARRY PLOUGH, 2015
Recorded December 31 2015; uploaded January 6 2016
Another Marty Lefkowitz recording of one of the band's semi-regular New Year's Eve shows at a favourite venue.

'YOU DID' IN MILL VALLEY, 2016
Recorded January 8 2016; uploaded January 14 2016
There are countless versions of this available, but this one benefits from a great mix courtesy of Marty Lefkowitz and a sky-high solo.

'TIME AIN'T NOTHING' DAN STUART SOLO PERFORMANCE, TIVOLIVREDENBURG, 2016
Recorded and uploaded March 5 2016
This tender reworking of the Green On Red staple features Tom Heyman on slide guitar. The poignancy of the performance is impossible to capture in words.

'IN THE MAUSOLEUM' LIVE IN THE STUDIO, 2017
Recorded March 29 2017; uploaded May 13 2017
A fierce workout for James DePrato on this pro-shot recording, live in the studio at WFUV Public Radio.

'THE WAITING' AT THE MAKE OUT ROOM, 2017
Recorded October 7 2017; uploaded October 8 2017
A terrific performance of this Tom Petty song, beginning with Chuck and Stephie playing as a duo—Chuck on Tele and Stephie on acoustic, as they had done regularly almost thirty years earlier at the Albion—with the band joining halfway through, and James DePrato nailing Mike Campbell's solo.

'HIGH AS JOHNNY THUNDERS' WITH AARON LEE TASJAN, 2019
Recorded 2019; uploaded November 15 2019
Filmed around the time *The Land That Time Forgot* was finished, this string-laden take on one of the key tracks features Aaron Lee Tasjan, who accompanied Chuck on a cultural tour around San Francisco, available here: southwest.fm/sites-and-sounds/episode-3/

DISCOGRAPHIES

Key *MLP*—mini LP; *LP*—full-length vinyl album; *MC*—cassette; *CD*—compact disc; *CDS*—compact disc single.

GREEN ON RED

1981 USA *Two Bibles* MLP Green On Red—R-714 (red vinyl)

1982 USA *Green On Red* MLP Down There—DT-3

1982 USA *Green On Red* MLP Enigma—E-1026

1982 Greece *Green On Red* MLP Virgin—VG 10261

1982 Holland *Green On Red* MLP Enigma—1026-1

1982 Spain *Green On Red* MLP Dro—4D-212

1985 UK *Green On Red* MLP Zippo—ZANE 002

1982 USA *Green On Red* MC Enigma—71026-4

1983 USA *Gravity Talks* LP Slash—23964-1

1983 Australia *Gravity Talks* LP Big Time—BT-7021

1983 Canada *Gravity Talks* LP Slash—92 39641

1983 France *Gravity Talks* LP Virgin—70262

1983 Greece *Gravity Talks* LP Virgin—VG 50071

1983 Sweden *Gravity Talks* LP Planet—23964-1

1984 Japan *Gravity Talks* LP Rough Trade/Slash—25RTL-19 (with printed insert & obi)

1986 Spain *Gravity Talks* LP London—828 036-1

1987 Germany *Gravity Talks* LP Metronome—828 036-1

1987 UK *Gravity Talks* LP Slash— SR 207

1987 UK *Gravity Talks* LP London—SLMP 16

2003 USA *Gravity Talks* CD Wounded Bird—WOU 3964

1983 USA *Gravity Talks* MC Slash—SLA 23964-4

1987 UK *Gravity Talks* MC London—SMMC 16

1983 Australia 'Gravity Talks' 7-inch Big Time—BTS-1213

1985 USA *Gas Food Lodging* LP Enigma—72005-1 (green vinyl)

1985 USA *Gas Food Lodging* LP Enigma—72005-1 (black vinyl)

1985 USA *Gas Food Lodging* LP Enigma—ST-73249 (re-release with different label design and different catalogue number)

1985 Canada *Gas Food Lodging* LP Enigma—ST-73249

1985 France *Gas Food Lodging* LP New Rose—ROSE 65 (black vinyl)

1985 France *Gas Food Lodging* LP New Rose—ROSE 65 (red vinyl with green streaks)

1985 Germany *Gas Food Lodging* LP Rough Trade—RTD 29/EFA 12-3029 (black vinyl)

1985 Germany *Gas Food Lodging* LP Rough Trade—RTD 29/EFA 12-3029 (red/green splatter vinyl)

1985 Greece *Gas Food Lodging* LP Virgin—062-VG 50127

1985 Holland *Gas Food Lodging* LP Torso—33004

1985 Japan *Gas Food Lodging* LP Wave—SP25-6012 (with printed insert and obi)

1985 Spain *Gas Food Lodging* LP Dro—4D-164

1985 Sweden *Gas Food Lodging* LP Planet—MOP 3028

1985 UK *Gas Food Lodging* LP Zippo—ZONG 005

1986 Brazil *Gas Food Lodging* LP Young/Enigma—308.7105

1985 USA *Gas Food Lodging* CD Enigma—72005-2 (in longbox)

1985 USA *Gas Food Lodging* CD Enigma—72005-2

1985 USA *Gas Food Lodging* MC Enigma—4XT-73249

1985 UK *Gas Food Lodging* MC Zippo—ZONG CASS 005

1985 Holland 'Gas Food Lodging' 7-inch Torso—TORSO 70004

1986 USA 'Gas Food Lodging' 10-inch Restless—72090-0

1985 Spain 'Black River' 7-inch Enigma & DRO—1D-175 (split release: Rain Parade)

1985 USA *No Free Lunch* MLP Mercury—422-826 346-1 M-1

1985 USA *No Free Lunch* MLP Mercury—422-826 346-1 M-1 (promo)

1985 Australia *No Free Lunch* MLP Mercury—826 346-1

1985 Canada *No Free Lunch* MLP Mercury—MERM 2

1985 Greece *No Free Lunch* MLP Mercury—826 346-1

1985 Holland *No Free Lunch* MLP Mercury—826 346-1 (printed inner sleeve)

1985 Japan *No Free Lunch* MLP Mercury—25PP-183 (with printed insert and obi)

1985 Spain *No Free Lunch* MLP Mercury—826 346-1

1985 UK *No Free Lunch* MLP Mercury—MERM 78 (die-cut sleeve with print on inside back sleeve; printed inner sleeve)

1994 USA *No Free Lunch* CD One Way—OW 30015

2003 UK *No Free Lunch* CD Acadia—ACA 8054

1985 USA *No Free Lunch* MC Mercury—422-826 346-4 M-1

1985 Australia *No Free Lunch* MC Mercury—826 346-4

1985 Canada *No Free Lunch* MC Mercury—MERM4 2

1985 New Zealand *No Free Lunch* MC Mercury—826 346-4

1985 UK *No Free Lunch* MC Mercury—MERMC 78

1985 UK 'Time Ain't Nothing' 7-inch Mercury—MER 202 (die-cut sleeve)

1985 UK 'Time Ain't Nothing' 7-inch Mercury—MER 202 (die-cut sleeve; with limited edition printed insert; no. 1 of 5: Dan 'Big Daddy' Stuart)

1985 UK 'Time Ain't Nothing' 7-inch Mercury—MER 202 (die-cut sleeve; with limited edition printed insert; no. 3 of 5: Jack 'Jake' Waterson)

1985 UK 'Time Ain't Nothing' 7-inch Mercury—MER 202 (die-cut sleeve; with limited edition printed insert; no. 4 of 5: Keith Mitchell)

1985 Australia 'Time Ain't Nothing' 7-inch Mercury—884 234-7

1985 Holland 'Time Ain't Nothing' 7-inch Mercury—884 234-7

1985 Spain 'Time Ain't Nothing' 7-inch Mercury—884 234-7

1985 UK 'Time Ain't Nothing' 12-inch Mercury—MERX 202 (promo with printed insert; promo only)

1985 USA *Spin Radio Concert* 2xLP Spin—C 002 (produced for radio stations only; three-sided, side 4 is blank)

1985 USA *Spin Radio Concert* 2xLP Spin—NC 002 (produced for radio stations only; printed insert)

1985 UK *In Concert—Glastonbury Festival 1985* LP BBC—CN 4670/S (produced for radio stations only; two printed inserts; split release: The Untouchables)

1987 USA *The Killer Inside Me* LP Mercury—422-830 912-1 Q-1

1987 USA *The Killer Inside Me* LP Mercury—422-830 912-1 Q-1 (promo. sticker on cover)

1987 Canada *The Killer Inside Me* LP Mercury—830 912-1 (printed inner sleeve)

1987 Greece *The Killer Inside Me* LP Mercury—830 912-1 (printed inner sleeve)

1987 Holland *The Killer Inside Me* LP Mercury—830 912-1 (printed inner sleeve)

1987 Italy *The Killer Inside Me* LP Mercury—830 912-1 (printed inner sleeve)

1987 Spain *The Killer Inside Me* LP Mercury—830 912-1

1987 UK *The Killer Inside Me* LP Mercury—GOR LP 1 (Printed inner sleeve)

1987 UK *The Killer Inside Me* CD Mercury—830 912-2 (Front page of booklet is die-cut)

1987 USA *The Killer Inside Me* MC Mercury—422-830 912-4 Q-1

1987 Canada *The Killer Inside Me* MC Mercury—830 912-4

1987 UK *The Killer Inside Me* MC Mercury—GOR MC 1

1987 UK 'Clarkesville' 7-inch Mercury—GOR 1

1987 UK 'Clarkesville' 7-inch Mercury—GOR 1 (one-sided acetate)

1987 Holland 'Clarkesville' 7-inch Mercury—888 344-7

1987 Spain 'Clarkesville' 7-inch Mercury—888 344-7

1987 UK 'Clarkesville' 12-inch Mercury—GOR 112

1987 Spain 'Clarkesville' 12-inch Mercury—888 344-1

1987 USA 'Clarkesville' 12-inch Mercury—PRO 497-1 (promo; same track both sides)

1987 UK 'Born To Fight' 7-inch Mercury—GOR 2

1987 UK 'Ghost Hand' 12-inch Mercury—GOR 212

1988 USA *Spin Radio Concert* 2xLP Spin—no catalogue number (produced for radio stations only)

1989 UK *In Concert* LP BBC—CN 5342/S (produced for radio stations only; printed insert)

1989 UK 'Keith Can't Read' 7-inch China—CHINA 16 (sticker on cover)

1989 UK 'Keith Can't Read' 12-inch China—CHINX 16 (sticker on cover)

1989 USA *Here Come The Snakes* LP Restless—72351-1

1989 France *Here Come The Snakes* LP Accord—102311

1989 Germany *Here Come The Snakes* LP Rough Trade—RTD 85

1989 Greece *Here Come The Snakes* LP Virgin—VG 50392

1989 Holland *Here Come The Snakes* LP Red Rhino—RED LP 93

1989 Italy *Here Come The Snakes* LP Ariola—209 475 (black vinyl)

1989 Italy *Here Come The Snakes* LP Ariola—209 475 (green vinyl; limited numbered edition of 1,000 copies)

1989 Sweden *Here Come The Snakes* LP Sonet—SLP-3142

1989 UK *Here Come The Snakes* LP China—839 294-1

1989 UK *Here Come The Snakes* 12-inch China—CRAWL 1 (promo; one-sided; in plain stickered die-cut sleeve; 4 tracks)

1989 USA *Here Come The Snakes* CD Restless—72351-2

1989 France *Here Come The Snakes* CD Accord—102312

1989 Germany *Here Come The Snakes* CD China—4509-95204-2

1989 Italy *Here Come The Snakes* CD China—WOLCD 1013

1989 Sweden *Here Come The Snakes* CD Sonet—SLPCD-3142

1989 UK *Here Come The Snakes* CD China—WOLCD 1013

2005 USA *Here Come The Snakes* 2xCD Belle Sound—IRT 7021 (fold-out digipak)

1989 USA *Here Come The Snakes* MC Restless—72351-4

1989 Greece *Here Come The Snakes* MC Virgin—TC-VG 50392

1989 UK *Here Come The Snakes* MC China—839 294-4

1989 Germany *Here Come The Snakes/Gas Food Lodging* CD Rough Trade—RTD CD 85

1989 UK *Live* 10-inch China—841 013-0 (sticker on cover; limited numbered edition)

1989 UK *Live* MC China—841 013-4

1989 Germany *Here Come The Snakes/Live* CD China—CHI 9014-2

1989 UK 'This Time Around' 7-inch China—CHINA 21

1989 Germany 'This Time Around' 7-inch China—873 170-7

1989 UK 'This Time Around' 12-inch China—CHINX 21

1989 UK 'This Time Around' 12-inch China—CHINX 21 DJ (promo)

1989 UK 'This Time Around' CDS China—CHICD 21

1989 UK *This Time Around* LP China—841 519-1

1989 UK *This Time Around* LP+7-inch China—841 519-1 (sticker on cover; 7-inch catalogue number: SNAKE 2)

1989 Australia *This Time Around* LP China—841 519-1

1989 Holland *This Time Around* LP China—841 519-1

1989 Italy *This Time Around* LP Ariola—210 443 (printed inner sleeve)

1989 USA *This Time Around* CD China—841 519-2

1989 Germany *This Time Around* CD China—4509-96203-2

1989 Japan *This Time Around + Live* CD Polydor—POOP-20312 (with obi)

1989 UK *This Time Around* CD China—841 519-2

1989 USA *This Time Around* MC China—841 519-4

1989 UK *This Time Around* MC China—841 519-4

1989 Italy *This Time Around* MC Ariola—410 443

1989 UK *This Time Around* CD China—No catalogue number (promo)

1989 UK 'Dan Stuart And Chuck Prophet Interviewed By DJ Johnny Walker' 7-inch China—SNAKE 2 (given away free with *This Time Around* LP)

1989 USA 'Reverend Luther' 12-inch China/Polydor—PRO 837-1 (promo)

1989 USA 'Reverend Luther' CDS China/Polydor—CDP 258 (promo)

1990 UK 'You Couldn't Get Arrested' 7-inch China—CHINA 22

1990 Germany 'You Couldn't Get Arrested' 7-inch China—873 746-7

1990 UK 'You Couldn't Get Arrested' 12-inch China—CHINX 22

1990 UK 'You Couldn't Get Arrested' CDS China—CHICD 22

1990 Germany 'You Couldn't Get Arrested' CDS China—873 747-2

1991 UK 'Little Things In Life' 7-inch China—WOK 2001

1991 UK 'Little Things In Life' 5-inch China—WOKF 2001 (limited; sticker on outer PVC cover)

1991 Australia 'Little Things In Life' 7-inch Liberation—K 10492

1991 UK 'Little Things In Life' 12-inch China—WOKT 2001

1991 UK 'Little Things In Life' CDS China—WOKCD 2001

1991 UK *Scapegoats* LP China—WOL 1001 (printed inner sleeve; sticker on cover)

1991 Germany *Scapegoats* LP China/Edel—CHI 9016-1 (printed inner sleeve)

1991 Italy *Scapegoats* LP China—WOL 1001 (printed inner sleeve)

1991 Spain *Scapegoats* LP China—WOL 1001 (printed inner sleeve)

1991 UK *Scapegoats* CD China—WOLCD 1001

1991 France *Scapegoats* CD Vogue—600335

1991 Germany *Scapegoats* CD China—CHI 9016-2

1991 Holland *Scapegoats* CD China—656.694-2

1991 Italy *Scapegoats* CD China—WOLCD 1001

1991 Japan *Scapegoats* CD Pony Canyon—PCCY-00286 (with obi and printed insert)

1991 USA *Scapegoats* CD Off-Beat—OBR 1001-2

1991 UK *Scapegoats* MC China—WOL MC 1001

1991 France *Scapegoats* MC Vogue—706335

1991 UK 'Two Lovers' 7-inch China—WOK 2005

1991 Holland 'Two Lovers' CDS China—146.038-3 (card sleeve)

1991 UK *Little Things In Life* CD Music Club—MCCD 037

1991 UK *Little Things In Life* MC Music Club—MCTC 037

1991 UK *The Best Of* LP China—WOL 1021

1991 Italy *The Best Of* LP China—WOL 1021

1991 Spain *The Best Of* LP China—WOL 1021

1991 UK *The Best Of* CD China—CHI 9022-2

1991 Italy *The Best Of* CD China—WOLCD 1021

1991 Japan *The Best Of/Live* 2xCD Pony Canyon—PCCY-00311 (in oversized gatefold jewel case with obi and 2 booklets)

1991 Australia *The Best Of* MC China—C 30758

1992 UK *The Killer Inside Me/No Free Lunch* CD Mercury—514 187-2

1992 UK *Too Much Fun* LP China—WOL 1029

1992 Italy *Too Much Fun* LP China—WOL 1029

1992 UK *Too Much Fun* CD China—WOLCD 1029

1992 Germany *Too Much Fun* CD China—CHI 9034-2

1992 Holland *Too Much Fun* CD China—656.812-2

1992 Italy *Too Much Fun* CD China—WOLCD 1029

1992 USA *Too Much Fun* CD Off-Beat—OBR 01029-2

1992 UK *Too Much Fun* MC China—WOLMC 1029

1992 UK 'She's All Mine' CDS China—WOKCD 2029 (promo)

1993 Philippines 'Rainy Days And Mondays' 7-inch Pony Canyon—PG-0033 (same track both sides)

1992 UK *Gas Food Lodging/Green On Red* CD Mau Mau—MAUCD 612

1994 USA *Rock 'N' Roll Disease—The Best Of* CD Off-Beat—752792102126

1994 Germany *Rock 'N' Roll Disease—The Best Of* CD China—4509-96106-2

1997 UK *Rock 'N' Roll Disease—The Very Best Of* CD Nectar—NTMCD 556

1997 Australia *What Were We Thinking?* LP Corduroy—CORD 026 (gatefold sleeve)

1997 Australia *What Were We Thinking?* CD Corduroy—CORD 026-CD

1997 Germany *Archives Vol. 1—What Were We Thinking?* CD Normal—NORMAL 194 CD

1998 UK *Here Come The Snakes/Scapegoats* CD Edsel—EDCD 590

1998 UK *This Time Around/Too Much Fun* CD Edsel—EDCD 591

2003 USA *Gas Food Lodging/Green On Red* CD Restless—REST 72999

2005 USA *Live At The International Manchester March 27, 1987* CD Belle Sound—No catalogue number (folded card sleeve with extra flap)

2006 USA *Valley Fever* DVD Brink—00029566

2006 Germany *Valley Fever* CD+DVD Blue Rose—BLU CD 0442

2007 UK *BBC Sessions* CD Maida Vale—MVRCD002

CHUCK PROPHET

1990 UK *Brother Aldo* LP FIRE—FIRE LP 22 (printed inner sleeve)

1990 Germany *Brother Aldo* LP Rough Trade—RTD 185.1119.1 (printed inner sleeve)

1990 UK *Brother Aldo* LP FIRE—FIRE LP 22 (printed inner sleeve)

1990 Germany *Brother Aldo* LP Rough Trade—RTD 185.1119.1 (printed inner sleeve)

1990 UK *Brother Aldo* CD FIRE—FIRE CD 22

1998 UK *Brother Aldo* CD Cooking Vinyl—COOK CD 164

1990 Germany *Brother Aldo* CD Rough Trade—RTD 185.1119.2

1990 USA *Brother Aldo* MC FIRE—FIREUS5-4

1993 UK *Balinese Dancer* LP China—WOL 1031

1993 Italy *Balinese Dancer* LP China—WOL 1031

1993 UK *Balinese Dancer* CD China—WOLCD 1031 (sticker on cover)

1993 Germany *Balinese Dancer* CD China—4509-96104-2

1993 Germany *Balinese Dancer* CD China—CHI 9046-2

1993 Italy *Balinese Dancer* CD China—WOLCD 1031

1993 UK *Balinese Dancer* CDS China—WOKCD 2032 (promo)

1993 UK 'Heart Breaks Like The Dawn' CDS China—WOKCD 2036 (promo stickered cover)

1993 Germany '110 In The Shade' CDS China—CHI 9051-5

1993 Australia A Thousand Footprints In The Sand LP Corduroy—CORD 033 (as 'Jim Dickinson With Chuck Prophet And The Creatures Of Habit')

1997 France A Thousand Footprints In The Sand CD Last Call—3018392 (as 'Jim Dickinson With Chuck Prophet And The Creatures Of Habit')

1995 UK A Taster From The Forthcoming Album Feast Of Hearts CDS China—WOKCDP 2063 (promo; digipak)

1995 UK Feast Of Hearts CD China—WOLCD 1061

1995 Germany Feast Of Hearts CD China—0630-10416-2

1995 UK 'What It Takes' CDS China—WOKCD 2062

1995 Germany 'Longshot Lullaby' CDS Warner—0630-10415-2

1997 UK Homemade Blood CD Cooking Vinyl—COOK CD 114

1997 Canada Homemade Blood CD True North—TNSD 0148

2000 Australia Homemade Blood LP Corduroy—CORD 101 (printed insert; limited numbered edition of 250 copies)

1997 UK 'Til You Came Along' CDS Cooking Vinyl—FRY CD 061 (promo)

1998 UK Balinese Dancer/Feast Of Hearts CD Edsel—EDCD 592

1999 Australia Homemade Boot CD Corduroy—CORD 077 (as 'Chuck Prophet And The Bible Dusters')

2000 Australia The Hurting Business LP Corduroy—CORD 102 (limited numbered edition of 250 copies)

2000 USA The Hurting Business CD Hightone—HCD8113

1999 Holland The Hurting Business CD Cooking Vinyl—4964512

1999 Japan The Hurting Business CD Buffalo—BUF-104 (with printed insert & obi)

1999 UK The Hurting Business CD Cooking Vinyl—COOK CD 159

1999 UK 'The Hurting Business' CDS Cooking Vinyl—FRY CD 087

2000 UK 'Dyin' All Young' CDS Cooking Vinyl—FRY CD 092P (promo)

2001 UK Turn The Pigeons Loose CD Cooking Vinyl—COOK CD 215 (as 'Chuck Prophet And The Mission Express')

2001 US Raisins In The Sun CD Rounder Records—11661-3177-2 (as 'Raisins In The Sun')

2001 UK Raisins In The Sun CD Evangeline Records—GEL 4018 (as 'Raisins In The Sun')

2001 US Raisins In The Sun CD Rounder Records—11661-3177-2A (as 'Raisins In The Sun'; promo)

2002 USA Selections From The Upcoming Album No Other Love CDS New West—NWE 0001 (promo)

2002 Germany No Other Love LP Blue Rose—BLU LP 0273

2002 USA No Other Love CD New West—NW 6039)

2002 Germany No Other Love CD Blue Rose—BLU CD 0273

2002 USA 'Summertime Thing' CDS New West—NWS 1015 (promo)

2002 USA 'I Bow Down And Pray To Every Woman I See' CDS New West—NWS 1018 (promo)

2002 USA Hotel San Jose CD Innerstate—INNERSTATE 7014 (as 'Go Go Market')

2002 UK Hotel San Jose CD Evangeline—GEL 4043 (as 'Go Go Market')

2004 UK 'Heavy Duty' 7-inch Casual—LOUPE012 (as 'Dan Penn & Chuck Prophet'; split release: Razzy)

2004 Germany Age Of Miracles LP Blue Rose—BLU LP 0350 (printed insert)

2004 Germany Age Of Miracles CD Blue Rose—BLU DP 0350 (US CD and digipak in German card slip-case)

2004 USA Age Of Miracles CD New West—NW 6062 (digipak)

2004 UK Age Of Miracles CD New West—NW 6062 (promo)

2004 USA 'Pin A Rose On Me' CDS New West—NWS 1029 (promo)

2004 USA As Seen On TV CD Wonderama—CD 124 007 (limited edition of 250 copies; CD in paper bag inside a tri-folded printed brown card sleeve)

2007 USA Dreaming Waylon's Dreams CD Evangeline—EV 0003 (limited numbered edition of 1,000 copies; in rectangular card cover stapled with booklet)

2010 UK Dreaming Waylon's Dreams CD Decor—DECOR 022 CD (digipak)

2007 USA Soap And Water LP Coppertree—CTR 004 (printed inner sleeve)

2007 USA Soap And Water CD Yep Roc—YEP-2173 (digipak)

2007 UK Soap And Water CD Cooking Vinyl—COOK CD 417

2007 UK Soap And Water CD Cooking Vinyl—COOK CD 417 PROMO (promo)

2007 UK Soap And Water CD Cooking Vinyl—COOK CD 417 CDR (promo)

2007 UK 'Freckle Song' CDS Cooking Vinyl—FRY CDR 321 (promo)

2008 UK 'Would You Love Me?' CDS Cooking Vinyl—FRY CDR 352 (promo; 2 stickers on cover)

2010 UK Let Freedom Ring LP Diverse—DIV 021 LP (printed inner sleeve)

2013 USA Let Freedom Ring LP+CD Yep Roc—YEP 2201 (sticker on outer PVC cover; printed inner sleeve; download card included)

2009 USA Let Freedom Ring CD Yep Roc—YEP 2201 (digipak)

2009 USA Let Freedom Ring CD Yep Roc—CD-YEP-2201 (promo)

2009 UK Let Freedom Ring CD Cooking Vinyl—COOK CD 499

2009 UK Let Freedom Ring CD Cooking Vinyl—COOK CD 499 CDR (promo)

2009 UK 'American Man' CDS Cooking Vinyl—FRYDL CDR 397-CDR (promo; 2 stickers on cover)

2009 UK Cry Tomorrow CD Belle Sound—BS-007 (as 'Stephanie Finch And The Company Men'; fold-out card sleeve)

2011 Spain London Calling Live! DVD Geztea Live—DVD LO 90410 (as 'Chuck Prophet And The Spanish Bombs'; card sleeve)

2012 USA Temple Beautiful LP Yep Roc—YEP-2255 (printed inner sleeve; download card included)

2012 USA Temple Beautiful LP+CD Yep Roc—YEP-2255 (sticker on outer PVC cover; printed inner sleeve; download card included)

2012 USA Temple Beautiful CD Yep Roc—YEP-2255 (digipak; download card included)

2012 USA Temple Beautiful CD Yep Roc—CD-YEP-2255 (promo)

2012 USA Temple Beautiful MC Burger—BRGR 246 (limited numbered edition of 150 copies)

2012 USA 'White Night, Big City' CDS Yep Roc—No catalogue number (promo)

2012 UK 'White Night, Big City' CDS Yep Roc—No catalogue number (promo; sticker on outer PVC cover)

2012 UK 'The Left Hand And The Right Hand' 7-inch Decor/Trash/Yep Roc—DECOR 027/TA 710 (limited numbered edition of 500 copies; 4 printed inserts)

2012 USA 'Castro Halloween' 7-inch Yep Roc—SI-YEP-2306 (orange vinyl; 2 stickers on outer PVC cover)

2012 UK 'Tulare Kiss' 7-inch Belle Sound—000019 (as 'El Depravo'; folded sleeve)

2014 USA Night Surfer LP+CD Yep Roc—YEP 2406 (printed insert; download card included)

2014 USA Night Surfer CD Yep Roc—YEP 2406 (digipak; download card included)

2014 USA Night Surfer CD Yep Roc—No catalogue number (promo in card sleeve)

2014 USA Night Surfer MC Yep Roc—YEP 2406

2015 USA Night Surfer 7x7-inch Yep Roc—6 34457 24541 9 (in card box; 3D glasses included)

2014 UK 'Tell Me Anything (Turn To Gold)' 7-inch Decor—DECOR035 (limited numbered edition of 500 copies)

2017 US Bobby Fuller Died For Your Sins CD Yep Roc—YEP 2490 (cardboard wallet style case, foldout leaflet)

2017 US Bobby Fuller Died For Your Sins CD Yep Roc—YEP 2490 (promo; jewel case; no booklet)

2017 UK Bobby Fuller Died For Your Sins CD Yep Roc—CD-YEP 2490 (promo; plastic sleeve; foldout insert)

2017 US Bobby Fuller Died For Your Sins LP Yep Roc—YEP 2490 (gatefold sleeve including integrated button badge; download card included)

2020 US The Land That Time Forgot LP Yep Roc—LPYEP 2691X (first edition; limited red vinyl; download card included)

2020 US The Land That Time Forgot LP Yep Roc—LPYEP 2691 (download card included)

2020 US The Land That Time Forgot CD Yep Roc—CDYEP 2691

2020 UK The Land That Time Forgot LP Yep Roc—LPYEP2691RT (Rough Trade exclusive; limited splatter vinyl; 250 copies)

BIBLIOGRAPHY

(n.d.) indicates a reference with no identifiable date. *[CPA]* indicates an article sourced from Chuck's paper archive. Some items do not have full dates or page numbers, but all references are given in as complete form as possible. Full URLs are available at jawbonepress.com.

Adams, Ryan (2019) Instagram post, November 19.

Aginghipster (2014) 'Talking with the Night Surfer: an Interview with Chuck Prophet', *No Depression*, September 16.

Almond, Steve (2007) 'Chuck Prophet', *Miami New Times*, September 20.

AMA (n.d.) The Americana Music Association, 'What is Americana music?'

Armstrong, Stephen B. (2002) 'Chuck Prophet: No Other Love', *Popmatters*, August 29.

Ashare, Matt (2001) 'Raisins in the Sun: Raisins in the Sun', *CMJ*, February [CPA].

Aston, Martin (1985) 'Green On Red: Electric Ballroom, London', *Melody Maker*, July 13 [CPA].

Ave the Sound (2017) 'Meet Chuck Prophet … "Songwriter out of Time"', November 5.

Azerrad, Michael (2001) *Our Band Could Be Your Life*. New York: Bay Books/Little, Brown and Company.

Bailie, Stuart (1989) 'Green On Red: This Time Around', *New Musical Express*, November 11 [CPA].

Baker, Brian (2000) 'Chuck Prophet—The Hurting Business', *Cleveland Scene*, February 17.

Baker, Brian (2009) 'Chuck Prophet, Let Freedom Ring', *Cleveland Scene*, October 30.

Barron, Jack (1985a) 'Red Alert', *Sounds*, April 13 [CPA].

Barron, Jack (1985b) 'Food for Thought: Green On Red: No Free Lunch', *Sounds*, October 12 [CPA].

Baruth, Seana (1996) *Bay Area Magazine*, January 5.

Batey, Rick (1993) 'The Road to Bali: Chuck Prophet', *Guitarist* magazine, May, pp. 130–4.

Baym, Nancy K. (2018) *Playing to the Crowd: Musicians, Audiences, and the Intimate Work of Connection*. New York: New York University Press.

Belcher, David (1995) 'Feeling the retro vibes', *Glasgow Herald*, May 26 [CPA].

Bertin, Michael (1997) 'CHUCK PROPHET *Homemade Blood*', *Austin Chronicle*, March 14.

Blackbook (2013) 'Musician John Murry Talks Addiction, Artistic Integrity, and his New Album "The Graceless Age"', *Blackbook*, March 13.

Blackstock, Peter (1992) 'SXSW Notes', *Austin-American Statesman*, March 15 [CPA].

Blackstock, Peter (2009) 'Let Freedom Ring', *No Depression*, November 3.

Bray, Ryan (2016) 'How Boston's Fort Apache Studios Captured the Sound of an Era', July 11.

Brazeau, Jules (2017), 'Klipschutz Steps out of the Shadows', *No Depression*, April 29.

Breen, Joe (2007) 'Chuck Prophet, Soap and Water', *Irish Times*, August 30.

Breznikar, Klemen (2011) 'Green On Red Interview with Dan Stuart', June 18.

Brown, Jules (2017) 'Chuck Prophet: *Bobby Fuller Died for your Sins*', *Spill Magazine*.

Burnett, Robert (2002) *The Global Jukebox: The International Music Industry*. London: Routledge.

Caligiuri, Jim (2000a) 'Chuck Prophet: The Hurting Business', *The Austin Chronicle*, January 21 [CPA].

Caligiuri, Jim (2000b) 'Review: Chuck Prophet Cactus Cafe, September 26', *Austin Chronicle*, October 6.

Caligiuri, Jim (2012) 'Chuck Prophet: Temple Beautiful', *Austin Chronicle*, March 16.

Cameron, Keith (1999) 'Chuck Prophet: Underworld, London ****', *Guardian*, November 17.

Cantwell, David (2002a) 'Chuck Prophet—the beating heart', *No Depression*, June 30.

Cantwell, David (2002b) 'Chuck Prophet / Go Go Market—No Other Love / Hotel San Jose' in *The Pitch*, June 20.

Carlyle, Thomas (1864) 'Goethe', in *Critical and Miscellaneous Essays*. New York: D. Appleton & Co., pp. 73–94.

Carroll, Jim (2016) 'A Word From The Management: Five Lessons for Creative Business from the World of Music Management', Jim Carroll's Blog, April 8.

Cavanagh, David (1991), 'Chuck Prophet: Brother Aldo', *Select* [CPA].

CBC Radio (2016) 'Christopher Ricks on why Bob Dylan is "the greatest living user of the English language"', October 24.

Christgau, Robert (1985) 'No Free Lunch' review republished at robertchristgau.com.

Christgau, Robert (1987) 'The Killer Inside Me' review republished at robertchristgau.com.

City Pages (2010) 'She was Unwanted in 17 States', *City Pages*, October 15.

Clark, Pete (1991) 'Green On Red: Scapegoats', *HiFi News*, June [CPA].

Cohen, Jason (1992) 'Chuck Prophet: Chicago House, Friday 13', *Austin Chronicle*, March 27 [CPA].

Commonplace, Constance (1985) 'Rockin Tucson in the '80s', reprinted in in Robert E. Zucker (ed.), *Entertaining Tucson Across the Decades Volume 1: 1950s–1985*. Tucson, AZ: BZB Publishing, Inc., pp. 96–8.

Cook, Dennis (2007) 'Chuck Prophet: A Thousand Stolen Kisses', jambase.com, November.

Copsey, Rob (2018) 'The Official Top 20 best-selling cassettes of 2018 so far', officialcharts.com, July 25.

Crossing, Gary (1995) 'I've got a shoebox of songs to sing you', *Big Issue*, June 27 [CPA].

DeCurtis, Anthony (1986) 'No Free Lunch: Green On Red', *Rolling Stone*, April 10 [CPA].

Deming, Mark (2017) 'Chuck Prophet—Bobby Fuller Died for your Sins', allmusic.com.

Denselow, Robin (1986) 'Shot in the heartland', *The Guardian*, March 27, p. 19 [CPA].

Denselow, Robin (1989) 'The serpents are beguiling: Green On Red: Here Come the Snakes', *Guardian*, April 7 [CPA].

DiGiacomo, Frank (2017) 'Chuck Prophet Says "People Are Exhausted by Pop Culture—But I'm Not', *Billboard*, March 10.

Doggett, Peter (1991) 'Green On Red', *Record Collector*, November [CPA].

Doyle, Patrick (2011) 'How Rockers Helped Free the West Memphis Three', *Rolling Stone*, September 1.

Drozdowski, Ted (1986) 'No Free Lunch for Green On Red', *Sweet Potato*, Mass Music, May, pp. 2–3 [CPA].

Drummond, Paul (2007) *Eye Mind: Roky Erickson and the 13th Floor Elevators*. Port Townsend, WA: Process Media.

Easlea, Daryl (2017) 'Chuck Prophet—Bobby Fuller Died for your Sins', *Record Collector*, February.

Elbourne, Martin (1985) letter to Green On Red band members [CPA].

Elliott, Paul (1989) 'Coming around again: Green On Red: "This Time Around"', *Sounds*, November 4 [CPA].

Elliott, Paul (2007) '80s Roots-Rock Survivor Now Hitting His Peak'. *Q*, October.

Ennist, Holly (1997) 'Chuck Prophet: Homemade Blood', *East Coast Rocker*, March 19 [CPA].

EQ (2010) 'Let It Bleed: Recording in a Small Mexico City Studio Helped Chuck Prophet Get Aggressive', *EQ Magazine*, January 8.

Fertig, Beth (1986) 'Green On Red—No Free Lunch', *Michigan Daily*, April 21 [CPA].

Foucault, Jeffrey (2019) 'The Answer That Got Cut', Facebook post, October 25.

Fortune, Ross (2002) 'Chuck Prophet, Borderline, Mon', *Time Out London*, May 15–22 [CPA].

Foster, April (2010) 'Alive After Five: Chuck Prophet with Sleepy Seeds', August 25.

Fricke, David (1985) 'Food for thought: Green On Red: Gas Good Lodging', *Melody Maker*, May 18 [CPA].

Gendelman, David (1990) 'Chuck Prophet, Stephanie Finch & Creatures Of Habit, September 15, Noe Valley Ministry, SF', *BAM*, October 5 [CPA].

Gill, Andy (2017) 'Music reviews', *Independent*, February 8.

Gilmore, Mikal (1985) 'Welcome to L.A.—the newest pop boom town', *Los Angeles Herald*, May 7 [CPA].

Gittins, Ian (2006) 'Green On Red: Astoria London', *Guardian*, January 14.

Gleason, Holly (2012) 'Chuck Prophet: *Temple Beautiful*', *Paste*, February 8.

Gonzales, Greg & Parisa Eshrati (2016) 'They Called It T.H.C.: A Glimpse Into Tucson's Punk History', trialanderrorcollective.com.

Goodman Frank (2007) 'A Conversation with Chuck Prophet', puremusic.com, December.

Graham, James (2018) 'Gig ticket prices have doubled since 1990s', February 8.

Green, (2015) 'The 50 Best Glastonbury Festival Performances', *Daily Telegraph*, June 16.

Gundersen, Edna (2007) 'Chuck Prophet: No Other Love', *USA Today*, November 12.

Halliday, Josh (2012) 'Music magazines suffer sales decline', *Guardian*, February 16.

Hann, Michael (2013) 'The Paisley Underground: Los Angeles's 1980s psychedelic explosion', *Guardian*, May 16.

Harms, James (1986) 'No Free Lunch—Green On Red', *Steppin' Out*, June [CPA].

Harward, Randy (2006) 'Valley Fever: Green On Red Live at The Rialto review', *Harp*, October 31.

Hawkins, Paul (2007) 'Chuck Prophet: Can a Woman's Voice Drug You?' An Interview with Chuck Prophet, *The Lazarus Coporation*, November 2.

Heller, Greg (2000) 'Prophet Takes Care of "Business"', *San Francisco Chronicle*, January 16–22 [CPA].

Hernandez, Raoul (2008) 'Tony Visconti Part 1', *Austin Chronicle*, June 19.

Himes, Geoffrey (1986) 'Green On Red Forages Ahead', *Washington Post*, June 27 [CPA].

Hoinski, Michael (2009) 'On the Haunting Songs of Chuck Prophet', *Village Voice*, November 10.

Holland, Duncan (1989) 'Everything's Gone Green', *Music Week*, April 17 [CPA].

Holt, Fabian (2010) 'The economy of live music in the digital age', *European Journal of Cultural Studies*. Vol. 13, No. 2, pp. 243–61.

Horowitz, Hal (2017) 'Chuck Prophet: Bobby Fuller Died For Your Sins', *American Songwriter*, February 9.

Howe, Zoe (2014) *Barbed Wire Kisses: The Jesus and Mary Chain Story*, extract in Q, July.

Huffman, Eddie (1993) 'Chuck Prophet: Balinese Dancer, Option, No. 53, Nov–Dec [CPA].

Hughes, Rob (2002) 'Green On Red: Paisley Source', *Uncut*, October.

Hurt, Edd (2008) 'Nashville Rebel', *Nashville Scene*.

Hutton, (1999) 'Dan Penn and Spooner Oldham #2: Memphis Women and Chicken', *Bucketfull Of Brains*.

IFPI (2017) *Global Music Report 2017: Annual State of the Industry*, ifpi.org.

Ingalls, Chris (2017) 'Garland Jeffreys: 14 Steps to Harlem', *Popmatters*, June 19.

Island Ear, The (1986) 'No Free Lunch: Green On Red', *The Island Ear*, New York, April 29 [CPA].

Jelinek, Russell (2013) 'Interview: John Murry talks about Graceless Age', April 9.

JG (2000) 'Chuck Prophet: The Hurting Business', *Guitar Player*, April [CPA].

Johnmurry.com (n.d.) 'Biography', johnmurry.com.

Johns, Glyn (2014) *Sound Man*. New York: Blue Rider Press.

Johnson, Brian F. (2006) 'Chuck Prophet Finds Solace in This Age of Miracles', *Marquee Magazine*, August 3.

Jones, Allan (1986) 'Green On Red: The Killer inside Me', *Melody Maker*, March 14 [CPA].

Jones, Allan (1990) 'Green On Red: The Killer inside Me', *Melody Maker*, August 4 [CPA].

Jones, Cliff (1995) 'Chuck Prophet: Slim's, San Francisco', *Mojo* [CPA].

Judge, (2011) 'Talk about the Passion', *Blurt*, November 15.

Jurek, Thom (2002) 'Go Go Market—Hotel San Jose Allmusic Review', allmusic.com.

Kaleta, Sabrina (2000) 'Chuck Prophet: The Hurting Business', *New Times Los Angeles*, January 20 [CPA].

Kamiya, Gary (2017) 'How Emperor Norton rose to power', *San Francisco Chronicle*, April 1.

Kane, Peter (1991) 'Chuck Prophet: Brother Aldo', Q [CPA].

Kent, Nick (1985) 'Lunch Ain't Nothing but Old Meal: Green On Red: No Free Lunch', *New Musical Express*, October 19 [CPA].

Kimpel, Dan (2006) *How They Made It: True Stories of How Music's Biggest Stars Went from Start to Stardom!* Milwaukee, WI: Hal Leonard Corporation.

Kinghorn, Peter (1991) 'Recording all over the world', *Newcastle Evening Chronicle*, March 28 [CPA].

Knopper, Steve (2009) *Appetite for Self-Destruction: The Spectacular Crash of the Record Industry in the Digital Age*. New York: Free Press.

Knopper, Steve (2018) 'The Grunge Gold Rush: Is there a lesson here?', NPR.org.

Krueger, Alan B. (2019) *Rockonomics: What the Music Industry Can Teach Us about Economics (and Our Future)*. London: John Murray.

Lanham, Tom (2011) 'Chuck Prophet Still "Chasing the San Francisco Dragon"', *SF Examiner*, October 26.

Lazarski, Todd (2010) 'Chuck Prophet: Let Freedom Ring', *Shepherd Express*, January 25.

Lee, Craig (1985) 'A Paisley Coming of Age: "Gas Food Lodging": Green On Red', *Los Angeles Times*, June 27.

Lee, Stewart (1995) 'Glastonbury Diary: Fest of Fun', *Vox*, September.

Leonard, Michael (1990) 'Green Fingers: Chuck Prophet IV', *Guitarist*, February, pp. 56–62.

Leviton, Mark (1984) 'Slash: L.A.'s Maverick Label Meets the Majors' in *BAM*, February 10.

Leviton, Mark (1985) 'Green On Red: Gas Food Lodging', *BAM*, June 21 [CPA].

Lewis, Catherine P. (2007) 'Chuck Prophet, *Soap and Water*'. *Washington Post*. November 8.

Ling, Dave (2017) 'Former Green On Red guitarist Chuck Prophet discusses life back on the road', *Classic Rock*, February 22.

Lomas, Maurice (1985) 'Green On Red: Leeds', *Sounds*, July 13 [CPA].

Lundy, Zeth (2004) 'Chuck Prophet: Age of Miracles', *Popmatters*, October 27.

Lurie, Robert Dean (2009) *No Certainty Attached: Steve Kilbey and The Church: A Biography*. Portland, OR: Verse Chorus Press.

McLeese, Don (2001) 'Raisins in the Sun: self-titled', *No Depression*, March–April [CPA].

McLenon, Andy (2005) 'Al Kooper—Don't ask me no questions', *No Depression*, June 30.

Maddux, Blake (2017) 'Blake Maddux Interviews Singer-Songwriter Chuck Prophet', December 1.

Martin, Gavin (2007) 'Green On Red man's ode to San Francisco', *Classic Rock*, March 4.

Malitz, David (2012) 'In "Temple Beautiful", Chuck Prophet Reflects on his Bay Area Home', *Washington Post*, May 21.

Marchetto, Pete (1985) 'Red Alert: Green On Red: Sheffield', October 30 [CPA].

Margolis, Lynn (2004) 'Chuck Prophet couldn't predict radio would play him', *Austin American Statesman*, October 6.

Martin, Douglas (2007) 'Jim Mitchell, 63, Filmmaker, Is Dead; Made "Behind the Green Door"', *New York Times*, July 19.

Martin, Gavin (2007) 'Green On Red man's ode to San Francisco', *Classic Rock*, March 4.

Mehr, Bob (2002) 'It Takes Two', *Seattle Weekly News*, September 18.

Mehr, Bob (2003) 'Chuck Amok' in *Seattle Weekly*, December 31.

Mehr, Bob (2010) 'Chuck Prophet's adventures in music-making lead back to Memphis', October 19.

Melis, Matt (2014) 'Chuck Prophet—Night Surfer', *Consequence Of Sound*, October 2.

Micek, John L. (2002) 'The Paisley Underground Reconsidered', *Popmatters*, April 30.

Miller, Cody (2009) 'Chuck Prophet: Let Freedom Ring', *Popmatters*, October 28.

Milliken, Joe (2015) 'SRO Interview with Grammy Award-Winning Producer/Engineer Paul Kolderie', standing-room-only.info, August 21.

Mills, Fred (2009) 'Chuck Prophet: *Let Freedom Ring*', *Blurt* magazine, November 23.

Mills, Fred (2014) 'The College Rock Chronicles, Pt. 4: Green On Red', *Blurt*.

Mitchell, Lincoln A. (2019) 'Dead Kennedys in the West: The Politicized Punks of 1970s San Francisco', *Literary Hub*, October 22.

Mojo magazine (1997), *Homemade Blood* review, November 15.

Mojo magazine (2012) 'Chuck Prophet: Temple Beautiful', *Mojo*, April 20.

Mojo magazine (2014) 'Chuck Prophet: Night Surfer'.

Morris, Chris (1997) 'Declaration of Independents', *Billboard*, March 22 [CPA].

Morris, Steve (1991a) 'Green On Red: Scapegoats', *Brum Beat*, April, p. 14. [CPA].

Morris, Steve (1991b) 'Green On Red: Best Of …', *Brum Beat*, September [CPA].

Mudd, Jonathan (1992) 'Chuck Prophet: Balinese Dancer', *BAM* [CPA].

Mueller, Andrew (1995) 'Chuck Prophet: Feast of Hearts', *Melody Maker*, June 3 [CPA].

Munson, Kyle (2000) 'Prophet's proclamations rooted in past', *Des Moines Register*, January 13 [CPA].

Murray Winters, Pamela (2004) 'Age of Miracles: Chuck Prophet', review, *Washington Post*, October 17, p.N07.

Murry, John (2007) 'Waylon, are you Pissed?', chuckprophet.com.

Murry, John (2012) 'Interview: John Murry', *Uncut*, August 6.

Myers, Mitch (2005) 'Green On Red: *Here Come the Snakes: After the Goldrush*'. Liner notes to 2CD reissue of *Here Come the Snakes*. Belle Sound, IRT 7021.

Newsreal (1983) 'Serf's up for Green On Red', February 11–March 11, Robert E. Zucker (ed.), *Entertaining Tucson Across the Decades Volume 1: 1950s–1985*. Tucson, AZ: BZB Publishing, Inc., pp. 130–33.

Nickson, Chris (2007) 'Chuck Prophet: No Other Love', allmusic.com.

Niesel, Jeff (2017) 'Singer-Songwriter Chuck Prophet Talks About How He Launched His Career Via a 'Great American Joyride', *Cleveland Scene*, March 16.

No Depression (1997) 'Chuck Prophet: Bringing it all back home'.

No Depression (2003) 'Review: Green On Red—Self-Titled'.

Ochs, Meredith (2000) 'Chuck Prophet', *The Boston Phoenix*, February 17–24 [CPA].

O'Reilly, Daragh, Gretchen Larsen & Krzysztof Kubacki (2013), *Music, Markets and Consumption*. Oxford: Goodfellow Publishers Ltd.

Palmer, Robert (1987) 'The Pop Life: in Green On Red's new "Killer," a nod to film noir', *New York Times*, April 15.

Palmer, Waiyde (2013) 'Halloween in the Castro: Then & Now', *hoodline*, October 31.

Passarelli, James (2011) 'Chats with Chuck Prophet', *Inflatable Ferret*, Vol. 2, No. 1, January, pp. 16–19.

Pawsey, Pete (1997) 'Factor Eight: Chuck Prophet' in *Hearsay* #15.

Peache, Mal (1993) 'Nice n' Balineasy: Chuck Prophet: Balinese Dancer', *Vox*, March [CPA].

Perrone, Pierre (2008). 'Obituary: Tony Kostrzewa: Founder of Red Rhino Records', *Independent*, May 8.

Perry, Andrew (1991) 'Green On Red: Best Of', *Select*, November [CPA].

Petridis, Alex (2011) 'The rise of the super-deluxe box set', *Guardian*, December 22.

Pitter, Charles (2014) 'Chuck Prophet: Night Surfer', *Popmatters*, September 25.

poet, j. (2014) 'Chuck Prophet explains how he created his new album, "Night Surfer"', *Press Reader*, September 21.

Pouncey, Edwin (1984) 'The Green Party: Green On Red: Soho, Alice in Wonderland', September 29 [CPA].

Pouncey, Edwin (1985) 'Green On Red: *Gas Food Lodging*', *Sounds*, May 18.

Pouncey, Edwin (1991) 'Chuck Prophet: Brother Aldo', *Vox* [CPA].

Prophet, Chuck (1995) 'Press Releases: *Feast of Hearts*', chuckprophet.com, February 1.

Prophet, Chuck (1997) 'Interview with Chuck for the reissue of Brother Aldo', chuckprophet.com.

Prophet, Chuck (1999) *Homemade Blood* Press Release, chuckprophet.com.

Prophet, Chuck (2000) 'The Uncut Tour Diary (2000)' chuckprophet.com, November 1.

Prophet (2002a) 'New Year 2002', chuckprophet.com, January 2.

Prophet, Chuck (2002b) 'Track By Track: *The Hurting Business*', chuckprophet.com, April 30.

Prophet, Chuck (2005) chuckprophet.com, 'Talkin' Tracks: No Other Love', January 1.

Prophet, Chuck (2006) 'Day 12: A Field in Norway'. chuckprophet.com, August 28.

Prophet, Chuck (2007a) 'Kelly Willis Sessions', chuckprophet.com, April 6.

Prophet, Chuck (2007b) 'Because It's Nashville', chuckprophet.com, April 18.

Prophet, Chuck (2007c) 'Vanderslice in 08', chuckprophet.com, July 26.

Prophet, Chuck (2007d) 'Alex Chilton', chuckprophet.com, August 31.

Prophet, Chuck (2008a) 'Dirty Work in Lexington', chuckprophet.com, January 2.

Prophet, Chuck (2008b) 'Letterman: Moths to the Flame', chuckprophet.com, January 23.

Prophet, Chuck (2008c) contribution to tdpri.com forum discussion thread, October 29.

Prophet, Chuck (2009) 'Jim Dickinson (1942–2009) R.I.P.', chuckprophet.com, August.

Prophet, Chuck (2012a) 'Alex Anderson', chuckprophet.com.

Prophet, Chuck (2012b) 'My 1984 Fender Squire Telecaster Is Gone …', chuckprophet.com.

Prophet, (2014a) 'Okay, We've Got Tour Dates. New Record Too', chuckprophet.com.

Prophet, Chuck (2014b) 'Cut Along Dotted Line' chuckprophet.com, November 6.

Prophet, Chuck (2017) Facebook post, December 18.

Q (1997) *Homemade Blood* review, November 15.

Q (2002) *No Other Love* review [CPA].

Q (2014) *Night Surfer* review.

Racer (2012) 'Chuck Prophet—The Hurting Business', *Ripple Effect*, March 5.

Reed, Bryan (2012) 'Q&A with Chuck Prophet', *Magnet*, February 6.

Riverfront Times, The (St. Louis, Missouri) (1986). 'Green On Red: *No Free Lunch*', March 12–18 [CPA].

Robbins, Ira (1986) 'Green On Red: *No Free Lunch; Rain Parade: Crashing Dream*', *Creem*, July.

Robbins, Ira (n.d.), Trouserpress.com

Rock And Roll Confidential (1986) 'Green On Red: *No Free Lunch*', March [CPA].

Romney, Jonathan (1985) 'Rhinestone Cowboys: Green On Red: Cambridge Guildhall', *New Musical Express*, November 23 [CPA].

Rosen, Steven (2017) 'Acclaimed singer/songwriter Chuck Prophet still believes in Rock'n'Roll', *CityBeat*, March 22.

Rounder Records (2001) *Raisins in the Sun* Album Profile/Artist Bio, February [CPA].

Sanchez, Daniel (2018) 'What Streaming Music Services Pay (Updated for 2019)', *Digital Music News*, December 25.

Schacht, John (2004) 'Chuck Prophet—*Age of Miracles*', *Paste*, October 1.

Schonbeck, Carl (2012) 'Chuck Prophet: Temple Beautiful', *Popmatters*, March 1.

Scott (2017) 'Album Of The Week', 50thirdand3rd.com, March 6.

Sekerka, John (2002) 'The Tape Hiss Interviews: Chuck Prophet', January 1.

Simkin, Stevie (2014) *Cultural Constructions of the Femme Fatale: from Pandora's Box to Amanda Knox*. Basingstoke: Palgrave.

Simmons, Sylvie (2009) 'Made in Mexico: Bringing it all Back Home', *Mojo*, December 3.

Simon, Jane (1985) 'Greed On Red: Lotta Bottle', *Sounds*, November 16, pp. 26, 28, 45 [CPA].

Simpson, Dave (1989) 'Green On Red: The Irish Centre, Leeds', *Melody Maker*, December 2 [CPA].

Sinclair, David (1989a) 'Musical pearls on a gutsy string: Green On Red: *Here Come the Snakes*', *The Times*, April 1, p. 40 [CPA].

Sinclair, David (1989b) 'Green On Red: Town & Country', *The Times*, April 10 [CPA].

Sinclair, David (1989c) 'Albums: Green On Red: This Time Around', *The Times*, November 3, p. 17.

Sinclair, David (1990) 'Birdsong, blues and patchy warbling', *The Times*, November 9, p. 19.

Sinclair, David (1991) 'Moyet mixes to match as usual', *The Times*, April 19 [CPA].

Sinclair, David (1995) 'Prophet motives', *The Times*, May 26 [CPA].

Sinclair, David (1997) 'The Week's Top Pop Releases', March 29, p. 20.

Sinclair, David (2006) 'Reviews First Night: Pop: Green On Red: Astoria', January 12, p.22 [S].

Sinclair, Mick (2004) *San Francisco: a Cultural and Literary History*. Oxford: Signal Books.

Sisario, Ben & Karl Russell (2016) 'In Shift to Streaming, Music Business Has Lost Billions', *New York Times*, March 24.

Sky (1989), 'Green On Red: *This Time Around*' [CPA].

Small, Christopher (1998) *Musicking: The Meanings of Performing and Listening* (Hanover, N.H.: Wesleyan University Press, 1998).

Smith, Andrew (1989) 'Snake Charmed: Green On Red: Powerhaus, London', *Melody Maker*, September 2, p. 20 [CPA].

Smith, William Michael (2007) 'Chuck Prophet, *Soap and Water*', Houston Press, November 21.

Snow, Mat (1985) 'Octane O.D.: Green On Red: Gas Food Lodging', *New Musical Express*, May 25 [CPA].

Snow, Mat (1991) 'Weathered Prophet: Chuck Prophet: Brother Aldo', September 15 [CPA].

Solnit, Rebecca (2016) 'Death by Gentrification: the Killing That Shamed San Francisco', *Guardian*, March 21.

Soref, David (2012) '"Temple Beautiful": Chuck Prophet and Friends' San Francisco Masterpiece', *positivelyturkstreet*, December 13.

Sounds (1989), 'Green On Red', *Sounds*, April 1 [CPA].

ST (1997), 'Chuck Prophet: Homemade Blood', *Sunday Times*, April 6 [CPA].

Steiner, George (1989) *Real Presences*. London: Faber & Faber.

Storey, Jon (1987) 'Green On Red: the Prophet's tale', *Bucketfull Of Brains*, Issue 21, Summer, pp. 17–19.

Strutt, Anthony (2010) Interview with Chuck Prophet.

Stuart, Dan (1989), 'Dan Stuart (Green On Red)', *Melody Maker*, December 23 [CPA].

Stuart, Dan (2014) *The Deliverance of Marlowe Billings: A False Memoir*. London: Cadiz Music.

Sullivan, Denise (1997) 'Homemade Prophet', *Bam*, April 18.

Sullivan, Denise (n.d.) 'Chuck Prophet: Homemade Blood', *All Music Guide*.

Sutherland, Steve (1988) 'Barroom Blitz', *Melody Maker*, July 2, pp. 32–4 [CPA].

Sutherland, Steve (1989) 'Glory Daze: Green On Red: Town & Country Club, London', *Melody Maker*, April 15 [CPA].

Sutherland, Steve (1990) *Brother Aldo* interview, October 5.

Swedlund, Eric (2009) 'Chuck Prophet: Let Freedom Ring', *East Bay Express*, December 16.

Swedlund, Eric (2012) 'Chuck Prophet: Temple Beautiful', *Tucson Weekly*, February 2.

Sweeting, Adam (1985) 'Red Menace: Green On Red: Dingwalls, London', *Melody Maker*, March 30 [CPA].

Sweeting, Adam (1989) 'Town & country: Green On Red', *Guardian*, April 10 [CPA].

Sweeting, Adam (1990) 'Remorselessness of the long-distance runners: Chuck Prophet: Brother Aldo', October 25, p. 26.

Sweeting, Adam (1993) 'Chuck Prophet: *Balinese Dancer*' *Guardian*, February 5 [CPA].

Sweeting, Adam (1997) 'Prophet Margin', *Guardian*, March 28, p. A15.

Sweetman, Simon (2014) 'Chuck Prophet: Night Surfer', *Off The Tracks*, October 1.

Swift, Steve (2014) 'Chuck Prophet: Night Surfer—album review', *Louder Than War*, September 25.

SXSW (2017) 'SXSW 2017 Event Statistics', sxsw.com.

Tanzilo, Bobby (2014) 'Chasing Down Peter Mulvey', *On Milwaukee*, May 5.

Temple Beautiful iBook, unpublished, undated.

Thane, Rich (2012) 'Album Stream: Chuck Prophet—Temple Beautiful', *The Line Of Best Fit*, January 30.

The Times (2009) 'Chuck Prophet: Let Freedom Ring, September 13.

Tomashoff, Craig (1987) 'Platter Du Jour: Green On Red: Gas Food Lodging', *Spin*, September [CPA].

Top (1995), *Feast of Hearts* review, *Top*, May [CPA].

Torn, Luke (2012) 'Chuck Prophet: Temple Beautiful', *Uncut*, February 26.

Traitor, Ralph (1989) 'Green On Red: Ugly but Honest', *Sounds*, January 28.

Traitor, Ralph (1991) 'For Their Country', *Sounds*, March [CPA].

Tucker, Ken (2010) 'Stephanie Finch: The Power of Simplicity', npr.org, July 8.

Tucker, Ken (2012) 'Chuck Prophet's "Beautiful" Homage to San Francisco', *Fresh Air*, February 8.

Tunis, Walter (2018) 'Chuck Prophet has never been in sync with the times. But he's always come to Lexington', kentucky.com, July 2.

Uncut (2014) *Night Surfer* review.

Unterburger, Richie (1999) *The Rough Guide to Music USA*. London: Penguin.

Vaziri, Aidin (2004) 'Chuck Prophet: Age of Miracles', *San Francisco Chronicle*, September 12 [CPA].

Vaziri, Aidin (2011) 'Chuck Prophet doing "London Calling"', *SF Gate*, January 16.

Vernon, John (1986) 'Green On Red: No Free Lunch', *Illinois Entertainer*, April 1 [CPA].

Vincent, Nigel (1991) 'Green On Red: Newcastle Riverside', *Northern Echo*, May 1 [CPA].

Weiss Neal (1999) 'Chuck Prophet—The Hurting Business', *No Depression*, December 31.

Weiss, Neal (2003) 'Green On Red—*self-titled*' review, *NoDepression*, February 28.

White, Darryl (2015) 'R.E.M. Timeline: The Complete R.E.M. Concert Chronology'.

Williams, Simon (1989) 'Green On Red, The Blue Aeroplanes, London Town & Country Club', *New Musical Express*, April 22 [CPA].

Wilson, Steve (2010) 'Chuck Prophet—Let Freedom Ring', *KC Free Press*, January 30.

Witt, Stephen (2015) *How Music Got Free: the Inventor, the Mogul and the Thief*. London: Penguin.

Wolf, Kurt (1990) 'Chuck Prophet, Brother Aldo', *San Francisco Bay Guardian*, December 19 [CPA].

Wolff, Carlo (1985) 'Green On Red: No Free Lunch', *Boston Globe*, May [CPA].

WR (2004) 'Chuck Prophet: Age Of Miracles', *Billboard*, September 25, p. 54.

Youbloom.com (n.d.) 'Mike Lembo'.

Zimmerman, Lee (2014) 'Chuck Prophet—Night Surfer', *Blurt*, September.

ENDNOTES

INTRODUCTION

1 Steiner 1989: 182–4
2 Small 1998: 197
3 CBC Radio 2016
4 Carlyle 1864: 75
5 Krueger 2019: 12, 7
6 Pitter 2014
7 IFPI 2017: 12, 34
8 Carroll 2016
9 Niesel 2017
10 AMA, n.d.
11 Scott 2017
12 Sanchez 2018
13 Foucault 2019
14 Witt 2015: 79
15 Reed 2012
16 Witt 2015: 191
17 O'Reilly et al, 2013: 24
18 Sisario & Russell 2016
19 Tunis 2018
20 Petridis 2011
21 Copsey 2018
22 Witt 2015: 260
23 Holt 2010: 246
24 Krueger 2019: 37
25 Graham 2018

CHAPTER ONE

1 Harward 2006
2 Stuart 2014: 30
3 Stuart 2014: 27
4 Commonplace 1985: 96
5 Mills 2014
6 Gonzales and Eshrati 2016
7 Mitchell 2019
8 Azerrad 2001: 6
9 Unterburger 1999:39
10 Barron 1985a
11 Mills 2014
12 Stuart 2014: 30
13 Newsreal 1983: 131
14 Breznikar 2011
15 Newsreal 1983: 131–2
16 Azerrad 2001: 9
17 Hann 2013
18 Hann 2013
19 Micek 2002
20 Hughes 2002
21 Hann 2013
22 Stuart 2014: 58
23 Hann 2013
24 Kimpel 2006: 84
25 Mills 2014
26 Stuart 2014: 65
27 Leviton 1984
28 Ave The Sound, 2017
29 Racer 2012
30 Storey 1987: 17
31 White 2015
32 Judge, 2011
33 Prophet 2008c
34 Hughes 2002
35 Storey 1987: 18
36 Cantwell 2002a
37 Stuart 2014: 72
38 Stuart 2014: 90
39 Howe 2014
40 Howe 2014
41 Pouncey 1984
42 youbloom.com n.d.
43 Storey 1987: 18
44 Drozdowski 1986
45 Drozdowski 1986: 2
46 Storey 1987: 18
47 Breznikar 2011
48 Mills 2014
49 Mills 2014
50 Leviton 1985
51 Simon 1985: 28
52 Mills 2014
53 Hann 2013
54 Azerrad 2001: 4
55 Hann 2013
56 Hann 2013
57 Gilmore 1985, Lee 1985
58 Tomashoff 1985
59 Pouncey 1985
60 Snow 1985
61 Fricke 1985
62 Hughes 2002
63 Barron 1985a
64 Stuart 1989
65 Hughes 2002
66 Cantwell 2002a
67 Weiss 2003
68 Cantwell 2002a
69 Mills 2014
70 Drozdowski 1986: 3
71 Sweeting 1985
72 Green 2015
73 Lomas 1985
74 Marchetto 1985
75 Aston 1985

CHAPTER TWO

1 Cantwell 2002a
2 Mills 2014
3 Simon 1985: 28
4 Drozdowski 1986: 2
5 Island Ear 1986
6 Rock And Roll Confidential 1986
7 Riverfront Times 1986
8 DeCurtis 1986
9 Harms 1986
10 Wolff 1986, Himes 1986
11 Christgau 1985
12 Robbins 1986
13 Fertig 1986
14 Vernon 1986
15 Barron 1985b
16 Kent 1985
17 Romney 1985
18 Elbourne 1985
19 McLenon 2005
20 Mehr 2010
21 Traitor 1989
22 Mills 2014
23 Sekerka 2002
24 Christgau 1987
25 Palmer 1987
26 Denselow 1986: 19
27 Jones 1986
28 Jones 1990
29 Mills 2014
30 Mills 2014
31 Mills 2014

CHAPTER THREE

1 Perrone 2008
2 Myers 2005
3 Traitor 1989
4 Stuart 2014: 102–3
5 Traitor 1989
6 Prophet 2009
7 Prophet 2007d
8 Traitor 1989
9 Sinclair 1989a
10 Sinclair 1991
11 Robbins

12 Traitor 1989
13 Sounds 1989
14 Williams 1989
15 Holland 1989
16 Sinclair 1989b
17 Sweeting 1989
18 Sutherland 1989
19 Smith 1989
20 Cantwell 2002a
21 Leonard 1990: 57
22 Leonard 1990: 57

23 Johns 2014: 267
24 Leonard 1990: 57
25 Kinghorn 1991
26 Bailie 1989
27 Elliott 1989
28 Sinclair 1989c
29 Sky 1989
30 Simpson 1989
31 Traitor 1991
32 Traitor 1991
33 Morris 1991a

34 Sinclair 1991
35 Clark 1991
36 Perry 1991
37 Morris 1991b
38 Doggett 1991
39 Vincent 1991
40 Stuart 2014: 117
41 Stuart 2014: 139
42 Leonard 1990
43 Stuart 2014: 142
44 Cantwell 2002a

CHAPTER FOUR

1 Storey 1987: 17
2 Storey 1987: 19
3 Sutherland 1988: 33
4 Baruth 1996

5 Cantwell 2002a
6 Gendelman 1990
7 Wolf 1990
8 Sutherland 1990

9 Sutherland 1990
10 Prophet 1997
11 Snow 1991
12 Sinclair 1990

13 Sweeting 1990
14 Kane 1991
15 Cavanagh 1991
16 Pouncey 1991

CHAPTER FIVE

1 SXSW 2017
2 Cohen 1992
3 Blackstock 1992
4 Prophet 1995
5 Knopper 2009: 43
6 Burnett 2002: 45

7 Knopper 2018
8 Brazeau 2017
9 Pawsey 1997
10 Brazeau 2017
11 Batey 1993: 134
12 Prophet 2014b

13 Batey 1993: 133
14 Prophet 1995
15 Prophet 1995
16 Huffman 1993
17 Mudd 1992
18 Peache 1993

19 Sweeting 1993
20 Prophet 2014a
21 Prophet 2014a

CHAPTER SIX

1 Lurie 2009: 206
2 No Depression 1997

3 Lee 1995
4 Sinclair 1995

5 Mueller 1995
6 Belcher 1995

7 Crossing 1995
8 Jones 1995

CHAPTER SEVEN

1 Pawsey 1997
2 Milliken 2015
3 Bray 2016

4 Prophet 1999
5 Pawsey 1997
6 Morris 1997

7 Ennist 1997
8 Bertin 1997
9 Sweeting 1997

10 Sinclair 1997
11 ST 1997
12 Q 1997

CHAPTER EIGHT

1 Hutton 1999
2 Passarelli 2011
3 Mehr 2003
4 Cantwell 2002a
5 Mehr 2002,
   Cantwell 2002a
6 Cantwell 2002b

7 Mehr 2002
8 Jurek 2002
9 Ashare 2001
10 Prophet 2012a
11 Foster 2010
12 Prophet 2002b
13 Prophet 2002b

14 Cantwell 2002a
15 Munson 2000
16 Kaleta 2000
17 Weiss 1999
18 Ochs 2000
19 Caligiuri 2000a
20 JG 2000

21 Baker 2000
22 Sinclair 2004: 234
23 Prophet 2000
24 Caligiuri 2000b

CHAPTER NINE

1 Adams 2019
2 Prophet 2002a
3 Prophet 2002a
4 Prophet 2007a
5 Prophet 2005
6 Jelinek 2013

7 Fortune 2002
8 Cantwell 2002b
9 Prophet 2005
10 Armstrong 2002
11 Gundersen 2007
12 Nickson 2007

13 Mehr 2002
14 Margolis 2004
15 Johnson 2006
16 Prophet 2017
17 Doyle 2011
18 Schacht 2004

19 Lundy 2004
20 Murray Winters 2004
21 Simmons 2004
22 Vaziri 2004
23 WR 2004

CHAPTER TEN

1 Goodman 2007
2 Gittins 2006
3 Sinclair 2006
4 Cook 2007
5 Prophet 2006
6 Ling 2017
7 Murry 2007
8 Hurt 2008
9 Hawkins 2007
10 Goodman 2007

11 Prophet 2007b
12 Smith 2007
13 Almond 2007
14 Lewis 2007
15 Elliott 2007
16 Breen 2007
17 Prophet 2008b
18 Prophet 2007c
19 Murry 2012
20 johnmurry.com, n.d.

21 Murry 2012
22 Blackbook 2013
23 Prophet 2008a
24 Prophet 2008a
25 Hernandez 2008
26 EQ 2010
27 City Pages 2010
28 Lazarski 2010
29 Wilson 2010
30 Miller 2009

31 Swedlund 2009
32 Hoinski 2009
33 Blackstock 2009
34 Simmons 2009
35 Mills 2009
36 Baker 2009
37 Times 2009

CHAPTER ELEVEN

1 Tucker 2010
2 Vaziri 2011
3 Prophet 2008b
4 Reed 2012
5 Lanham 2011
6 Baym 2018: 15

7 Martin 2007
8 Martin 2007
9 Schonbeck 2012
10 Palmer 2013
11 TB iBook
12 Soref 2012

13 Kamiya 2017
14 Halliday 2012
15 Swedlund 2012
16 Tucker 2012
17 Malitz 2012
18 Caligiuri 2012

19 Torn 2012
20 Gleason 2012
21 Martin 2012
22 Schonbeck 2012
23 Thane 2012
24 Prophet 2012b

CHAPTER TWELVE

1 Aginghipster 2014
2 Aginghipster 2014
3 Melis 2014
4 Pitter 2014
5 Simkin 2014
6 poet 2014

7 Pitter 2014
8 Zimmerman 2014
9 Swift 2014
10 Sweetman 2014
11 Ingalls 2017
12 Tanzilo 2014

13 DiGiacomo 2017
14 Maddux 2017
15 Solnit 2016
16 Ave The Sound 2017
17 Gill 2017
18 Easlea 2017

19 Horowitz 2017
20 Deming 2017
21 Brown 2017
22 Rosen 2017

CONCLUSION

1 DiGiacomo 2017
2 Heller 2000

INDEX